Melissa Richmond

Peter Richmond has been an award-winning reporter and feature writer for *GQ* for two decades. He has covered everything from Rosemary Clooney to sports, and his work has also appeared in *The New Yorker, Vanity Fair, The New York Times Magazine,* and *Rolling Stone.* He has appeared often on National Public Radio's *Morning Edition.* He lives in Dutchess County, New York.

Fever

Fever

THE LIFE AND MUSIC OF

Miss Peggy Lee

Peter Richmond

PICADOR

HENRY HOLT AND COMPANY

NEW YORK

www.picadorusa.com

Picador® is a U.S. registered trademark and is used by
Henry Holt and Company under license from Pan Books Limited.

For information on Picador Reading Group Guides,
as well as ordering, please contact Picador.
Phone: 646-307-5629
Fax: 212-253-9627
E-mail: readinggroupguides@picadorusa.com

Drawing of Peggy Lee by Robert Richards

Library of Congress Cataloging-in-Publication Data

Richmond, Peter, 1953–
    Fever : the life and music of Miss Peggy Lee / Peter Richmond.
       p. cm.
    Includes index.
    ISBN-13: 978-0-312-42661-3
    ISBN-10: 0-312-42661-5
    1. Lee, Peggy, 1920– 2. Singers—United States—Biography. I. Title.

ML420.L294R53 2006
782.42164092—dc22

                                                                2005052782

First published in the United States by Henry Holt and Company

First Picador Edition: May 2007

10 9 8 7 6 5 4 3 2 1

To my daughter, Hillary,

who makes the music

God will not have his work made manifest by cowards.

— RALPH WALDO EMERSON

Contents

PROLOGUE: *White Night*   1

PART I: *Dreamland on the Train*

1. *In Dakota*   15
2. *Pick Up Your Telephone*   34
3. *The Most Beautiful Street West of Minneapolis*   49
4. *The Magic Aquarium*   70
5. *Benny Blows In*   84
6. *Don't Be That Way*   108
7. *A Cool Quality*   128
8. *Do Right*   146

PART II: *The Lady in the Limelight*

9. *Our Little Dream Castle*   163
10. *On Air*   181
11. *Borderline*   193

12. *You Was*   208

13. *Home*   224

14. *Lovers*   240

15. *Modern Screen*   258

16. *Coffee Break*   271

17. *Kelly Girl*   283

18. *High on a Hill*   297

19. *Things Are Swingin'*   314

20. *Rainy Nights in London Town*   333

PART III: *Angels on Your Pillow*

21. *The Best Is Yet to Come*   355

22. *All There Was*   374

23. *Grand Tour*   387

24. *Diplomacy*   393

25. *Mirrors*   413

26. *Piano Players*   426

27. *One-Woman Show*   441

28. *Hip Angel*   462

29. *I Won't Dance*   471

30. *Take Me Back to Manhattan*   498

ACKNOWLEDGMENTS   515

NOTES   517

INDEX   537

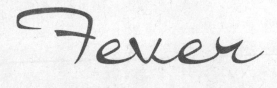

White Night

THE HALF NOTE was dark, Coltrane uncharacteristically silent. Birdland was battened down. Buddy Rich and his boys had taken a one-night holiday. Lonely chords serenaded the empty rink at Rockefeller Center, not a single skater to hear them. On this February evening in 1961, the blizzard of the century had all but locked the great city down. The silence of a foot and a half of newly fallen snow had blanketed the island from river to river. An edict from Mayor Robert Wagner had swept all but essential vehicles from the streets. Bars, restaurants, shops—everything was shuttered; most of the town's famously bright lights were extinguished. Hardly a sound could be heard in the muffled night, save the winter wind whipping from alley to alley.

Hardly a soul could be glimpsed on Manhattan Island, except

for the intrepid pedestrians gathering in the immediate vicinity of East Forty-eighth Street and Lexington Avenue, where the most elegant of parades was making its way through the blowing flakes and the gathering drifts. Laughing couples seductively attired in minks and tuxedos, giddy revelers swathed in mufflers and mittens, all hurried through the glow of streetlights, braving the wind, lured by an unseen gravitational pull toward what was, on this singular evening, the city's undisputed nexus. The long, rarely silent, and usually smoky room was known as the nightclub of nightclubs, and despite the climate's extreme hostility, people packed the space—wall to wall, table to table, knee to knee, stranger to stranger—as if all the energy of old New York, banished from the streets, had been channeled and gathered into this single place, for one single night, one single show.

They had come to catch her fever. They had come to bask in her cool. They had come to Basin Street East to hear the Queen. That's what Ellington had ordained her: "If I'm the Duke, man, Peggy Lee is *Queen.*" *The New Yorker,* describing this particular engagement in typically omniscient style, had settled simply for calling her "practically the hub of the universe," drawing no argument from the cognoscenti. At any rate, the semantics were irrelevant. No one in Basin Street needed convincing. The only phrases that mattered on this night were melodic—jazzed, bluesy, heartbroken, hopeful—and all absolutely American. And the woman who could sing them all, from the classic phrasings of the standard popular songbook to adventurous melodies out on the rhythmic fringe, and everything in between—was about to seize the small, empty stage and claim the whole magical New York night as her very own.

There was never a question that the show would go on. Even with the weather wreaking havoc, nothing could have waylaid the faithful. With delivery trucks banned from the streets, the club's publicist had enlisted local schoolkids to scour nearby grocery stores for all the provisions they could load onto their sleds. For this evening's show, the guests would feed on impromptu cuisine and fuel themselves on a more limited range than usual of their favorite cocktails—as if to prove the Richard Rodgers dictum that our need for melody is as strong as our need for sustenance. The club held 340 people, legally. On this occasion, it would accommodate nearly twice as many. As the listeners shook off the snow and settled into the cramped confines, the low murmur of anticipation became a rising undercurrent. On this night, instead of the usual three shows, she'd be doing just one. This crowd would be hearing everything the woman had to offer.

They were here because no one would dare miss any occasion to see the undisputed female champion of pop-jazz at the top of her game, in a city and time where beat and Beat were almost interchangeable. Down on Washington Square a handwritten sign stuck to a snow-covered fence read: "Be Abstract." But unlike Kerouac, Pollock, Ferlinghetti, and all of their friends in the avant-garde, Peggy Lee, on February 4, 1961, was not out on the fringe looking in, railing at the soullessness of it all. After years of feeling herself the outsider, she had reached the top of her game and was finally enshrined inside the big room of fame where the lights burned late and her ballads and jazz and rhythm and blues spanning every emotion reached every kind of listener, from martinied-up suburban types to the visiting jazzmen and players who had come to pay homage, to tap the tiny tables as her informal accompaniment, nodding *Yes. Yes.*

The roster of faces in the crowd during her four-week stint at Basin Street that winter would say all that had to be said about her peers' regard for her status in the pop pantheon. Making the pilgrimage to East Forty-eighth Street were Ray Charles and Count Basie, Ella Fitzgerald and Lena Horne, Marlene Dietrich and Judy Garland. (Garland once called Peggy her favorite girl singer.) Then there were Cary Grant, Jimmy Durante, Sammy Davis, Jr., Joan Crawford, Art Carney, Louis Armstrong, and a young arranger named Quincy Jones. (Tony Bennett called late one night after a gig in Detroit, hoping for a seat at the 2:30 A.M. show.) None would have thought of missing out on this engagement, not at this time, in this era when popular jazz singing was not only a craft but an art of the highest order, a universal language that touched the hopes and longings of a generation of American dreamers.

The crowd wasn't privy to her preshow rituals: first, the physical transformation from woman to Stage Presence. (One night in the elevator up to the hotel room where the singer would make up, do her hair, and don the gown, a stranger asked, "Are you Peggy Lee?" Her answer: "Not yet, I'm not.") Then came the hugging and kissing of the musicians, for good luck. Then the healthy slug of cognac, from a large glass, followed by a drink of cool water—not just for the rush of energy, but for the added release the alcohol brought, the little bit of extra freedom. For every show had to be special—they expected no less of her, and she demanded no less of herself. An element of unpredictability could only add to the mystery. She wanted to seduce them all. She wanted them to hear each word, and feel every emotion that lay behind it. She wanted perfection. She *needed* perfection.

Then, as the band set up out front, she said a quiet, intimate prayer behind the curtain. Now the musicians launched into the brassy intro: a medley comprising a few measures each of Peggy's standards, a signature string of great sounds—a snatch of a chorus from one of her original hits with Benny Goodman, a melody line from one of her own compositions from the forties, a measure of a memorable bridge from the glorious early fifties, a lilt from some recent swingy triumph.

Then came the voice offstage: "Ladies and gentlemen, Basin Street East takes great pleasure in welcoming . . . Miss Peggy Lee."

Behind the curtain, she'd let out a scream—just loud enough to start her own engine—and stamp her foot, once. Then she'd yank open the curtain and step into the light.

And there she was: an hourglassed platinum doll, forty years old, shrouded in a metaphoric glow, an aura she had earned, step by step, from her first, unlikely low-down blues hit for Goodman in 1942 to the hypnotic finger-snapping "Fever" a few years back—and a whole lot of everything in between: an Oscar nomination; a turn doing the voices for a couple of Siamese cats in a Disney animated feature; the mambo-and-sex-soaked "Lover," which made it to the top three on the charts. Not to mention *Black Coffee*, the jazz-vocal album that had raised the pop-jazz bar to unheard-of heights.

But just as obvious as her celebrity on this night was her sensuality, a confection of cosmetics, jewelry, and hairstyle, of glance and wink and half smile, that spoke as much of illusion as it did of authentic female. Her appearance told more than a few half-truths. She was the image of glamour and independence, but there was something artificial about the strength she displayed beneath the lights, for with three failed marriages and another broken Hollywood romance already behind her, the music increasingly defined her whole world. Her artistry had risen from a childhood without real family, and by now her audience and her public had become a very large part of what sustained her. Her nightclub theatricality was as spectacular as her art, but the elaborate gowns and masquerade could not conceal the vulnerability beneath. At this crossroads of her life she found her love in those who crowded the clubs from coast to coast.

The applause had not yet died when she plunged into her opener, "Day In, Day Out," a rollicking jazz-infused arrangement of a Bloom-Mercer standard she'd recorded just that week, and immediately she had the place hooked. Her notes rushed and leaped, insistent, playing with the beat, moving behind it, shadowing it, toying with it. The horns swung a high-speed brassy subtext. The pace was breakneck; in their adrenaline rush to get the thing going, the band and the singer nearly outran themselves right out of the gate. The opening number was finished in a minute and forty-five seconds.

"Thank you—thank you very much," she said—just breathily enough. A knowing smile passed across her lips and her eyes darted off to the side. It was the coy, flirtatious expression that would ride her features all evening long, suggesting that something was being mysteriously withheld. She always kept some secrets behind the curtain, even when she insisted otherwise; even when she was exchanging giggles and laughing at double entendres and she and the crowd were meeting halfway, in perfect harmony; even when she confided about the cold she felt coming on: "See? I tell you *everything*." It was a ruse, though; she never confided more than just enough.

The rest of this show fell into place exactly as she had choreographed it, song by song, so that the moods balanced perfectly between highs and lows, and every rhythm, every genre, had its say. "Call Me Darling" brought scattered laughter at the mention in the lyrics of the word "affair." "The Most Beautiful Man in the World" evoked a late-night-to-dawn jam, and she stretched the beat to mirror the flights of the band's solos. This much was constant: No matter what the rhythm of the song, her body moved as if being guided, as if the notes were caressing her. But there was no mistaking who was running the show. Beneath all the artifice, beneath the glamorous mocha gown and the lacquered nails and the sequins that caught the glint of the lights, she was in complete control—of every note, of every pause. Her pianist and conductor Joe Harnell responded to a single lifted finger, to a single lifted eyebrow. Her bassist Max Bennett, entrusted with the beat, was on high alert to her every physical nuance. The multiple lighting cues in every song came neither a second too early nor a second too late.

When she wove her way through the melancholy languor of Jimmy van Heusen and Sammy Cahn's "The Second Time Around"—one of the most lush and heartfelt of all her ballads, it sounded like a Shakespearean soliloquy—she was completely in the moment, measure by measure, tone by tone, syllable by syllable. So utterly given over to the song was she that to disturb the spell would have been to risk a fissure in the universe. By now, anyone who had begun the evening sitting back had unconsciously shimmied forward, hypnotized. Her midsong pauses and silences brought an answering silence out in the room: not a knife scraped a plate, not a cigarette was stubbed out, not a chair was dragged, not even an inch. It would have been like coughing in church.

Her rendition of "Fever" was liquid, all slow drips of honey; she brought the audience to her, entwined and entrapped it, note by note, with the gestures of a single hand, a single snap of the fingers against Bennett's thumping stand-up bass. Then she turned the room loose again with brassy, polytonal high jazz: Ellington's "I'm Gonna Go Fishin'" with the lyrics she'd written at Ellington's request. The music mounted and mounted, key change by key change, the horns going octave, the arrangement turning almost anarchic. But she would never lose sight of the melody. She never did.

Her tribute-medley of songs recorded by Ray Charles—a man for whom she held extraordinary admiration—offered a taste of everything, from the slow, sultry, dazzlingly cool "Just for a Thrill" to the galloping "I Got a Man" to a raucous, hip version of Sy Oliver's "Yes Indeed!" On this last one, with a wide smile on her face, she seemed to offer an affirmation of just about everything that this night, this world, this life could possibly have to offer.

It was over as quickly as it began. The show spanned less than an hour and a half. The final ovation lasted for several minutes, and at last her audience reluctantly trudged out to the sidewalks, where they were met by horse-drawn sleds summoned by the club, the perfect finish to an evening of New York romance in an era that still believed in the possibility of enchantment.

And she? Her night was hardly done. The music was over, leaving a space she would rush to fill. The late, late hours were those she would always call her own, and she would surround herself with company. She could never bear to be alone. And so, again, picture another curious parade on another Basin Street evening, after one particular late show. Picture another odd assembly of souls, this time not out on the sidewalks but in a hallway of the luxurious Waldorf Towers apartments, outside her very own door. The elevator bell pinged, the doors slid open. Out spilled the singer and some of her friends: Cary Grant, Sammy Davis, Jr., Art Carney. But before she turned the key in the door, she indulged a sudden whim. She ordered them all to the floor. "Lie on your backs," she told them. "Now put your head on the stomach of the person lying next to you." And they did.

"Now say 'Ha.'"

"Ha," said one. "Ha, ha," said the next. And within seconds they'd convulsed in laughter. No doubt, had the elevator opened again, the sight would have been hard for a stranger to explain, this cluster of celebrities playing a Cheeveresque suburban-living-room party game—unless our observer understood that on this night, the woman in the beaded dress, after a lifetime of using her pain to create her art, was finally in command of her own universe, as well as ours.

During the two decades when popular music spoke a universal language, Peggy Lee's star blazed brightly. She sang the Great

American Songbook, flavored by jazz and blues and swing and pop and bop and Latin and soul. The music and the culture would soon change, and when the lights finally dimmed, she would be increasingly lost in the darkness. But in a time when art still shaped our popular media, from writing to film to music, she reigned supreme. It was not a time, as now, when "popular" and "disposable" were interchangeable terms. It was a brief, never-to-be-revisited era when popular novels were also literary and enduring, when popular movies were crafted and inspired and lasting. When music had meaning and resonance. The cultural chaos and cacophony that have ensued have done much to obscure the soft brilliance of this particular past. But artistically, it was a golden age in America, and Peggy Lee was in its pantheon—not only as a singer but as a lyricist, and not only a lyricist but a lyricist whose poetry spoke worlds. A Peggy Lee lyric told a story, felt a feeling. She was one of the first important female singer-songwriters, and several of her hits were her own compositions. Few other songstresses of the time could make such a claim.

At the time of her Basin Street triumph, she'd had five recent albums in the top twenty, an annual salary ten times Mickey Mantle's, album sales of many millions. She was a given. She was an icon. She was a cultural emblem in a culture that had not yet radically changed. She wasn't one of our *girls*, like Rosemary Clooney or Dinah Shore or Patti Page or Doris Day; there was more richness to her, more complexity, more undercurrents that couldn't quite be controlled. Ella, of course, was widely held to rule the pop-jazz roost, but she was never quite able to bring a true broken-heart ballad to the depths of the soul that Peggy could. She wasn't Billie, or Sarah, or Anita—all of them brilliant in some ways, but limited in others. She had some of all of them in her, but she was a great deal more. She was singular. No one occupied Peggy Lee's place, because only one woman could:

platinum-pretty, but beholden to no one. Perky and bouncy, but genuinely soulful and world-weary, and resigned.

Musically? She was possessed of nothing less than extraordinary intonation and perfect time—so much so that many of her musicians and collaborators regularly use the word "genius" to describe her innate musical skills. Her personality? Forever in discord. Born Norma Deloris Egstrom, a child of the Depression Great Plains, shy and insecure, she had gradually blossomed—on the surface—into another lady entirely. But the glittering, seductive façade only hid, never erased, the girl beneath, and it was the interplay of the two that produced the woman's art.

"She had an image to uphold," the producer of one of her final albums says. "The dichotomy, I think, was between that girl in North Dakota who she never stopped being, and Miss Peggy Lee, whom she invented and became. Once I asked her if Norma Deloris Egstrom was still there in her. She said yes. I think that was the whole thing about Peggy Lee. The dichotomy between the two."

Peggy Lee was not in a class by herself. There were three others who shared her particular greatness. Armstrong, Crosby, Sinatra, Lee—these are the faces on the Mount Rushmore of American pop, the greatest generation of American music, singing at the height of an era when the American Songbook was the expression of the national heart and soul.

Others sang the songs, of course—countless others, and often brilliantly—but these were the four who perfected an art form now lost to mainstream history—now filed, in a fringe wing of our cultural archives, under "popular jazz singing," which was one of American music's truest contributions. If jazz was our nation's invention, our absolutely original music, it was popular jazz singing whose lyrics and melodic sentiments reached us all and embodied America's dreams of romance, dreams we can no longer even imagine. Peggy and the three men who were truly her peers were the voices of our lost American innocence, of sweetness and gentleness, of longing and melancholy, but always of the *rightness* of things. They were the artists entrusted with expressing the yearnings and desires of an entire culture. No less than that generation of distinctly American writers, they were given a mandate to tell a nation's tale.

History has told us all we need to know about the three men, and more. Their legends live on not only because they lived in a time when men ran the legend-making machinery, but because each had extraordinary talents layered with an unforgettable image. Louis Armstrong brought jazz to the pop mainstream in a tempered manner and entertaining guise that, at the time, we could understand and easily accept from a black man. Bing Crosby brought the gift of a vocal instrument without equal, along with a paternal demeanor, to a country that once admired him more than any other man alive. And Sinatra brought a taste of solo swagger to his swing; as a man, his attitude could be countenanced and embraced and revered in the spirit of the Great American Individualist Pioneer.

History has told us very little of the woman. The musicians know of her stature, of course. But when the music changed and rock altered the landscape, her art had difficulty adapting in the popular eye. Neither could her image adapt. And nor could she. When our dreams died—our hopes for a house on the hill, our certainty that our train would always arrive to carry us forward to the next place, the place where we'd find what we were searching for—her dreams died, too. She grew old, and not always gracefully. For too many years, we forgot her and overlooked what she had achieved as an artist.

Now it is time to remember, and celebrate, and enjoy anew, one of the greatest female singers of that American century, and the music that animated an entire land. It is time to come to know, for the first time, Miss Peggy Lee.

PART I

Dreamland on the Train

ONE

In Dakota

ON THE BARE stage of a small town hall in the middle of an isolated farm village in a large, empty state, a blond girl sat at a piano with her back to the audience, playing the music she loved more than anything else in life. She was ten years old. The year was 1930. The town was Nortonville, North Dakota.

Friends and neighbors had gathered on folding chairs on the floor below. Like most of the people in those times, they had little to spare. The Depression was as unrelenting as the summer winds that scoured their parched topsoil and buffeted the town hall's six narrow windows that day. But the people of Nortonville were happy enough to listen to the girl play, and not only out of a sense of obligation—everyone knew she had troubles at home—but because the fifth-grader with the remarkably upbeat disposition was an obviously talented child.

Norma Egstrom had never performed in a venue as grand as the Nortonville town hall. The biggest room she'd ever played before was the practice space behind the sanctuary over at the modest Methodist church, where she sat at the Washburn upright piano. The town hall was the big time, the social anchor of a community boasting one bank, one hotel, three grocers, a restaurant, a bowling alley, a blacksmith, a livery, a hardware store, and a railroad depot. A long, thin clapboard structure, free of architectural adornment, the hall had been raised from the dirt a dozen years before, in all of three weeks, by townspeople eager to see their crossroads claim some sort of recognition in the beleaguered grassy outback of the southeastern part of their state.

It was here that Nortonville gathered to watch the motion pictures, as kids chewed the sunflower seeds that grew in the endless ocean of fields surrounding their homes. It was here that citizens came to hear the lectures that brought news about the world beyond the plains horizon. It was in the hall that they skated, played basketball, and danced. And it was in the town hall that Norma Deloris Egstrom made her public debut in a recital on that summer afternoon in 1930.

Finishing her song, she rose from the piano stool and heard the applause: the unequivocal and tangible affection that only an audience can provide, a feeling that can be especially gratifying when acceptance is hard to come by in the usual places. She had always been a shy girl; she would later say that she'd sung before she talked. Now she'd spoken, and she'd been heard.

People in Nortonville who recall that day won't go so far as to say that the girl was the best child pianist they'd ever heard, but they still marvel at her dedication. They speak of her with pride, though some concede that even before she played a note, the members of the audience were already disposed to like her. Norma Egstrom's dad, a father of seven, the station manager for the humble Midland Continental Railroad depot just down the street, was a gentle, kind, whimsical man. But he was also a drinker. He wasn't morose, or somber, or violent, but neither was he responsible or accomplished. Marvin Egstrom was a "rail"— an itinerant depot manager and agent—at a time when depots and railroads dotted the landscape of America.

Before his sixth child's birth, Marvin's curriculum vitae had been a checkered one. He'd been a superintendent with the South Central Dakota line down in Sioux Falls until his drinking prompted the railroad to demote him to station agent. After that, he'd hooked up with the Midland Continental, up north in Jamestown, North Dakota, where, according to documents from the archives of the railroad's owner at the time, Egstrom had been associated with a scandal involving fraud and larceny. The railroad had exiled him to Nortonville, with a significant cut in salary, when Norma was eight.

Most people who knew him would say that Marvin Egstrom and the everyday did not, in general, make a good fit, especially in a part of the nation where a man was defined by the acreage he owned. The railroad people had no real place there. They worked for a machine that signified transience in a state that was still enough of a frontier to pride itself on roots, literal and figurative. The Midland, not one of the more impressive lines, comprised only seventy-seven miles of track running north and south from Wimbledon to Edgeley with just a dozen stops in between.

Marvin Egstrom was a pleasant, ineffectual man who, like nearly all of his family's members, had music in his soul. It manifested itself in unconventional ways, like the performance of an impromptu jig in the post office in the middle of the day, or a solo sung to the rails at two in the morning. "A couple of drinks," recalled one of Norma's classmates, "and her father could do the best soft-shoe dance you ever saw."

Marvin's wife, Min—Norma's stepmother—cut a very different figure. She was stout, dour, congenitally cross, and surrounded by rumors. One concerned the freak accident in South Dakota—involving a torch and a frozen valve on a drum of gasoline—that had blown her first husband's head off. Speculation would persist that the man had killed himself. His widow's stern and humorless demeanor did little to lessen the credence of the tale.

Other stories came closer to home, and were far more credible: Min Egstrom, it was whispered, beat her stepdaughter.

The people of Nortonville (population 125) knew little about Norma's early childhood up the road in Jamestown, the county seat. Jamestown could boast the college and the mighty Northern Pacific's terminal, as well as the headquarters station of the humble Midland. It was also the home of the "bughouse"—the state mental institution, south of town.

Norma's real mother, Selma Anderson Egstrom, had died in Jamestown at the age of thirty-nine, when Norma was four. In April 1924, she had given birth to her last child, a daughter named Jean, and was confined to her bed after that. On August 6, Selma passed away, leaving seven children: Norma, her five older brothers and sisters, and her infant sister. Marvin and Selma Egstrom had been married for twenty-one years.

With the Reverend Joseph Johnson of the Scandinavian Lutheran church presiding, the memorial service was held in the Egstrom home. Too small to peek over the coffin's side, Norma was lifted up to peer into her mother's casket. She would recall seeing a frail woman at rest. Selma Egstrom's remains were sent to her family's hometown of Volga, South Dakota, where she was buried. Norma's infant sister, Jean, went to live with Selma

Egstrom's sister until the girl's death, at age fourteen, of "a heart ailment of long standing."

Norma was now the youngest in the household: a four-year-old with no mother, an alcoholic father, and her music. It was upon the occasion of her mother's death that Norma wrote her first song. "I remember writing a lyric to the song 'Melody of Love' when my mother died, when I was four," Peggy Lee would recall, many years later when her imagination and sense of her own myth had been heightened. "It wasn't a brilliant lyric, but I think it was interesting that a child would write one. I would walk around the house singing, 'Mama's gone to dreamland on the train.'"

Norma's memories of her mother's home were vivid. In later years she would recall Selma's crystal and fresh linen, the scents of her baking, and the melodies her mother sang and played on the keys of her prize possession: a Circassian walnut piano. As in so many households of the time, entertainment in the Egstrom house was left to the creativity of the family, and music had always been part of the Egstroms' lives. Years later, a classmate would remember that both Della and Marianne Egstrom, Norma's two older sisters, had exceptional voices. "But they did not," recalled the classmate, "have the oomph to do anything about it."

Six months after Selma's death, the Egstrom home burned to the ground. Until the family relocated to another place in Jamestown, Norma lived with the former in-laws, and then the parents, of Min Schaumberg, who had been working as the nurse for Norma's married sister Della's first child.

Norma enjoyed her time with the elder Schaumbergs as best she could. The old man's meerschaum pipe, his German-language newspaper, his old-world ways—these intrigued and comforted her. Best of all, they had a player piano. During the afternoons, the Schaumbergs would try to coax the girl into taking a nap in the parlor, but she spent more time on her knees pumping the pedals with her hands than she did sleeping.

More often, Norma would be in the yard outside, peering out through the black iron picket fence as she waited for her father to visit and take her away, if only for a meal. One day Marvin Egstrom arrived with news: Min Schaumberg would be Norma's new mother. Min's son, Edwin, would be her stepbrother. One year to the week after her mother's death, Marvin Egstrom officially took a new wife. The unusual figure they cut—the thin, pleasant Marvin and the fat, frowning Min—would prompt many remarks.

"I didn't want to imagine him loving her after mama," Norma would later write in her memoir, *Miss Peggy Lee*. "I often wondered why Daddy and Min got married. Was it because of what Marianne and I heard . . . about Daddy being asked by [his supervisor] to 'fix the books a little for the good of the railroad'? It was something about the per diem reports. Was it because Daddy was drinking and Min knew and might tell on him?"

Far likelier was that Marvin Egstrom, a widower with several children, wanted a woman who could run his household while he tried to hold down his own job and his children did their share around the home and in the community. Like all the kids in Jamestown, Norma and her siblings who still lived at home— Marianne and brother Clair—would be sent out to help on local farms. It was Clair she was always closest to, though he did torment his little sister in the universal fashion of older siblings. When they had to harvest pails of gooseberries in a local park, Clair would stuff the bottom of his own bucket with grass and leaves and talk Norma into exchanging pails. When they'd help out on a local farm, Clair would get Norma to milk the cows that he was supposed to milk. As for Min's own son, Edwin, neither

Norma nor Clair was particularly fond of him. The feeling was said to be mutual.

It is not hard to imagine bashful, quiet Norma acceding to her older brother's schemes. Self-conscious about her weight and no doubt baffled by the inexplicable (to a young child) disappearance of her mother, Norma had trouble meeting someone's glance. Her reticence even extended to the legendary local barnstormer whose aerial antics above the fields outside Jamestown provided prairie entertainment. Still, despite her shyness, Norma was fascinated with Ole Olson's Curtiss; it was said he could pick up a handkerchief with the wingtip of his plane. Norma wanted to go up into the sky so badly that one day, when Olson told her he'd take her if she'd dance the Charleston for him, dance she did, and up she went.

The escape was fleeting. Within days of her father's wedding, Norma's stepmother had wielded the willow switch she'd commanded the girl to pluck for punishment. Whatever the woman's motivation, discipline was frequent and formidable: "Florid face, bulging thyroid eyes, long black hair to her waist pulled back in a bun, heavy breathing," was Norma's later recollection of Min. "Obese and strong as a horse, she beat everyone into a fright. Even the men were afraid of her."

Added to the physical beatings were psychological ones. Her stepmother would criticize Norma's physical attributes: She weighed too much; her hands were too big. "I grew up terribly self-conscious of [my hands]," Peggy Lee once said, many years later. "I would hold them behind me . . . fold them up, never present them flat to view but edge-wise only. I was one of the quickest handshakers you ever saw."

When the Midland relocated Marvin and his family down to Nortonville, the Egstroms didn't have much to move. Norma took her love of music, and a subtle sound that had imprinted itself in her head during the years she'd lived just a few blocks from the busy Northern Pacific tracks: the downbeat of iron boxcar wheels clacking one after another, hundreds of them, forever on end. She would carry the rhythm wherever she went—just as she carried the songs she had learned to love—for the rest of her life.

Music surrounded her. With radio in its infancy, and with most of the prairie towns not yet electrified, it was routine for folks to play instruments in their homes. As Norma played her recital in 1930, windup Victrolas and Columbia Grafanolas across the land were featuring anthems designed to buoy the listeners: "Happy Days Are Here Again," "Puttin' On the Ritz." Even the instrumentals, like Ted Lewis's "On the Sunny Side of the Street," had a skip to them, a rhythmic current whose spirit could carry a girl along, afloat, away from the plains, with their infinite horizons. If Peggy Lee would grow to master the minimal, to practice the art of less-is-more, perhaps the empty, featureless plains of her childhood are owed some of the credit.

Make no mistake: Nortonville, North Dakota, was not a desperate place. It was a village where life was simply lived, and lived simply, a place where people would not abide self-pity. Largely of sensible Scandinavian stock, the residents did not complain about the things they couldn't control, like the windstorm that razed half of Bismarck, the state capital, one hundred miles due west, in 1929. Or the drought that made that same summer the driest in the state's history. The soil, already loosened by too many years of punishing droughts and settler farmers tearing up the prairie, was raked by wind that swept the Midwest from Texas to Canada and back again. The dust settled into people's pores, and the silt piled up a half-inch deep on the sills of Nortonville's windows. Women would hang sheets wetted at the town pump to keep the grit out of their homes. But nature's indifference wasn't personal, and it was best just to play the cards you'd been dealt.

Like any small town, Nortonville was full of characters. Harmless little Hoover, a dim-witted boy, would dip his bucket into the pond outside of town again and again, in an effort to drain it and catch the duck out in the middle. Odd, boozy Fred Bitz's in-laws, who sold Fred their moonshine, were the last folks to see him alive before his body was discovered in his old pickup in the middle of a bean field. The suspicion was suicide by carbon monoxide. No one was surprised; life was growing increasingly unsettled. New faces arrived every day, men and boys dripping off the sides of the boxcars. The hoboes, many of them young— at the Depression's height, the army of men on the road included a quarter-million teenagers—came to the door asking for food. They passed word along about who gave a "lump" (a bit of food in a bag) and who was a "knee-shaker" (a more giving sort who dispensed a full tray). The odd markings on the pole at the end of one street had a secret significance: They were a private code that pointed out where to go for food, shelter, or work.

Norma, as generous as she could afford (or was allowed) to be, gave the workers—among them the first Negro men she had ever seen—bread and butter. She felt for the boys turned out from their homes, their parents unable to support them. She felt for the older men stripped of their pride. But their freedom was intriguing, too. "I'll leave," Norma Egstrom thought, "when I find out where these railroad tracks lead."

The train, coming up from Edgeley, to the south, and down from Jamestown, to the north, carried more than vagrants. It brought news of life in Jamestown; reports of the biggest moonshiners' bust in history west of Chicago; news of farmers blockading roads to drive prices up. In Nortonville, the concern was more immediate: heating the homes. Local farmers had taken to burning the grain they couldn't sell, to keep their families warm.

The winter of 1930 was typical for North Dakota. The snow

didn't stop until it had completely buried one house. The neighbors had to dig it out, starting with the chimney. It was the kind of winter in which a little girl, loaned out to help with chores, found her hands frozen by the water from the cistern. She thawed them by running them through snow.

On the bitterly cold day of January 5, 1930, the Nortonville Midland depot burned. It was the second time in ten years that fire had taken the Egstroms' residence. "A lot of the residents were in church," recalled Mattie Brandt, one of Norma's schoolmates. "The door burst open and someone yelled, 'The depot is on fire!' Everyone left church and went to the fire. When we got there, the fire was beyond control. And there was a second accident to be dealt with: Min had come down the stairs to get a pail of water and had slipped on the ice around the old pump and lay there with a broken leg."

' The cause of the blaze was unknown. A cinder, perhaps, from a Midland engine's coal stove. Or perhaps the recklessness that curses an alcoholic home. The family moved into a tiny gabled clapboard house one block behind Main Street, which Clair and Marianne—Norma's only siblings still at home—would both soon leave: After the family's arrival in Nortonville, Norma helped Marianne run away to her sister Della's home in the eastern part of the state. Norma suffered a beating for not revealing where her sister had gone. Some years later, she would also be complicit in Clair's escape. "Marianne, Clair, and I seldom found much happiness" was her concise assessment, years later, of their time in Nortonville.

The house lay less than a hundred yards from the school, and for Norma, whose chores began early, the proximity was fortunate; her teacher would ring the schoolhouse bell extra long on the mornings that the young girl hadn't yet arrived. He'd keep ringing it until he saw her run out the door and sprint to school, lest she be marked tardy and have to face the consequences back home.

Next door to Norma lived a woman named Pearl Buck (no relation to the famous author), beloved in the county, the epitome of the independent North Dakota pioneer. So firm in her opinions was Mrs. Buck that she voted only once in her life. (Displeased with the outcome, she never voted again.) But Pearl was the best pianist and organist for counties around. She played the piano in the Methodist church, and would teach music to many girls before she finally passed away at the age of one hundred and three. Pearl found Norma Egstrom a delightful, funny little child. When Norma watched the older woman's hands on the piano keys, she became very serious. It was as if, somewhere inside her, something had opened up.

The day that the Otter Tail Power Company electrified Nortonville was an occasion for villagewide celebration. No one was more delighted than Norma. Before the power company had harnessed the current of the Otter Tail River back east in Minnesota, villagers had been forced to rely on the largesse of those few folks lucky enough to have basement generators. The arrival of power in every home brought new possibilities. What mattered most to Norma were the radios.

On a grand scale, radio changed the world, opening the doors to a new kind of town hall: a place where not only news but music could reach us all, from the hymns that were so dear to the staunch Lutherans to new sounds from distant cities—the orchestra of Duke Ellington, Chick Webb's rollicking band, the revolutionary trumpet solos of a man named Louis Armstrong.

But on a smaller scale, for a certain kind of child, radio wove together the disparate elements of a dream. For a young girl searching for a place to belong—a place that, until recently, she could only try to imagine—the melodies of a single song, from a distant city or an exotic rooftop ballroom, became more than tunes. They carried the first glimpse of an alternate life, facets of a picture of a very different future.

When Norma was eight years old, another little girl could ask her, "What are you going to be?" and Norma could answer, without really knowing what it meant, "I'm going to be in show business some day."

Picture Norma Egstrom like this, then, if you need a few snapshots: Imagine her at the piano by Pearl Buck's side, or, a few years later, splayed on her stomach listening to her family's new Atwater-Kent five-dial radio in the mahogany cabinet with the bell-horned speaker that looked like nothing so much as a blooming flower. Picture her singing along to the tunes of the day: "Night and Day," or "Georgia on My Mind," or a song that particularly appealed: "My Blue Heaven," with its lyric "Just Molly and me, and baby makes three." Or, to Norma's ears, "Just Mama and me, and Daddy makes three." To a girl with no mother, the lyrics of popular romantic ballads lent an idea of the way it might have been. *If.*

Lots of little girls were sitting in front of radios in 1930s North Dakota, but very few were hearing what Norma Egstrom did. This was obvious to those who hired Norma to babysit, only to discover quickly that she was not the most reliable of girls if there was a radio or a piano in the house. Not reliable *at all.* As a Nortonville neighbor recalls, "We had a new baby, and she was supposed to help out with the chores, but she wasn't very helpful. She just *sang* all the time."

Norma's generally buoyant nature concealed, but couldn't erase, a more confused, darker disposition. Though she tried to avoid it, she occasionally lingered on the shadowy side of the street. One particularly gloomy day, all alone, Norma raised a glass full of cleaning fluid emblazoned by a skull and crossbones to her lips. Interrupted by her stepbrother, she wound up pouring the bottle down the sink. It was all likely no more than a theatrical gesture—and a natural impulse for any child who had lost a parent at too young an age to understand death as anything but abandonment.

One day when she was ten, Norma's stomach started to hurt, and she had to ride eighteen miles to the south over unpaved roads to have her appendix removed. The procedure was performed in a doctor's office on the second floor of a dark brick building on the main street of Edgeley; in the next room, Norma heard the moans of a patient "taking the cure"—presumably, withdrawing from alcoholism. But she was back at her chores within a week. She cooked for threshing crews for good money, $2.50 an hour. She fed the pigs and the sheep of the neighboring farms. She also fed and plucked the chickens, which delighted her. One day, in a rainstorm, she watched a small bird open its beak, tilt its head back, fill its gullet with water, and tip forward to the ground dead, a scene so absurd as to be cosmically comical to her. Not surprisingly for a bright, creative kid looking for ways to deal with a difficult life, she was already developing an ironic and unconventional sense of humor, an irreverent and skewed way of looking at the world. She and her friend Ebbie told the same joke over and over, the one about the man whose toe and nose had been cut off and reattached in the wrong places: Whenever he had to blow his nose, he'd take off his shoe. It would make her laugh for the rest of her life.

She washed clothes, and scrubbed floors, and cleaned out barns. She delivered milk and eggs to neighbors. She was diligent and reliable, careful not to drop an egg or spill a bottle of milk. The consequences would have been severe, though no one in town was absolutely certain about the beatings. They never saw Min shove Norma's head into the garbage pail, or use the willow switch or the leather razor strop. Peggy Lee would say, years later, that these things happened. She would tell the stories again and again. One time, Norma related famously, Min used an iron skillet as her weapon, and the girl felt a crack inside her jaw. Decades hence, when every detail of the girl's face had become widely known, a distinctive sideways rocking of her jaw would come to be a signature, along with her coolness and hip nonchalance.

Norma did not generally confide in her father. She would later say that she had no desire to burden him any more than he was already burdened. She did not want to rely on his help. She would depend on her own ability to survive.

She would depend on her own resources—her talent, her inner muse, her growing determination to lighten the burdens she was now bearing at a very young age.

And they were considerable. It would have been difficult enough for an insecure and reserved child to suffer the inexplicable loss of a mother and the functional absence of a dad whose love was earnest but incomplete. Add to that the physical and psychological abuse rendered for no good reason at all, and Norma Egstrom's determination to break away, to use her gift as a passport to a promised land as soon as possible, is hardly baffling. Within a very few years, she would turn her back on the desolate, dark monotone of her prairie upbringing to seek love and acceptance in the multihued palaces of another land entirely. But for the time being, she would shoulder her burdens within.

By the time she was twelve, Norma was snapping her fingers to music featuring a beat decidedly at odds with Lutheran hymns. The sound bouncing out of radio speakers was hardly new to the people filling the clubs of New Orleans and Kansas City, Chicago and New York, or to the sophisticated listeners who had spent the previous decade imbibing the music called jazz. Norma, getting her first taste of the music that would change her life, didn't know that Cab Calloway and Duke Ellington were packing them in over in London, where—as always—the Europeans were light-years ahead of the Americans.

She didn't know about the Paul Whiteman Orchestra, rocking New York's Paramount Theater, or the wild act of two kids named Bing Crosby and Al Rinker, or the cornet accompaniment of Bix Beiderbecke, the first white jazzman to prove that the new music crossed racial barriers. She hadn't heard of the work of Louis Armstrong, who seemed to be dreaming up something absolutely original every time he set foot on a stage. Norma had not yet listened to the new female voices, either. She hadn't encountered the women who had supplanted the soprano males whose megaphoned warblings had traditionally accompanied dance bands: Bessie Smith, who was packing them in at the Alhambra in Harlem, and Al Rinker's cousin Mildred Bailey, who would be considered the greatest white female jazz singer for a few more decades, until a girl named Peggy Lee stole her crown.

Norma's ears were more attuned to devotional melody and sentimental pop. She had never read R.W.S. Mendl's *The Appeal of Jazz*, written in the late twenties. But as her treasured radio began to introduce her to the rhythms, beats, and inflections that would change her from the inside out, she would have appreciated Mendl's boast: "Jazz, or syncopated dance music, appeals to more people in the world than any other form of music."

Untrained (and never to be) in music theory, she couldn't have explained what was happening technically. She couldn't have sensed that the European canon—the backbone of the music she sang at church—was blending with African rhythms coming out of the South, out of Bill Basie's stride piano over in Kansas City, out of Fletcher Henderson's wild piano stylings up in Harlem. She would not, could not have known that the frenzied, insistent 2/4 ragtime beat of the jazz of the last few decades was stretching out into 4/4—the tempo of a heartbeat, as an arranger named Nelson Riddle would say years later.

She certainly knew nothing of the place where the siren song of jazz was coming from most entrancingly: a block of about-to-be-famous speakeasies on West Fifty-second Street in New York City. Halfway between the Village and Harlem, West Fifty-second sampled from both of the island's extremes. The block that drew musicians of all stripes fronted a total of thirty-eight speakeasies boasting bad liquor, good music, and a heady haven from Prohibition. Norma knew nothing of an occurrence on West Fifty-second one night in 1933, when, at 10:30 in the evening, two men met in a club called the Onyx. They were men whose backgrounds would have made their acquaintance unlikely, if not impossible, outside the world of the new music. And they would alter not only Norma's life, but those of a million musicians who would change the sound America loved.

On that fateful night in New York, John Hammond, society swell, uttered the Onyx's three-syllable password—Eight Oh Two, the local of the musicians' union—then walked through the door to wait for the arrival of a clarinet player raised in the Jewish ghetto of Chicago.

At first glance, or on paper, the handsome, twenty-three-year-old Hammond, a familiar Fifty-second Street patron, didn't fit the profile of the average "speak" denizen. He'd been raised in a household of sixteen servants and owed it all—Hotchkiss, Yale—to the New York Central Railroad, founded by his grandfather, Commodore Vanderbilt, one of the most influential railroad barons in history. But the grave black-and-orange volume of the annual Social Register was not the book where John Hammond's name was destined to be most prominently featured.

In 1922, on a trip to London at the age of twelve, Hammond had heard his first jazz band: Paul Specht's Georgians, led by one of the first bandleaders to experiment in that decade with "arranged jazz." At first listening, something had shifted inside Hammond. Thereafter, on vacations from his red-brick prep school in Connecticut's Litchfield County, or later from the Yale campus in New Haven, he did not hang out in the family mansion. He visited Fifty-second Street, and the Village, and Harlem, where he became a regular at some of the hotter clubs: the Yeah Man, the Hotcha, the Alhambra Grill.

Hammond was not the first white kid of privilege to be drawn to places where music defies societal convention. Nor was he the first prep-Ivy sort to discover the effect of unfamiliar rhythms on the bluest of bloods. But he was one of the first to devote his life to the marriage of black beat and white convention. From behind the scenes, John Hammond would do more to change the course of American popular music than any other single musician ever did.

By his early twenties, Hammond was a correspondent for *British Gramophone* and *Melody Maker* magazines, reporting for Londoners on the burgeoning U.S. jazz scene, and when he was back home, rounding up jazz musicians for English recordings. Britannia had a taste for the new stuff. In particular, British record executive Sir Louis Sterling wanted to make records with the young clarinetist Benny Goodman, a white kid from Chicago who had made a name for himself. Did Hammond know Goodman? Could he sign him?

Hammond may not have let on that they had met and hadn't clicked—hardly a surprise, given Benny's reserved demeanor and Hammond's confident strut. Then there was Hammond's obvious bias toward black musicians. To top it off, Hammond had been less than enthralled by Benny's playing ("I felt that Benny was a good clarinet player," Hammond would write in his autobiography, "although no better than Jimmy Dorsey, and less good than several black clarinetists I could think of").

But business was business, and Hammond promised to deliver four sides by Goodman. Hammond's mission at the Onyx on that fateful night in 1933 was to bring home the bacon. "I have a British contract," he told Benny, who was persuaded to listen: Goodman was, at the time, bringing in the sum total of $50 a week for a radio show. When Hammond relayed the news that Sterling wanted a "mixed" band, with Lionel Hampton on vibes and Teddy Wilson on piano, Benny balked—not out of prejudice, but pragmatism: The times were not enlightened enough for Goodman to record with Negroes. Nonetheless, there were some white guys around who might be able to do a passable job: Benny's quintet would ultimately include drummer nonpareil Gene Krupa and fabled trombonist Jack Teagarden.

Their first two sides were a pleasant enough Fats Waller tune called "Aintcha Glad" and a number called "I Gotta Right to Sing the Blues," written for a Broadway revue called *Earl Carroll's Vanities of 1932* by a couple of guys attracting a lot of attention: Harold Arlen, a cantor's son from Buffalo, and his wordsmith partner, Ted Koehler.

Hammond wasn't overly optimistic when Benny's band arrived at the Columbia studios in New York; he thought both songs too commercial for what he'd promised to deliver—until Benny took the reins in the studio. "He suddenly abandoned the commercial considerations that had dominated his thinking about the date up to now," wrote Ross Firestone in his biography of Goodman, "and began to tear the arrangements apart, setting riff backgrounds here, assigning solo spots there, giving himself over to the spirit of the music that Hammond had been trying so hard to instill in him."

The feel was infectious. The record sold an impressive five thousand copies—the first ripple of a wave that, in a very few years, would buoy a whole nation. A wave that would lift and carry Norma Egstrom away.

In 1933, as a thirteen-year-old, all Norma could hope for was to catch the stuff riding the airwaves out of distant Fargo, a hundred miles east, on WDAY: Basie's work with Benny Moten's band, which she loved, and Lester Young's tenor sax, with the Blue Devils of Minneapolis, Arlen's dark, langorous, enduring "Stormy Weather," and Ellington's ultimately cool "Sophisticated Lady." Maybe, if she was lucky, she got to hear Fletcher Henderson's orchestra itself, from a New York studio.

All of them were coming from the same place: a land where any outsider with a taste for a beat might belong. With their joyous urgency, their rhythmic flow, these songs and anarchic stylings spoke to a girl whose true language, from the very start, had been the music inside her. They took her someplace the straighter rails never ventured.

TWO

Pick Up Your Telephone

WHEN NORMA WAS fourteen, the Midland Continental found itself in need of a new depot manager up at the northernmost stop
of the line, in Wimbledon. The railroad reassigned none other
than Marvin Egstrom. The town that was to be Norma's new
home lay thirty miles north of Jamestown. Its lifeblood pumped a
little more urgently than Nortonville's.

Two railroads served the transportation needs of Wimbledon.
The Midland teed into the east-west line of the Minneapolis, St.
Paul and Sault Sainte Marie—the Soo Line. The confluence of
two lines of steel made Norma's new home something of a rail-
road nexus, and Marvin Egstrom a slightly more important man.
Min Egstrom, who also worked for the railroad, was assigned to

the depot down in Millarton, though she continued to spend much of her time in Wimbledon.

When her father was transferred, in the spring of 1934, Norma was in the ninth grade down in Nortonville, and she moved in with the Erickson family for the final month of the school year. The talk, of course, was that Norma and Min had been fighting and the Ericksons had taken in their daughter's friend. Years later, however, one of the Erickson girls would recall no motive for housing Norma other than her need to finish the school year where she'd started it; it was simply the neighborly thing to do.

When Norma eventually moved to join her father and stepmother in Wimbledon, she rode the Midland up and disembarked at her new home: the Midland Continental depot. Not surprisingly, it looked exactly like the depot in Nortonville that had burned down. The paint scheme, bright yellow with green trim, was just the same. The family resided in the four rooms of the second-floor apartment, with its crank-and-holler Bell telephone: "Pick Up Your Telephone," implored the two-page directory's legend, "and the Barriers of Time and Distance disappear."

In Wimbledon, the Midland Continental's northernmost station, the last stop before open prairie, the depot manager had more responsibility. Marvin Egstrom wasn't always up to it. It was a good thing his daughter was. Norma didn't mind taking over the management of the depot when her dad's drinking rendered him all but useless. "The part I loved about running the station," she would later write, "was that daddy was around, even though he was drinking. He was fun."

The poignancy of that last sentiment is hard to ignore; having a father who was known about town as sometimes unable to man his post because of his love of the bottle could have hardly been fun. But who could blame her for wanting to gloss her world? For putting the best spin possible on her plight? For the rest of her life, Norma would forever forgive her father, never lay blame. Her love for Marvin Egstrom was, in some ways, the one true, pure, uncompromised love of her life.

She ran bills of lading—the Midland's freight included grain and grain products, lignite coal, and crude oil—across the tracks to the Soo depot, which was run by the father of a new school classmate, a kind man named William Brenner. Norma got to sit in her father's chair and look down the tracks and watch the Soo's big train—Train 13, the *Twin Cities*—heading back east. In her new town, the tracks out the window didn't end in a field down in Edgeley, they beckoned: Follow those tracks east, and there was no city's allure they wouldn't offer.

Norma wasn't the only kid in town who found the railroad romantic. Ethelyn Olson was a few years older than Norma, but she took to the younger girl immediately and enjoyed visiting after school at the Midland depot. "She wasn't a wild-acting person," Ethelyn recalls now. "Or a loud person. She was always a little on the plump order. I remember she wore one dress so much of the time . . . it was almost like a satin . . . but it was muslin. She was just plump enough; it fit her quite tight. I remember it pulling apart at the side seam."

Norma's weight would forever fluctuate, although it wasn't until much later in her life, when she was a public persona subject to the public's fickle scrutiny, that it would be an issue. In adolescence, she was a pretty girl, but hardly beautiful; photographs of Norma posed with a church choir at fourteen or fifteen depict a slightly plump girl in her midteens, with a sunflower smile framed by a blond coif, simply a cute face in the crowd.

Kindred spirits, Ethelyn and Norma sang in a trio at the school and wrote poetry and music together. Ethelyn dreamed idly of being a singer, but not as seriously as her new friend did. During the summer of 1934, when they were working at different farms, Norma had the good luck to be working at a place with both a piano and a telephone. The latter, of course, was connected to a party line, but as Ethelyn tells it, Norma didn't care. She'd hear a song on the radio, transpose it by ear, and call her friend up: " 'Hey Ethelyn, listen to this!'—and then I'd hear her put the phone down," her friend remembers, "and she'd play a song she'd heard on the radio."

Ethelyn wondered what the other people on the line must have thought when they'd pick up their phone and hear Norma Egstrom's impromptu midsummer recital of "You Oughta Be in Pictures," or "Moonglow," or "April in Paris." But she doubted that anyone was really annoyed.

During the school year, Ethelyn never kidded herself about why Norma liked to hang out with her. It wasn't just that the two liked each other; Ethelyn's folks' piano figured into the friendship. "She'd say, 'Ethelyn, if you would come home with me after school and help me do the dishes, I'll come out and stay at your house tonight.' We lived at the very edge of town, and she would come out to our place and bang on that piano. My mom was classically trained, and Dad was a pianist, but they didn't hurt her feelings—they would go out and sit on the front porch."

At the Midland depot, once they'd finished their chores, the girls would sit at Marvin's desk in the depot manager's office, right off the waiting room, with its woodstove and its view of both the Soo and Midland tracks. "It was so exciting for me to go down to her dad's office, sitting at the counter with those tall stools," Ethelyn recalls. "I thought, 'This is something different for an old farm girl.' It was sitting on those stools we got the idea of writing songs. I'd start writing the words to a song, and she'd start humming and write the notes. How many songs did the two of us write, just sitting there?"

Some of Ethelyn and Norma's tunes weren't bad. On occasion, Norma sang some of them at PTA meetings. Ethelyn was happy to have them heard—and especially happy for Norma, whose hardships at home were obvious to her friend ever since the day Ethelyn saw Min Egstrom's unusual demeanor up close. The girls' arms were plunged elbow-deep in sudsy dishwater when Ethelyn felt someone approach, and turned. "That stepmother, I swear, she weighed three hundred pounds," Ethelyn recalled. "The sight of the two of them—her father was so thin—was something to see. I was scared to death of her. When Norma used to ask me if I would come home after school, I'd always ask, 'Will your stepmother be there?' She'd say, 'If she's around, we'll just have to be kind of quiet.' But I was scared to death of her.

"That day, her stepmother came out to the kitchen. She came over and Norma and I were giggling, doing the dishes, and she came over and slapped Norma across the face: 'Get those dishes done! Quit your fooling!' I remember seeing the mark. We really toned down. Norma didn't dare complain. We were all business after that. We sobered right up."

Min had few fans among Norma's friends. "Her life growing up with that stepmother was pretty sad, but she never made any bones about it," recalls her friend Mary Rose. "She never really complained. If you ever got inside the depot, and got your first impression of the stepmother, you knew she was not good to Peggy. She made her work so hard. . . . She used to have to scrub those old wooden floors. I can still see her yet, down on her hands and knees."

"Norma didn't have too happy a home life," says another friend, Lillian Wehler. "But old man Egstrom was nice—he just couldn't drink. My mother would cook for him when his wife was down in Millarton. The stepmother we tried to stay away from as much as possible. She had a nasty tongue. She was just *cross*. I don't think she had a kind bone in her body. But Norma was a good kid—a nice kid. She had her dad on her side, but her dad wasn't strong enough to do much good for her. She never knew if she could go home or not: What kind of welcome would she get from the stepmother? I was sure glad it wasn't me. I had so much, and she had so much sorrow."

But despite the difficulties, there were things in which Norma Egstrom took pride. For example, she was proud of her railroad, the way a mother would be proud of her runt. The Midland Continental was as much Norma Egstrom's as anyone else's. Who else had lived in two of its depots? Who else had managed a depot by age fourteen? It pained Norma that her railroad was the subject of local jokes about its reliance on used equipment—a Model T car on rail wheels, two converted buses. She must also have been a bit sensitive about the grandeur of its competitors: Down in Jamestown the Great Northern ("Great Freight") boasted of locomotive power so herculean it could pull the mile-long *Empire Builder* through the Cascade Range on its way out west. The Midland, on the other hand, with its typically humble motto— "Satisfying Service"—boasted of the tiger lilies that bloomed in the fields that flanked its route.

A railroad that tried to appeal to passengers by implying they could step off and gather flowers didn't suggest speed or timeliness. The Midland's meager rise and subsequent fall mirrored any number of industrial concerns in the "Dirty Thirties." With 95 percent of its oil freight lost to the development of Canadian oil fields, Norma's railroad was, by 1934, struggling as much as the town of Wimbledon, itself the victim of a recent bank embezzlement. The stolid red-brick railroad hotel next to her depot was long deserted and downright spooky.

The two-story brick high school on the other side of town, though, was a going concern, and Norma was one of its stars. She found time to join the glee club. Students walking past the gym during rehearsals could hear strains of "The Whiffenpoof Song" lilting from the windows as the group practiced for the countywide glee-club competition being held over in Valley City to the east. If Val City wasn't exactly the big time, entertainment-wise, it was definitely the bigger time. Val City boasted of a thriving main street, and a teachers' college, and the lovely three-story Rudolph Hotel, bedecked by columns and architectural detail at every turn. The Rudolph offered fine dining, nice lodging—and a new radio station, which had just gone on the air. No surprise that Norma soon felt the pull east.

The Wimbledon glee club finished second in the Valley City competition. But Norma had other prizes in mind. On one day trip to Val City, she sat in the audience for a local talent show and, unimpressed by the entrants, took the stage, sang—and won.

By now, Min Egstrom was more or less alone in not believing in Norma's future as a singer. Her high-school music teacher, Janet Stein, coached high-school music groups, and the enterprising Egstrom girl would "whip up a skit to be presented between acts during school plays," Stein would recall. One day she showed her teacher a notebook in which she'd written a song called "Purple Hills in the Sunset." She even professed her wish to sing with the budding star crooner of the radio waves, Bing Crosby. "She didn't know the meaning of *can't*."

Bob Ingstad, the young man who was the voice of Valley City on KVOC, had more than a few things in common with the girl he was about to meet: ambition, a wild imagination, and a love of the new music. One of his first hires at KVOC had been a local girl named Edith Butcher, who sang the traditional tunes that the farm folk enjoyed on their Atwater-Kents after a day of work in the fields. But Ingstad knew he needed to look to the future. The popular songs in 1934 clearly showed that the times were changing. Along with Guy Lombardo's "Winter Wonderland" and Paul Whiteman's band's "Smoke Gets in Your Eyes," there was more adventurous fare—Chick Webb's band's "Stompin' at the Savoy" was a big hit nationwide. Benny Goodman himself had recently sat in, uncredited, on the recording by a still-unknown singer named Billie Holiday of a fine new side called "What a Little Moonlight Can Do."

Ingstad needed an original act to put his station on the map, and he found it in his back yard. The Doc Haines Orchestra was not an orchestra, really, just college kid Lyle "Doc" Haines at the piano, and a rhythm section. Doc was a pretty compelling character—tall and handsome, with an athletic build, a soft face accented by wire-rimmed glasses, and a shock of thick brown hair combed straight back. Back over in Wimbledon not long before, when Doc's boys hit the Roxie, some of the locals had pointed out the Egstrom girl to him. "She's our star," they said. "You ought to use her in your band."

Ingstad had hired a staff pianist for the station, a girl with serious experience. Belle Ginsberg had played for a sorority band over in Grand Forks at the University of North Dakota. She knew her stuff. When a young teenager named Norma showed up one day to ask Ginsberg for an audition, Belle liked the kid immediately. The voice itself wasn't extraordinary. But her delivery was. She could hit the notes, but more: She could play with them. And how could your heart not go out to her? She wasn't dressed too well—she clearly came from the sticks—but Belle asked Ingstad to give Norma Egstrom an audition. When he consented, the pianist took care of a little business first. She bought Norma a pair of stockings and sat her down for a few rehearsals. Then Norma took her place in the studio, behind the glass and in front of Doc Haines and the boys.

Bob Ingstad, prepared for just about anything, sat down and half-listened as Norma Egstrom started to sing "You Oughta Be in Pictures," a hit for Rudy Vallee. Fairly quickly, she had his full attention. That night, Bob told his brother that something special had happened. "We had a girl on with Doc's boys," Bob Ingstad boasted to his friend, "and she's the real thing." His opinion was shared by a local restaurant, which offered to sponsor a show for the girl. Norma's quarter-hour aired just before Edith Butcher's fifteen-minute spot on Sunday afternoons.

"Norma would come and listen to me and have her nose right up to the window," Butcher remembers now. "I had classical music. She had jazz. Afterward we had so much fun talking about how it went. We'd go have a Coke together. We didn't have to do a lot of things. We'd just enjoy. Norma always wore a black dress when she sang. And she'd have an artificial flower hanging on it. It got so that flower just looked so terrible, I'd say, 'Can't I get you another dress?' She'd say, 'No way! I'm going to wear it forever. It's what I started with, and I'm going to keep wearing it for luck.'" Edith didn't know if the girl could afford another.

Soon Doc made Norma another offer: to come sing with his band. She didn't have to be asked twice. Doc was happy to have a pretty girl who could bring in a few more people. His outfit, known as a "territorial band," played percentage dates: They got their cut only if folks actually showed up. On a good night, Norma could clear a dollar; on an average night, fifty cents. One night she made more than the bandleader. Doc didn't mind. He knew he had a good thing in "my little blues singer."

The money was better at KVOC, but sitting in the studio behind the glass didn't hold a candle for Norma to standing on a stage and seeing the college kids dancing to the rhythms she herself was feeling. The special camaraderie of being part of a band on the road—even a band covering a small territory—also offered a heady thrill for a fourteen-year-old girl; it gave her a family to belong to. One night, their trailer fishtailed into the snow, and someone had to go back to town to find a clothesline to retie all the instruments onto the platform. When they finally got to the gig they found only three couples waiting to dance to the orchestra. Norma wound up buying Doc a bowl of chili with her profits.

Norma Egstrom made her wider public debut with Doc's boys

at a New Year's Eve party on December 31, 1934, at the Valley City Eagles' Lodge, on the third floor of an office building on Main Street. Some of the audience members snickered at her dress: a shabby black thing, they would remember, adorned by a single bedraggled artificial flower. The Valley City locals believed that a small-town girl from over in Wimbledon was way out of her league in their town. In just a few years, she would prove them right.

In the meantime, obligations back home did their best to delay Norma's journey. Her life was chores and schoolwork. The latter problem was solved fairly easily. The principal at Wimbledon High School could deny some of his students special privileges, but not the Egstrom girl: If she got her work done early, she was free to pursue her new professional calling.

More vexing was the question of logistics. There were no paved roads between Wimbledon and Valley City. She'd hitch an occasional ride with the driver of the Holsum bread truck, and the Soo Line train was also a handy option. (Her father's position with the Midland entitled her to a pass on the sister railroad.) But sometimes the timing wasn't right. One day, her counterpart in the Soo depot came to the rescue. William Brenner had a special tie to the girl across the tracks: Selma Anderson Egstrom, Norma's real mother, had been a high-school classmate of Brenner's down in Volga, South Dakota. And on this afternoon Norma was due for a gig in Valley City. Bill Brenner remembered the girl running across the tracks, crying.

"Here came Norma," Brenner recalled: " 'She won't let me go to Valley City today! She says I can't sing, and I'm just wasting my time going down there.' Well, Henry Fehr and I were both on the school board at the time, so I said to Norma, 'You are going down there to sing whether your stepmother wants you to or not, and I'll see to it that Henry takes you this evening.' And that I did."

Though the people of Wimbledon felt the hardships of the times—they were impossible to ignore—Norma also took advantage of the attractions of a town whose pastoral quiet was broken only by the train's whistle, the moan of the wind, and the thrum of powerful Rumely gas tractors out in the fields, with their ten-inch bores and twelve-inch strokes. In the summers, the best escape lay south of town. Norma and her buddies—Lillian Wehler, Stanley Stroud, Genevieve Thomas, and Edith Locket—could often be found in a dinghy down at Spiritwood Lake, the girls in summer dresses, Stanley in his shirt and tie. Though the season was hot and dry, the pleasures were fresh.

"In the summertime, every Wednesday night they would have a band concert on Main Street and all the farmers and everybody congregated," her schoolmate Mary Rose recalls. "They had a big old wagon, and this hometown band would play all kinds of old music. That was the highlight of the week."

In winter, the snow could be friend as well as adversary: "On weekends my dad would hitch up a team of horses and a bobsled and every kid in town would hook on with their sled and he'd take us sleigh-riding," Mary Rose remembers. "The farmers would all come to town on Saturdays in the wintertime with their sleds and horses. They would put them in the barn when they went shopping and did their business. I remember those horses vividly. We'd sneak in and go up in the hayloft and look down, and here's all these horses stomping in the cold. Scared the wits out of us."

Despite the mammoth drifts, the Midland still ran—occasionally. The railroad's equipment included a unique snowplow, custom-fitted to the front of one of the old Alco engines, but this seldom guaranteed punctuality. One winter night the Courtenay High School basketball teams, eight miles northwest of Wimbledon, were scheduled to play a tournament in

Jamestown, and traveled down to Wimbledon to catch the Midland the rest of the way.

"We got to Wimbledon with no trouble," recalled Florence Anderson, a member of the girls' team at Courtenay, "but the train was late—very late. It was getting close to midnight and our coach was pacing the floor. Norma went upstairs and came back soon to tell us she had a good fire started in their parlor furnace, and invited the girls to their living room upstairs to nap or rest. The boys could stretch out on the waiting-room floor downstairs. We were just starting up the steps when we heard the train whistle. We quickly left Norma standing in the stairway with dirty coal-dust hands."

By the time Norma was a junior, her talent was a source of pride for her friends. No matter where her gang was gathered, they'd ask Norma for a song. One Friday night, a constable on horseback patrol noticed a '32 Chevy sedan parked down by the stockyards. As he approached the car with four kids in it, he heard a girl's voice raised in song drifting out the open windows. Live music wasn't the usual parked-car activity for a carful of Wimbledon kids, but it was for Norma and her date, Chad Darkenwald, and their friends Leo Radke and Jeanne Souter.

Leo liked his girlfriend's friend well enough, but he didn't really care for Norma's singing. He thought it was too "loose and familiar."

Somewhere around this time the Jack Wardlaw Orchestra came through town. He wasn't a major artist, but banjo wizard Wardlaw was the real thing, his band a national outfit. His first band, the Carolina Tar Heels, had grown big enough to play on ocean liners plying the Atlantic, where passengers were treated to Jack's particular and distinctive brand of "speed banjo." In Europe, he'd accompanied the dancing of the legendary enchantress Josephine Baker, when she wasn't parading the Champs Elysées with her leashed cheetah. His current outfit had opened for Guy

Lombardo at the Steel Pier in Atlantic City. Wardlaw would never merit much mention in the halls of big-band history, but he was good enough to merit a sponsor: Jack's trailer, in which he plied the backroads, was emblazoned with the words "Castleberry's Chili."

In the summer of 1936, Norma became the Wardlaw outfit's singer for a short, indeterminate time—a chapter that, strangely, would go largely undocumented. Jack didn't mention it in an unpublished autobiography in later years; Peggy Lee mentioned Wardlaw only two or three times. Maybe this gap in history has something to do with Norma's young age.

By mid-decade, the Dirty Thirties had taken their toll on Wimbledon, on the economy, and on Norma Egstrom. One day she walked past a deserted milliner's shop in the middle of a struggling downtown main street. Behind its smudged window sat a near-empty display: just two hats, waiting on a hatstand. Curious, Norma tried the door. The wind that rushed into the stale air stirred letters and papers around the deserted rooms. In the back, in the kitchen, Norma found pots on the stove filled with caked, moldy food—the remains of the last dinner eaten by the widow who ran the failing business. It was a Flying Dutchman of a store, anchored not in the sea, but in the ocean of nothing that separated Wimbledon, and Jamestown, and Nortonville—all of the farm towns she scuttled through in her fractured childhood—from the outside world.

As soon as school ended, Norma told herself she was going to be gone—but not before, as editor of the school newspaper, in response to the snide asides she heard around town, she'd penned a defense of the poor Midland Continental.

In June 1937, a few days after the graduation ceremonies for Wimbledon High School, the town newspaper ran the graduates' class poem on the front page: "Success Awaits at Labor's Gate," written by Norma Egstrom. Her first published lyrics were a paean to the prairie ethic of hard work.

Her twenty-four-line poem, written in rhyming couplets, hammers home the lesson she's drawn from a childhood of endless chores: The things that are "truly worthwhile," she writes, are the things that are achieved "when work is in style." In Norma's view, it's the work we've put in that will determine our fate "on eternity's day." Not surprisingly, interwoven through the surprisingly sophisticated verse of a girl who has spent most of her short life looking for a way out of her sorry station is the promise of opportunities that lie ahead: There's "always a morrow where there's been to-day." We are told to "look to the future," and "what it might bring"—a future where, for the conscientious soul, "success is the thing."

Her concluding line—"Success awaits at labor's gate"—is nothing less than this teenaged girl's manifesto. Her verse is a shout of defiance into misfortune's face: A future of "darkened hue" was not going to be Norma's fate, not as long as she was able to do the work.

As her first set of figurative lyrics, Norma's ode is sophisticated, a strong voice overlaying a steely, determined will. Clearly this is a girl who, if still shy and insecure about her station in life, most definitely had something to say.

It was another great lyricist, Johnny Mercer, soon to be a friend, who would one day observe that writing music may take more talent, but that writing lyrics takes more courage—something that Norma clearly did not, nor would ever, lack.

College was not an option for Norma, financially. According to friends, her lack of a higher education would now add another insecurity to her psyche: The girl without love, beaten and confused, wouldn't have her college degree for another forty years, and that one would be an honorary sheepskin. But that same shortcoming here began to fuel the intellectual curiosity that marked her personality for years to come; it was another hurdle to overcome, another motivation to spur her on. She would eventually become a reader of the most eclectic tomes, from philosophy to physics, and seek out the company of deep thinkers both celebrated and eccentric, both mainstream and marginal. She would forever seek out as many intellectual boundaries to cross as musical ones.

She obviously could have handled the academics. Belle Ginsberg's husband had once confided to her that Norma was known to pick up extra funds by helping some of the teachers'-college students with their papers. And so, after graduation, she headed back down to Jamestown, the place of her birth. And when she turned her back on Wimbledon, Norma Egstrom took the train with her: In 1937, the northern branch of the Midland—Jamestown to Wimbledon—ceased scheduled passenger service. Her railroad had decided that it could not survive without her.

"She shook the dust of Wimbledon off her feet," Lillian Wehler says now, "and I don't blame her."

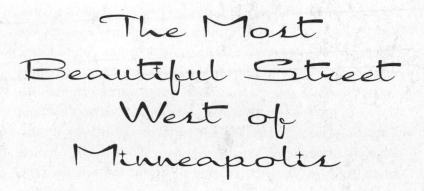

The Most Beautiful Street West of Minneapolis

IT WAS A different Jamestown that welcomed the prodigal daughter home. The climate in Stutsman County was no different—in the winter of 1936–37 the mercury touched forty below in Jamestown—but the town had a face and a name now, known to the rest of the nation. The previous summer, Jamestown's enduring Depression hardships had drawn President Roosevelt, who visited the town, leaning out of his chauffered convertible to chat with farmers in overalls who were harvesting virtually nothing from the thin, swirling topsoil of the county. Farmers plowing behind teams of horses would lose their way in their own fields, so thick were the clouds of dust, so harsh the winds that would erase the path of the row they'd just tried to plow.

WPA work crews planted trees for shelterbelts around the

town to hold back the wind. Sheep died of malnutrition; corn, when it did sprout, topped out at two feet. More than fifty thousand local folk were working on public projects in the county, thanks to Roosevelt's New Deal, and Horseshoe Park was now full of hoboes who leaped off the boxcars as they pulled into the roundhouse; one night, the crack of the yard dick's gun rang out, and one of the rail-riders was dead.

But hardship begs diversion, and business was holding its own. The Coca-Cola Bottling Company had set up shop, and there was a 7UP franchise, too. The opera house still drew crowds. The Palace of Sweets had opened its doors, with its new Art Moderne decor. Next to the opera house, the Gladstone Hotel was doing good business; it was a grand place whose rooms featured balconies sitting directly over the Northern Pacific tracks, which—at the height of rail travel in the land—were invariably busy. Passengers of the Northern Pacific's twice-daily *North Coast Limited,* according to an unsigned account of life in town at the time, would "dash into the NP lunchroom for food, while the engine takes on water, and in the winter . . . billowing up great clouds of steam, while all the time the brakeman is moving from car to car checking for hot boxes. The train . . . was it #1 or #2?—has come from the wonderful east, heading for the exciting west, firing our imagination and envy. I was sure the people riding that train— and especially the ones in the dining car—were all rich and probably movie stars. Lucky dogs to have the money to ride a train like that!"

Radio station KRMC, broadcasting out of the hotel's second-floor studios up the ornate staircase, boasted more power than its Valley City sister as it broadcast its good-time anthems, trying its best to buoy the spirits of a struggling young city.

The first place Norma would ever call truly her own was a basement room for rent in a house in downtown Jamestown. Conveniently, it was located just a few blocks from the three-story clap-board Gladstone. Norma's new digs were furnished with a bed, an orange crate, and an alarm clock that (usually) kept her from being late for her job as a relief girl at the Gladstone's coffee shop. Rather quickly, the young waitress also managed to get herself on the radio, accompanied by a minister's daughter on piano. This young lady, happily, had a feel on the keyboard for the new sounds—jazz, blues, all of the music that was influencing Norma's creation of herself as a performer.

The airwaves of KRMC carried a variety of new music ema-nating from New York (of course), where Swing Street still thrived, and swing was now undisputed king. Count Bill Basie's band was packing the Roseland Ballroom, and Goodman's boys were in full sway. By now, Benny had become the preeminent musical figure on the national landscape. But a relatively un-known female singer had recently begun to capture Norma's imagination. Maxine Sullivan, a diminutive (four-foot-ten) black woman from Pittsburgh who sang for pianist Claude Thornhill's group, had released a seemingly unlikely song: the Scottish folk tune "Loch Lomond," set to a swing arrangement. Sullivan's voice was good enough, but it was her style—her "suave, sophis-ticated swing," as a later critic heard it—that intrigued Norma. As the more full-throated bluesing of Bessie Smith and the other pioneers of the new music gave way to women with more sub-tlety, Sullivan's trademark was her restraint. She reined the notes in, and they carried all the more power for it.

Years later, Peggy Lee would cite her three favorite, and most influential, woman singers: "You have to pick Maxine Sullivan for her simplicity; Billie Holiday for her emotional appeal; and Ella Fitzgerald for her 'great heart.'" It was Sullivan's "soft tone and marvelous sense of time," as Peggy would put it, that informed a great deal of what Norma was to become, and she would fre-quently, for the rest of her life, cite Sullivan's influence: "[She] had a happy talent for knowing where to draw the line, having the good taste to cut some things. . . . She sang very lightly, like a painter using very light brush strokes. She communicated so well that you really got the point right away."

Not every listener in the Midwest appreciated the grafting of swing onto traditional music. A radio station in Detroit pulled "Loch Lomond" from the air, prompting Sullivan to go so far as to contact Eleanor Roosevelt, asking for the First Lady's opinion on the appropriateness of swinging traditional tunes, since she and bandleader Claude Thornhill had it in mind to do it again. The First Lady replied that she saw nothing wrong with the practice.

On March 1, 1938, Sullivan recorded "It Was a Lover and His Lass," a song that had first enjoyed popularity on the stage— Shakespeare's stage, in fact; composed circa 1590, it was included in original productions of *As You Like It*. Sullivan's version merits a footnote concerning the accomplished jazz guitarist she and Thornhill had often used: There was no part in the song for Dave Barbour's guitar, so the native of New York City had been reduced to manning a bird whistle and, at the song's end, in a sound effect that Sullivan herself didn't understand, closing a door.

It is not known whether Norma Egstrom ever heard "It Was a Lover and His Lass." It would be a few more years before she heard the guitar stylings of Dave Barbour. But it was likely around this time that she was first exposed to another Sullivan recording, "The Folks Who Live on the Hill"—a song that she would never forget.

Down in Jamestown, belying her Wimbledon reputation for paying little attention to boys, Norma fell for an American archetype. Red Homuth had already graduated from Jamestown High, where he had served as captain of both the football and basketball teams. He'd passed up any further higher learning to take a job with the Nash Finch Company out of Fargo, delivering wholesale groceries to the Jamestown grocery stores, along with his buddy Don Ingstad, Bob's younger brother.

Girls weren't a problem for Red. But the first time he walked up the stairs of the Gladstone to the radio-station studio and saw, behind the glass, seventeen-year-old Norma singing, he was instantly intrigued. She was a little plump, but pretty cute. Before long, they were dating, very innocently. One night, after a late-night watermelon shared over Red's family's kitchen table, it was too late for Norma to go back to the apartment she was now sharing with an older woman named Izzy. So Norma slept over at Red's—in Red's mother's bed.

Norma was a little young for Red, but he liked being by her side; she was becoming a minor celebrity around town. "I just thought it was nice to go out with somebody who could sing like that" is the way Red remembers it now.

One night, after a long day of work for Red, Norma asked for a ride up to Wimbledon to see her folks. Red borrowed his mother's car. He was lucky enough to miss meeting Min, but enjoyed Marvin's company as they walked around outside the depot. "Her dad liked to take a little nip once in a while," recalled Red, "but he and I got along fine that night. He respected me. I respected him."

The trouble began on the ride home. "She thought I should have some sleep so I could drive the truck right the next day," Red recalls. "We'd stayed out pretty late. I let her drive, and I guess I was sleeping when she hit the herd of horses. She wrecked the car." Red's bad luck with vehicles had just begun. That summer, in the middle of a stifling heat wave, Red, his buddy Bob Deery, and the Ingstad brothers, Bob and Don, piled into the Ingstads' Ford after a carnival in Valley City. "We'd been nipping on a little something, and we thought Bob should drive because the three of us had been drinking a little bit. It was a two-seat coupe. Bob got behind the wheel. Deery and I were on Don's lap. About 4 A.M. Bob fell asleep, veered off to the right, made a U-turn, and we landed on the other side and rolled. We ended up in the Jamestown Hospital." Red's arm was broken. Don fractured his spine, and was confined in the same ward; the others were unhurt.

Norma's typewritten letter to Homuth two weeks later, after she'd already paid him several visits in the same hospital where she had been born, revealed a great deal about the girl: her affection for Red, her budding perfectionism in her music, her insecurities about her appearance.

After chatting about the oppressive heat—and making a pointed reference to her own "excess poundage" and the need for a diet—she complains that her gifts of flowers and candy have gone unappreciated: "So I guess that I haven't got what it takes, eh wot?" But her self-deferential tone is balanced by a display of her spunk, in a phrase that seems to nicely sum up her growing confidence about her abilities as a singer: After advising Red to catch a song she's going to perform on the radio, she adds, "Listen, if you can stand it. If not, I can't help it."

Spiced with the vernacular of the day ("a Hey-nonny-nonny and Howzeverthin?") the missive ends with a typical dose of her delightfully off-center sense of humor: "You can fool some of the people some of the time but you can't fool some of the people some of the time!"

By now, Norma had picked up on Red's waning interest: Her cloyingness was a little bothersome. "We respected each other," says Red, "but she was younger, and there were other girls around who were more attractive."

Another athlete, four years older than Norma, showed up in the coffee shop another day. Bill Sawyer, a bighearted ballplayer sprung straight from the pages of American archetypes, managed to catch her eye, before turning her life right around. But unlike Red, Sawyer had nothing in mind but friendship. "He was the first big brother in the outside world I ever had," she would recall. "He was the opposite of a wolf."

It was a rowdy bunch that had come in that day: the Fargo-Moorhead Twins, the top farm club of the Cleveland Indians, had just moved into a brand-new stadium back in Fargo. Barnett Field could boast, without argument, of being the finest ballpark to be found anywhere between Chicago and Seattle. The freely flowing Grain Belt Beer didn't hurt the image at all.

They loved teasing the waitress. When one guy broke away to sit at the counter, she could tell he was different. The Twins' left fielder had attended college at Western Reserve University back in his hometown of Cleveland. For Bill Sawyer, baseball was just a way station; he would one day make his livelihood as a teacher. Looking back later, Peggy Lee would call him an angel.

The ballplayer and the waitress fell into conversation, and before long, Sawyer ventured a bold proposition: "Would it be all right if I wrote you a letter?" She was too nice to say no. A few weeks later, Norma got her first note from Bill Sawyer, whose greeting included the titles of a few books she might like. She wrote him back. Over the next months, she found herself looking forward to his correspondence.

And one of his letters mentioned that he was a good friend of a radio guy in Fargo. Well, more than a radio guy. Ken Kennedy was the program director of WDAY in Fargo. If Norma wouldn't mind, Bill Sawyer wanted to make arrangements for her to audition for him.

It was time to follow the swirling winds east, time to sample the biggest city in the state, where Fargo's skyline challenged the endless plains sky. At the city's heart, the Black Building dominated the horizon. With its eight stories of solid sandstone and

Deco detail, it anchored Broadway—"The Most Beautiful Street West of Minneapolis"—both literally and symbolically dwarfing the old three-story buildings on the avenue: Rosen's Clothing, Luger's Furniture, Harrington & Houghton Hardware. They were family shops all, artifacts from an innocent era, now giving way to the bustling face of the future. A half dozen theaters with fancy names—the Princess, the Isis, Fargo's own Crystal Ballroom—hinted at big cities and distant lands.

Like folks in just about every city in the land, Fargoans sought to shed the Depression blues by gathering en masse to dance the night away. The new jazz-infused music had started to sweep the country, even if no one was quite sure what to call it, as evidenced by the divergence of definitions that appeared in the pages of *Variety* in May 1936: "It's carefully conceived improvisation," opined singer Red McKenzie. "It's not just the old-style jazz," vibes wizard Red Norvo said. "It's a livelier tempo," said trumpeter Wingy Manone; "you know, it's swingy-like."

The Black stood at the epicenter of town, equidistant from the Northern Pacific station on the south side and the Great Northern depot to the north, just down the street from the ornate Fargo Theater. From its perch on the eighth floor, WDAY beamed its signals to the prairies, to the farms. For a girl raised out in "the toolies"—rural slang for "the sticks"—walking into the skyscraping studios of WDAY took courage.

"Bill [Sawyer] literally had to push me in the door," Peggy would later recall, in *Interview* magazine. "I was terrified, very shy. The thought of getting in front of a microphone terrified me. But as soon as I could open my mouth and sing, I was okay." The girl who had always shied away from speaking had learned to express her personality in song. She had made a name for herself singing the current stuff back at Val City, and she stayed the course at her audition. Spurning the safe classics, she chose to sing "These Foolish Things," a hit for Benny Goodman and his vocalist Helen Ward the year before. It was a ballad full of evocative images: daffodils, long excited cables, candlelight on little corner tables, the sigh of midnight trains in empty stations, silk stockings thrown aside, dance invitations.

"Oh, how the ghost of you clings," she sang, as seductively as she knew how. "These foolish things remind me of you."

Ken Kennedy put her on the air that afternoon.

Like so many of Fargo's folk, Ken Sydness hailed from a railroad clan; he was the son of a detective on the Great Northern who yo-yoed from Minneapolis, in the east, up to Whitefish, Montana, to the west. But railroading was never in Ken's blood. Playing the drums held far more fascination. His choice of Augsburg State, a Lutheran college, was a little inappropriate, since the school forbade dancing. So Ken did what any enterprising college musician did at the time: He changed his name, and on the sly formed Ken Kennedy and the Kanadians. Later he moved back to Fargo and got the Kanadians a regular gig playing the Crystal Ballroom, performing fare ranging from standards like Bing Crosby's "Pennies from Heaven" to the hipper stuff such as Benny's lively arrangement of "Goody, Goody," and Tommy Dorsey's bouncy, ragtime-jazzy version of "The Music Goes Round and Round."

One night, when the WDAY studio announcer failed to show up on time for a Kanadians gig, Ken plugged in all the right wires himself, grabbed the microphone, introduced the band—and was summarily hired by the station manager. For the next thirty years, he would be the station's voice, conscience, and majordomo. It was Ken who cultivated the local talent. It was Ken who organized the popular Hayloft Jamboree, a cadre of entertainers who visited the halls of local towns dressed in Early Hee-Haw, and played their music while they did their hayseed comic routines.

Kennedy got the most out of his crew, no matter how young

or inexperienced. The Egstrom girl had to perform on the Noonday Variety Show (for $1.50 an appearance) as well as play "Freckle-Faced Gertie" with the Hayloft Jamboree and lend her voice to the Georgie Porgie Breakfast Food Boys. And singing was only part of her job description. She wrapped gifts for contestants on station contests. She addressed envelopes. And she filed music scores—a gig that sounded boring on the face of it, but which intrigued Norma Egstrom no end. As she put away the music composed by the likes of Jerome Kern, Rodgers and Hart, Cole Porter, and the Gershwins, she scrutinized the lyrics, sang the tunes, and very quickly became an amateur scholar of the Great American Songbook. WDAY's file cabinets of scores were her academic library, and she was now earning her metaphoric master's.

Norma's WDAY gig didn't pay the rent. But her other new job—a twelve-hour shift at the sprawling brick Regan Bakery factory—did. From 4 P.M. to 4 A.M. she made the time pass by slicing and wrapping the loaves in rhythm.

By now Norma had moved up in the world, literally; she was living aboveground, in a large red-brick apartment building a few blocks south of First Avenue, within walking distance of the Black Building. The place was just a tiny one-room flat, but Norma didn't feel she had much to complain about. Her neighbor, Peggy Grant—née Magda Christina—worked two jobs, supporting her two young sons (six-year-old Joseph William Grant and his four-year-old brother, Duane Lee Grant) as well as her sixteen-year-old sister, Edna. All were squeezed into a two-room space on the other side of the wall from Norma.

Joseph and Duane, who slept in the closet, were particularly fond of their pretty, affectionate, musical neighbor, whom they knew as Deloris—"the name she used around the apartment," Joe Grant remembers now. When the boys made too much noise in their closet, which shared a wall with Deloris's place, they were quick to heed her warning whacks. They knew that if they didn't quiet down, Deloris would tell their mom. But for the most part, the brothers were entranced by her attentions.

"My little brother, always in need of a smile and a hug, looked at Deloris with his incredibly large deep-brown eyes which were shaded under a canopy of eyelashes that women drooled over—and Deloris was hooked," Grant recalls. "She and Duane stopped for hugs whenever they passed." When his mother was working over at the Black cleaning offices, Deloris would tuck Duane in, singing him to sleep with "You're a Sweet Little Headache," or "Little Sir Echo," a popular children's song of the time with a curiously poignant subtext: the tale of a lonely child beseeching his echo to visit him. "Little Sir Echo, how do you do? Little Sir Echo will answer you." (If Deloris added a little something extra to it, she was ahead of her time; trumpet great Roy Eldridge would later record a jazz version.)

On the night when Joe and Duane unwisely took it upon themselves to walk to the Black Building to help their mom scrub the floors, they found themselves wandering the halls of the vast building, quite lost. Up on the eighth floor, they ran into Deloris, who quickly hunted Peggy Grant down and then took the boys back home.

On one particularly memorable night, it was Joe who was privy to a tearful discussion at the kitchen table between his mother and Deloris about a crisis in the building. Some of Deloris's conservative neighbors felt that it was inappropriate for a young girl to be living alone, unsupervised. "Everyone thought it odd that such a young girl was out on her own," Joe recalls. " 'What's to stop her from bringing men to her room?' The women didn't want their kids to be around her, and damned sure didn't want their husbands hanging around 'that girl Deloris!' "

A petition had been circulated: The Egstrom girl, it declared, had to go. Joe didn't really understand what all the crying and cursing was about until the following day, when his mother complained. Peggy Grant was quiet by nature. "But they were a couple of tough Norwegians, and my mother understood how difficult it was making a living during those Depression years. My mother said she'd see that it was stopped. When mother told the other women that [Deloris] was singing in a radio station, it helped. When they found out Deloris was occasionally singing in bars—'Places that sold whiskey . . . and underage . . . my God, sixteen years old?'—they were upset. Fortunately, it didn't go anywhere."

Ultimately, the petition disappeared. The police were not called. And soon, with some help from Joe Grant's family, Deloris underwent a transformation. The next thing little Joe knew, Deloris had taken on a new name.

"One day, Deloris was walking down the sidewalk, and she told me, 'Tell your mom to check the front of the Powers Hotel.' Mother wasn't getting home for a while, and we were about the same distance from the hotel as we were from the Black Building, so I walked over to see what she was talking about. There on the marquee was 'The Powers Hotel presents Peggy Lee.' "

Ken Kennedy always told his new hires to change their names. After all, *he* had. Everyone in the business did. Kennedy had told her that "Norma Deloris Egstrom" wasn't going to cut it. As Peggy herself wrote in her autobiography, and related countless times, it was Kennedy who came up with her new name, out of thin air. But in fact Peggy had chosen her neighbor's first name and little Duane's middle name to begin her new life. "My mother joked about it," Grant says now. " 'Peggy Lee' was a much better choice than 'Peggy William'—my own middle name. Not long after that, we moved from the downtown area—and Peggy Lee moved on."

Curiously, the former Norma Deloris Egstrom wasn't the only

Peggy Lee of note at the time. A few years earlier, writer Anna Andrews had published four books for adolescents in a series called "the Peggy Lee Stories for Girls," including such titles as *Peggy Lee of the Golden Thistle Plantation* and *Peggy Lee and the Mysterious Islands.* Heroine Peggy Lee, in the Nancy Drew vein, did her sleuthing in exotic locales. In 1936 the books had just been anthologized and reissued for popular sale.

Peggy Lee never made mention of her fictitious counterpart, but she found an exotic locale of her own. A letter from an old schoolmate named Gladys Rasmussen arrived postmarked "Los Angeles," and it suggested that her old friend try her luck in the growing city where fantasies could become reality. Peggy took the bait. When she mentioned the trip to her father, he stunned her by allowing her to go. He would let her use his railroad pass for the voyage. And she would finance her journey by selling her Elgin graduation watch to her landladies for thirty dollars.

"She wanted Hollywood," Edith Butcher, her singing companion back in Valley City, says. "We all thought, 'You're crazy.' But we had a little get-together in Valley City before she had to leave. We were all there to wave and holler as she got on the train back to Fargo.

"I know that Fargo thinks they made her," Edith adds. "But we started it."

Peggy's railroad journey to the City of Angels represented an extraordinarily long exodus for a teenaged girl by herself, and it immediately grew longer when she found herself seated next to an older man with wandering hands. "He began to give me little touches and pats," she recalled in her biography. "I was a babe in the woods, only seventeen . . . so I didn't know how to handle the situation. Luckily, a woman noticed the hanky-panky and came over and said, 'I'll sit by you.' She was large, and she was wearing an electric blue dress, and she . . . lit up the whole car. I ended up in the middle, like a sandwich." This generous soul took Peggy off the train at her hometown of Salt Lake City for a bath, a meal, and a sightseeing trip to the Mormon Tabernacle.

Gladys Rasmussen was waiting at the huge southwestern-Deco Union Station in downtown Los Angeles on the day of Peggy's arrival. With some friends, she provided a stylish welcome: a drive to the beach—Peggy's first glimpse of an ocean—and a tour of Hollywood Boulevard. "It was beautifully clean, as polished as someone's marble living room," Lee would remember. "The ocean has never looked so big, and the Hollywood streets never looked so clean."

A car-radio broadcast of "Milkman's Matinee" furnished the soundtrack of her first night in town. The hit New York City radio program of one Stan Shaw, an ex–orchestra leader out of Kansas City, the live late-night show attracted, as *Time* magazine expressed it, "dunkers in all-night coffee pots and diners, cabbies dozing on the late-trick hack lines, night watchmen, charwomen, belated motorists, bakers, lighthouse keepers, lobster-trick pressmen, the boys in the bars and all the other sun dodgers." In other words, the denizens of the time of night that, in the years to come, would be Peggy Lee's favorite hours.

Between songs like "Mexicali Rose" and "The Very Thought of You," Stan liked to use his perch on the airwaves to provide help to his loyal listeners, should they need it; he was best known for his on-air pleas that had considerable success in persuading runaways to return home, wherever home was. By the time Peggy hit town, Stan had returned more than a dozen kids to their parents.

Peggy wouldn't need Stan's help quite yet, but her first trip to the promised land on the Pacific quickly furnished a wake-up call about life on the road. The newly named Peggy Lee would pack enough intrigue into a few short months to fill more than a few volumes of the Peggy Lee Stories for Girls.

There was no work to be had in Los Angeles in the spring of 1937. California remained as depressed as North Dakota. When she arrived, Peggy had $18 left from the sale of her watch. She and Gladys shared a flat, spent their days taking streetcars to the employment office, and tried to stretch the dollars. "We broke the money down so we could each have twenty-five cents a day for the 'big little rib-eye steak' at the Cunningham Diner, plus twenty cents apiece for streetcar fare," Lee wrote in her autobiography. "When our funds hit an all-time low—[enough for] one jar of peanut butter and one loaf of bread—I lost my shyness, walked up to the [employment-office] desk, and said, 'I can do any job you have here.'"

The job was an opening for a cook and waitress in Balboa, fifty miles down the coast, and Peggy hitchhiked all the way. The owner of Harry's Café found her lodgings in a cabin park, but the short-order work dried up when Easter break ended. The owner of the cabins had a carnival called the Fun Zone, and Peggy went to work as a barker, joining an eclectic workforce made up of veteran carnival geeks.

For one dollar a day, she fronted such depressing booths as the "Dunk the Wino" attraction, where she found herself cringing at the poor guy's lot in life: "Time after time, the poor soul would crawl out and get back on his perch. I never knew his name." But she struck up a friendship with the scar-faced lion tamer, who also owned the Ferris wheel. He let her ride for free if she let him tell her the tales that lay behind his scars: "The scars were his identity, and he appreciated someone caring."

Untethered for the first time in her life, she found herself moving freely and naturally among her cohorts living on the fringe. The Depression made brothers of a lot of folk who would otherwise have never crossed paths, and now Peggy's set of pals numbered a band of equally footloose and resourceful teenagers. Trips to the docks for fish, to the bakery for day-old bread, to the orchards for oranges, all of it spiced the routine for a very shy barker. "I discovered a lot of teenagers in the same impoverished position," she later wrote, "but they didn't know as much about survival as I did."

Music was not a part of her daily Balboa routine, although she did manage to slide a few spare nickels into the jukeboxes around town, endlessly playing her favorite song of the time: "Don't Be That Way," a hip, infectious swing serenade by the Benny Goodman Orchestra. The arrangement featured a couple of wild clarinet flights by the master himself, and some terrific tom-tomming by the madman drummer Gene Krupa, and a quick trombone flight by the virtuoso Jack Teagarden that was then, and still is now, just too cool to be believed.

The popular-music landscape was truly transforming, and Peggy soon claimed a part of it for her own. That time came on an early-summer night in 1937—a typical evening at the Fun Zone, when she found herself at the far end of the pier that stretched out over the sand into the surf. Poised over the Pacific, she was accompanied by the setting sun, the lap of the waves, and a couple of boys with guitars—nephews of one of the concessionaires. She'd told them of her love of singing, and they'd offered to back her up.

"What do you want to sing?" asked one—fully expecting that, being a good Dakotan, she'd ask for some Western fare—say, "Bury Me Not on the Lone Prairie." Instead, she asked for "The Man I Love," the lovely Gershwin brothers standard—in A flat, no less: "They were absolutely bowled over that I knew the key." Clearly, her hours studying the charts back at WDAY had paid off.

"You shouldn't be here," one of them said. He told her of a club he knew of back up on Hollywood Boulevard, a small room where the singers came in all shapes and sizes and persuasions, from those on the way up to those arcing in a different direction. So she hitchhiked back north again to find her place in a new fraternity, in a city just coming into its own in the jazz world.

Los Angeles in the thirties had the feel of a wide-open lotus land, peopled by westward-bound lemmings of every kind: budding movie moguls, prizefighters and athletes, and the wanderers who'd found their way as far west as west could take them. Among the immigrants were a new wave of jazz artists, led by the likes of Jelly Roll Morton, the most prominent of the many black musicians from New Orleans who'd migrated to Los Angeles after the First World War. By 1937, Los Angeles' Central Avenue rivaled Swing Street back east—in talent, if not in legend. Art Tatum played piano at Lovejoy's till dawn. Jack's Basket Room, the Alabam, the Flamingo Lounge—all were havens for the new sound. In the words of memoirist Arna Bontemps, "Los Angeles in legend became Paradise West to Negroes still languishing in the Egyptland of the South."

The summer before, in fact, in Los Angeles, Armstrong had cut a record with Jimmy Dorsey's orchestra, a disc that included "Dippermouth Blues," "Swing That Music," and "When Ruben Swings the Cuban" with vocals by national singing idol Bing Crosby.

The Jade was owned by one Larry Potter, the proprietor of a number of spots all over town, from Melrose, to the south, north over the hills to Ventura, and right on down to Burbank. The Jade wasn't well known, but to some musicians it was a favorite venue. It had some soul, and it had a heart: Potter was known to hire out-of-work entertainers—albeit for very little money. Decades later, a legendary Los Angeles nightclub owner named Steve Boardner would recount the night he was filling in at the bar back in 1937, and Potter sidled over:

"Steve, come here. I want you to listen to this girl sing. See what you think of her." Potter was auditioning a new girl from North Dakota.

"Does she drink?" asked the bartender. The reason he asked was that she didn't look a day over seventeen. Which, actually, she was—by a couple of days.

She didn't look too glamorous, either. "I wore a beige pants suit made of hopsacking that had a large, colorful sash," Peggy would remember. "The tops of my beach shoes had worn and pulled away from the cork soles, and there was no money for new ones. I had cut a piece from the sash and sewed it to the cork sole. It lasted until I started walking toward [the club]. It lasted for a couple of blocks. By then, I was at the Jade. Barefoot, I went in and auditioned."

Potter signed her up: The job paid $2.50, with fifty cents kicked back to Potter.

"She was what we used to call 'an Oregon apple,'" Potter would recall—"cornfed, milk-cheeked, and with hay practically falling out of her hair." None of this disqualified Peggy from joining the ragged roster of performers in the vaguely exotic little room.

"The Jade had an air of mystery about it," Peggy recalled, "dark, with Oriental decor, the smell of the gardenias and the Chinese food; the waitresses in their satin coats and pants moved silently on the thick carpet. An enormous carved dragon formed the bar, where you could see a movie star, an FBI agent, or some-one who was looking for a tourist to roll."

Peggy's new fraternity included singer Hal March, who would go on to fame as the host of a television show called *The $64,000 Question*, and dancer Louis DeProng, who would one day work as dance director at Twentieth Century–Fox. Most conspicuous of all was the woman who called herself Jabuti, whose specialty was playing "Wang-Wang Blues" on her slide trombone. Peggy remembered she had "magnificent long red hair, which she used to great advantage as she bumped and ground her near-perfect body over the slide trombone. Between shows she read big, thick books."

Peggy's stage persona was a little less exotic. Potter would smile at her self-consciousness about her hands. Potter's wife, for her part, became the first in a long and distinguished group of women who would do their best to upgrade the singer's costume over the next several years; she took Peggy to the May Company department store to buy her a simple gown to perform in—and, presumably, some shoes.

Potter was soon paying her $30 a week—a huge raise, but hardly enough to stock a costume trunk. A big-hearted singer named Mary Norman selflessly came to Peggy's rescue, even though the new girl was, in effect, replacing Mary: "She gave me a magnificent red pleated gown to wear." Soon the only thing left of Mary at the Jade was her dress, worn by the only girl singer: Peggy Lee. Mary had been shown the door.

Mary Norman's legacy endured, too: She'd given her replacement some advice on what songs to sing. While the record-buying public was starting to lean toward jazz—Basie's "One o'Clock Jump," Ellington's "Caravan"—the vocal favorites of the day were swing-band versions of pop fare—Porter's "It's De-Lovely," the Gershwins' "They Can't Take That Away from Me," Rodgers and Hart's "My Funny Valentine."

When she wasn't singing, Potter encouraged Peggy to mix with the clientele. The night that Potter asked her to join him and another man at their booth, the guy asked if he could drive her home. Not relishing the mile-and-a-half trek back to her room, she acceded. But her escort drove her instead to a shabby, peep-holed joint in the wilds of downtown, where, bewildered and frightened, she found herself sitting in a booth with the guy and his friends, all of them growing increasingly drunk. A man on the other side of her suddenly leaned over and said, "I'm going to get you out of here. Follow me, and stick close."

Following a bout of shoving and thrown fists, the man had her out in his car, and they were fleeing to safety before he spoke: "Look, you don't know what you just got away from, but I'm going to tell you. I don't know why I should do this, but you remind me of my little sister. You were headed for white slavery, and no one would ever have heard of you again. Nobody."

If his dire warning sounded dramatic, its sentiment rang authentic: In a time of desperate economic straits, in a city founded on the twin promises of entertainment and escape, girls did disappear into the sex trade. The Mann Act, which had arisen out of the same progressive movement that had given rise to Prohibition, was also known as the White Slave Traffic Act—a legislative act designed not to keep underaged girls on their sides of the state lines, but to keep them from being sold into sexual slavery.

The Potters thereafter doubled their security at the Jade, but they couldn't keep the teenager from falling prey to her propensity for infirmity. All-night singing, bad food, weird hours, a three-mile round-trip hike to her flat down on Gower—not to mention near-abductions—all had taken their toll on Peggy's throat. Repeated trips to a public clinic confirmed she was sick, until one night—for the first time, but hardly the last—she simply fainted on stage. After an ambulance ride to Hollywood Presbyterian, she was diagnosed with tonsillitis. "You don't belong here," the doctor said. "You should have surgery, and you need to be near your family."

Then he asked a question that needed no answer:

"Why don't girls like you go back home where they belong?"

The family Peggy needed now lived in another small town back in North Dakota, on the eastern border of the state, north of

Fargo, just south of Grand Forks. Her sisters Della and Marianne were living in a crossroads called Hillsboro, and when Peggy wrote to ask if she could come home, their response was swift: They sent Hubert Sweeney, one of her former on-again, off-again boyfriends back in Fargo, on a rescue mission. "Sweeney went out on holiday from college," recalls Bill Snyder, a friend down in Fargo at the time. " 'I'm going to go get her,' he told me. But Hubert was really hot for her."

Later, Peggy would regret that all the way back to North Dakota, she was barely civil to poor Hubert. But she couldn't help it; she was coming home with her tail between her legs. The girl who was going to storm the entertainment world had been chewed up and spat back out. She hadn't been prepared this time around. The next time she visited to the city of anything-but-angels, she'd be all business.

A doctor in Hillsboro named Cuthbert performed the tonsillectomy on Peggy soon after her return. As she would tell it years later, the surgery was not a success; within twenty-four hours she was hemorrhaging and on her way to Deaconess Hospital in Grand Forks, North Dakota. But she rebounded quickly. Not long after, she took to visiting a place called the Belmont Café, where she caught the act of another young singer named Jane Leslie, who was on the rise. Lee took to the spotlight at the Belmont herself, singing on occasion. Post-surgery, something had suddenly changed in the Peggy Lee timbre: Her voice had an added huskiness. A throatiness.

It was time to give Fargo another shot. The Powers, right where she'd left it, needed a singer. With family in tow—Della and her young son, and Marianne—Peggy returned to the big town, savvier, stronger, and, as always, hungry as hell.

FOUR

The Magic Aquarium

ON MIDWINTER NIGHTS, the wind that raked the broad streets of Fargo scraped them clean of man and beast, but behind the bright Deco façade of the Powers Hotel Coffee Shop, just around the corner from the Great Northern depot, stood a warm, well-lit sanctuary for the assorted travelers just off the *Empire Builder*, as well as high-school kids, faculty and frat boys from the college, railroad crews—all drawn by the food, by the lights, by the fellowship, and by the singer. Once again—as would often be the case—the next real step up in Lee's career meant a gig in a hotel. For a girl from a family whose natural state was fracture, it was hardly surprising that she often found her footing in places where people were on the move and rootless.

The Powers Hotel prided itself on being the best lodging in

town: "Fargo's Center of Social and Commercial Life" read the legend on the menu of the restaurant, which was accessible through the hotel lobby as well as through its Deco outside doors. The bistro's recent renovation had attracted national attention in the pages of *Hotel Monthly* magazine, whose correspondent was impressed not only by its enticing menu—Sautéed Deep Sea Scallops with Saratoga Potato Flakes, Fried Fillet of Walleyed Pike, Two-Star Lamb Chops (for a pricey ninety cents)—but by its modern phone communication between chef and waitresses. Not to mention the stunning new façade with its wine-colored Carrara glass and bright neon lettering, which the magazine described as "a magnetic influence attracting people to its door."

There was no mention of the entertainment. Lloyd Collins, the organist, was a wire-rimmed, already balding churchmouse of a guy who, despite being only in his mid-twenties, had the mild demeanor of a middle-aged man. During the day, Lloyd sold musical instruments across the river in Moorhead, Minnesota. By night, he plied the keyboard of the Hammond organ at the Coffee Shop, perched on a little raised stage against the north wall. It wasn't exactly the big time, but for Lloyd, it was more than enough. Lloyd loved the Powers. It was a family. The night clerk held a Christmas party every year at his apartment; Beauchamp, the manager, liked to peek over transoms to make sure that nothing illicit or out-of-wedlock was going on upstairs. Pete, the doughnut delivery guy, earned a sandwich in exchange for his wares. Marty, the supervisor, would send a waitress back to the kitchen if she so much as touched her hair before she served the food. Lloyd played songs not only for the diners; he played for the staff, his family and friends. If he wanted to do something special for a waitress who needed a little picking up, he'd choose "Ain't She Sweet."

It was in the WDAY studios, where Lloyd did organ stylings on the morning slot, that he caught his first glimpse of his new partner. The Powers was upgrading, and they'd hired their own canary—someone easy to listen to and easy to look at. By now, Norma Egstrom had matured in more ways than one. Living dime by dime on the coast on a peanut-butter diet, she'd lost the farmgirl figure, and slimmed down. The cute oval face had grown into wholesome, even striking beauty. "Someone said, 'That's the gal you'll be working with,'" Lloyd recalls. "She made Dolly Parton look bad. She was just so beautiful." Lloyd couldn't believe his luck. Still can't.

With the renovation, and facing competition from the other clubs around town, the Powers stepped up in class. With Peggy Lee, their entertainment took on a whole new look and sound. The conventional musical library being played by the man wearing a suit and tie began to sound a little progressive.

Lloyd would never forget their first number together: Half a minute into their first song, chosen by Peggy Lee, he knew that this new team was going to work. The song was "'Tain't What You Do," a swingy little thing:

> Ain't what you do, it's the way that you do it
> That's what gets results.

He wouldn't forget the way she looked, either—a white shirt and a black skirt—or the way she moved: Compact and comfortable in her cramped space on the small stage, beneath the spotlight (blue in summer, red in winter), she didn't swing her body or make a big show of her physicality. She just sang the notes, with a smile. But it didn't take Lloyd long to realize that Peggy Lee understood that the package was as important as the tunes. It wasn't just her perkiness; she'd taken a Dale Carnegie course, and before long, she'd managed to memorize the names of all of her regular customers. If the first thing anyone noticed about

Peggy Lee was her homespun beauty, her personality also became infectious.

For Lloyd, Peggy's arrival signified a happy way to test his collegiate training in music. "I had theory, and she had unlimited range. When she wanted to go into another key, I could do it. And she never rode me . . . if I forgot a chord, it didn't matter. It always worked just perfectly." Nor was there anything of the selfish diva about her. On the night when a railroad crew hit town to paint the depot, they came in for the show. One of the more generous guys tipped her a full ten bucks. She split it down the middle with Lloyd, of course. That was how she was.

One thing did bother Lloyd, though: Peggy's music sometimes displayed a quality he wasn't familiar with. "To be truthful, she had a *different* style. I didn't like it to start with: She sort of sang and spoke at the same time. But I grew used to it." It would forever be a Peggy Lee trademark: making a song almost conversational in parts, if the lyrics lent themselves to it. Eventually, her ability to mix song and spoken word would earn the greatest recording triumph of her career.

Peggy and Lloyd did two shows a day during the week—a lunch set and a dinner set—with late shows on Friday and Saturday. Their ease with each other was obvious: The staff called them Ma and Pa, so comfortable was their vibe. When she rested a hand on his Hammond, he'd reach up and flick off one of the fake fingernails she'd so studiously applied, prompting a good-natured rebuke: "Lloyd, you're a horse's ass." If he'd eaten onions at lunch and she leaned too close, she'd give him grief. He wouldn't eat onions again, either. And if Lloyd was dragging that day, she'd prod him, with a sisterly smile: "Come on, Lloyd—get a hatpin in you."

Ma and Pa notwithstanding, they were hardly alike. Lloyd was solid, unrufflable, day in and day out. Peg wore her heart on her sleeve. "She was an emotional gal" is how Lloyd puts it now. "She wasn't moody, but when she sang, she sang the meaning in the words."

For the most part, the tastes of the crowd dictated their playlist. Patrons would fill out "Powergrams" at their tables, which the waitresses would pass to Peggy: "Red River Valley," if a farmers' group came through. "Dipsy Doodle." "Stardust."

But Lee also helped Lloyd learn some of the stuff she'd come to love, material being penned by the significant composers of the time. The one he would never forget was a slow, bittersweet ballad written by Johnny Mercer and Jimmy Van Heusen called "I Thought About You." It told the story of a man taking a cross-country train. At every stop, Mercer's lyrics proclaimed, the villages out the windows made him think about his gal:

> *I took a trip on a train*
> *And every stop that we made*
> *Oh, I thought about you.*

Sometimes, Lloyd noticed, a slow ballad would send Peggy into a melancholy mood. Her sister Marianne, living with her in the Hogan Apartments, had tuberculosis. By now, it seemed as if half of Peggy's family lived with her in the Hogan Apartments. There was her brother Clair as well as two of her sisters and Della's son Tyke and a stray male friend of the clan named Ossie Hovde, all in a small second-story apartment in a chancy part of town.

To make things even tougher, one night, when a member of the audience requested "I Dream of Jeannie with the Light Brown Hair," the blue mood that engulfed his singer prompted Lloyd to ask what was wrong. "It was her little sister Jeannie," Lloyd recalls. It was in November 1938 that Jeannie Egstrom, whom Peggy had never really known, finally died, back in Jamestown, from her chronic heart ailment.

It was no wonder that by now Peggy Lee was determined to

perfect a sunny disposition and a Dale Carnegie–honed winning personality. She needed to lacquer over the deeper emotions that accompanied her new station: the youngest kid in the family, earning the money, paying the rent, but seemingly unappreciated for it. No wonder she had dreams of moving on. She didn't want to get wrapped up in people, loves, and loyalties that would overwhelm her. Instinctively she seemed to keep her distance, out of self-protection.

Lloyd thought it odd that none of Peggy's brothers or sisters came to hear her sing. On nights when no boyfriend dropped by and she had no one to take her home, Lloyd would walk her down the deserted streets where the wind that came in from the north still occasionally carried the scents of farmland and livestock.

One time, Lloyd recalls, their talk naturally turned to their respective aspirations.

"What's your dream, Lloyd?" she asked. "To lead a symphony orchestra," Lloyd responded.

"Some day," Peggy confided, "I want to sing with a big band."

But there were plenty of nights when she had male companionship, Lloyd recalls, and didn't need him to walk her home. If Lloyd was her big brother, her casual boyfriends up at North Dakota State in the Greek House—Alpha Tau—were her buddies. She stayed away from serious commitment. She wanted to keep her reputation on the up-and-up. On the night when a professor whose tastes ran to raccoon coats and stiff drinks wanted to take it further, she refused, and never saw him again. She wanted to be viewed well by the college kids—one in particular.

"She always used to have a lot of men around her," Hubert Sweeney's buddy Bill Snyder remembers. At the time, Bill was dating a girl at WDAY who had a cooking show, and he saw Peggy often. He liked her, but never understood why she seemed to settle for men who weren't as classy as she was. "I used to say of Peggy that she always went with the chauffeur when she coulda gone with the guy in the backseat, you know what I mean?"

Of course, there was another kind of reputation to uphold: a musical reputation, a professional reputation. She was growing increasingly known around town—so much so that the Chateau, the Powers's competition, imported a singer from out of town. It was Jane Leslie, the singer Peggy had first seen up at the Belmont in Grand Forks.

"Jane turned out to be one of my best friends," Peggy would later recall. "I loved Janie's clothes. Of course, I had so little [in the way of dresses]—'that one and the other one'—that that nice girl said, straight out, 'Would you like to borrow some of my clothes?'"

The friendship lasted a lifetime, and Jane would be by her side as Peggy took her next career steps. Peggy, in fact, would introduce Jane to a man named Leonard Feather, a music critic. As the years went on, Jane Leslie would put aside her own career and marry Leonard Feather, a fulfilling relationship that would last the rest of their lives. Leonard, for his part, would be there to chronicle firsthand, at every step of the way, the career of Peggy Lee, and her own lifelong, successful relationship . . . with her art.

Lloyd had more than a passing interest in Peggy's boyfriends. And if someone filled out a Powergram asking for "I'm in the Mood for Love," well, that one was easy for Lloyd to play along to. He was smitten when his partner was around, although he kept his affections to himself. But Lloyd had another girl, too— until they broke up because her mother frowned on Lloyd: He wasn't a Lutheran. When Lloyd needed a shoulder to cry on that time, Peggy was there. But Lloyd never really let on about where his own affections lay. "It was a dream I never expected to have," he says now, "but that I *did* have."

Their actual interactions remained innocent. "One time, Carl, the guy at the dessert bar, called us over after the show and let me fix up a couple of hot fudge sundaes," Lloyd remembers. "I said, 'Feel how hot this fudge is,' and when she put her hand over it, I squashed her hand into the fudge. She chased me all the way downstairs. Another time, she came in dressed in a new outfit. 'Hey Lloyd, I want to show you something,' she said, and she lifted this formal dress, to show me the stretch in her new stockings."

That was a little much, Lloyd thought, but he knew that she was innocent, and he wasn't about to make any moves. That wasn't the way it was between Ma and Pa. Besides, before long, "her new boyfriend wouldn't let anyone else near her."

Johnny Quam's education, like his new girl's, had topped out at high school. "I was too smart to go to college—or too broke," Quam says now, with a laugh. "Or I lacked ambition."

As Lloyd recalls it, Johnny was a sharp-dressed guy, but that was easily explained. Johnny worked at a dry cleaner's, which gave him a leg up on his romantic competition: "She had only one or two gowns. I saw they were kept clean."

But it wasn't Johnny's sartorial splendor that made him stand out at the Coffee Shop as much as his habit of sitting alone, checking his watch, counting the minutes until the end of the show when he would get the blond canary to himself and take her out on the town. It wasn't that he didn't want to hear her sing. "She didn't have a big voice," Quam recalls, "but she was so articulate, you could understand every word. She wasn't as sexy as some girls, but boy, she sang sexy. She had that mole, a little birthmark. I guess it was later she found out you're supposed to enlarge those things with a pencil." Johnny was impatient only because, after a long workday cleaning clothes, he was looking for some fun. A typical night would start at the Coney Island diner near the Fargo Theater, followed by a nightcap. Fargo's city statutes at the time prohibited the serving of liquor in a dining establishment, so they would usually make at least a couple of different stops and end up in Moorhead, across the state line.

"Peggy was always hungry, so after ten o'clock we'd go to the diner," Johnny remembers. "We'd have coffee and one order of french fries. Peggy would take the catsup and the Worcestershire and mix them together to dip the french fries into. She loved doing that. She didn't have much money to spend—it was me that bought, and I was working for fifteen dollars a week. She had an older brother up in Grand Forks [Leonard], I think he managed the YMCA. As I remember, her brother Clair was kind of a ne'er-do-well. I'd always have to give him a buck just to get him off my back. They all lived in a little two-bedroom second-story apartment. She was the breadwinner [though] she was the youngest."

For liquid libations after their fries, several options were available, but Johnny and Peggy favored a place with a touch of fantasy to it. "In those days, at a bar a mixed drink was twenty cents. The one we frequented was called the Magic Aquarium in Moorhead. It had a long bar with red-plastic-covered stools. And live fish in the back bar. Northern pike and walleyes and bass. The real McCoy.

"Peggy didn't have much training at drinking," according to Quam. "She had one whiskey and Coke, she'd loosen up . . . get funny and giggly. She loved to tell jokes."

She didn't use profanities—"I don't know that I ever heard her use a swear word," he says. But she did like slightly scandalous jokes and, considering their surroundings, they tended to involve drunks. "Her favorite was, 'These three drunks are sitting in a bar. The middle drunk turns to the drunk on his right and says, "Did you pee down my leg?" "Of course not!" says the guy. So he turns to the drunk on his left. "Did you pee down my leg?" The other guy, with a look of astonishment, says, "Of course not!" "Well," says the drunk in the middle, "it must be an inside job." '

"The other one she told all the time was, 'These two drunks are driving in a car and they're driving pretty fast. One says to the other, "We must be getting close to town." "What makes you think so?" says the other guy. "We're hitting more people." '

"But she couldn't hold her liquor at all," claims Quam. "She liked to have a drink. We didn't have much to drink—places that served food couldn't serve liquor—so when we did, we didn't know how to handle it. Whiskey and Coke . . . and of course . . . Seagram's Seven Crown and 7Up . . .

"One night when we'd been drinking I took her home. She was really, really loaded. I got her up the steps to her apartment, one of her sisters came to the door and grabbed her by the hands, and she fell all over the place. I said 'Good night' and hightailed it. I never heard the last of that. I had a hard time living that down."

The neon that so pleasingly lit the comforting, warm, dark cave; the giggly jokes; the blurred, soothing release, the ebbing of the pressure that had come with the spotlight, the stage, and the need to please the crowd—all of this was the magic of the Magic Aquarium. Peggy Lee had joined a universal fraternity of performers in which drinking came with the territory. Countless members of the fraternity never left this place. Alcohol claimed more than its share of the talents of the times.

It was natural enough for artists who plied their trade in the late-night hours, who fancied themselves of the avant-garde, to seek out the comfort of a drink, or two, or a whole lot more, in the years when the liquor was once again gloriously legal (and less likely to make you blind). But what about a young girl leaping from a childhood marked by drink, straight into a profession

practically based on booze? Even without a genetic predisposi-
tion, it would hardly have been surprising for Peggy Lee to de-
velop a taste for the stuff.

As Johnny Quam now concedes, a little reluctantly, he and
Peggy were never lovers. "At that time, I was playing the field,
and she was, too. When you got serious in those days you gave
someone a ring and got married. There are going to be many guys
who say she was an easy mark. But she was not. Or maybe I just
didn't have the talent."

Soon, of course, Peggy was ready to move on again. Johnny
was not surprised when Ken Kennedy got his girl an audition
with Kennedy's cousin's band out of town. "She was just a cute,
wonderful gal—bubbly and sincere, fun to be around—and I will
say this: She had ambition."

It only made sense that Kennedy's introduction to the bigger
time would take her farther east, where the cities grew bigger and
busier in increments. Sev Olson's band in Minneapolis wasn't
much more than a local nine-piece outfit, but still that was a good
deal more sophisticated than Ma and Pa. When Ken told Peggy
that Sev's band was the house group at the very top-end Radisson
in Minneapolis—in a lounge called the Flame Room, in the heart
of another hotel—well, how could she not be drawn to it?

The Minneapolis that greeted Peggy Lee was a city of worldli-
ness and style. The fragrance that rode the north wind down
Nicollet Avenue was redolent not of cattle, but of the exhaust of
taxis and the electric ozone scent of the streetcars that delivered
dancers to the doors of the Marigold Ballroom, where jitterbuggers did their best to bring credence to the ballroom's famous
sign: "Never Grow Old Dancing at the Marigold."

Countless clubs and dance rooms crowded the town, culminating across the river at the Saint Paul Hotel. The city's jazz fans were on nodding terms with the best bands in the land. At the time Peggy arrived, both Benny Goodman and Tommy Dorsey had recently been in town. Minneapolis was a place where Peggy Lee could legitimately test, challenge, and further her art.

The entrance to her new home, the Radisson Hotel, greeted guests with the promise of luxury. After strolling under a fifty-foot-long canopy, they entered through three huge doors flanked by marble columns, flowing into a French Renaissance lobby. "The Jewel of Seventh Street" the Radisson called itself, and its grand tower was once the tallest reinforced concrete structure in the land. "It was heaven to me," Peggy recalled. "I'd plow around on those thick carpets, overcome by the grandeur."

The Radisson had its own library, its own coffee, and its own crest and motto: *"Labore et Honore."* Fine diners would be seated in the grand Château Room. More relaxed fare could be sampled in the Viking Room, with its Nordic mural. And loyal seekers of casual sounds would enter the Flame Room to hear the house band, led by a hometown favorite. Well, how much more wholesome could a bandleader be than a handsome, modest dental student who never frowned?

Sev Olson was blond, good-looking, and as straight, honest, and innocent as the day is long. "He always had a smile, ear to ear," recalls Lloyd Luckman, who played trumpet behind Sev in those years. "Handsome and charming—and Peggy recognized it."

The Flame was an intimate space that drew an impressive crowd. "It was fairly small, good food, good drinks—a favorite room for professional people." Behind Sev's drums, the band had been known to swing a little, with the three tenor saxes lending a low, smooth sound filled out by the trombones. Sev's little band didn't partake of the booze that the big boys were known for. "We didn't need it," Luckman says. "The big bands, over at the

Marigold, they had all that traveling and such—I think that's why they did the drinking."

Sev's boys simply did the standards, and did them well. His sidemen were nothing world-class, but they were good enough to dream. Peggy sang "Body and Soul" for her audition. She suspected that, thanks to Ken, the job was a done deal, but she gave the tryout her all. "She was just gorgeous," recalls Luckman. "And she had a gorgeous voice. She didn't need a big accompaniment, and she didn't need hyped-up music. She could make a song into a single moment. Her voice was very good, but I'll tell you, her presentation and everything—you could hear a pin drop. For lots of the things she did, there was practically no accompaniment—maybe Willy Peterson tinkling on the piano—but she didn't need anything else."

As Luckman recalls it, she had no trouble holding the attention of the room—or of one man in particular. "Sev went bananas over her," Luckman recalls. "I'll tell you this—Sev Olson was in love with that gal. He was enthralled. His every thought was of her. And they really cared about each other. But you might have thought he'd be better off without her," Luckman adds—naturally, because Sev Olson, budding dentist, was married.

Their affair lasted only a couple of months. "He was handsome and kind of funny," Peggy would recall. "I was practically dizzy just being around him, and he, unfortunately, shared my feelings. I knew I was in deep water now, and I kept wondering what I would do to get away. I spent the next few months between pleasure and pain."

By now the band was regularly booked into larger local venues—Billy Rose's Aquacade, the Marigold—and Peggy's exposure had earned her some airtime on the Standard Oil broadcasts over KSTP in Minneapolis. When bandleader Will Osborne, one of the bigger boys on the dance-band scene, came through town, he happened to be in the market for a singer, and asked a radio columnist to pass the word. Peggy went for it. Osborne offered not only a national band with a record contract, but a way out of her messy romantic entanglement. She auditioned for Osborne with "I Can't Give You Anything but Love," and got the job. Then she broke the news to Sev: "It really hurt me to do it. He brought his wife, Martie, down, and we all wound up crying. She was willing to give him up. But I knew it was wrong, so I stuck to my guns, and told them I would be leaving in the morning."

When Peggy left town with the Osborne band, she left behind the first serious relationship of her life. It had been impractical, impulsive, destructive, and without a hope in hell of lasting in the long run. It would set the pattern for many of her relationships to come. Sev Olson, the dutiful dentist, stayed married to Martie for the rest of his life. For Peggy's part, she'd been faced with a choice between two relationships. She'd chosen to stay with the one that would last the rest of her life. She chose her career. It wouldn't be the last time she made that decision.

FIVE

Benny Blows In

WHEN PEGGY STEPPED into the car of Osborne trombonist Gene Nelson, accompanied by Gene's wife and a backseat loaded with trombones, heading for the band's next engagement at the State-Lake Theater in Chicago, she was taking a huge step up. Osborne's outfit was a national dance band. The Canadian-born drummer with a crooner's voice employed seasoned professionals. Osborne's venues were hotels of stature—the luxurious Netherland Plaza in Cincinnati, the staid, stone-faced Ritz-Carlton in Montreal, the Bellerive in Kansas City, the Park Central and the Lexington in New York. His safe, commercial sound attracted the attention of sponsors a tad more high-profile than Jack Wardlaw's Castleberry's Chili. The manufacturers of such household necessities as Mazola salad oil, Karo Syrup, and Linit

Dye & Starch sponsored time for Will's group on national radio broadcasts.

In a bandscape littered with hubris—it came with the band-leading territory—Osborne was known as a truly good guy, though musically he was not at the cutting edge. Peggy had joined an outfit associated more with danceable ballads and novelty songs than musicianship. Like many bandleaders, Will figured his audience wanted to smile and laugh, and he wasn't above goofing around. The infectious "Listen to the Glissen" (glissando) was a showcase for the band's unique slide-trombone sound, which was augmented by its even more unique section of slide trumpets. (The custom-made horns were Osborne's own invention.) In "Glissen," Osborne's male singer, the personable Dick Rogers, introduced the brass section and explained their sound—if he didn't happen to be engaged in hitting on a gal at the time. (Befitting a band that indulged in humor, Osborne's outfit seemed to enjoy itself. The night that Rogers left the stage at the Book-Cadillac Hotel in Detroit and proposed to a young lady who was dancing on the floor, she accepted, right on the spot. The marriage lasted about a week.)

In the second week of November 1939, the band left Minneapolis for a tour that took them to a Christmas engagement at the ornate Fox Theater in St. Louis, en route to the West Coast. St. Louis, of course, was steeped in jazz history dating back to the twenties when, on land, Frank Trumbauer's outfit had a guy named Beiderbecke blowing his horn, and on the river, Fate Marable's orchestra rode the nightclub of the steamer *St. Paul,* led by young Louis Armstrong, working his way up from New Orleans and blowing his horn on the riverboat six nights a week. The *St. Paul* would drift down the Mississippi and then turn around and go back upstream. It was said that young Armstrong always did best playing against the current.

With a repertoire that mixed novelties and show and film songs such as Cole Porter's "It's De-Lovely" with brassier fare, the Osborne band was so successful in St. Louis that the engagement had to be extended into the new year. The new girl was obviously working out. On New Year's Eve, befitting the atmosphere around the wild Osborne crew, the lights went out at the Fox and the box office was robbed of its gate receipts before the late show. Peggy had to put her makeup on by candlelight.

Within weeks, her career with Osborne was unexpectedly extinguished, too—victim of a patented Peggy Lee illness. She'd awakened one morning to feel a lump in her throat. She visited a local doctor and asked him to excise it immediately. He told her to return for surgery the next day.

By any reckoning, a professional singer who has just joined her first national band asking to have a throat operation on the spot in a strange doctor's office seems a little unusual. Perhaps Peggy just liked the attention of doctors. Whatever the case, her decision brought disastrous results. She found herself alone in a St. Louis operating room with the anesthetist preparing her for ether. She asked if she could have gas instead. Ether, this veteran of the operating room told the man, always made her sick.

"He didn't answer," she later recalled. "He seemed annoyed. He quite deliberately pushed me down on the table. He fastened the straps, put gauze over my nose and mouth, and began *pouring*, not dripping, the ether onto the gauze. I was fighting to stay awake as I felt the ether dribbling down the side of my face."

When she awoke, she found herself clawing at stitches on her mouth, with Osborne's band manager Max Schall by her side, trying to calm her down: "Don't pull at those, Peggy—they're stitches. You've had a little accident." It seemed that in transferring her from one table to another, the medical staff had dropped Peggy Lee on her face. Her front teeth were broken, and they'd split her lower lip. A dentist capped her teeth, and she recuperated in the hospital, whose nuns were relieved when she consented to absolve them of blame. Whether the growth was ever removed from her throat is unknown.

One thing did disappear during her hospital stay: her job. Unfortunately—as was not unusual at the time—Will Osborne didn't have the funds to keep the band going, and by the time Peggy got out of the hospital, he had literally disbanded.

After her recuperation, Peggy accepted another invitation: to join Max Schall and the band's pianist for a drive out west, back to California and straight back to the Jade, where the crew welcomed her with open arms. But when a new guy in town, songwriter Jack Brooks, heard her sing, he suggested a venue with a little bit more style and class, down in a town that was a little less woolly than her current environs: Palm Springs, a vacation spot once known as nothing more than the home of the Cahuilla Indian tribe's hot springs, had suddenly become a mecca for the wealthy. Here an aspiring singer might easily catch an A-list eye.

Seasonal home to the Hollywood glitterati—Gable, Lombard, Bette Davis, Errol Flynn, Gary Cooper—and vacationing captains of industry alike, by 1939 Palm Springs had sprouted four large hotels to accommodate tourists in season, when the population jumped from five thousand to eight. Entertainment was plentiful: golf, gambling (in nearby Cathedral City), and nightclubs, from the top-end Chi Chi Club to the Doll House to the more atmospheric Western-themed Mink and Manure. The Doll House would become a legend as the room where Lorre and Cagney did their drinking, where Sinatra would court Gardner . . . where Peggy Lee, fronting a band called the Guadalajara Trio, caught the eyes and ears of a baseball magnate and a Chicago hotelier who would give her the biggest boost of her career.

But first she had to undergo an inadvertent transformation of her singing style—thanks, indirectly, to radio giant Jack Benny. One Saturday night, Benny and his radio entourage were in the crowd at the Doll House. Peggy was petrified. Benny and his admirers were a boisterous bunch, and singing over the din was not her style; when she started to belt, she lost something, style-wise. She realized this.

"When I sang quietly I felt more emotion," she would say many years later in an interview. "My voice seems to have a center core surrounded by rings of overtones, and when I sing loud, I lose some of those overtones. When I sing softly, they're all there. I like getting into that very careful place." But on a Saturday night at the Doll House, there wasn't a lot of room for nuance. Frustrated, nervous, and a little pouty—"I was thinking people didn't want to listen to me, so I'd just sing to myself"— she decided not to try to sing over the noise, but under it.

"In a moment of intense fear, I discovered the power of softness," she recalled. "The more noise they made, the more softly I sang. When they discovered they couldn't hear me, they began to look at me. Then they began to listen. As I sang, I kept thinking, 'Softly, with feeling.' The noise dropped to a hum; the hum gave way to silence. I had learned how to reach and hold my audience—softly, with feeling."

On another night, one of the luminaries turned out to be very influential. Fred Mandel, owner of the Detroit Tigers, and his wife were as intrigued by Peggy's voice and personality as Lloyd Collins and Lloyd Luckman had been. When the Mandels returned for a second show, they brought along another Palm Springs vacationer.

Frank Bering was a slightly paunchy guy with a Midwestern pallor. He didn't look like a cutting-edge music guy, but he'd spent three decades in the employ of Chicago's Sherman Hotel, where he'd risen to the manager's post. For music people, this made Mr. Bering someone to be reckoned with, for the Sherman was the home of both the Panther Room and the College Inn restaurant. (The College Inn had introduced Chicago's white, non–South Side denizens to the music of Isham Jones, the twenties bandleader whose clean, popular, lively, uncompromising style would make his outfit the paradigm for swing bands worried about wandering too far afield. Isham Jones wrote songs that lasted, including "It Had to Be You," and he knew a musician when he saw one; young Woody Herman, on sax and vocals, cut his teeth with Isham.)

By the time Frank Bering dropped in to the Doll House, he wasn't thinking about the Sherman; he had other hotels on his mind—the two others he owned, on the northeast and northwest corners of State and Goethe streets in Chicago, the Ambassador East and the Ambassador West. The East housed the Pump Room, a storied, spacious place with pomp and plush written all over it. The West housed the Buttery, a very posh and Waspy venue.

At the Doll House, Bering asked Peggy to audition for his Buttery back home. The Guadalajara Trio had packed up for the evening, but the band over at Claridge's played longer into the night, and after Bering issued his invite, the party relocated across town, where the Claridge's musicians fronted Peggy on "The Man I Love" (presumably in A flat). She couldn't have known that at nearly the exact same time, back east, one of the best canaries in the land, Helen Forrest, had recorded the same song with the band she'd been fronting for nearly two years: Benny Goodman's. Goodman wouldn't release the song until after Forrest had quit, whereupon it would become the first hit and only Number One song Helen and Benny would ever produce. But by then Forrest would have been replaced in Benny's band by an unknown novice.

Like most of the men in the business who had thus far crossed her path, Bering was as entranced by Peggy Lee's personality as by her pipes. "I'm hiring you more because of your enthusiasm than anything else," he told her. She jumped at his offer. For one thing, the acoustics in Chicago had to be better. She wrote her friend Jane Leslie back in Minneapolis and implored her to come to Chicago and bring along her favorite song, their good-luck charm: "Wishing (Will Make It So)."

Peggy arrived in Chicago. She was living close to the vest, monetarily; the Mandels had paid for her plane ticket east. She found he'd given her a room at the Ambassador West, where she was immediately impressed, of course, by the thick carpets, among other amenities. But when she reached the reception desk, she was momentarily flustered, as she recounted in her 1989 memoir *Miss Peggy Lee:* "Self-consciousness flooded my face. 'Will you please write your residence on the register?' 'Oh yes, of course,' I stuttered, and then became confused, because I really didn't have a home at that point. 'Well, I guess it's here.' I shrugged, trying to be nonchalant. . . ."

At the start, before Peggy knew that she could have picked up the phone to order room service, she and Jane lived on cookies Jane's mother had sent—and the room-service leavings of other guests, left by the chambermaids.

In fact, she'd landed in the lap of luxury. Before long, the Mandels took her to a party up the shore in their exclusive Lake Forest digs, where they introduced her to society. The guest list included one Mme. Oppenheimer—of the Lake Forest Oppenheimers, don't you know. And there was an extra perk to performing in a room that attracted an upscale crowd—including, one night, the famed and controversial muralist Diego Rivera; she had acquired an agent: William Morris, the agency she would stay with for another twenty-four years.

As Peggy began to find her musical footing, word got around among the music stars in the Second City. Visitors included the likes of bandleader Claude Thornhill, who was so impressed that he offered her a job. It would seem to have been a terrific fit: It was in Thornhill's outfit that Peggy's muse Maxine Sullivan had blossomed. The problem, she wrote a friend at the time—on the swank Ambassador stationery—was that she'd have to leave Morris for the agency associated with Thornhill.

"Everything has been fine," reads her missive of June 2, 1941, to a friend named Linny—"except that I was so far in debt when I got here. I've paid the [Morris] agency $110 since I've been here. . . . Trying to make up my mind again. The agency that pushed [Artie] Shaw and [Glenn] Miller up so fast is working on Claude Thornhill now, and they want me to join him. In order to do that, I'd have to break my contract with Wm. Morris. I wouldn't feel badly about that cuz they pulled a very fast one on me. . . ."

She goes on to provide a little news: Mme. Oppenheimer had thrown a little money her way, having Peggy model some of her gowns, and sold her a couple of dresses "for practically nothing." Peggy adds a few social notes: Jane and she—"and some fellas"— caught a White Sox–Cleveland Indians game, where she met the star pitcher Bob Feller. But her main feller seems to have been a popular, widely respected singer named Buddy Clark, who was appearing on the radio a half dozen times per week on CBS with Wayne King's staid, schmaltz-waltz band: "[Clark] is a very special friend of mine, lives at the hotel. Did you see that heart and key on *Life*'s cover? He brought me one from Pittsburgh." She doesn't elaborate on Buddy, whom she never mentioned again. Nor does she explain the nature of the "fast one" pulled by her agency; presumably, Morris interfered in some way and kept the job with Thornhill from happening. As would soon become apparent, however, her inability to sign on with Thornhill was a blessing in disguise. Had she gone with Claude, she wouldn't still have been chirping at the Buttery when another bandleader came through town.

In retrospect, the story of Benny Goodman and his band before the arrival of Miss Peggy Lee makes her ultimate appearance seem almost inevitable. Benny and Peggy *had* to meet. They were too alike not to hook up, although you'd never have known it at first glance, given that Goodman was a perpetually preoccupied, misanthropic, stiff-looking guy with the outward demeanor of a bored accountant, and few true friends. Truth was, Benny and Peggy had always been on the same journey—just taking parallel tracks. Both were artists who'd fled troubled childhoods. Both needed their art to help them navigate the world.

At the time of Peggy's arrival at the Buttery in the summer of 1941, Goodman had just arrived in town to play the College Inn. He was a troubled man. Long gone, by now, were his mainstays Gene Krupa (percussion) and Harry James (trumpet). But he was facing more than these losses; by 1941, a buzz about the death of swing was in the air. The buying and dancing public was starting to favor "sweet" bands that produced a music that needed no further explanation. Despite topping both the *Down Beat* and *Metronome* polls once again, Benny had just witnessed the specter of waning interest up close: a three-band swing-dance extravaganza in Madison Square Garden with Goodman's and Charlie Barnet's and Larry Clinton's outfits had failed to draw the expected crowds.

So serious was the siege that Benny wrote an impassioned defense of his chosen musical form (the magazine essay appeared under his name, at any rate) equating the blossoming of swing with the virtues of democracy and declaring that "if Swing dies, it will die over the dead body of American freedom." As odd as it sounds, midway through August 1941, Benny Goodman may have needed Peggy Lee as much as she needed him.

Before this turning point, Benny's story had been a twisting American tale with a difficult beginning, though it wasn't the featureless void of the North Dakota plains from which Benny Goodman broke away but the clustered, crowded Chicago ghetto tenements he'd fled at age sixteen, reeds in hand. Goodman's father, an immigrant sweatshop tailor, had insisted that his sons learn a craft they could enjoy—and perhaps profit from. So he'd bestowed on his three youngest boys instruments whose size corresponded to the pecking order in the family. Benny, the smallest and last, was given a clarinet.

Benny honed his craft in grade school and later with the marching band affiliated with Hull House, the urban social settlement founded by pioneer activist Jane Addams to better the lives of inner-city immigrants. Out in the countryside at Hull House band concert picnics, Benny found time to break off and jam. His dedication was admirable, his proficiency remarkable, but he was not a boy given to emotion; it was as if his notes spoke for him. Any question as to whether little Benny embraced the route his father willed for him was erased on the day Harry Goodman saw his kid brother kiss his clarinet.

If the Hull House band taught Benny discipline, the jazz clubs on the South Side, in black Chicago, showed him where music could go if let loose. In twenties Chicago, it was routine for white kids to show up in clubs where the new music was evolving. Teenaged Benny got his first real lessons in the small hours of the morning, listening to jazzmen whose names have been lost to time, with the notable exception of Louis Armstrong. Like Benny, Louis had made a kind of escape with his instrument— the horn he'd picked up at the Waifs' Home for Boys, thirteen years after his birth.

In August 1925, when a Chicago drummer named Ben Pollack, now leading his own band, wired Benny from Los Angeles to come play, Goodman headed west to the Venice Ballroom. It was here that the West Coast jazzmen first got to hear the clarinetist who was already considered a prodigy. But when Pollack's band returned to the Midwest in 1928, Chicago's jazzmen were migrating east, where new things were happening. Armstrong was up in Harlem now, recruited by Fletcher Henderson for his own band.

Benny joined the diaspora eastward, where he hooked up with Red Nichols's boys, alongside Krupa, Glenn Miller, and Jack Teagarden. Within a couple of years, Benny had put together a couple of combos—Benny Goodman's Boys was one—but it wasn't until John Hammond walked into the Onyx and hooked him up with Columbia that Benny's name began to be spoken with real respect. After the success of Goodman's first records in 1934, it was Harry Goodman who suggested that his kid brother front his own real band.

Benny put together an ensemble known for its style. They scored a considerable break when impresario Billy Rose, famous for his Casino Paree, announced plans to open a lavish club on Broadway and agreed to audition Goodman. Rose was unimpressed at first, but interested enough for a second listen. This time Benny brought along a girl singer. And thus did eighteen-year-old Helen Ward, already a veteran of the band scene, become the first member of the distinguished, long-suffering sorority of Benny Goodman's girl singers (of whom there were several; only the most prominent will appear in these pages). Goodman, in Ward's own words, would always consider canaries "a necessary evil." She had a tendency to warble in a high pitch, but she could hit a note, and hit it on time; she would sing on five songs that hit the top for Benny.

At the time no one was asking any band's girl singer to be an artist, although so many truly were. She had to have looks though. Ward seemed a little girl in terms of both voice and appearance. (Her amply applied lipstick did its best to make her seem older—but failed rather miserably.) Still, she presented a more visually intriguing picture than did Benny, whose stage expression veered between bland, blank, and oddly uninterested: a mask that reflected his true personality. One of the most influential musicians of the twentieth century was also the most self-absorbed, selfish, and inconsiderate performer on the face of the earth. It would take a very special brand of musician to plow through his personal baggage and become his friend. Very few ever did.

Ward saved Benny's bacon at the second audition, and Benny's band got the Rose job. But they'd barely begun before the club's reputed-mobster backers balked at the musicians' fees, and the band was let go. Benny's next funds were to come from a more legitimate enterprise: The National Biscuit Company, hoping to ride the growing dance wave, decided to sponsor the radio show of shows, a Saturday-night affair called *Let's Dance*. It would feature not one but three bands on the same cavernous soundstage. "Have a Dance Party on Saturday night!" sang the promo. Xavier Cugat and Kel Murray's ensembles were signed, along with Benny's Boys. The show debuted on December 1, 1934.

Goodman's band was the most adventurous on *Let's Dance*, but it still hadn't reached the artistic heights he envisioned. "It's too Dorseyish," Goodman said. "We're too routine." John Hammond suggested that Benny bring in Krupa, the percussionist whose onstage persona was as wild as his rhythms. And by some accounts, it was Red Norvo's girlfriend, hall-of-fame jazz singer Mildred Bailey, who suggested that Benny find an arranger up in Harlem to give the band some style. Someone like Fletcher Henderson.

When Mildred Bailey talked jazz in 1934, only a fool wouldn't listen. The sister of Bing Crosby's partner Al Rinker, she was "discovered" by Paul Whiteman when Crosby and Rinker invited the bandleader to hear her sing at Rinker's home in Spokane. She became not only one of the most influential jazz singers of her era, but also an infallible judge of talent. Years before, she had suggested that young Bing Crosby, then an unknown partnered with her brother, listen to a singing trumpet player out of New Orleans named Louis Armstrong.

It was Fletcher Henderson who'd first brought Armstrong to Harlem, to join the likes of Coleman Hawkins and Don Redman in the remarkable Fletcher Henderson Orchestra—the one band that virtually every musician on Manhattan Island listened to. But it was Fletcher Henderson who now, in 1934, was looking for work.

What Henderson had and always would have was an ability to chart a popular song. That is, he could take a tune and arrange the scoring for a bigger band. The likes of Irving Berlin's "Blue Skies" and Jimmy McHugh's "I Can't Give You Anything but Love," when orchestrated by Henderson, took on new life. He could make an ensemble sound like a person doing a solo.

Goodman was by now firmly committed to jazz, explaining, "I wanted to play dance music in a free and musical style . . . in the way that most good musicians wanted to play, but weren't allowed to on the ordinary job." But his bands had been straitjacketed by their Dixieland backbone. Approached by Hammond, Henderson agreed to help Benny cross the jazz bridge. He would arrange a couple of songs and write a few more. With Henderson's arrangements spicing the way, Krupa's drumwork adding driving rhythm, and trumpeter Bunny Berigan blowing as well as any man alive, the band started to do something it had never really done before. It started to cook.

The *Let's Dance* show ran from 10:30 in the evening until 4:30 in the morning, Eastern Standard Time. Near the close, Benny brought out the Henderson arrangements, and the band began to poke around the edges of conformity and sobriety. One night Berigan got so drunk he literally fell off the bandstand. (He had a compartment for his gin bottle built into his case—lined in red velvet.)

Then, in early 1935, just as Benny's beat was starting to capture the masses, Nabisco's workers went on strike. After just twenty-six weeks, the sponsor had to pull the plug on *Let's Dance.* Benny's agent, Willard Alexander, booked a cross-country tour for the group, to start in July.

The historic Goodman cross-country odyssey of the summer of 1935 threatened to end with a whimper as it moved westward. It seemed that Benny's brand of jazz and swing had no grip on non-Eastern imaginations. "The West had a reputation for being corny," Benny recalled. "They had all those . . . Mickey Mouse bands. So I said, 'This has got to get worse the farther west we go. I don't see any future in this at all.' "

In Lansing, the band drew eighteen people. In Grand Junction, Colorado, they played behind wire netting. In Denver, they were booked into a hall on the grounds of an amusement park called Elitch Gardens. It seriously looked as if Benny and the boys would call it quits before they made it over the Rockies.

But pianist Jess Stacy suggested that they try to keep going: "What do we have to lose?" And so they limped on. In Oakland, the reception warmed, but Benny was still worried. After an ominous stop in Pismo Beach ("We played in a fish barn," Helen Ward recalled, "and I mean that literally—the place stank of fish"), Goodman's band was booked into the huge Palomar Ballroom in downtown Los Angeles. Born as the staid Rainbow Ballroom, where fancified couples in gowns and tails once danced beneath soaring Moorish arches, it had morphed into a room where all things modern were at home. The "Dining, Dancing and Entertainment Center of the West" was a sixteen-thousand-square-foot dance floor that could hold nine thousand dancers, not counting the diners up in the Promenade Cocktail Lounge, replete with palm trees and cocktails.

The demoralized band didn't know what to expect. But they had not foreseen that, unlike the corpses back in Lansing, the

L.A. fans had been listening to the *Let's Dance* late sets. Three A.M. in New York was midnight in Los Angeles, and unbeknownst to Benny, the Henderson-styled swings had developed a following beneath the palms. And so, on the night of August 21, 1935, the band stood at an evolutional crossroads.

They started out with standard stuff, but the room was dead, and by the second set, Benny heard implorings, the urgings of a crowd looking for swing. "Let's cut the shit, Benny," the Dionysian Berigan famously said. "If we're gonna die," added the wild man Krupa, "let's die playing our own thing."

Benny obliged, and they cut loose with a cool, slightly bluesy, very jazzy rendition of "King Porter Stomp." It opened with Berigan's playful trumpet intro, then mounted into a full-blown jazz jam giving flight to Krupa's drums. After Berigan got turned loose for a wild solo, the stomp ended with a loud, emphatic question-and-answer between the brass and the reeds.

"To our complete amazement," Goodman would later recall, "half of the crowd stopped dancing and came surging around the stand. That was the moment that decided things for me. We finally found people who were up on what we wanted to do. That first big roar from the crowd was one of the sweetest sounds I've ever heard in my life."

If Duke Ellington had announced the birth of the style three years before with "It Don't Mean a Thing If It Ain't Got That Swing," swing music—and the liberation its rhythm both promised and delivered—took real flight in the space of five minutes in an L.A. dance barn. For years, the feel and the sound of jazz had been thriving just a few blocks to the east, on Central Avenue. But on that summer night, Benny's Boys, swinging an aircraft-hangar-sized ballroom on Vermont Avenue, leashed a wave whose currents would sweep a generation of Americans to a different, deliriously happy place.

The new sound, the new feel, of swing did more than make

feet and hips move of their own giddy accord. Embedded in the solos of Berigan, Krupa, and Goodman lay the themes of true blues and true jazz. As a nation, we had come to a place where we were ready to embrace a sound with some depth, a buoyant rhythm with distinct undertones—of wistfulness, of longing. Swing was more than mindless exuberance: It suggested soul. Driving it all was Benny's reed.

Basking in its success, the band stayed in Los Angeles and was chosen to appear in a movie called *The Big Broadcast of 1937*. It was in this film that a version of "Sing, Sing, Sing" revealed to a mass audience the unrestrained emotions that drove their music. Most notable was the drum solo that Krupa literally refused to finish, pounding the skins until they seemed about to explode. When Goodman returned to the Palomar (at triple the admission price they first commanded), he unveiled some tunes with a small combo featuring Teddy Wilson, the man John Hammond would call "the only piano player I could conceive of with the same technical facility Benny had." This was probably the first time anyone in Los Angeles had seen a black man playing with a small white group.

Goodman would soon add Lionel Hampton to the quartet that played between big-band sets at his concerts—Goodman, Krupa, Wilson, and Hampton. John Hammond would later describe the combo in lovely detail: "The quartet was a beautiful sight: Teddy cool, correct, the impeccable piano; Gene, with the chomping jaw, shaking head and falling lock of hair, crouched over his powerful drums . . . Benny with clarinet an inch or two from his mouth so he could smile beatifically at some little four-mallet riff of Lionel's, then answering with one of those perfectly controlled, razor-edged, scintillating Goodman runs."

Ward was antsy, but Benny had used guile to keep her, buying her gardenias, suggesting romance on the horizon. "You know,

I'm going to marry that girl," Benny said to Helen's date at the Brown Derby one night. He even persuaded her to come back east with the band instead of quitting. Then, in Atlantic City, he told her he had changed his mind: "You know, it's so early in my career, I'm not ready for marriage." The official end of Helen Ward's tenure was made public in a restaurant, when she quit and Benny threw a menu at her.

Enter Martha Tilton, a trouper who would see few nights off during her two-year tenure with Goodman and Company. It was a hard life, and a girl who could show up and do her bit was worth her weight in gold.

Once he had captured the soul of Los Angeles, there was only one jazz town left for Benny to impress, and two very different Manhattan venues to do it in. The soaring Paramount Building was the brainchild of Paramount Pictures head Adolph Zukor, who had figured back in 1926 that a thirty-six-hundred-seat theater planted in the heart of Times Square would give him a chance to showcase both his films and the Paramount studio's stable of stars.

Zukor crowned the building with a glass globe clock twenty feet in diameter, a vainglorious design motif meant to signify the motion-picture medium's rule over the rest of the world. But through the years, the Paramount's stage had hosted a singularly impressive roster of Jazz Age superstars, from Maurice Chevalier, Eddie Cantor, and Rudy Vallee to Danny Kaye, Jack Benny, and Bob Hope, as well as a significant number of purveyors of popular music. Glenn Miller's band had earned its stripes here, as had Tommy Dorsey's. It was here in 1931 and 1932 that Bing Crosby took his final steps into the pantheon of the greats.

Any performer who could fill the cavernous Paramount—performing between the motion-picture shows—was a certified phenomenon. But Goodman's band did more than fill it. They nearly rocked the old girl off her moorings. On March 3, 1937—

opening day—teenagers lined up as early as seven in the morning, standing five abreast on the sidewalk, for the first of six shows. That night, as the huge Paramount stage began to rise up from the pit, with the band playing "Let's Dance," the room went crazy. For the first time in musical history, the theater audience left its seats, rushing the stage.

For the next few weeks, they danced in the ticket lines, they danced at their seats, they danced in the aisles. For the first time, white kids were allowed to groove in public, en masse, without apology. But that's not all they were doing, claimed swing's growing army of detractors. The director of the New York Schools of Music spoke of scientific studies proving that young people exposed to swing would neck. (Classical music would keep them chaste.)

And now a publicist named Wynn Nathanson, at the agency that handled Benny's *Camel Caravan* radio show, came up with the idea of capitalizing on the controversy. Following the examples of European shows given by Armstrong and Ellington in sacred concert halls, why not have Benny play Carnegie Hall?

"You must be out of your mind" was Benny's first response. But the classical clarinetist in him soon warmed to the idea. "Maybe swing is dying, as some guy wrote," Benny told the *New York World Telegram*. "Maybe the public is tired of it. I can't prove it. But I can prove the opposite." Carnegie Hall had been sold out for weeks when, on January 16, 1938, the sidewalks filled with dowagers in mink as well as more casually dressed teens and jazz buffs. Benny himself had to buy scalped tickets for family members in from Chicago. "I feel like a whore in church," Harry James said as the band took the stage, but before long—after a Krupa solo in the opening number, "Don't Be That Way," demolished the tension—the old hall shook loose. They danced in the hallowed aisles as Goodman mixed proven fare with an all-band thirteen-minute jam on "Honeysuckle Rose."

But the night's most hypnotic stuff came from Goodman's trio and quartet. Teddy Wilson received a huge ovation as they swung into "Body and Soul." Soon "Avalon" snapped at full speed, with Lionel Hampton's mallets dancing over the keys of his sweet vibes like butterflies flitting from flower to flower, effortlessly keeping up with Krupa's driving beat behind him. At one point, Krupa's cymbal flew off its stand. Hampton caught it in midair, tapping it in time with his mallet without missing a beat.

When Krupa began frantically pounding his skins to announce "Sing, Sing, Sing," with its hyper downslant of a vibe, it wasn't just the kids who were moving, but some of those in private boxes, too. "Sing" stretched out into a twelve-minute semi-jam of dark, hip, blue jazz at its brassiest best, backstopped all the way by Krupa's insistent tom-toms. Everyone took a solo, from Harry James's triple-tonguing to Benny's flights of fancy.

Then Jess Stacy began to cook. "Yeah, Jess!" Benny shouted, bringing a rolling laugh from the audience, and notching the hitherto-uncelebrated pianist up to a musical plateau that would be called the greatest two minutes of his career: a soulful, light-touching triumph. The rest of the musicians backed off to near silence, and the storied hall suddenly found itself host to a truly hip journey into places that until now had belonged in clubs on Fifty-second Street or Central Avenue, on Basin Street or Chicago's South Side.

It was a new kind of concert. The final ovation rang as loud as the applause usually reserved for Toscanini. "I *like* that jazz," a stagehand said to Hampton afterward. "What is it?"

"If you don't know what it is," said Hampton, "don't mess with it."

Despite all the acclaim, Benny still needed a girl. Martha Tilton had moved on, and he was auditioning again. Mysteriously, he passed over a thin, pretty, gutsy young woman named Anita

O'Day, whose blood flowed pure jazz—when it wasn't diluted by other intravenously induced substances. O'Day had been singing at a Chicago club called the Off-Beat in the late 1930s when Goodman was playing the Chicago Theatre, the huge, ornate downtown space known as a palace for white jazz. O'Day had heard that Benny was searching for a girl, but during the actual audition someone handed her a song so bland that history has forgotten its name. As O'Day would later recount in her brilliant memoir, she let the pianist do the introduction as written, then went off on a flight of O'Day fancy. She paid attention to the melody—at the beginning, and at the end. In between, she took some liberties with the notes and the timing. When she was done, Benny weighed in. "What was *that*?" he snapped. "You didn't sing the melody! In my band, the girl singer sings the melody!" O'Day stomped out.

Helen Forrest, who had gained national notice for years with Artie Shaw until the recent dissolution of his band, was next in line. Goodman offered her the job without as much as a listen: If she was good enough for Artie, Benny's only rival, she was good enough for him. Forrest's voice had a smooth, flawless tone—"a creamy voice and trumpet sound," spoke *The New York Times,* "at once spunky and wistful."

From the start, Goodman and Forrest were oil and water. Benny's fans now demanded jazz, and Benny had the band to deliver it. Relegated for long stretches to sitting in the wings, out in Siberia, in a straight-backed chair, alone with her thoughts, the canary was likely to find the gig depressing, if she had any ego at all. When the singer's song was finally called, the band still had at least two instrumental choruses before they changed the modulation to the singer's key, which was her cue to walk to the center of the stage, find her place in front of the microphone, sing her chorus or two, then bow and return to the shadows as Benny wailed into his solo.

Not for nothing was the frustrated Forrest called "the Madonna of the middle chorus." In 1939, live crowds weren't in the mood for ballads; all they wanted was the energy that Goodman could deliver nonpareil.

Forrest was never sparing of her praise for Benny's musicianship: "Artie's band didn't need Artie, but Benny's band didn't come to life until he got on the stand," Forrest would later say. "Then it really started to rock. I grew with Benny because of the caliber of musicians he had. . . . He wanted great musicians so much that he, more than Artie, broke the color barrier. It took courage to feature blacks in his band, but he did no more for them than he did for the white musicians."

But that assessment was possibly Forrest's only good memory of her eighteen months with the man. Forrest's own memoir, *I Had the Craziest Dream*, painted a picture of a collaboration from hell. Acquaintances of Benny Goodman's would weigh in on his eccentricities for years to come, but none would ever paint the vitriolic portrait Helen Forrest did: "Benny Goodman was by far the most unpleasant person I ever met in music. . . . The twenty or so months I spent with Benny . . . felt like twenty years. Looking back, they seem like a life sentence. He was strictly an instrumentalist and the need to have vocals were a pain to him. . . .

"He never said one kind thing to me about my singing, but then, he never said one kind word to anyone about anything. He practiced more than any musician I've ever known, and when he wasn't playing or practicing, he was thinking about his music.

"He didn't have a best friend," she continued. "He didn't have a friend. Maybe John Hammond, or [his agent] Willard Alexander. Perhaps because he had so few friends, Benny relied a lot on family. He ran his band like a family business, like the corner deli. At one time or another, Benny had in his band one brother, Harry, on bass; another, Irving, on trumpet; Eugene took care of the music, Freddy was the road manager. Ethel, his sister, ran the office. The rest of us were really just outsiders. . . . Fortunately, he drove to most of his dates, like most of the bandleaders. None of the musicians ever drove with him that I remember."

It's safe to say that there was virtually nothing Forrest liked about Goodman, certainly not his insistence on calling everyone "Pops"—including Forrest—because he couldn't be bothered to learn names. No surprise that Helen Forrest was eager to give her notice by the beginning of the summer of 1941. Years later, Benny spoke of the singers who played a significant role in his band's greatness. He fondly recalled Helen Ward, Martha Tilton, and Peggy Lee. But he never mentioned Helen Forrest.

"But she sang with you for two years," a friend reminded him. "She did?" Benny responded. "Really?"

By the summer of 1941, if better pure-jazz musicians— Armstrong, Basie, Pee Wee Russell, Earl Hines—were selling records and filling the radio airwaves, Goodman's band was at the top in terms of national saturation. He had lost Gene Krupa and Harry James, but it was inevitable that he'd reassemble a new crew to beat off the inevitable challenges of the other bands. Before long, into the vacuum rushed a handful of promising newcomers. Big Sid Catlett was a musicians' musician of a drummer, the temperamental opposite of the crazed Krupa—a big, quiet, consistent anchor ("He had delicacy as powerful as a bomb," said one Benny band member). Trumpeter Cootie Williams was a legend among the players.

More significant were a couple of true new prodigies. The first was young guitarist Charlie Christian. Hammond had been tipped off about the tall, scrawny phenomenon laying down electric licks in the Ritz Café in Oklahoma City, and made a side trip to see what the fuss was about. Christian's band was earning $2.50 a night. When Hammond first met him, Christian was bedecked in purple shirt and yellow shoes. His clothes weren't the only unusual thing about the man; his electric guitar work—something of a novelty at the time—had "the phrasing of a horn," said John Hammond, who sent him to Benny, who had him playing not only in the band, but in the sextet.

Far more important to Benny, who had always considered the piano to be the second most crucial instrument in any of his bands, Goodman had compensated for the loss of Teddy Wilson and Jess Stacy with the addition of a blond teenager precocious way beyond his years. Writer George Simon (a music critic who would briefly date Peggy) had seen the kid playing piano in the Village and passed on the word. Benny took a chance with the young man from the Bronx. The arrival of Mel Powell would forever change the fortunes of both the band and the young Peggy Lee.

Né Mel Epstein, the kid had grown up on 161st Street in the borough of the Bronx in New York, across the street from Yankee Stadium. His heroes were Babe Ruth, Debussy, and FDR. Epstein had been classically trained, but jazz hooked him at the age of thirteen, when he saw his first concert from the front row at the Paramount Theater, featuring Benny Goodman. In the middle of the show, Lionel Hampton's mallet flew out and landed in the boy's lap.

Mel sat through five showings of the movie *Maid of Salem* to hear five Goodman sets, at which point his classical training went out the window, at least for the time being. Soon the teenaged Epstein was playing a club in the Village; underage, he'd duck into the men's room whenever a union official dropped in. After one particular set, he was led to a table where a big, dour-faced guy had been sitting expressionless, pounding the table in time with one hand. It was Art Tatum himself, the partially blind piano genius. "You gonna be a real one," Tatum said to the kid.

He changed his name to Powell, a bowdlerized version of the

family's original name back in Eastern Europe, Poljanowsky, and joined Goodman's outfit. Before long, the eighteen-year-old was not only playing piano, but arranging some of Benny's songs.

With Catlett, Williams, Christian, and Powell on hand, and with legendary arranger Eddie Sauter writing for the band now, *Metronome* called the April 1941 version of Benny's new group "in many ways, the best stage band that Benny Goodman ever had."

They had just never yet found a woman who could improvise herself a real role in their music. They were waiting for her arrival.

SIX

Don't Be
That Way

In Chicago in August 1941, preparing for an engagement at the College Inn, Benny Goodman was staying at Frank Bering's Ambassador East. One night, Benny's fiancée, Lady Alice Duckworth, suggested that he come next door to the Buttery and catch the new girl singer. The imperious, handsome granddaughter of Commodore Vanderbilt—founder of the New York Central Railroad—Lady Duckworth was also John Hammond's sister.

"So the next evening she brought Benny in, because they were looking for a replacement for Helen Forrest," Peggy would remember. "I didn't know it, but I was it. He was looking at me strangely, I thought, but it was just his preoccupied way of looking. I thought that he didn't like me at first, but it was just that he was preoccupied with what he was hearing." As a rule, Benny listened to his fiancée's musical opinions. She had the pedigree. Alice Hammond Duckworth was the "rebel" of the family, according to Hammond, and coming from John, these words had some weight. Alice's first marriage, to a member of Parliament—of the Tory party, to boot—hadn't worked out. Now she was engaged to Goodman.

Alice shared more than a streak of rebelliousness with her famous brother; she'd always been intrigued by John's milieu, and the people in it. She knew her way around the jazz world, and she knew that her fiancé would be intrigued by the blond girl fronting the quartet across the street. And so on a night in mid-August 1941, she dined with Benny and Powell on steaks in the Buttery.

"I guess we've got to get somebody for Helen" was Mel Powell's recollection of what Benny said over their steaks (with no mention of Benny's table manners). And thus did the world's most famous bandleader—"the most talked-of jazz instrumentalist in all the country," as *Esquire* had recently put it—choose, as a singer for the world's most famous band, a young girl with virtually no experience, fronting a quartet in a hotel coffee shop, based on a single night's performance.

The group was the Four of Us. The song that Peggy would remember singing was "These Foolish Things," Benny's old hit with Ward, the one that had gotten her into Ken Kennedy's studio just three short years earlier. Ward's vibrato version had been a hit, but Peggy's richer, more languid tones were far better suited to the poetic wistfulness of the tale of foolish reminders of a lost love:

> *A cigarette that bears a lipstick's traces*
> *An airline ticket to romantic places . . .*

"Mel thought [Benny] decided to hire me on the spot," Peggy would later write. "It certainly didn't look that way to me. . . .

From where I stood it looked like he was just staring at me and chewing his tongue."

It wasn't personal, of course; as Powell would soon reassure her, "The question with Benny is whether the plug is in or out."

"I wish he'd enjoyed it," Peggy said after the show, to the Four of Us.

When her roommate Jane told Peggy that Goodman had called their room the next day, she was understandably incredulous. But Jane persuaded her that it wasn't a hoax, and that she should respond. Goodman was typically terse and all business. There was no "I'm going to make you a star" moment. "Do you want to join my band?" he rasped. Peggy's answer was a stunned affirmative. "Come to work," Benny said, "and wear something pretty." No mention of a rehearsal. That night, at the College Inn, Benny's band appeared with two canaries, the new and the old. Benny had insisted that Forrest play out her contract, but never gave her another chance to sing.

"He said, 'Stick around until your contract runs out,'" Forrest would recall. "I sat alongside Peggy on the bandstand and didn't sing a note for four weeks. She'd get up and sing, but I never got up. When people would ask me why I wasn't singing, I'd say, 'Ask Benny.' They'd ask him and he'd say, 'She's got laryngitis.' That was the longest month of my life."

"Helen Forrest Out; Peggy Lee Joins BG," read the *Metronome* story, calling it "a surprise Chicago move." The magazine's priorities were obvious: Peggy's arrival was played beneath another item: news of Benny's engagement, announced in a larger typeface: "Goodman Wedding Imminent." Alice Duckworth had received her Reno divorce from George Duckworth. "A British paper," read *Metronome*'s account, "commenting upon the future alliance, noted that Mrs. Duckworth was known in London as a swing fan."

At the beginning of the College Inn engagement, Peggy impressed no one. She knew the songs, but they were all in Forrest's higher keys. For now, as far as Goodman was concerned, she was just a necessity, a little something pretty for the guys in the audience (and the players who got to sit behind her and admire a part of her physique that some of her close male admirers would never tire of praising).

At the time of Peggy Lee's entrance, Benny had a less flamboyant troupe than in previous years. Peggy fit in perfectly. What the audience saw onstage was a girl who clearly hailed from the American outback. A local scribe referred to one of her outfits as "one of those Yukon Lil" dresses. A particularly low point came on the night when the crowd chanted "Sing! Sing! Sing!" and she thought they were screaming at her critically.

For one critic with a keen-edged pen, Peggy's early performances with Benny evoked a woman "gripping the mike as if it were a baseball bat she was clinging to in midocean after a shipwreck." To others with less flair, she was "a cold dish of tea." *Down Beat* ran a photograph of her farmgirl face with the caption "Sweet Sixteen and she'll never be missed" (a reference to "sweet sixteen, and never been kissed").

"I was terrified," she told a newspaper reporter years later. "I remember how the spotlight reminded me of a freight train bearing down on me." She developed a "psychosomatic" cold, she said, a result of the pressure of not only performing, but replacing a woman she'd been listening to herself for so long.

Within days, Peggy approached the man she'd spent all her nickels on back in Balboa's jukeboxes, with an offer: "I'd like to quit, please." Until now, she had been embraced on every level, ever since Valley City. Maybe she feared she had hit her ceiling. It wasn't as if she didn't have other options. She was twenty-one years old. She could make a good marriage and have a family. But she would later say that she knew in her heart that if Benny fired her or allowed her to quit, she would never sing again. She knew she'd turn her back on that world.

"I won't let you" was Benny's response.

On their national radio broadcast from the hotel's Panther Room on August 21, the *Metronome* critic would praise not only Powell's playing—"a brilliantly flexible ivoryman"—but his ability to lessen the pain of listening to the girl: "His little runs back of Peggy Lee . . . helped relieve [her] stint of a routine quality. . . . Singing here was only fair, and the arranging and playing couldn't compensate for the deemphasized vocal element."

According to Forrest, if Benny was encouraging Peggy to keep on trying, he wasn't showing it to the band. His intractability, his obliviousness, and mostly his stare—the Ray, it was called—would all conspire to reduce the newcomer to tears: "Benny kept glaring at her. When she asked him what was wrong, he muttered something about her phrases. She didn't know what she was doing wrong. One night Harry James stopped by to hear the band and Peggy told him tearfully of the problem. Having worked with Benny, Harry understood. He told her to tell Benny before the next performance that she now knew what the problem was and would do what he wanted. But Harry also told her to sing exactly as she had been singing, and she did this, too. When she was done, Benny smiled at her, pleased. It was one of the few times he ever showed approval of anything."

More trying still was Peggy's first recording date. The Columbia recording crew was in town to record more fodder for the bottomless maw of jukeboxes and ballrooms; a new Benny record was expected monthly, if not more often. John Hammond was in the studio, keeping an eye on Benny, as he liked to do. And so, on August 15, in her first week with Goodman, Peggy Lee went into the studio to record "Elmer's Tune," a lightweight standard that had been a hit for Glenn Miller—and was terribly difficult to sing. The key changes were frequent. The lyrics were borderline novelty, and quite silly: "Why are the stars always winkin' and blinkin' above? What makes a fellow start thinking of fallin' in love?" Half a century later, Lee would confide that she still hated the recording so much she'd leave a room if someone played it.

It was now that Benny's piano prodigy went above and beyond the call of duty. Mel Powell might have been just a kid, but he knew talent when he heard it. Powell appointed himself musical mentor of the girl who was routinely quaking in the spotlight, trying to sing in Helen Forrest's key in front of the most sophisticated band in jazz history. Mel Powell would go on to write symphonies so complex that he'd teach theory at Yale. But his first student in music theory was a canary.

"Peggy must have been a nervous wreck," Powell recalled. "She met Hammond in the control room, and he handed her the sheet music for 'Elmer's Tune.' This was a pretty tough rap for a kid. There was no taping those days, you just made the record. If you blew something, you just started from the beginning. You didn't say, 'Let's take it from measure 39' and splice it. She was so nervous. The sheet music John handed her made such a racket it sounded like a forest fire that was going over the brass, over the saxophones. Peggy had . . . been up all night learning this thing, and the arrangement was disorienting because 'Elmer's Tune' was very clever, very fancy, full of stuff.

"So I led her into an adjacent studio, and we sat down and ran through a couple of things that were in the arrangement, especially her cues. I was constantly cuing her, and I told her that during the recording of the arrangement I could always improvise something."

The key to it all, Powell explained, was giving Peggy her first note before she had to sing it, so she wouldn't come in blind. "I told her, 'Benny won't know, nobody will know. I'm just gonna pop that [note] in there in the midst of what seems to be a ramble over the band, while the band's playing. You catch it from that; that'll be the cue: count four, and go.' I think she's never forgotten it."

She never did. "God bless him, he was such a help to me," Peggy recalled. "Mel would give me four bars, and I would count, and listen hard for where I was supposed to come in—jumping in at the last moment, hoping for the best."

Adding to the general tension was Hammond, whose decade-long collaboration with Benny was beginning to fray. Benny was growing tired of John's constantly taking credit for the band's success. On the day of Peggy's first recording with the big boys, the animosity came to a head. Noted audio engineer Bill Savory sat in the control booth that day. His recollection of Hammond's behavior reflected the general dislike of the workers for Hammond.

"It was a tense situation," Savory remembered. "John started hassling Benny about Peggy's deficiencies. 'Benny, she *cahn't sing*. She just *cahn't sing*.' Finally, out of exasperation, Benny picked up a chair and hurled it across the studio at him.

"John was amazed, and very upset. 'What does one do?' he asked. 'Does one fight?' 'Just forget it, John,' I said. 'The sight of blood would probably make you faint.'"

In September, Benny took part in a doubleheader, a half-classical, half-jazz show with the Chicago Women's Symphony Orchestra. The Mozart Clarinet Concerto was followed by jazz featuring Cootie's trumpet. "One o'Clock Jump," according to one newspaper report, "produced a screaming 'E-e-e-e-e-yow-e-e-e-e-e!' from the crowd. You would have sworn the whole crowd had been inducted into paradise; there was a strangled quality of unbearable excitement in their shouts and ejaculations."

Peggy made every effort to find a way to fit in and not embarrass Benny. Alice Duckworth had started to buy Peggy some more glamorous stage outfits, and Peggy had taken to visiting

Rush Street to catch various true jazz singers, to refine her sound. But the critics had panned "Elmer's Tune"—"Very poor and dull," noted *Metronome*.

It was a tough entry into the very big leagues. Peggy had not only stepped onto a white-hot stage at the College Inn, she had joined a crowded stage nationally. On the night Goodman unveiled his new girl, 339 other bands were playing theaters or doing tours coast to coast—from Basie, Calloway, Dorsey, Shaw, and Miller on the top shelf, to Will Osborne (on tour), Sev Olson (still at the Radisson in Minneapolis), and Jack Wardlaw, speed-banjoing the Club Royale in Savannah. Such were the times that Frank Dailey, player and proprietor of the Meadowbrook Gardens ballroom back east, had recently declined to form a band of his own: There were too many great men out there already.

But numbers weren't the only concern in the weird world of the big-band caravan. Increasingly, the wandering tribe of swing and jazz musicians comprised a distinctly loose fraternity. In the summer of 1941, an industry founded on bringing good times was beset by more than its share of tragedy, danger, and narcosis. "Musicians in general are being subjected to a terribly unfair licking these days," editorialized *Metronome*, the monthly jazz bible, in its August issue. "The general public is getting a totally unfair impression of what musicians are really like. They get these impressions from magazines, from books, and even from radio. . . . After reading and listening, we thought it over: We decided to forget, momentarily, what we knew musicians were really like. We decided to let a new impression be formed from what we saw printed and heard spoken. Our new impression of the average musician then went something like this: 'He's never happy unless he's drunk. He never plays well unless he's drunk. If he isn't drunk, he's elated because he's been smoking marijuana—pardon, he's been "toting tea." He's up all night. He sleeps all day. He talks only in jive language. He has no interest in anything except swing, or anything that will make him enjoy swing more. He's either running after women, or running away from them. He has no sense of responsibility whatsoever.' Now, that's brutally unfair to the average musician."

The claims came back to haunt the magazine—very quickly. The lead story in the next month's issue recounted the deaths of two of swing-jazz bandleader Charlie Barnet's sidemen, guitarist Bus Etri and former Goodman trumpeter Lloyd Hundling, in a traffic accident in Los Angeles. Their car had collided with a truck at the corner of La Cienega and Venice boulevards early in the morning. The police found marijuana in the car, then proceeded to the home of the couple that was housing the two, where they found more marijuana, and busted the couple, too.

The taint of scandal tying the weed to Goodman's band surprised few. If Benny's boys' musical reputation was extraordinary, they were hardly immune to temptation. "There were the same marijuana-smoke-filled buses and rooms with Benny's boys, just as there had been with Artie's outfit," Helen Forrest recalled. "Some drinking. No hard drugs." (Her intense dislike for Goodman no doubt compelled her to add, "Benny's boys were not as much fun as Artie's had been.")

After Chicago, the Goodman band hit the road, en route to an all-important gig in New Jersey at Dailey's high-profile Meadowbrook Ballroom, with several one-nighter stops in between. Once again, Powell took to smoothing out the rough edges on the bus rides between various burgs.

"Mel and I would ride on the bus together and sing," Peggy later recalled. "He'd sing the brass parts sometimes, and I'd sing the reeds or vice versa, to things like 'Down South Camp Meeting' and 'Stealin' Apples.'" Before long, Powell and Peggy weren't singing just old standards. They were singing the scores of the Benny Goodman library—including such challenging fare as the instrumental "Clarinet à la King," in which Goodman's instrument takes off like a bumblebee—a challenge for any a cappella voice to imitate. Sometimes they'd run through the band's entire catalog of scores.

As was the custom with most bands, Benny, as leader and marquee star, didn't ride the bus. Usually, he drove with a member of his family. But he was apparently favoring his new girl singer, for soon after they left Chicago, as the band made a short jaunt from Syracuse to Toronto by bus for an August 30 date at the Dance Pavilion of the Canadian National Orchestra, Benny gave Peggy a ride—until the car broke down. Efforts to charter a plane were futile, and Benny ended up hiring a private sleeping car to attach to a train. The lodgings were more than luxurious for Peggy, if strangely stifling. Soon, Benny arrived at her berth: "Wait a minute!" he said. "I can't have you sleeping here . . . the car isn't air-conditioned!" His singer couldn't have cared less. She wasn't about to give up a private sleeping berth.

The instruments on that trip fared worse. The truck had stopped to be searched at customs, and broke down on the spot. Benny's brother Fred scoured the town for instruments and showed up at the Toronto train terminal, horns and all, accompanied by a police escort. The dance came off without a hitch.

Metaphoric bumps in the road paled next to the actual vehicular chaos that increasingly beset the industry. More disturbing than the ubiquity of the evil weed, as the number of bands increased, was the mounting toll on the highways. In July, the American Federation of Musicians proposed a ban on overnight trips of longer than four hundred miles between one-nighters, with obvious good reason. Two months later, bandleader Red Sievers's bus collided with a cattle truck ten miles south of Owatonna, Minnesota, at 5:30 in the morning, killing Sievers and five of his musicians. It was the culmination of a brutal year in which accidents had affected the bands of everyone from Hal Kemp, killed in a train wreck, to Benny Carter and Anson Weeks.

Most of the top bands traveled by train, at least over long hauls. But the bus trips were the ones that tried their patience—full of travails like the routine during the Helen Ward years, when Benny's band was traveling in an old four-cylinder Coney Island sightseeing bus so aged and feeble that on large hills the band had to get out and walk up, carrying their instruments. If you were carrying a clarinet, you were fine. If you were carrying a trumpet with a special case for a fifth of hooch, it was a little uncomfortable. And if you were carrying a bass, forget it: That instrument commanded a seventy-three-pound, seven-foot iron maiden of a case, big enough to hide a man in.

"Traveling never was fun, of course," Helen Forrest wrote. "Maybe I didn't mind it as much when I was starting out and it was new to me. It was kind of exciting to see all the cities. But before long you realized you didn't see the cities. You saw the countryside as you drove in, you saw the four walls of the hotel. You saw the ballroom or the theater or the fieldhouse. Then the countryside as you drove out. It all became a blur—the town, the time of day, the day of the week, the date. Someone else told you when to do and where to go, and you went."

"Pretty soon, people and places become pretty much a blur," Benny wrote in 1939. "You start thinking (if you ever get a chance to), was it in Scranton that Lionel sat in on 'Sing, Sing, Sing,' and gave that tough old set-up the workout of its life, or was it Buffalo? Was it in Detroit that we first started doing those descending trumpet runs in the last chorus of "One o'Clock Jump," so that everybody started referring to it as "Two o'Clock Jump," or was it Philadelphia? . . . After a while it really doesn't matter much . . . as long as when it's happening you get a lift out of the band, and the audience feels it, too, and you know you're swinging."

His choice of cities wasn't just a matter of literary license, either; even the coal towns were hopping now, as an October issue of *Metronome* noted, in a one-paragraph blurb that captured the tone of the times: "Wilkes-Barre jumps to the flow of the cash registers of local niteries doing big-time business."

And oddly enough, if you were lucky enough to catch the band in Scranton, or Erie, or Wilkes-Barre, you probably saw them at their best. "There's no better way to get an all-around picture of a jazz orchestra's ability," wrote George Simon, "than by catching it on a dance date known as a one-night stand. On these dates they loosen up, play anything they like in their library without concessions to song publishers, and have no time limit on any number if they're in the mood to stretch it by several choruses."

After Toronto, Benny's band had a hiatus until it was due at the Meadowbrook. Peggy's public was not exactly clamoring for her craft. "Peggy at that time," *Down Beat* later recalled, "was very unsure, nervous, and confused." But Benny told Peggy to ignore them: "I've heard you when you were really singing, and I know what you can do. Stick it out and don't let them scare you."

No wonder Peggy used her furlough to return to her home state for a family reunion with Della, Marianne, and Clair. "She actually seems more thrilled about coming home than she does about her new contract," Della told the Fargo paper. By now, Della had married, and Marianne was living with her; Della's husband was overseas in combat from which he would never return. Clair and his new wife were living in Fargo, too.

Peggy performed a special show from WDAY, backed by the station's studio orchestra—and the Four Jacks, reunited with their Jill for a quarter of an hour.

From the beginning, Benny's relations with his new singer bore little resemblance to his frosty goings-on with Forrest. But then, neither Forrest nor any of the other previous canaries had made use of her considerable downtime on stage to write songs in her head. But, though audiences would never have known it to look at her during the shows, that was exactly what Peggy was doing as she sat in her chair in the wings, waiting for her number. She was not idling the measures away; she was beginning to compose lyrics, an ambition that would eventually distinguish her from nearly every other female singer of her era, as well as produce some of the most remarkable musical poetry the American songbook would ever see.

Surprisingly, Goodman immediately went out of his way to promote her songwriting. The *Chicago Sunday Herald-American* ran a weekly feature in which they published a selected song from a given band's library, and in the fall of 1941, Goodman sent the newspaper the music for an original Peggy composition called "Little Fool," which Benny would occasionally perform but Peg would never record. The name of the author of the accompanying blurb is lost to history, but whoever he was, he had a way with hyperbole: "Here is the tune all of America has been waiting for, written by Peggy Lee, 21-year-old vocalist for the band. 'Little Fool' is a first, and a must. Also, it's her first published tune. . . . There aren't many songwriters who turn out both lyrics and music. Hoagy Carmichael and Cole Porter and Noel Coward are the first names that come to mind."

Of course, mindful of the commercial climate, Benny was going out of his way to trumpet his girl singer to a public buying "sweet" band stuff more than ever before. Benny knew the market value of a good, sweet song sung by a young girl with a matching disposition and an appearance that was growing increasingly easy on the eyes.

Not everyone supported the changes. "The Goodman followers immediately set up a howl, crying into their minimum's worth of beer," noted *Down Beat* some years later: " 'What's with Benny and all this balladry?' "

In September 1941, the band settled in for a four-week engagement at the Meadowbrook in northern New Jersey, and the jitterbuggers turned out in droves—as did the critics, with their sabers sharpened. Peggy still wasn't comfortable with the range or complexity of the arrangements, or the high stakes. To have vaulted from Olson to Osborne to Goodman was like nothing so much as spending a few weeks in baseball's minor leagues before having to don a major-league uniform and play in the World Series. "I was afraid one of those nights someone was going to grab my ankles and pull me off the stage," she later told *Look* magazine. "She was so scared for about three or four months," Goodman later said, "I don't think she got half of the words out of her mouth."

Benny's shows from Dailey's ballroom-barn in Jersey included several radio broadcasts over CBS, which generally featured about a half dozen songs by the band. Peggy was usually given one. She sang "Let's Do It" on September 16, and on the next night, "I See a Million People"—a song written by Una Mae Carlisle that should have carried a bluesy undercurrent, but given the big-band constraints that was apparently difficult to achieve; one review of her show on the seventeenth was particularly cruel. The writer for *Down Beat*, after noting that Goodman's new girl singer had been everything from a milkmaid to a waitress to a carnival barker, wrote that "Lee was better suited to any one of those earlier chores than she is to singing with one of the great dance bands of all time." The writer was Dave "Dex" Dexter, the former Kansas City scribe who'd discovered Basie. He would come to regret the assessment—a particularly harsh judgment considering how severely the big-band format shackled any songstress.

One week later, Peggy went back into the studio for Columbia, and this time the results were a little different. In fact, they were downright encouraging. In Chicago, she'd caught Laura Rucker singing down on Rush Street with Baby Dodds, the drummer, doing a version of the Cole Porter standard "Let's Do It" that hipped up Porter's little parlor tune. On September 25, Peg laid down her version, in fairly routine fashion—until she threw in her own phrase: "Well, let's *do* it," she uttered, in a semi-spoken style that sounded almost impatient, like a casual nod thrown over her shoulder at some panting schoolboy. It was the first recorded example of the technique that had bothered Lloyd Collins back in Fargo: her blurring of the barrier between song and the spoken word.

To Peggy Lee, it was a natural device, a way of making her relationship with the audience casual and conversational. It also made her seem warmer, more personal and accessible. Then, it hardly hurt that the song had such sultry undertones. The fact that Porter's "it" actually refers to "fall in love," and not the "it" that the imagination first conjures, doesn't detract from the suggestiveness of the lyric—and as phrased by Peggy, the suggestiveness was obvious. Befitting the style of the time, most of the song was instrumental, but the bluesy vamping of the band was lively, loose and infectious. The first sung verse came in only after Benny's reed had had its say. But when it was over, it was a Peggy Lee song—the first Benny tune claimed by its young singer. But hardly the last.

"Peggy Lee lets loose an infectious vocal" was *Metronome*'s characteristically terse appraisal. But it was a start, and it paled next to the second song recorded in the same September 25 session, another kind of tune entirely. Alec Wilder's "That's the Way It Goes" is a lyric laden with longing, and Peggy's version included very little instrumental decoration. Morty Stuhlmaker's bass led the way before Cootie Williams's horn and Benny's reed took their melancholy turns. But it was all just a quick setup for Lee's voice, which delivered the breathtaking lament of a woman falling head over heels—and bemoaning every second of it. Peggy summed up so much resignation and world-weariness that it was hard to imagine she hadn't felt that way before.

Possibly, Goodman had put some thought into finding material that would showcase his new girl singer in a manner appropriate to her particular gifts. But if he had, this ran contrary to his history; just as likely is that Peggy's rendition furnished a strong example of how easily her innate talent could overcome big-band convention. Big-band numbers were seldom designed to set up a vocal. At any rate, the record earned good notices, and her confidence grew. She even began receiving fan mail. One missive especially moved her: "Some singers," wrote the admirer, "hit you over the head the first time you hear them. You're the kind it takes a while to catch up with."

Something was happening in the Goodman band that had seldom happened before: The girl singer was starting to thrive. Peggy actually thought *and* felt time and rhythms, as a musician would—or at least a musician with an instrument that allowed a performer to play with its notes, to slide and bend them, to stay behind the beat, to experiment within the framework of the measure.

On stage, she was developing a persona of her own, emphasizing an increasingly minimal, held-back kind of styling that was unique and that would stay with her from here on. "Her minimalist gestures were deliberate," said one later fan. "But the music ran up and down her entire frame." It was under the auspices of Benny Goodman that her trademark economy—of volume, of movement—really began to take hold. Some years later, after pianist, composer, and maestro André Previn had become a fan, and a friend, he described her demeanor evocatively.

"She would not move a muscle." Previn says. "That was so attractive. It concentrated you on the song so much. But," he added, "it's wrong to get off on how she looked. She was just the best there was. Billie Holiday, yes, and of course she influenced her, but after Billie there's never been anyone as good as Peggy was. She had the best sense of time, in the jazzman's sense, of any singer. She was remarkable. As the jazz guys say, she was right in the pocket. Her sense of time was nothing short of perfect. And if it was a song about being in love, she meant it, she understood it, she lived through it."

The fact that she didn't give obvious expression to the swing beneath her skin made the rhythms that much more effective. To make the beat overt would have been to lessen its power. Peggy Lee was learning to keep the lid on everything on stage; her gestures were small. This would forever be her paradox: Possessed of the surest time of any singer of any era, she would never express it physically. Ella would bop and sway and snap and groove as naturally as one of the God of Rhythm's own marionettes, but Peggy seemed to move uncertainly, as if genetically encased by the straitjacket of her Lutheran church-song heritage. Or her stepmother's upbraidings.

Peggy Lee's lack of physical grace had an upside: It put more emphasis on her beauty, which seemed all the greater because she was so quiet, still, and apparently mysterious. She gave the crowds little but a smile and the sidelong glance she was starting to perfect—a look that spoke a thousand words, accompanied by a little sideways drift of the jaw, with the gaze dropping off to the side and her eyelids falling to half-mast. It was nothing but shyness, of course. She was afraid to look someone in the eye—the legacy of too many times as the childhood whipping post—but she transformed her uncertainty into an art form.

In October 1941, Peggy visited the studio again to record what would become her first legitimate chart hit. It could hardly have been good luck or coincidence that the song wasn't a mechanized dance ditty but a bluesy, soul-rich Ellington tune. From the opening measures, "I Got It Bad" was the perfect meld of vocal and instrumental: Goodman's band didn't get in the way of the singer. The instrumental intro lasted a scant half dozen measures, with the trumpeting, melancholic flourish slowly parting like a curtain to reveal Peggy's world-weary complaint, "Never treats me sweet and gentle, the way he should / I got it bad, and that ain't good."

If there was still a little too much varnish on her voice, there was a new quality to her tonality. Her sound was racially indistinct. To a listener perched by a radio speaker, it was virtually impossible to say whether this songstress was black or white. When she purred "But when the fish are jumpin', and Friday rolls around, my man and me, we gin some, and pray some, and sin some," Lee's voice came close to cracking. Benny's clarinet talked back to her before Williams's trumpet came in, heavy with the melody, squawking and singing the blues. On the big finish, the whole band stepped on the syncopated notes and swung to high heaven.

This was a record that truly represented a new sound. To be sure, women had been singing plaintive blues since before Bessie Smith, and big bands had featured jazz singing since Paul Whiteman brought Bing Crosby on board; Benny had been swinging melancholy for five years. But no band had ever featured a white canary as blue as this one.

Goodman's band left New Jersey just as the Tommy Dorsey band, featuring Buddy Rich on drums (and a young kid from Hoboken named Sinatra on vocals), rolled in. Next, Goodman's troupe set up shop at the glamorous Terrace Room in the goliath Hotel New Yorker—a highly scrutinized Manhattan engagement, given the wholesale personnel changes in the band. Cootie had just split to form his own band—he'd open up at the Apollo with a hot combo featuring legendary Eddie "Cleanhead"

Vinson—but replacement Billy Butterfield was no slouch on trumpet, and Goodman's two-man trombone team of Lou Mc-Garity and Cutty Cutshall played as well as anyone out there.

The long-anticipated Terrace Room booking turned out to last a good deal longer than anyone would have guessed. Goodman's new band, breaking all records, wouldn't surrender the room until five months later, by which time some twenty thousand revelers, drinkers, and listeners and dancers had paid them homage.

In New York, Peggy moved to a hotel called the Victoria, a humble little haunt she'd chosen after Columbia executive Morty Palitz told her to steer clear of the musicians' hotels. The Victoria was not among the city's palaces, but it was tall, and impressive enough for her to note later that as she checked into her room, she was physically higher than she had ever been in her life (except during her barnstorming jaunt back in Jamestown with stunt pilot Ole Olson).

Equally intriguing was the view, albeit in a very different way: "The Roseland Ballroom sign," she recalled, "was blinking at me—ROSELAND, ROSELAND, ROSELAND. I felt a little tickle in the pit of my stomach." In her new digs, she had some company: a spaniel puppy named "Torchy"—the first in a long line of canine companions who would be by her side for the rest of her life.

Other than the dog, the boys in the band furnished most of her company at first. Peggy didn't meet a lot of people; that wasn't the life she had chosen.

In November, the band went into the studio and turned out two more tunes featuring the new singer. "Somebody Nobody Loves," the legacy of one Seymour Miller, was pop-froth dance fare at its best. Benny's clarinet took the first verse, bouncing lightly from note to note like a sing-along dot above a cartoon lyric. Peggy's voice managed to display her almost uncannily true pitch, but it functioned here as just an instrument delivering a nice set of notes.

But the second song, the Gershwins' "How Long Has This Been Going On," was simply a killer. "I could cry salty tears," she sang, scraping her upper register, tempting listeners to tear up right along with her, even though she was singing about finding, not losing, the joy of love: "Kiss me once, then once more," she implores. "How long has this been going on?" The strange thing was how *down* she made the song, which spilled over with far more emotion than she'd shown on vinyl.

By now—and this was no small thing—the anonymous three-judge star-chamber rating panel of *Metronome* seemed to be on her side at last. The magazine gave "How Long" an A minus, citing "great work by Peggy Lee." As for "Somebody," it merited a B plus: Lee "lifts 'Somebody' a bit higher," said the magazine.

The clarinetist who had brought jazz to mainstream America had a jazz singer on his stage, and in his recording studio. Not a jazz singer by label, perhaps, but a singer with an obvious dose of jazz in what she sang.

SEVEN

A Cool Quality

"PEGGY LEE, WHO wasn't too impressive till she got over the shock of finding herself with Benny's band, is slowly turning into one of the great singers in the field. The lass has a great flair for phrasing—listen to her on those last sets at night, when the band's just noodling behind her, when there aren't any complicated backgrounds to sing against. That she gets a fine beat, that she sings in tune and that she's awfully good-looking are more self-evident."

The writer of this paean, George T. Simon (of the Simon & Schuster Simons), was considered the premier critic of the time. He also briefly dated Peggy, but that doesn't mean he was off the mark in his review of Benny's band at the Terrace Room in December 1941. By now, Benny's new girl singer was gaining notice in all the trades.

At the Terrace Room, the band broke all kinds of records. There was little question that Lee's "unforced, cool quality"—in Simon's words—was a huge part of the attraction. Perhaps it had something to do with her venue: singing in a hotel, next to a train station—it was almost like home. Of course, by now, the station was Pennsylvania Station, the land's largest, and the train was all-star industrial designer Raymond Loewy's fantastic, streamlined *Broadway Limited,* which pulled in underground and debarked passengers right at their hotel. And not just any hotel. When the Hotel New Yorker opened its doors in 1930, it was the tallest in the United States. A Deco palace of a more than 2,500 rooms, the New Yorker was a "Vertical Village" whose advertising boasted the world's largest barber shop (forty-two chairs); the world's largest private power plant (five steam engines and an oil-burning diesel producing enough light, heat, power, and refrigeration for a city of thirty-five thousand); 856 miles of carpeting; twenty-three elevators that traveled nine hundred miles a day and were capable of transporting an entire city of two hundred thousand people in twenty-four hours; bellmen "smart as West Pointers"; an acre of kitchens "as sweet and clean as a mother's cookie jar"; secretaries on every floor; and French maids to assist with cosmetics in the ladies' lounge.

Peggy Lee had found the ultimate hotel, a place at least a hundred yards closer to the Penn Station platforms than any other establishment. Suites with "sky-terraces where you can literally say, 'Good morning, Mr. Sun!' " went for $11 per night. At dusk, on their terraces, where they could see the Hudson cutting "through the twilight haze like a silver ribbon," guests could enjoy a cocktail. Ever since the repeal of Prohibition, when thirty thousand New York speakeasies gave way to the new nightclubs, the hotels had been ramping up their entertainment with fresh, attractive venues such as the Blue Room at the Lincoln, the Astor Roof, and the Green Room at the Edison.

At Christmastime in 1941, the band competition around town was fierce. Basie and Teddy Wilson's new band played the clubs, and hotels turned their attention to the big bands: Glenn Miller at the Pennsylvania, Harry James in the Blue Room. The jitters of war seemed to hurt only those musicians making livings on the steamship trade; on solid ground, Americans were seeking the big-band sound wherever they could find it, in either of the current flavors: swing or sweet.

Outside the clubs and hotel ballrooms, Manhattan was an island of contradictions. Over on East Forty-third, cattle roamed the street outside the slaughterhouse, and tenement kids swam in the East River next to pipes spewing sewage. Downtown, between Broadway and the Bowery, the sidewalks were crowded with houses fashioned of crates, elaborate structures the homeless made. But inside the Terrace Room, on a December night, the guests would have finished their Kennebec Salmon Steak, their Lake Erie Trout, their Fried Spring Chicken Maryland— dishes all named for places, the better to impress diners with how far-flung the chefs' search for provisions had been. They would have sipped on a Bronx Cocktail, or a Clover Leaf, or a Peruvan Pisco, a Southern Honeysuckle, a Sam Ward, or a Sidecar. Adele Inge, the Youthful Skating Sensation, would have packed up her skates for the night and the hotel's small rink would be covered by portable flooring that could withstand dancing. Some of the guests simply wanted to listen—at tables up on the terraces where couples could sip and snuggle beneath the Deco sconces. A fantasy in maroon and silver and black and gold, the room was a resplendent court, glittering and discreet at once.

No one in the Terrace Room could have guessed the full ramifications of the Japanese attack on Pearl Harbor. But then, nobody wanted to know. Accounts of Benny's 1941 Terrace gig never mention the fact that the war had the whole town spooked. Maybe because the Terrace was where they went to forget.

What no one would forget was the singer popping up from her chair and chiming in with a verse after all the instruments had had their say. She was awfully hard to miss. Physically, she was growing up. Her face had no hint of classical glamour, but reflected a clearly All-American beauty. She had the smile of a cheerleader and a hairstyle that framed her face perfectly: two waves of blond hair swept back above her broad forehead, to either side.

During the band's time at the Terrace Room, the one song that would particularly have caught veteran Benny-watchers by surprise was a blues-drenched classic. As she stood just a few hundred feet from the Pennsylvania tracks, what could have been more appropriate for Peggy than one of the most evocative train songs ever penned?

"Blues in the Night" would be the first song she'd sing *and* record on Christmas Eve; it was written by Harold Arlen and Johnny Mercer, as good a songwriting team as America would ever produce. Arlen's songs would eventually earn him mention in the same sentence with Gershwin and Berlin, and Mercer's lyrics would deserve every accolade ever thrown Cole Porter's way. In collaboration, the two would voice an authentic strain of the American soul. Wildly different in personality—Mercer could be a volatile, dark man, while Arlen was a gentleman's gentleman—they shared a seminal childhood experience. Each had grown up close to African American families. Each wrote American anthems that seemed to come from a metaphoric place where white and black cultures overlapped and intermingled, a place few songwriters of the time visited.

And to the delight of aficionados of poetry, blues, and story-telling, Peggy Lee would never stray far from their influence for the next fifty years. Mercer would become a friend, an important figure in her recording career, and a mentor in lyric writing. Five decades later, when she recorded the final great album of her career—of Arlen songs exclusively—Peggy would say, "We had something in common. Harold Arlen and I both loved the blues."

Arlen's father had come to the States through New Orleans, where he developed an appreciation of slow Southern stylings be-fore taking up his true calling as a cantor in Buffalo. "My parents rented a home they owned to an African American family," Arlen's son Sam recalls. "Very early on he was exposed to differ-ent kinds of music, and in that era that was unusual. His father wanted to expose the family to other cultures and religions and ideas. You start to pick up those two idioms—the cantorial chants, the African American music—and that carried over to so much in his life."

For his part, Arlen never considered himself a blues composer. He felt that only two of his songs were true blues: "Blues in the Night" and "I Gotta Right to Sing the Blues," the song he'd writ-ten with Koehler for *Earl Carroll's Vanities of 1932.*

"When he did the Cotton Club," Sam recalls, "at a time when there was so much segregation—at the Cotton Club, the staff was black and the clientele were white—my father was accepted as one of their own people. He could say things and use slang and terminology, and get right in the midst of any conversation, and he was accepted. He was not trying to be one of them; that's who he was." Years later, a portrait painted of Harold Arlen depicted him as a black man.

By his late teens, Harold was playing keyboards and singing jazz in New York speakeasies. By 1929, he'd sold his first song,

"Get Happy." By 1933 he and Koehler had written the astoundingly melancholy "Stormy Weather," which debuted in 1933 at
the Cotton Club, sung by Ethel Waters. In 1939, seven years after
penning "Paper Moon," he and collaborator Yip Harburg turned
in some songs for an MGM movie about a little girl in a land
called Oz, including an anthem about longing titled "Over the
Rainbow."

But by 1941, Arlen's relationship with the notoriously difficult
Harburg had temporarily cooled, and he hooked up with a guy
he'd worked with before, a man who, as a singer of some renown
himself, understood the songwriting process, and who, as a native
of the Deep South, seemed to hear the same rhythmic voices as
Arlen—as well as a few dark, dour others that no one else was
hearing.

A child of privilege, the direct descendant of one of George
Washington's generals, Johnny Mercer had spent his childhood
between the family house in Savannah, Georgia (within earshot
of Five Mile Bend, where Savannah's trains turned around on the
coast to get back to the station in the city), and on the island the
Mercer family owned off the coast to the south, where Mercer
got to know the coastal black population, with their Gullah
(Geechee) dialect, through his black playmates. Introduced to
popular music by song-pluggers—men hawking sheet music
across the land for firms back in Tin Pan Alley—at a Savannah
carnival, the youthful Mercer began hanging out on West Broad
Street, over in the black part of town, combing stores for "race
records." At prep school in Virginia, he wrote poetry, and sang,
and moved with the gait of a man forever exhorting his classmates
to feel the animating force of life. "Get hot!" was Johnny Mercer's motto.

On a trip to New York in the twenties, Mercer caught Paul
Whiteman's band at the Paramount, featuring not only Bix Bei-

derbecke, the shooting star doomed to be doused in drink, but also the Rhythm Boys, the trio known for the jazz-tinted stylings of the young singer out of the Northwest, Bing Crosby.

From the beginning of his career as a lyricist, Mercer would show a love for the railroad; his first songwriting gig was as a staff writer for Miller Music, the company owned by William Woodin, president of the American Locomotive Company. When Mercer married his childhood sweetheart, Ginger Mehan, in 1931, it was with an affection that was equal parts physical and emotional; it was to Ginger that he'd lost his virginity; it was to her that he wrote from a Pullman car on the *Super Chief* to California of his fondness for the act of making love. "Music [became] my sun on a dark day," he would later write, "my solace in time of pain and disappointment, my best friend. I know of no joy like it, outside of sex." To those two pals he could have added "drinking," for he also had a strong affection for alcohol, although it increasingly brought out his brooding, angry side.

In 1932, Mercer and Hoagy Carmichael wrote "Lazybones," a tuneful paean to the languid Southern pace of life, which, sung by Mildred Bailey, hit big and conferred instant stardom on the kid from Savannah. By the mid-thirties, Mercer was drinking with Cole Porter and Lorenz Hart in his suite at the Waldorf Towers. In 1935, Mercer's "The Dixieland Band" became one of Benny's first hits. And for a movie called *Hollywood Hotel,* Mercer wrote the lyrics for "Hooray for Hollywood," the song that will forever be the anthem of the industry, despite Mercer's derision of the movie folks' shallowness ("That phony, super Coney Hollywood"). Like that of Tennessee Williams, Mercer's Southern stance let him see his land and its people from a distance, through a lens both critical and loving. Johnny Mercer was a singular figure on the American song landscape, a man who knew rhythm and despair—the feel, as well as the sound, of the beat of a boxcar on the rails.

Mercer's pen also proved to be commercial: The peppy "Goody, Goody" had gone to the top of the chart for Benny and Helen Ward in 1936, and in 1939, Mercer's railroad poem "I Thought About You," Peggy's favorite rail song with Lloyd Collins back at the Coffee Shop in Fargo, was recorded by Benny and Bailey.

In the early forties, Mercer and Arlen were asked to write a blues tune for a movie called *Hot Nocturne*. They came up with a number told from the point of view of a black man sitting in a jail cell. "I went home and thought about it for two days," Arlen would say. "After all, anybody can write a blues song. The hard thing is to write one that doesn't sound like every other blues song."

And Mercer? He just opened a vein and let it all spill out. How to find a way to bemoan the cruelty of a woman, a worrisome thing—"who'll leave you to sing the blues in the night?" Easy: Let a train whistle—the loneliest sound there ever was—underscore the sentiment. Then layer it across the land with some vintage Mercer lyrics: "From Natchez to Mobile, from Memphis to St. Joe, wherever the four winds blow."

And now trust it to find its voice: in the most incongruous of places, in this Terrace Room overfull of finery. Trust the girl who's singing, who's started to attract notice with a cross-cultural style that perfectly lent itself to Arlen and Mercer's way of seeing the world. "Here," Henry Pleasants would write in *The Great American Popular Singers*, "was a white girl of Scandinavian origin, sounding like a sister . . . of Nat King Cole."

The Benny Goodman version of "Blues in the Night," as sung by Peggy Lee, was truly remarkable music, the stuff of late-night laments, of a lonely 4 A.M. with empty bottles strewn across the landscape. Peggy's voice is sexy, slow, and wounded: as the rains "are fallin'" the train's "a-callin'"—the "lonesome whistle," the echoing of the "clickety clacks"—all the railroad imagery of a

North Dakota childhood add up to nothing less than . . . the blues . . . in the night.

Befitting Benny's obsession with his music—at the expense of his musicians' personal lives—he took a sextet into the studio on Christmas Eve to record "Blues in the Night." His new sextet comprised himself, Powell on piano, Sid Weiss on bass, Tom Morgan on guitar, and Benny's two trombone aces, Cutshall and McGarity. Their studio was Liederkranz Hall, the ornate New York auditorium built for German symphonies in the nineteenth century. It had become renowned as the finest acoustic hall in the land and was a favorite recording venue for jazz musicians.

The recording of "Blues" went well, but it was a second song from this session that truly opened another door deeper into the maturing style of Peggy Lee. That song was "Where or When." A soon-to-be-standard from the Rodgers-Hart musical *Babes in Arms*, the ballad represents the musings of a woman wistfully recalling a long-ago encounter. "Where or When" was possibly the most subdued, wistful, quiet ballad that Benny Goodman would ever play or record. Not a single unnecessary note was either played or sung. McGarity's trombone intro is a thing of restrained beauty; never has the belled instrument sounded so plaintive. Never was Benny's tone so lyrical. And never had Peggy Lee sung so simply. Well, *technically* she was singing, but the tone was as hushed and intimate as a quiet conversation between friends on a back porch in the middle of the night. Backed for most of the tune by nothing but Morgan's hushed strums on the guitar—so soft they sound like brushes on a snare—and Mel Powell's beautiful fingerings on a celeste, she sang just louder than a whisper.

Part of this effect could be directly traced to the unusual method Benny used to record the song. There was only one microphone in the hall that day, hung from above, to pick up all of the instruments. It hovered high above, with a pyramid of crates beneath it. To get close to the microphone, to play a solo or sing one, it was necessary to climb the crates.

"Lou would first crawl up in the air on boxes," Peggy later remembered, "then for the vocal we had to pass each other as silently as possible while I crawled up and he crawled down. Those recordings were moody, but it was also a little dangerous. But if Benny said do it, we did it."

Finally, on a record, Peggy Lee had let the record-buying public hear the technique she'd discovered back at the Doll House. But now her minimalism had grown more assured, conscious, elegant. "It's something like painting," she would say many years later, referring to that particular recording session. "If you were drawing little lines, doing little images . . . you wouldn't have the broad brush: you'd have a finer one, and just touch it to the canvas, to get a very interesting effect."

Metronome's three-judge panel was split on "Where or When": "Plenty of reviewers' dissension on 'Where,'" read the magazine's analysis, with "two handing it a straight A, the third unmoved by the mood. Cited for honors were Miss Lee's intimate, sincere vocal and her noble Powell backing."

"Blues in the Night" earned an A minus with a "commendation for Miss Lee's blues yodeling." (Never mind that it was Lou McGarity doing the yodeling.)

In January, the band released a couple more numbers that featured Peggy prominently. During their five months in New York at the Terrace Room, Benny recorded some forty songs. Almost two-thirds of them featured vocals, a few with Art London, Benny's oft-overlooked male singer of the time (later known as Art Lund), but most with Peggy Lee.

"That Did It, Marie" and "Somebody Else Is Taking My

Place" both earned A minuses from *Metronome*. "Somebody Else" was pure pop froth, and Peggy was pitch-perfect, making her way skillfully around the bouncy horns, the boppy beat, the solos surrounding the melody. "Somebody" quickly became one of the biggest hits Peggy and Benny would have.

By now Peggy was finding her footing in the city as well as the studio. Benny began taking her to his haunts on Fifty-second Street to catch the cutting-edge competition. They were seen frequently enough for gossips to wonder, but Peggy would later assure a questioner that their relationship had always been platonic.

On the night they sat through all of pianist Fats Waller's sets at a club on Fifty-second Street, Waller came to the table, and Peggy found herself asking for the first autograph she'd ever requested. Fats signed an ace of spades for her, which seemed only appropriate: It was during the New Yorker engagement that Count Basie gave her the compliment that she would later confide to a close friend she would cherish as the highest praise she'd ever received.

"I was singing 'That Did It, Marie,' when Count Basie danced by the stage. He winked up at me and said, 'Are you sure you don't have a little spade in you, Peggy?'" Ellington and Armstrong visited the Terrace, too. In a very short time, Peggy had been given access to the stratosphere. But if the celebrities excited her it was one of the soldiers who touched her.

It was wartime now. The military men who found their way to the Terrace Room weren't the boozy enlisted men combing the bars around town. They were visitors looking for a different kind of experience. Peg's heart went out to a kid from Illinois who was so eager to get into the fight he'd enlisted in the RAF, but was now on his way home, sporting a pronounced limp and a depressed demeanor. He requested one sad song after another, and when Peggy sat down after one of her sets, he told her how much he enjoyed her singing. For the rest of the evening, she'd return to his table between sets. They agreed to meet again the next day, after the lunch matinee. This time he brought her a bracelet from the gift shop: "Please," he said when she demurred, "you've been so good to me."

After the afternoon set, she took him up to her room and he poured out the cause of his gloom: He didn't think he could ever recover from the guilt of having bombed innocent people. Peggy would later recall the moment:

" 'I'm a coward,' he said.

" 'No, of course you're not,' I said. 'You've just been through something pretty terrible.'

" 'But what do I do with my life now?' He gestured to his injured leg.

" 'Maybe you could be a commercial pilot,' I said weakly, and he gave me a wistful smile, as if to say, 'You just don't understand.' I didn't.

"He suddenly said, 'I want to give you these,' and he took off his wings.

"I was taken aback, and said, 'You're not supposed to take these off unless . . .' and fell silent."

Left unspoken was what they both knew: that a pilot who bestowed his wings on a girl was proposing marriage. "I'll keep them for you," she said. He left, and they met again between sets that night. They talked idly until she excused herself to go to the powder room. When she returned, her friend was gone. "Isn't it terrible about that young pilot?" she heard someone say later. She fled to her room, and the phone was ringing. It was Benny. "Don't talk to anyone," he said. "That pilot you've been talking to just shot himself through the head." Through the shock, she heard her boss tell her to come back down and go to work; it would keep her mind off it. Freddy Goodman plied her with cognac, and she went on stage. The next day, the pilot's brother came to town, and he told her he'd been on the phone with his brother when he shot himself.

"He made me feel a lot better," she would recall. "'You mustn't blame yourself for anything,' he said. 'I'm just glad you made his last hours as pleasant as you could.' I gave the wings to his brother to give to his mother and dad. There was nothing else to do but say a prayer for him."

The grim incident did nothing to dissuade the crowds at the New Yorker, nor did Benny need any prayers. The hotel was so delighted with attendance that it asked him to stay on. "BG stays in NY, cancels concerts to remain in the city till March 12," trumpeted *Metronome*. "Business has been exceptionally good and hotel management wants to keep Benny and the business going together as long as possible."

Another dispatch—"From the City Desk," back in North Dakota's *Valley City Times-Record*—spread the word in a folksier tongue: "The foreign correspondent from Japan, James B. Young, who spoke at the auditorium last Friday night as a windup to the Winter Show, brings good news of another North Dakotan who has done well—Norma Egstrom, singing as Peggy Lee for Benny Goodman's band. Young, who is known from the China coast to Manhattan's Stork Club as Jiminy, saw Peggy two nights before he came to Valley City as she finished 'Deep in the Heart of Texas' to the delight of a contingent of navy officers. Their show at the Hotel New Yorker, with an ice carnival, has been rated top in drawing capacity crowds among all hotel name bands. Nearly 20,000 have paid the cover charge to hear the Wimbledon-born girl [sic], who made the lights of Broadway via Valley City and Fargo."

An unexpected brush with her past added a personal note to Peggy's Terrace Room success: She encountered an old classmate from Wimbledon, George Brenner, who was stationed over at Fort Monmouth in New Jersey and had crossed the river to catch the act. As Brenner would later recount the tale, he visited on a night when they were turning people away at the door; the place was packed. But George gained entrance—likely with Peggy's help—and Peggy gave him an autographed photograph: "To George! I will never forget those good old days at Wimbledon HS."

Benny's musicians managed to maintain a degree of fondness for the guy despite his self-absorption—a trait that Peggy witnessed firsthand. While driving through Westchester, near Benny's new suburban house, with Benny and his brother Fred, Peggy experienced another instance of Benny's legendary lack of empathy. The rain was coming down in drops the size of grapes. The windshield wipers were sloshing and it was nearly impossible to see anything out the windows of the automobile. "Benny," said Freddy, "I have bad news: The lead alto sax gave two weeks' notice." Just as Benny was absorbing the news, their car slammed into a huge deer.

The group got out of the car and walked to the front to see blood and fur on the grille, and the huge animal, which was heaving and nearly dead. Goodman's brother wanted to put it out of its misery, but of course no one had a gun. So they got back in the car and decided to drive around, knocking on farmhouse doors.

Through the entire incident, Benny had said nothing. The car started up again and pulled around the deer. Peggy was a basket case, sobbing for the suffering creature.

At last Benny spoke: "Did you offer him a raise?"

Peggy was saving her $60 weekly salary and keeping to herself. To the band, she was a polite kid, watching and learning while trying to fathom the man in whose hands her fortune lay. Benny could be inexcusably rude. Like the night he didn't care for the way she was singing a melody, and turned the bell of his clarinet right at her face. He blasted out the melody as he wanted it sung in a very unmistakable fashion.

Benny was a man who believed in rehearsal. He rehearsed. He rehearsed again. And then he rehearsed some more. Long after Peggy thought an arrangement was perfect, they'd go on practicing it. Years later, when she had earned her own reputation for endless rehearsing and unrelenting perfectionism, Peggy reflected on the lessons she learned from Benny's regimen: There was, she said, a "value in rehearsing. He would go over it and over it and over it. There is such a thing as overrehearsing something, but not in his case, because he was rehearsing the section pieces, then leaving the choruses open for free-form extemporizing." There were times, she later told *Zoo World* magazine, when she'd have to wait three hours before the band rehearsed a song with a vocal in it: a lesson in "patience and humility."

By March 1942, Peggy's domestic situation had improved: She'd moved out of the hotel and into a basement flat in the West Village with Jane Leslie. Jane was singing in New York, and they had hooked up to share the place, their clothes, and their cosmetics—a good arrangement.

"It had not one, but two fireplaces," Lee wrote. "We just flipped." The Lee-Leslie pad would become the first, but hardly the last, of the Peggy Lee domiciles known to keep their doors open to any and all. In his pseudonymous "Jimmy Bracken" column in *Metronome*, George Simon recounted attending the dinner Peggy threw to celebrate their new digs: "Their enthusiastic Greek cook that night was Benny Goodman's bandboy, Popsie Randolph." *Click,* a sort of *Life* magazine knockoff, photographed the girls for a layout: doing each other's hair, trying on dresses, needlepointing, listening to records, even looking at apartments. The furs they were wearing were likely on loan. Beneath the headline "Double Up for the Duration," the authorless block of text began with these words: "The advantages of 'single blessedness' are apt to be overrated at any time. In wartime they disappear. Women especially need the warmth of family life to strengthen their minds and hearts against war's buffeting."

The words rang truer than the copywriter probably knew. In fact, both women in question were thinking about families. Peggy had introduced Jane to music critic Leonard Feather, with whom she would enter into a satisfying lifelong marriage. Peg, in the meantime, had met another pilot, this one with a more optimistic take on life, and she fell hard. Frank Ladd had flown with Claire Chennault's heroic Flying Tigers in China, and was now stationed in Washington, D.C. Peggy and Frank seemed to spend most of their time together in train terminals, parting: Pennsylvania Station, across the street from the New Yorker, and Union Station, down in D.C. This time, Peggy was more than willing to accept the man's wings, and they became engaged.

"We had the rings, license, and all," she remembered. "The band was playing a theater in Bridgeport [Connecticut], and I was to meet him in New York the next day. During our half hour off stage, Frank managed to get a call to me, to tell me he couldn't meet me—they were flying out on a secret mission. I was shocked, and, broken-hearted. I stood there staring straight ahead, and Joe Rushton, our bass saxophonist, couldn't help but notice my pale face. Without a word, he handed me a bottle of gin. I tried to tell him I didn't drink, but he poured me a glass and said, 'Here, this will stiffen you up—you have to go out there and sing.' So I drank it. I had no idea I was allergic to gin.

"Benny was playing 'Skylark' "—a new Johnny Mercer–Hoagy Carmichael lyric—"beautifully, and I came staggering out to the microphone. 'Skylark . . . have you anything . . .' and nothing more would come out. I stared at the audience. They stared at me. They laughed. I tried to back away from the microphone, barely able to move. I was thinking, 'How cruel. They don't know about Frank.' Benny, meanwhile, trying to figure out what was wrong with me, just stood with his clarinet at his side, with the reed pointing at me at about midthigh.

"During those days Benny had a stream of dignified gentlemen who would visit him with a briefcase of reeds. Most of them didn't suit him, so he would promptly flip them into the wastebasket. Well, I crashed into the one good reed it had taken him so long to find, and smashed it. He put the clarinet to his mouth to play, but thanks to the ruined reed, it came out in squawks and squeaks. I ran off the stage and hid in the dressing room, sure he would fire me, but he didn't. His reed was gone—and so was my flier. During the following months, I sent candy and cigarettes and socks and wrote letters, but received only one piece of a letter. It said, 'Darling, I'm going to take a chance and tell you more than I should—' the letter was cut off at that point by the censors. I never heard from him again."

Her account of her relationship with Frank Ladd, in a letter dated March 4, 1942, to her friend "Donna Mae" back in North Dakota, fills in some of the gaps—and provides a few intriguing insights into Peg's romantic situation, as well as her romantic habits. For despite her later memories, it seems that Peggy and Sev Olson, the married bandleader from Minneapolis, had not completely cut their ties.

"Here's a little surprise—I've definitely broken off with Sev and I've found a new baby," she wrote. "We are terribly in love, even more than Sev and I were—if that's possible. He is a Lt. in the air corps. Name Frank Ladd—22 (get that—me getting back in my own age class!) years old—French and Scotch Irish and terribly good-looking. He's such a wonderful fellow, too . . . Mmm-mmm. He's in Wash. D.C., so I don't see him much, but we love each other much, and he's the one and only person I've ever written daily letters to, so you know what I mean. Furthermore, I couldn't think of being untrue to him, which is unusual for me—remember?"

On to news of the band: "We're going to be here until March 12, and then we have two weeks off. So I need a rest! Seems like we've been here for years. We've played a lot of benefits and concerts besides our regular work. There are days when I'm sure someone shot me out of a cannon. Then, of course, always records and rehearsals ... probably back there people think that in New York you take baths in champagne, etc., but I'm serious when I say that New York and Podunk all look the same from a hotel room, and if you think I wouldn't love an onion sandwich—just ask me. . . .

"My throat is better now (knock on wood). I'm taking electric needle treatments because I was afraid of another operation. . . . Donna, honey, I'm going to take a short nap because I got about 4 hrs. last P.M., and I'm a beat chick. Smootches! Peg."

Did Frank Ladd fly literally, or figuratively? Why did he leave her? Because men always do, by one means or another? If so, then, how do you solve *that* problem? Maybe by making sure that it can't happen that way again: by making wrong choices in men right from the start.

EIGHT

Do Right

IN APRIL 1942, the band hit the road—and the road hit back. Even by the standards of the time, their wanderings were astounding and exhausting. Benny's fans were legion, and he was determined to satisfy them all. By one count, they slept under a total of seventy-three different roofs in the next four months. It wasn't unusual for Benny's outfit to ride the bus hundreds of miles overnight. A typical three-day jaunt might take them from a club in Jersey to Rocky Mount, North Carolina, and back to Pottstown, Pennsylvania, on the third leg for a show the very next night. They drove all night after each gig, checking in to hotels in the morning, checking out that same day. They lost laundry. They ate deathly food. "It was hard schooling," Peggy later recalled. "We rode in buses and trains and occasionally planes—oh, I would rather've walked. And for some reason, until I had my daughter, I was fearless. I think I must have been a little bit insane."

Under Benny's watch, nothing untoward was permitted between the girl and the band members. She was just one of the guys. She carried her own bags and relieved herself in the woods. And she stayed out of trouble; tenor sax man Vido Musso made sure of that. Musso was Peggy Lee's "unofficial bodyguard," according to Benny biographer Russ Connor. Connor discovered Musso's unofficial role as watchman firsthand when, at a one-nighter stop, band member Lou McGarity tried to hook Connor up with Peggy—and Musso vetoed the idea. If a member of the general public wanted an introduction to Peggy, he had to go through Vido—a large, jolly fellow with a gift for malapropisms (the doctor who "glanced" his boil) and a talent on his instrument that was not trained, but heartfelt. He could blow jazz, and that was good enough for Benny.

A glimpse of a reel from a handheld movie camera from the time says it all: Peggy Lee steps off at some rest stop on some back highway, to see the camera rolling. She coyly lets Musso buss her on the cheek. But the body English is obvious: She was his little sister. Their teasing was good-natured. But when it came to the kidding, she could give as good as she got.

The success of Benny's band meant that some of the time they could travel by train. The men had to double up in sleeping compartments, which allowed for a more relaxed routine in their frantic city-to-city caravan. Peggy enjoyed her privacy. And it was Mel Powell who told the story in Peggy's book of the night when Peggy's sense of humor revealed itself fully to her cohorts.

"We were in Pittsburgh—next stop St. Louis. It was about eleven o'clock, and we had the luxury of a little time, because we weren't due to leave until two. My roommate at the time was a fellow named George Berg. He'd been on the road a thousand years. He proposed we go to a special ribs place, pick up a couple of portions, go down to the train yard, and get aboard early.

"Now, George used to be a big fan of marijuana. He never drank—just marijuana, very pure—whereas for me, a couple of shots of Scotch would do the trick nicely. So I thought, 'Terrific. After a hard night's work, we'll go out there and get rested, nobody to bother us.' If the other guys wanted to get loaded, let them.

"After stumbling around in the dark we somehow located one of the two coaches with 'Benny Goodman' painted on the side. We found the little drawing room we were to share, got into pajamas, and took out the ribs. George began to smoke, and I had a couple of drinks. There was a knock on the door. We jumped a foot. Shaken, I went to the door, and there was Peg, terror-stricken, panicked, in tears. I was really unnerved.

" 'What's the matter, Peg?' She could hardly speak. 'I came out early, I wanted to be alone. I went to my room . . . and there's a dead body.' It was the dead of night, she was hysterical, we'd all seen too many movies; you've got to be a hero. . . . She put her hand in mine. She was trembling. We walked down the little corridor to her compartment. And I sort of peeked in, already beginning to get weak-kneed. I was not a dead-body man.

"I saw a head—covered in blood. So it was not just a question of a dead body. There'd been bad business here. I didn't see the body. 'It's in my closet, Mel, I didn't even notice the head,' she said. 'Are you kidding?' I said. 'Look, babes, I think what we've got to do is jog down to the station. . . .' 'Well, gee, I wish you would get it out of here for me.' Just then, a couple of the guys, obviously feeling the other side of marvelous, arrived: Freddy Goodman and Lou McGarity. 'What's the matter?' Freddy asked. 'There's a body in the closet!' Peggy yelled.

" 'Wait!' I began, but Freddy was already opening the door. I'm three inches from the cadaver and I don't want to look, so I turn my head away just as it begins to fall on me. I feel this tremendous dead weight, and I'm pushing against it in absolute revulsion. I try to back off, but it's too heavy, and I go down with it on top of me, and I'm about to have a coronary, when I hear laughter—from the cadaver. I look, and it's Sid Weiss, the bass player. He's wild, shaking, and catsup from his face is dripping on mine.

"Peggy had set it up, and Sid was picking me up from the floor, too stunned to think, yet wondering even then at the labyrinthine plans the woman had gone to. The image that clearly remains with me is a pair of slippers aligned perfectly outside the door— George Berg's slippers. My friend, in a marijuana haze, had obviously seen what he supposed was a headless thing drop out of Peg's closet—and jumped clean out of his slippers."

Peg would later explain her motives. "I planned this little ghoulish joke because the fellows used to tease me so. Sid Weiss was the right size to fit into the closet, so I just talked him into it. They didn't tease me after that."

If their wanderings weren't as horrifying as the crucibles that were the foxholes of Europe or Guadalcanal, half a planet away, the big-band odysseys were hardly unrelated to events abroad. Their war effort, as a platoon in the virtual army of bands crisscrossing the land to keep the national mood upbeat, was being played out on stages, in clubs, on highways, on all-night train jaunts. Audiences needed cheering up and the band helped bring them back to life, from town to town, college dance hall to suburban casino, show after show after show.

"It was like boot camp," Peggy said. "Tremendously tough to endure. But if you come through it, you'll be in shape for anything that comes along. Johnny Mercer said something once . . . it had to do with sudden fame being so dangerous. So many people have sudden fame, and they can't handle it. If you have to pay your dues, you have to do it. I was being paid $75 a week, and out of that I had to pay for my gowns, my hotels, and my meals. I washed my own hair. I handled my own wardrobe. Once I remember ironing my gown in an auditorium light booth. It was always catch-as-catch-can for hotel rooms, trying to find the cheapest, cleanest room available. . . . We were all earning very little money, and we were constantly on the road. I averaged two hours of sleep a night. Being a blonde with long hair, I spent hours washing my hair every night—and no hair dryers in those days."

It was Maxine Sullivan who once put it most succinctly: "I often wondered how Ella and the other singers could do the one-night-stand thing, year after year. I did it once with Benny Carter, and when I got back to New York, I kissed the ground."

Despite the hardships, Peggy was coming up in the world. By now, no one talked about Benny without mentioning his singer, too. "Peggy Lee, Benny Goodman's star," wrote *Look* magazine in November 1942, "is a battering ram in a velvet glove. You can hear her electric-blue voice from every juke box in America."

As the nation found itself fully engaged in World War II, the band was pressed into performing war-bond rallies around New York. And at a war-bond show in Brooklyn, Peggy began to get a sense of how passionate New York crowds could be. "Somebody Else" had risen to the top of the charts, and in the outlying borough she got her first taste of rock-star status: "The crowd sort of went wild when I sang it," she would recall. "After one show, my gown was ripped off. Dick Haymes [the male vocalist who'd replaced Art Lund] and I ran to escape." An anonymous pilot helped them to get away from the crowd and into the subway. She never saw that airman again, either.

The war would affect different bands in different ways, as evidenced by a new policy announced by the federal Office of Defense Transportation, which had outlawed bus use by colored bands. The ODT was now allocating all of five buses for the use of colored bands, "to be distributed among these crews according to need."

In late May 1942, Benny's band returned to New York for a gig at the Paramount Theater—to the relief of all. The big bands loved New York in the spring and summer; it meant the resumption of the softball games in Central Park. Harry James had once said he'd rather play softball than his trumpet, and a newspaper photograph from the summer of 1942 poses the teams of the Jimmy Dorsey Band and Woody Herman's. Jimmy wasn't present in the photograph. Perhaps he was nursing an injury; it was about this time that Jimmy and Tommy got into a fistfight on the roof of the Astor, arguing over whose band could outdraw whose.

All over the city, jazz was doing its best to keep morale high. In addition to the war-bond rallies, there were weekly jazz jams at the Stage Door Canteen on Forty-third Street, which provided a haven for servicemen: Actors, musicians, and entertainers of all stripes volunteered their time to entertain the kids about to sail on the troopships anchored across the East River at the Brooklyn Navy Yard.

At the Paramount, site of his landmark concerts in 1937, Benny's band wasn't catering to the cocktail crowd as it had at the New Yorker. The Paramount drew the bobby-soxers, and Benny didn't let them down, despite tumultuous turnover in personnel. By some accounts the Goodman engagement in June 1942 was one of his greatest ever. "Benny Absolutely Stupendous" was *Metronome*'s giddy headline, and the review didn't spare the compliments for either the bandleader or the girl singer. At the show in question, after Benny had them dancing in the aisles with the infectious Mel Powell arrangement of "Jersey Bounce," Peggy "hushed the house completely with an extremely warm version of

'Where or When.' She was singing from deep down inside, and the crowd not only sensed it, but appreciated it as well."

The real raves were saved for Goodman, though. His solo and trademark finale, "Sing, Sing, Sing," lasted a full ten minutes—during which time, "before it was half over, not a person in the house was moving. And nobody moved till Benny was completely through with his passage. Whether or not Benny realized it, this was one tremendous gesture. It proved that a Saturday evening audience has a surprisingly fine appreciation of what's really way ahead in jazz."

At one show, at least a couple of patrons had shown up to see Peggy alone: two proverbial tough guys from Brooklyn with hearts of gold. They brought her drapes made of paper, and a paper bedspread, to turn her tiny dressing room into a palace. They brought her liverwurst sandwiches from Walgreen's. They made the girl sitting out in the wings feel as if she were the center of the universe.

Peggy was grateful for the grub. She'd already experienced Goodman's penuriousness firsthand: One day Benny sent Popsie Randolph out for soft drinks, at fifteen cents a cup. Popsy came back with the goods; Peg drank half a glass, and handed the rest to Popsy. Benny made her pay eight cents.

The significance of Peggy's first Paramount engagement would transcend the experience of just conquering the shrine for swing. For starters, we can credit the paper-thin walls of the Paramount dressing rooms for her biggest breakthrough to date. Given the logistical difficulties of travel from town to town, Peggy traveled light, but she never forgot to pack her windup phonograph. Among her favorite 78s, along with her Debussy record, was a slatternly, sloe-eyed, minor-keyed loll called "Why Don't You Do Right?" sung by Lil Green, who, with the death of Bessie

Smith in 1937, had—in the opinion of some critics, anyway—
ascended to the top of the pure blues singer pack.

Originally written for the Harlem Hamfats in 1936 by guitarist Joe McCoy with the title "Weed Smoker's Dream," the
song was recorded by Green with legendary jazzman Big Bill
Broonzy. Green's version was slow and mournful, just a couple of
chords of stride piano, played with the doleful rhythm of a half
dozen pallbearers on their way to a hole in the ground. "Why
Don't You Do Right?" gave us low-down, dirt-road, Deep South
black blues, as emotionally and stylistically removed from the
Northern Plains as it was geographically removed. Dark, sinister,
and stoned, "Do Right" didn't sound like a pop song a prairie girl
would be packing in her kit bag. "You love that record, don't
you?" Benny said to Peggy one day. "I really do," she admitted.
"Let's play it with the band," said Benny.

And so they did. As arranged by Mel Powell, the new version
was faster than Lil Green's pot-fueled plaint, but even sped up,
hepped up, swung up, it had the undercurrent of an opium
dream. But the remarkable thing about Peggy Lee's version is the
blackness of it. This isn't a half-white, half-black rendition; it's all
black. From the opening lines, it could just as easily have been
Bessie or Billie doing the narration: a woman who's been mis-
treated, who fell for her man's "jiving," and took him in—all for
the meager reward of a "drink of gin." So, quite naturally, she demands that he "do right" and do for her what he's done for his
other gals: Go out and "get me some money, too."

"It wasn't an imitation," Peggy said years later. "I understood
that character. That was a woman who had a lot of bad times with
that man. And yet it has some humor in it, too." Not that Benny
or Columbia had any particular love for the song. They made no
plans to release it. Like all of Columbia's artists, Benny was
stockpiling records in anticipation of the impending ban on

recording. The controversial president of the American Federation of Musicians, James Petrillo, had decided to draw a hard line at the widespread use of recordings as fodder for jukeboxes and radio shows without royalties for the musicians. On August 1, 1942, the ban kicked in. For the time being, Columbia kept "Do Right" in the vault.

The band went on the road again after the Paramount, hitting such locales as Canobie Lake, New Hampshire, and Detroit, Michigan, where the engagement was distinguished by little except the arrival of another new musician. It was from the wings that Peggy first heard the sounds being played by the new guitarist. Tom Morgan had left in mid-Paramount, to be replaced by a personable, talented veteran named Dave Barbour.

She'd just sung "These Foolish Things," the tune that had always held so much luck for her. "I was walking over to the iron steps that went up to the dressing room. The notes the guitarist was playing circled around me as I placed one foot on the step, moved back down, turned around, and went back to the wings to listen. David Barbour—the man of my life. I fell in love with David the first time I heard him play."

At the age of thirty, Dave Barbour had already traveled a great many musical miles. A native of Queens, New York, he'd played the banjo on the stage of Carnegie Hall at age twelve. In high school in the late twenties, he was the first guy in his class to form his own band. He switched over to guitar and began to get professional gigs. In 1934, at twenty-two, he had already hooked up with Wingy Manone's combo at Adrian Rollini's club on West Fifty-second. Manone was the real thing, a product of the streets of New Orleans, where a streetcar accident took off his left arm when he was a ten-year-old. The accident, however, had done nothing to hinder his trumpet virtuosity. Playing riverboats, like Armstrong, he worked his way north, hooking up with Goodman in 1929, when the combo was known as "Benny Goodman's Boys."

Throughout the thirties, Barbour's splendid guitar work appeared on the recordings of some of the greats in the business: Armstrong, Bunny Berigan, Teddy Wilson. He toured with vibe wizard Red Norvo's band, strumming behind Mildred Bailey. But in 1937, after a stint with Norvo's band, the impact of the lifestyle of a roving bandsman with a taste for the bottle started to show. He had a breakdown. It was two years before he reappeared, and worked with everyone from staid Southern bandleader Hal Kemp to the stride-jazz musician Herman Chittison, the black pianist who gained fame playing with Ethel Waters.

By the time Goodman hired Barbour, he was well known in the business, but not so prominent as to merit any serious mention of the move in the trades. It's unlikely that anyone even introduced him to Peggy. There were so many roster changes going on that the sight of a new face would have been routine. But then Barbour wasn't just a routine face: He was handsome, dimpled, likable, accessible. Immediately, there was a flirtation: Barbour stuck his foot out in rehearsal and tripped Peggy to make sure she noticed him. Or so Peggy would tell it. Dave's account differed: "I was sitting there minding my own business when a clumsy blonde came trampling across the bandstand and walked all over my feet. She didn't even say excuse me."

She thought he looked intelligent, so she started reading serious stuff such as Thomas Wolfe just to impress him. And of course he could most definitely play, even if he seemed less than enthusiastic about making the world notice it. Some chalked his reticence up to his alcoholic personality. Others simply called him shy.

In August 1942, Mel Powell left to join the Army—or, more specifically, to join Glenn Miller's America Armed Forces band, a collection of all-stars over in Europe. Despite his youth, Mel was simply worn out. "Playing for ten straight hours was nothing in the Goodman days, [and] the endless repetition of material in the Goodman band—playing the same tunes day after day and night after night—got to me," he later recalled. "That repetition tended to kill spontaneity, which is the heart of jazz and which can give a lifetime's nourishment." Mel Powell's career had just begun. While he was playing with Miller overseas, he began to write string trios and brass quintet pieces. By the late fifties, he was teaching "Late Renaissance Polyphony" at Yale. His unconventional symphonic compositions won him a Pulitzer Prize. But his last Goodman contribution was an immortal one. His arrangement of "Why Don't You Do Right?" was released in the fall of 1942. Powell was nineteen.

"The big surprise," opined *Metronome*'s one-sentence capsule, "is Peggy Lee's vocal of this Lil Green tune—the lass really chews it right off."

The song made it to Number Four, which was a great deal more impressive than it sounds these days. It was not a time when a performer had to be Number One to be considered a success, while everything and everyone else was a loser. In 1942, to sell more records than every other song in the land but three was to be in an elite pantheon. And it had happened not on the strength of Benny's band, or Benny's clarinet. They had done it on Peggy's rhythms, her time, her attitude, and her voice. Some years later, as quoted in a biography, Billie Holiday remarked, "She stole every goddamned thing I sang"—as high a (backhanded) compliment as the priestess could possibly bestow. While Peggy would sing tributes to Billie throughout her life, in this case it wasn't inaccurate. But no one disagreed that the voice coming out of the radio sounded uncannily like Lady Day's, as, on occasion, it would throughout the rest of her career—

occasions that seemed both intentional and praiseworthy of Holiday. Indeed, Peggy would praise Holiday's singing several times throughout her life.

"Why Don't You Do Right?" seemed to take on a life of its own. In the fall, when the band went to California, *Down Beat* magazine wrote, "Peggy and Benny were amazed to hear that more than 200,000 copies of the record were on order in Southern California alone." But it wasn't until the troupe returned to Hollywood in December to film *Stage Door Canteen,* a musical inspired by the servicemen's club, that "Do Right" announced itself to the world at large.

It was quite a show to steal, given that the cast included Katharine Hepburn, Merle Oberon, Katharine Cornell, Helen Hayes, Judith Anderson, Tallulah Bankhead, Lynn Fontanne, Paul Muni, Ed Wynn, Ray Bolger, George Jessel, and Johnny Weissmuller. Actually, they all had only cameos. *Stage Door Canteen* was a singularly charming ensemble show from United Artists, one of a bunch of morale-boosting Let's-Put-On-a-Show-to-Support-Our-Boys flicks. For those who liked their patriotism big and brassy, this was the ticket. The setting was the actual canteen, where the name performers, supported by legions of aspiring, wholesomely beautiful homegrown actresses who served as platonic dance-hall partners, gave the soldiers and sailors their send-offs. The corny but irresistible subplot featured a trio of GIs—"Dakota," "California," and "Texas"—who lost their hearts to the canteen hostesses. Hepburn herself, delivering the final soliloquy of the film to the girl whose sweetheart has just sailed, uttered the lines penned by the scriptwriter, Delmer Daves, with the earnestness of a grand dame doing Chekhov:

"He's fighting for the kind of world in which you and he can live together in happiness. In peace. In love. Don't ever stop—for a minute!—*working. Fighting. Praying.* Until we've got that kind of world for you, for him, for your children—for the whole human race. Days without end. Amen."

The shallow plot, of course, hardly bothered the audience; the nonstop parade of entertainers who graced the basement club's stage were this film's considerable attraction: Ethel Merman belting, Yehudi Menuhin playing classical violin, Gypsy Rose Lee doing a subtle, wholesome routine, removing nothing but her gloves and stockings yet making the routine every bit as sensual as if she'd stripped herself bare.

The roster of bands was as impressive as the cast of actors. Unfortunately, all but one performed instantly forgettable patriotic numbers written for the film by the songwriting team of Al Dubin and James Monaco. Basie's band accompanied Ethel Waters singing something excruciatingly faux-soulful called "Quick Sands," with the Count, cool as can be, caressing the keys. Kay Kyser's band, its leader vaudevilleanly frantic, and Guy Lombardo's—the leader stiff as a frozen lamppost—offered light military-themed ditties. Kyser's number was a hoot—"The gals prefer a private who can jive it!"—and Lombardo's was treacly: "Sleep, baby, sleep, in your jeep; far away across the deep blue sea may you dream of me."

Xavier Cugat's guys weighed in with "Bombshell from Brooklyn." Freddy Martin's band, with Martin's alto sax soothingly crooning, offered the soporific "Don't Worry Island," a place where "we can lease a piece of paradise."

Whether director Frank Borzage had the good sense to let at least one of the film's featured bands do its own thing, or whether Benny simply refused to perform a written-for-the-flick patriotism-theme-park ditty, audiences who'd waited through the whole movie received a payoff near the end, when emcee Allen Jenkins, who normally played comic gangsters, stepped to the microphone and announced: "And now, here's something for the *cats.* I'm gonna bring you a cranky brawl by a sharpie who plays a licorice stick that's out of this world. The guy who knocked them off their seats and rolled them into a groove . . . Benny Goodman."

Benny wailed a minor-keyed intro, and then out came Peggy, hair piled in a twist adorned by a single dark flower—the reverse image of Billie's white gardenia. Nervous at first, smiling stiffly, a twenty-three-year-old in front of hundreds of extras, her whole demeanor melted into nothing but High Cool as soon as she launched into the opening lines of "Why Don't You Do Right?" Despite the tangible impression of a schoolgirl all dolled up, she came across as flirtatious, and sexy as hell—and the camera loved her. Even Benny seemed swept away: His solo was stretchy and loose, featuring a high C that he held for several extra measures. When he handed the song back to Peggy, as she sang the second verse, even more low-down this time, he had a half smile as he gazed at her—and maybe, this time, even saw her.

Only serious music freaks would have stopped at this point and considered the significance of *this* band featuring *this* girl singing *this* song, but consider it now: Here was the giant, one of the best jazz musicians in the country, and he could have chosen from a hundred songs. From a thousand. And what's the one song they did? The song Peggy brought to Benny's table. Even oblivious, eccentric Benny knew he had something special here. It was in her smile, and his.

The band returned to the Paramount in New York after Christmas, where on December 30, 1942, another young singer made something of an entrance himself. He'd left Tommy Dorsey's band needing more work and polish. Someone had talked the Paramount's manager, Bob Weitman, into catching the kid's act in Newark. Weitman had booked him as an added attraction, and his name made it onto the bottom of the huge Paramount marquee.

And so it was that during one of the shows on the night of December 30, Benny Goodman paused and announced, in a thoroughly bored and monotonous voice, "And now, Frank Sinatra"—whereupon a skinny, hollow-cheeked kid parted the curtains and the audience immediately erupted into a shriek of such nails-across-the-blackboard pitch that Goodman was heard to say, "What the fuck is that?"

A couple of girls fainted in the aisles.

Frank wasn't the only singer to cause hysteria at the Paramount gig. One male fan leaped onto the stage to pursue Peggy Lee.

In March 1943, Peggy was nearing the end of her twentieth month with Goodman. Professionally, there was little left for her to attain. Personally, her buddies had long departed. And romantically, she had found her man.

By one account, Benny fired Dave Barbour in Los Angeles: He'd dated the singer, broken the rule. According to another account, Barbour had just quit. By both accounts, it was a rainy day in Los Angeles when Dave asked Peggy to have coffee and told her he was leaving the band. When Benny pulled out of town, he wouldn't be on the bus. She was devastated, but she didn't let on. They were standing outside the coffee shop, in the rain, and he was stroking her cheek. "Come on, Normer," he said. "Let's get married." The world-weary guitarist had fallen in love with the girl, not the star.

With bass sax man Joe Rushton as witness, Peggy became Mrs. Dave Barbour on March 8, 1943. Twelve days later, live from the Hollywood Palladium, Benny's band played "Slender, Tender and Tall," with Peggy Lee on vocals. It was the last song she would ever sing with the band. After the performance she bade goodbye to Benny Goodman. While he would score some big hits in 1945 for Columbia, and tour successfully through the fifties—notably in Europe—he would never again enjoy the same measure of success.

PART II

The Lady in the Limelight

Our Little Dream Castle

THE MARRIAGE WAS big news, both in the trades and back in Fargo: "Peggy Lee, the sultry-voiced warbler who has done much to put the Goodman band into the top popularity bracket," announced *Down Beat*, "disappeared from the bandstand at the Palladium a couple of nights recently, and when she returned it was revealed that wedding bells had chimed discreetly for Peggy and Dave Barbour, BG's former guitarist. 'It wasn't a secret wedding,' said Peggy. 'We just didn't want to publicize it. There's nothing to say except that we are very happy.'"

The Fargo *Forum* also chimed in, quoting from the trade magazine. "Although neither Peggy nor Goodman made any statements regarding her expected departure from the band, *Down*

Beat says it's pretty well established that she plans to remain in Hollywood with her husband."

Los Angeles was a natural starting place. Peggy had developed a taste for the city in her earlier forays to the coast, and now she had family here. Her sister Marianne lived in Van Nuys, her sister Della in Hollywood. But of course the real impetus for settling in California was Dave Barbour. Not only did he have friends in the music world, he had a taste for things bohemian, and in 1943, living in Los Angeles still signified an attractive alternative to a buttoned-up world.

Barbour loved the beach. It was the hip place to be, and Dave, a beachcomber at heart, was cool before anyone even know what cool was. He wore chinos rolled up at the cuff and white dress shirts with the sleeves rolled up. A very quiet, introspective man with a fabulous sense of humor, he was ready to put the cold winters of his New York birthplace behind.

And so in the spring of 1943, Dave and Peggy settled into a $35-a-month downtown apartment at 4239½ Monroe Street, near Los Angeles City College. While Peggy set about the business of establishing her first home, Dave went about getting a union card, playing every gig he could get, including a down-at-the-heels club with the evocative name of the "Waldorf Cellar"—on skid row. They entertained their fellow musicians on Peggy's culinary specialty—curry.

In homemaking matters, Peggy's expertise was questionable; among other problems, her stove regularly caught fire. But she was genuinely drawn to the domestic life. "Why Don't You Do Right?" had by now achieved the status of a bona fide hit, but when the telephone on the lacquered Chinese table rang and there were offers to sing, she would turn them down. When she discovered she was pregnant, she was overjoyed.

Her later recountings of Dave's reaction—"Why, Peg," Dave said, when she gave him the news, "I hardly know you"—suggest alternate interpretations. His words were likely an example of Dave's offbeat sense of humor. They had set up shop very quickly; they'd known each other for less than a year. When he said, "Peg, I hardly know you," it was funny, but it was also true.

In her Broadway show four decades later, Peggy added veiled subtexts to Dave's reaction to her pregnancy. In a monologue, she would tell the audience, "I always thought I would treasure whatever he said, and I do. But I expected something else." Perhaps in hindsight, she saw something that wasn't there at the time; by all other accounts, they were both delighted with the situation.

In November 1943, after nine months of marriage, Peggy gave birth to Nicki, by caesarean section. By Peggy's own account, it had not been an easy term; examinations disclosed the presence of two uterine tumors. And when the delivery date came, the labor was complicated: Peggy's blood pressure had soared dangerously high and she was on the verge of pneumonia. But the child was healthy. And her new daughter brought her pure joy. This was the verse she wrote on the headboard of Nicki Barbour's crib: "Blessed is the forest in which grew the tree from which came the wood that made the crib in which you lie." Despite their cash-strapped situation, the young couple sent out engraved birth announcements.

Behind the scenes, the pull between the hearth and the stage was taking its toll on Peggy. But she was settled, with a husband—who, at least at the very beginning of the marriage, had cut back on the drinking, possibly at his wife's behest—and a child, a garden, and a place to rest after a decade of running. She was genuinely happy.

"All I wanted to do was be a housewife and a mother," she would recall. "All I wanted was to have a family and cling to the children."

After the complications of the birth, she was told, she could have no more children. Whether this sobering news opened her up to the idea of getting her career back on track is something she never discussed. She later mentioned that she and Dave thought of adopting, but they never did.

It was more than "Do Right," of course, that had raised Peggy's profile to a national level; it was also two years of singing with the best-known musician in America. Those who hadn't seen her sing live knew her from *Stage Door Canteen* or another Goodman band appearance soon after, in a movie called *The Powers Girl*. After the settlement of the thirteen-month-long musicians' strike, Peggy found herself the musical equivalent of a prized free agent in modern-day sports. "It was strange to see Peggy changing the baby with one hand," her sister Marianne told *Redbook* some years later, "and refusing fabulous offers over a telephone held in the other."

There were plenty of girl singers, but "Do Right" had set Lee apart from the pack. There was no questioning the singer's affinity for jazz inflections, for interpreting songs with a soulful strain, and that immediately drew the interest of the newly promoted jazz producer at fledgling Capitol Records—Dave Dexter, the former sportswriter who, as a newspaper music critic back in Kansas City, had urged the world to discover Bill Basie.

The Capitol label had been Johnny Mercer's brainchild. In the early forties, there were only three major record labels—Decca, Columbia, and RCA—and they were all based in New York. Mercer, according to biographer Gene Lees, figured that there was a surplus of talent in Los Angeles, and with his partners (Paramount executive Buddy DeSylva, who brought financial expertise, and Glenn Wallichs, a technical master) he founded Capitol in 1942 and hired Dexter to write *The Capitol News,* a magazine designed to promote the label's new artists.

The label's early stable was impressive. On board were Mar-

garet Whiting and Nat King Cole, whom Mercer had heard at
the 313 Club in downtown Los Angeles, and Jo Stafford, whom
Mercer had come upon singing in the Famous Door back on
Fifty-second Street. (Stafford, stunned to see the famous singer-
songwriter in the audience, had asked for an autograph; Mercer
sketched a caricature of himself.) Martha Tilton was on board at
Capitol, too. Even Billie Holiday had done a recording for the
new company, but since she was under contract to another label,
she used a pseudonym: Lady Day.

By 1943, Capitol had promoted Dexter to "jazz producer,"
and he wanted to release a set of jazz 78s. The newborn company
was a natural destination for Peggy Lee, with whom Dexter was,
of course, familiar, having ripped her singing to shreds in print after her Meadowbrook Ballroom debut just two years before. He
would later admit that he'd been as wrong as a critic could be
about her performance that night in the fall of 1941. He was
clearly out to make amends.

But before contacting Lee, Dexter approached Dave Barbour
to do some jazz recording for the nascent label—a logical enough
move. Barbour's bona fides had been established even before he
hooked up with Benny. Barbour was a guitarist of no small talent; his rhythm was superb, his jazz sense authentic. He was also
a fine accompanist, and his single-string leads had a voice of
their own.

Barbour had never been at home in a big band. In Los Angeles,
he was hanging out with his drinking and jazz-loving pal, trumpeter and arranger Billy May, playing private parties, including a
few at the Pasadena Biltmore and the Roosevelt hotel. (May had
played with and scored for Charlie Barnet's adventurous band before hooking up with the Glenn Miller Orchestra; now he was
freelancing on the West Coast.)

Dexter had heard that Barbour was having trouble finding
work, and asked him to get a combo together for the new label.

They would not lack for talent: Dave would team with Jack Teagarden, one of the jazz trombone kings.

At the same time, Dex asked Peggy if she'd be interested in doing a couple of songs for a new Capitol album to be called *New American Jazz*.

"Barbour was delighted," Dexter later recalled. "His wife was hesitant." Barbour encouraged her; he thought she had too much talent not to use it. He told her she'd regret it later if she didn't pursue what she had always dreamed of. But what she'd always dreamed about was the family she had finally created. The dueling tugs of hearth and art, she admitted later, could reduce her to tears in the early years of her marriage. "I cried—I was the opposite of women wanting to get out of the house," she said.

A letter Peggy sent to her friend Modie da Costa soon after Nicki's birth provides a clue to Peggy's state of mind at the time. Peggy was fond of doing little sketches on her correspondence— the back side of the letter to da Costa featured a drawing of a little man with a square head saying, "Well just don't stand there staring—open de letter!" Inside, she'd drawn a sketch of herself and Dave. The drawing of her husband shows him playing a guitar and frowning. Peggy depicts herself with a smiling baby on her lap, and holding a bottle, but she's not smiling. She appears to be in the middle of a breakdown. Her hair is in disarray, and there are circles under each eye. But her sense of humor is intact. On the sketch is this note: "Nicki was crazy about the sweater. She ate every bit of it."

Despite her protestations, Peggy clearly couldn't quiet her muse: Even during pregnancy she had been writing down ideas for songs. "Finally," Dave Dexter recalled, "after I called Peggy a second time, she asked, 'What will it pay?'"

"I can get you a hundred dollars for singing two songs, and it will only take an hour," Dexter answered. Reluctantly, she went down to the MacGregor studio, where Capitol was doing its recording, and cut a couple of sides with the Capitol Jazzmen, a combo of big-band vets with whom Barbour had worked. Dave didn't play on Peggy's numbers, but Dexter used him with May on a couple of other cuts on the *New American Jazz* collection.

True to his word, Dexter had Peggy out of the studio within an hour. "Ain't Goin' No Place," a bluesy jaunt written by one Al Larkin, was lighter in tone than "Why Don't You Do Right?" but Peggy brought more than a little black-bluesy feeling to it. Her effort proved that she didn't need Goodman or heavyweights such as Mel Powell and Sid Catlett behind her. This time she flew solo with a song that strayed off the happy, sentimental American Songbook path.

The other song, "That Old Feeling," was an old standard about a woman who couldn't get rid of her feelings for a former flame. According to Dexter, L.A. deejays—Don Otis, Al Jarvis, and the rest—gave the two Capitol songs plenty of air time, and Barbour and Lee signed a long-term deal with Capitol. Dex Dexter had more than made up for nearly derailing her career back in Jersey.

It wasn't routine for singers to write their own songs; Johnny Mercer, more songwriter than singer, was one notable exception. For women, however, songwriting was virtually unheard of. To Peggy, it came naturally. With the baby on her lap, or doing housework, she started working on lyrics while Dave spun melodies. One tune came to her literally as she was doing the dishes. This time there was no stepmother standing by as she was elbow-deep in suds, but the chore still clearly evoked ambiguous sentiments. Lee's lyrics for "What More Can a Woman Do?" are full of subtext, hinting at a marriage that wasn't all it appeared to be and a woman whose notions of romance owed much to celluloid fantasies.

If he told me I should steal, I guess I would, the way I
  feel . . .
If he told me I should lie, I guess at least I'd have to try . . .
'Cause it's for him I'd live or die . . .
What more can a woman do?

Anyone looking for a subtext could find more than a glimpse of Peggy's real life.

And perhaps her first inklings of her husband's complexities. By now, Dave's manager was the legendary Carlos Gastel, whose reputation was as large as his stature; his clients included Stan Kenton, Woody Herman, Mel Tormé, and Nat Cole. His tastes leaned toward the good-time high life: "Carlos was a tremendous drinker," says Jack Costanzo, the famed bongo player, who would hook up with Peg in a couple of years. "When he was out, it was never without a glass in his hand. He was a gem."

"Carlos loved his gin," says George Schlatter, the manager of Ciro's, the hottest club of the era (he would also eventually produce the television classic *Laugh-In*). "If you hadn't talked to him in a while, he would say, 'Pal of my cradle days, why have you forsaken me?' So Carlos would say come by and I'd put a bottle of gin and a bottle of vodka on the bar, and by three P.M. the next day I'd have a contract for Cole to come to Ciro's."

But perhaps the best Carlos Gastel drinking anecdote came from trumpeter and arranger Billy May. "He smoked and drank all day long," May told music writer Will Friedwald, for *Sinatra! The Song Is You*, Friedwald's definitive study of Frank Sinatra. "If he wasn't smoking, he was drinking. If he wasn't drinking, he was smoking. When someone suggested he cut back on his excesses, he said, 'I have to take a drink just to think about that.'"

Gastel took two of Lee and Barbour's songs to Mercer at Capitol: "What More Can a Woman Do?" and something called "You Was Right, Baby." Mercer liked them. They recorded on December 27, 1944, with Dave on guitar and Billy May on trumpet. Like its companion number, "You Was Right" was anything but up-beat, and its voice was no housewife's; Lee adopted a a black ver-nacular and a tonal languor heavy with world-weariness. Peggy was portraying a woman whose man had tired of her wandering ways and left her, making good on his promise that one day he would "turn the tide":

> *You said some day you'd turn the tide*
> *and I'd be laughing on the other side . . .*
> *You was right, baby*
> *baby, you was so right . . .*

Neither of the two songs had the slightest echo of a canary's big-band chirping. Neither was obviously commercial or the sort of fare heard on the big radio shows then hosted by Bing Crosby and Jimmy Durante. Both were entertaining, but hardly uplifting or optimistic. Still, "You Was Right, Baby" was a hit, confirming Peggy's facility for translating jazz and blues for the masses. It sold three-quarters of a million records.

There was no going back. Peggy Lee the singer was now even more in demand, despite what Peggy Lee the mother might have wanted.

The downside of Gastel's involvement in the Barbours' new suc-cess was his love of liquor. Though he didn't exactly introduce Dave to the bottle, he was an obvious enabler, "a bad influence," as Peggy would write. Nonetheless, it was in her nature to trust Gastel. A few years later, she would confide that she and Dave had never signed a contract with Dave's manager. "We don't want one," she said, "and we don't need one."

"I was an idealist, and my ideal in those days was that being a wife and mother was a full-time career," she would later tell *Sci-*

ence of Mind magazine. "Only there was a lot of pressure—from MGM studios, from Capitol Records, from Dave, who felt I had too much talent not to use. . . . But I was very confused, very unhappy right then. When Nicki cried I would hold her and rock her, and I think I cried more than she did."

David's favorite drink was a boilermaker. "He even fed the goldfish bourbon," Lee would later recall in her book—an anecdote to which she added a postscript that spoke worlds of the coming changes in her life: Her early days with Dave, she wrote—with her infant daughter, their "beautiful, healthy" baby, who was "very early show[ing] signs of high intelligence" (she began to laugh early)—were among the happiest she'd ever known.

But there were strains, and adding to them was the unexpected arrival on the West Coast of Dave's mother—not for a visit, but for good. The relationship between the two women was not a good one. Peggy and her sisters found Mrs. Barbour an apartment nearby, but the mother-in-law was dissatisfied with the way Peggy had furnished it. She also charged the couple to babysit Nicki. She clearly got on Peggy's nerves, and apparently on Dave's. Peggy later wrote that it was after her arrival that Dave's drinking first began to get out of hand.

Peggy's health had become an issue, too. When Benny Goodman persuaded Peggy and Dave to join the band for an engagement at the San Francisco Theater, Mel Powell recalled, she took the stage one night with a spiking fever—and fainted. "As she was going out," Powell recalled, "she said, 'Oh, shit—I've killed myself,' as she gracefully fell to the floor."

This was the first reported instance of Peggy Lee's fainting on stage. It would not be the last. In the years to come, Peggy's fainting—in rehearsals, on stage, while entertaining at home—would become almost as legendary as her desire to stay in bed. Various causes for her blackouts are bandied about to this day.

Some mention the stress created by her intense desire to please her audience. Others bring up the innate shyness Lee had been trying—through song, Dale Carnegie courses, or drink—to overcome since childhood. The most plausible explanation for Peggy's frailty was the emotional exhaustion of performing. Her perfectionism, her repeated refusal to slack off on a single note for a single song, drained her completely. Even early on, she made stringent demands on herself. She was driven, uncompromising, often exhausted.

A neighbor in her apartment building offered Peg a welcome refuge—and forever changed Peggy's life. Raised in the bosom of the Lutheran Midwest, Peggy had never been overtly religious, but in retrospect it's obvious that the void within the confused young woman was crying out for a spiritual fix. Estelle Frombach was an attractive, cultured woman. When she left a note on Peggy's door ("I never see you go anywhere . . . I'd be happy to babysit with your child while you and your husband go to a movie"), Peggy took her up on it, and the two became friends. It was Estelle who suggested that Peggy acquaint herself with the life lessons of a man named Ernest Holmes, whose lectures at the Institute of Religious Science had begun to attract a following. Seeking spiritual enlightenment to temper the increasingly chaotic world, Ernest Holmes's legion of left-coast listeners was growing.

For two decades, California had been the center of a nationwide growth of fringe quasi-religions whose beliefs would today be characterized as "New Age." Their prevalence at the time spawned a sort of anticult mania in the mainstream media, fueled by the worries of conventional religious leaders that the American flock was wandering too far afield.

It would stand to reason that Los Angeles, a city founded on the notion of selling the art of illusion, would host more than its share of seekers of spiritual grounding.

One evening, Estelle took care of Nicki, and Peggy ventured downtown. She was the first to arrive at the hall Holmes used for his lectures. After randomly choosing a seat, she noticed a brass plaque on the back of the chair in front of her. It had been donated by Estelle Frombach. The coincidence, Peggy would later write, seemed like a sign. It would point her toward a man who would be a confidant and friend for several decades, until Holmes's death.

The youngest of nine children raised in the late nineteenth century on a farm in Maine, Ernest Holmes had found his way down the coast at an early age and taken a job in a Boston grocery store. From there, his immersion in the writings of Ralph Waldo Emerson and Christian Science founder Mary Baker Eddy set him on a spiritual quest that eventually led to Venice, California, in 1914, at the age of twenty-seven.

Holmes grew up to be a handsome man with an easy smile who was clearly comfortable in his own skin. But his charisma wasn't the stuff of tent-revival snake handlers. He was no charlatan. He was sincere, and his ego was not a driving force of his mission. His Divine Science church, which he'd founded in 1927 in a building on Wilshire Boulevard, was a nonsectarian institution whose teachings, distilled to their essence, preached positivity. All past trials, errors, and mistakes, he told his listeners, could be turned into the goodness of "now." Holmes held to no single deity's or mortal's strict beliefs: The teachings of Jesus, Buddha, Socrates, and all "Way-showers" were given equal weight in the Holmes doctrine. Essential to his teachings was Emerson's notion that the infinite divinity of creation is embodied in every aspect of our lives, that we are simple instruments of God's creation—a notion best illustrated by Emerson's notion of himself as nothing but a "transparent eyeball," a witness to all of creation. Years later, Peggy Lee grew fond of quoting a specific

Emersonian axiom: "God will not have His work made manifest by cowards." There is no question that Holmes was her first window not only into the Transcendentalists, but into seeking alternate ways of seeing the world. She would hereafter, and for the rest of her life, not only profess to being on a quest for knowledge, but walk the walk as well. She would hereafter and always be drawn to those whose minds might offer metaphoric windows into deeper meaning.

"This is what I've been looking for," Peggy thought that first night, and she would remain close to Holmes, his wife, Hazel, and the church's teachings for the rest of her life. Ultimately, she would preside at Holmes's memorial service. "Peggy," Holmes would say of his newest disciple, "radiates creativity in all departments. She has made contact with the Thing itself, and she accepts the way it works with complete trust."

Spirituality was not the only new avenue that Peggy Lee had started to explore. She had begun to branch out in other ways, too. Dave, himself an amateur artist, had begun teaching Peg to paint. Sculpting came naturally to her, too; she had a particular talent for busts. Years later, one of her paintings—according to her own account—fetched some $35,000.

The music world that Peggy was returning to was beginning to change. It was no longer one big happy pop-jazz family. The fissure suggested by the war between "swing" and "sweet" was widening. By 1945, as many postwar music lovers settled back to enjoy the sentimental ballads that increasingly ruled the charts, jazz started heading in a new direction—away from strictly danceable stuff to more adventurous fare. The new genre was called "bop," and the new practitioners—notably Dizzy Gillespie and Charlie Parker—were determined, in the former's words, to make music that was "fast and furious—with the chord changes going this way and that." Progressive jazz was now becoming the province of black musicians who, instead of sitting back and letting the likes of Goodman and Shaw dictate what swung, were determined to seize the new national day for their own.

In Los Angeles, the jazz scene down on Central Avenue was still a hotbed animated by the New Orleans influence of the black migrants of the twenties. But mainstream L.A. audiences—even cool ones—weren't ready for the harder stuff. In 1945, a man named Billy Berg set up shop smack in Hollywood, announcing "a California version of Manhattan's Café Society, offering jazz and welcoming black as well as white patrons," according to author Geoffrey Ward. But Berg's first big progressive engagement, in January 1946, with Gillespie's trumpet and Parker's alto sax splitting the night with stuff many patrons had never before heard, was not a success. Some members of the crowd left "dumbfounded," in Gillespie's words. Los Angeles wasn't ready for bop.

Most folks weren't ready to dispense with swing, with sentimental thoughts underlaid by hints of blues, by simple melodies that rode a rhythm of jazz.

That Peggy brought more power to her laments, that she had the blues lurking just beneath her surface, was by now obvious. In 1945, when perennial top jazz songstress Sarah Vaughan recorded Lee's "What More Can a Woman Do?" it was high praise; Vaughan would later speak of her fondness for Lee's blues work. And in the winter of 1945, Lee used her knack for mining the blues vein in a tune called "Waitin' for the Train to Come In," written by a well-known disc jockey named Martin Block and his partner, lyricist Sunny Skylar. From its opening measures to its final plaintive notes, "Train" seemed to speak the emotions of millions of wartime lovers. It told the story of a woman in limbo, alone, emotionally lost, waiting for her guy to come home from the war.

Opening with some lonesome reeds echoing an off-key late-night train whistle, the arrangement had a swing tempo evocative of the sway and rustle of the rails. The tempo changes signaled a singular hipness to the arrangement, which featured Barbour's riffling single-string notes backgrounding her lyrics like the plashing of waterfalls.

But the power behind this train was not the arrangement. It was Peggy's voice, with its new curvature and way of rounding the notes, bending and tweaking them. Her enunciation was, as always, precise, but she was becoming confident enough to play with her phrasing and with the beat. She had begun to allow the final syllables of a line just to dive off and disappear, but not affectedly. Hers seemed the natural phrasing of one resigned to fate. She was, in short, more haunting than ever.

"Train" is one of the first and best examples of Peggy's unusual propensity for acting the voice of each of the songs she sang. She was clearly not content to sing the lyrics of every song as just Peggy Lee. She had a way of becoming a different person every time out, of finding a singular mood and tone of voice for every number. In "Train," the woman waiting for her man was a Peggy Lee that listeners had never heard before.

"Train" was a perfect melding of song, stylist, and storytelling; it's not hard to believe that its success owed to the melancholy chord it struck in all of the wartime women whose husbands had not come home. It rose to Number Four.

Peggy's songwriting had by now become more than a hobby. It had become something that she and David could do together, common ground for a young couple struggling to stay on an even keel. Her original compositions with Dave are among the best work of her life: tunes that came, thematically, from so many elements of her own inner life. Six months after "Train," the Barbours composed the first song that would be included in her permanent canon, a song that would be covered and quoted for the next half century. It was another tone poem that seemed to draw on her own emotions and conflicts, but its upbeat rhythm was downright infectious, and Lee's refrain was nifty, with Porteresque echoes: "I know a little bit about a lot of things, but I don't know enough about you. I know a little bit about biology, and a little more about psychology. I'm a little gem in geology, but I don't know enough about you."

Recorded in December 1945, "I Don't Know Enough About You" was a pleasant, lightweight, swingy ditty. According to the credits, Barbour wrote the melody, but many years later Peg would confess that it was actually her own. At the time, though, it was the lyrics she was concentrating on, and she was proud enough of these to show them to the master: Johnny Mercer himself. He was encouraging, but suggested rewrites. That Peggy would later write of her admiration of Mercer during this time says much about her own character, for he wasn't exactly a puppy dog. "He was not fucking charming," George Schlatter says. "He was a tough sonofabitch."

"I loved his work," Peggy would later recall. "And he helped me. He said, 'You have a really good idea there, but I think you should rewrite this, and that.' I tore it up and rewrote it, and it made all the difference." Having been run through Mercer's brain, her song took on a new dimension.

She sang the song with Dave's band on a short film released by Universal Pictures called *Banquet of Melody,* between other numbers by the Delta Rhythm Boys and Matty Malneck and His Orchestra. It can hardly be disputed that the appeal of the song— it sold more than half a million records and spent seventeen weeks in the Hit Parade's Top Ten—lay in its languid, casual, major-keyed tone. Treading on the blues, but smiling with them, the song is irrefutably hip. "The definition of cool, and therefore the influence over what will enter the culture, generally comes from the fringes," a cultural critic would opine several years later, and

in this case, the thought was apt. If Peggy was physically searching for a spot at the mainstream hearth, psychologically she was
revealing a songwriting persona that seemed dissatisfied, in one
way or another, with the status quo. Of course, there was also, almost certainly, an autobiographical impulse at work in the song:
Lee obviously felt she didn't know enough about Barbour, a man
to whom she'd been attracted in part because of his mystery, his
quiet, and, of course, his flaws.

For, of course, alcoholics are much more exciting than
"normies," to use the modern addict's vernacular: Their personalities are more exciting. They are generally unavailable—at least,
their true nature is—which adds a dimension to their allure. The
more complex and alcoholic a man, the more he intrigues. It
seems more than likely that Peggy's belief that she could turn
Dave's life around was part of her attraction to him.

There's no question, though, that he was the real love of her
life—and that his musical chops had something to do with this.
He didn't want fame. He was a loner. He was a recluse. Some
people are simply happier being by themselves. And if no one
every fully got into Dave Barbour's heart, it would probably have
frustrated Peggy from the start, for when Peggy loved, she loved
absolutely.

In public, Peggy seemed to be a possessive wife, pulling Dave
out of parties to go home. In reality, she was learning his tipping
point when he'd had too much to drink. When she later wrote,
"There was some playful pushing when he was drinking, but
mostly he had a lovely, quiet disposition," we get the picture of a
man who kept most of his thoughts and feelings to himself, until
a drink turned a darker side loose. Later, in a magazine profile
discussing the forties, Lee spoke of how she and her husband
would fight when he'd been drinking. She implied that she might
have been pushed around by Barbour. Others confirm that there
may have been a single incident, but friends insist that Barbour

was the least violent man in the world, and the consummate gentleman. Perhaps, suggests one, she egged him on.

A young pianist named André Previn was barely sixteen but already a precocious keyboard talent when he got a call from Dave Barbour. "Are you working New Year's Eve? Do you want to play a gig with me?" Previn was excited, even if the gig was in some hall in the wilds of downtown Los Angeles. Even if, for reasons unknown to the boy, Barbour instructed him not to show up until eleven. When Previn arrived at the appointed hour, pianist Milt Raskin was sitting at the keyboard with Barbour's band. Previn was obviously surprised and not at all happy to see him there. But Barbour reassured him: "No, man, don't worry. Milt is almost drunk enough to fall off the bench. When he falls over, gently move him off the bench and shove him under the piano, and keep playing." And when Milt very sweetly fell off the bench, Previn played on.

Previn thought Barbour a good guitarist and an even better accompanist. He certainly considered him good enough to collaborate with. They would go on to record together occasionally, most notably on the single "Good Enough to Keep," with "Blue Skies" on the B side.

Barbour's talent wasn't the only thing he was known for musically; like Peggy, he was a perfectionist, and he had a forceful personality when it came to what he wanted artistically. "With Dave, the music had to be right," says bongo player Jack Costanzo, the most famous hand drummer of the era, who would later work extensively with Peggy Lee in the fifties. "I don't care how many times you do it, the end product has to be the best you are capable of doing. Dave was like that."

On Air

Selling records was only half of the equation for a popular singer in Peggy Lee's early days. In postwar America, it was radio that dictated the success of records. No artist could be declared major until she or he appeared on a network radio show. And no one had a network radio show to rival the *Kraft Music Hall*. On May 12, 1946, Peggy Lee took to the NBC airwaves and sang "I Don't Know Enough About You," not only for an immense audience—a few years earlier, the Kraft show had boasted a staggering fifty million listeners—but for the show's host, the most beloved performer in the history of American popular culture.

When Peggy stepped in front of the microphone that night, it was with the introduction and imprimatur of Bing Crosby, the reigning god of song. It was the first of some fifty appearances she would make on Crosby's shows over the next decade, a time during which Crosby would become a close friend and ally. Crosby's love for Peggy Lee's music, and for Peggy Lee the woman, was perhaps the single most important factor in the blossoming of her career—and how could it have been otherwise? As an artist, she was following a trail into pop-jazz that no woman had trod, but that Bing Crosby had not only discovered, but mapped. It was with Bing Crosby's sensibilities that Peggy Lee truly identified, on every band of the spectrum.

Harry Crosby was an industrious kid from northwestern Washington, the son of musical middle-class parents. From the start, his personality set him apart; he was wry and easygoing. By the end of grade school, he had shed the nondescript "Harry" moniker for "Bing"—a nickname bestowed by a friend who had picked it up from a humor feature in the Spokane paper called "The Bingville Bugle." The single syllable, with its absence of seriousness, fit the boy perfectly.

By 1926, at the age of twenty-three, Bing was one half of the Rhythm Boys—Mildred Bailey's brother Al Rinker was his partner. Crosby was performing with the groundbreaking Paul Whiteman band featuring Bix Beiderbecke. He was the first white kid to swing, pure and simple. The Rhythm Boys, wrote Crosby biographer Gary Giddins, were the "jazz age personified: two clean-cut white boys bringing a variation of black music to the vaudeville stage with panache and charm." The duo worked theater circuits out west, packing them in in Chicago and finally New York, where, in the mid-twenties, Harlem's swinging scene immediately seduced Crosby.

Though Rinker was half of the act, it was Bing, Giddins wrote, who was accepted into the "golden circle" of Whiteman and Beiderbecke, the men considered the true jazzmen in the first band to cross over the musical lines. In late-night jams at after-hours clubs, Bing's voice became a jazz instrument every bit as fluent as Bix's cornet. As Giddins wrote, to insiders Crosby was "a Bixian hero. . . . Just as Bix proved that a white musician could be an expressively nonconformist jazz player, Bing showed that a white male vocalist didn't have to sound like a Florodora girl."

In the words of Louis Armstrong, with whom Crosby became the closest of friends, "the man was a natural genius the day he was born." It was Armstrong who soon noted that as many black people seemed to buy Bing's records as white. And Crosby had something else in common with the true jazz world: he was a raging alcoholic in his early years. It didn't get in the way of his work, though, at least not usually.

But it wasn't just his swing that made his stuff special. It was his emotional way with a song. That descriptions of Crosby's interpretations eerily evoke later assessments of Peggy Lee's is no coincidence. The man she would listen to on the radio as a girl, and later in the wings of the radio-show stage, Giddins wrote, "knew the meaning of words, and how he wanted the band to accent certain things. He had exemplary . . . time and articulation." He had "sterling pitch."

By the late twenties, radio was beginning to muscle in on recordings as the main venue for music lovers. As radio grew, so did Crosby: By 1931, he had his own fifteen-minute show. By January 2, 1936, when he debuted as the new host of the *Kraft Music Hall,* he had his own half hour, and the extra fifteen minutes made all the difference: The format of his shorter shows prohibited him from talking directly to the audience; he just sang. Now that he could speak to listeners the charisma of his voice wove an even more potent magic. There was a new intimacy, and it seemed he was speaking (and singing) to each listener one-on-one. No doubt, as Giddins suggests, the debut six months earlier of Franklin Delano Roosevelt's homey "Fireside Chats" had had an influence, but equally important was Bing's ability to, in Giddins's words, "engage the listener's smile and sense of involvement, as if KMH were a family circle that just happened to comprise superb musical entertainers."

By the time Crosby welcomed Peggy onto the air, after ten triumphant years with *Kraft Music Hall,* he'd stopped performing concerts altogether and had compiled a movie career nonpareil. His fame was at its peak and his drinking was in the past. According to one national poll, Crosby was nothing less than the most admired man in the world—but his on-air, on-screen personality of casual, friendly self-assurance wasn't the whole story. He was, according to Giddins, "not unfamiliar with stage fright."

More interestingly, he had no time for troublesome people. "Bing could not abide pouting, and found emotional neediness as unpleasant as emotional dishonesty." The man who launched Peggy's radio career was "quintessentially American, cool and upbeat, never pompous, belligerent, or saccharine, never smug or superior." In other words, the man into whose microphone she sang her first national radio song did not abide fakes, phonies, or whiners. Peggy Lee would become one of his genuine favorites.

She would return to Bing's show. But in the meantime, on July 12, 1946, Peggy drew upon both sides of her ambivalent personality— the lonesome melancholic and the Holmesian positivist—when she hit the studio to turn out two contrasting originals. The slow, sad "Don't Be So Mean to Baby," recorded previously by Duke Ellington, wasn't particularly catchy musically, but the words were transparent: The narrator implores her man not to "leave me cryin' without even tryin' " because "baby's so all alone."

The flip side, though, was nothing less than an anthem of up, a paean to possibility, whose lyrics she'd been toying with for a couple of years. "One morning I got up to clean house," Peggy began, describing the song's inception. "I'm always happy when I'm cleaning, and besides, I had just found out that I was going to have a baby. I looked out the window and said to myself, 'It's a good day.' Then I started to hum, and Dave came out with his guitar, and before we knew it we had written the words and music for a song." (The day's blessings, she later wrote, included a friend's arrival with a bottle of wine, another showing up with a pheasant to cook, and telephone calls offering her work.)

Three years later, she and Dave were ready to record the song based on that good day—and it was unashamedly smiley. From the beginning of the ditty with Dave's playful major-key intro notes, through the big fat muted trombones, through a set of other solos that truly did cook, this was a blithely naive feel-good song, made entirely infectious by Peggy's optimistic choruses.

When she sang, "Good mornin', sun—good *mornin'*, sun!" her voice was so clear, so happy, it was as if she was swinging open the kitchen door and announcing the arrival of the postwar sunshine that would bathe everyone in its bright and beautiful light: It was not only "a good day for shinin' your shoes and a good day for losin' the blues," it was time to throw off other tyrannies: "It's a good day for payin' your bills, it's a good day for curing your ills, so take a deep breath and throw away the pills."

Years ahead of the fifties' string-spangled lush-life vision of a new America, the song was hard to resist, despite its complete lack of irony. It was as if she'd decided to stop moping about her marriage, worrying about her career, and letting negativity take hold. Again, Lee was pulling off an exquisitely convincing act: Gone was the sad, lonely bride of "Waitin' for the Train." "It's a Good Day" features Peggy Lee playing the optimistic wife and mother with such conviction that her sunny little number struck an enormously resonant chord. Disc jockeys opened their morning shows with it. "Come on, America," the singer seemed to cajole. "Get up and get to it: Grab a piece of the brand-new dream."

In September 1946, Peggy was back at the fabled Paramount, the site of earlier triumphs, but Sinatra was the star this time around. A column from the Fargo newspaper at the time quotes a woman who had visited Peggy backstage: "Next to her very glamorous dressing room is a room fixed up for Nicki's nursery. In spare moments Charlie Spivak and the boys in his band drop in to play with the baby." But it wasn't just Spivak: Frank Sinatra himself would look after the little girl. The gig marked the blossoming of a lifelong relationship between Peggy and Frank that would move from the studio to the bedroom and beyond without ever losing the genuine mutual admiration at its foundation.

Peggy, however, doesn't seem to have been thinking about Sinatra when she gave an interview to a reporter from *The New York Mirror*, an exchange that revealed a new candor on the part of the singer—and a store of memories she would never be able to put aside. "It's cold outside. I know. I was outside for a long time. There was practically no sun for the first twenty years of my life," she said.

The quote, a strikingly uncharacteristic utterance, marked the first time that her childhood, long a motivator for her drive and ambition, became fodder for public consumption. As her marriage became further complicated by her husband's drinking and her own conflicted ambitions, she'd given the world a glimpse at a facet of her personality that would eventually come to dominate her public image: the victim. It would stand to reason that as she was losing the affection of her husband, she'd turn to her fans for some sympathy and understanding. But opening a metaphoric vein to spill out a little self-pity to an audience marked a step toward being a star, a commodity—a persona rather than a person. But Peggy Lee needed to reach out for her audience's love, and even the *Mirror*'s writer got a taste of that need. "If you gathered all the stars and put them at the feet of Peggy Lee," he wrote, "she'd still be the kid from Fargo, North Dakota [*sic*]. Peggy is the singer with the silken voice who's just thankful that she's liked."

Down Beat named Peggy Lee the Number One Girl Singer of 1946. No doubt some of the acclaim owed to her music, but the fact that she had become ever sexier and more beautiful could hardly be discounted. Her looks made her a star to be sold. When Capitol issued *Rendezvous with Peggy Lee,* the cover art was hardly subtle, and it was clear that the marketing and publicity people were planning to emphasize her visual appeal. It was all sex-bomb stuff. Lee was photographed splayed on her back on some sort of divan, her blond hair in disarray on a pillow behind her, her sparkly green gown suggesting nightclubs, after hours, after sex. Dangly blue earrings framed bright red, seductively smiling lips. The eyes—bright blue, rather curiously, given that hazel was their natural shade—were cast askance. Her décolletage swelled enticingly—at least on the first pressings. On later copies of the record, only about a half inch of swelling breast was visible; the rest was covered by a black triangle on which the songs were listed in white type. One can only surmise that a backlash resulted in Capitol's reconsideration of all the flesh she'd revealed. But either way, the intent was obvious. From the beginning, Lee was given to understand that her looks and sexuality were as important to her commercial appeal as her voice. No wonder she later became obsessed with maintaining her appearance.

The liner notes spoke volumes about her status as a rising star, and her future place in history: "This is a rendezvous with Peggy Lee," read the anonymous blurb, "but be prepared to meet a dozen different Peggies." Peggy didn't just sing a song—with each, she would seek and find "its most appropriate tempo, tonal quality and style. As a result . . . each of her songs winds up being sung by a different Peggy Lee."

In 1947, financially buoyed by their string of hits, Peg and Dave decided to stop looking for their cottage and build it, on Blair Drive in the Hollywood Hills, an unpretentious ranch house with a garden. It was here that Peggy first professed to find her love of gardening—the yard boasted a bank of moss roses and baby tears. She described the house as being "on the sentimental side," with chintz fabric on the furniture. Her kitchen decoration mirrored the mood of her latest hit: She painted Norwegian aphorisms emphasizing positive thinking to hang on the walls. But she was spending less and less time in the kitchen; her music was increasingly her priority: "I never got around to making dinner, but the song is done."

A woman named Alice Larson, from back in Hillsboro, North Dakota, came west to work as Nicki's nurse. "Our house was filled with music and laughter," Peggy would later write.

Peggy Lee had matured from would-be singer through marriage and motherhood and emerged as a name performer. She seemed to have found a balance, and a life philosophy to carry her through the rougher currents. But as Dave became less and less reliable, the pressures were mounting: She wanted to keep the family intact, but she also needed to earn money. In her later years she would tell a friend that she lived daily with the fear of the poverty she grew up in. North Dakota was never far away. The work—on recordings, on radio, on stage—was ever more demanding, and Carlos Gastel, now her manager too, was undependable. She remained a shy and inexperienced young woman who faced many tough new challenges. The love of her audience and the record-buying public provided the affirmation she needed, but would it last?

When she was called to New York to substitute for Jo Stafford, Peggy flew east. She grew increasingly ill on the flight, and when she landed, she put through a person-to-person call to her spiritual adviser, Ernest Holmes. "You'll be fine," he assured her. "Come see me when you return."

"By air time, I was fine," she told *Science of Mind* magazine some years later. "My first experience of spiritual mind healing! When I got back to the coast I went to see [Holmes] at once. From then on Ernest and Hazel adopted me as one of those daughters they 'didn't have.' Now I began consciously to apply the principles he taught, and to experience their effect in my life. They even reached back into the past, into my childhood, for Ernest taught me to forgive what happened to me there."

Holmes maintained that the human body is a miraculous thing, its equilibrium essential for health to be maintained. Physicians, said Holmes, could lend assistance with medicines and surgery, but the primary responsibility for the body's care lay in the mind of its owner. Through the years, Holmes's messages to Lee would be simple and comforting: To grow, he would tell her, you must give love for hate. Joy for sadness. Beauty for ashes. And you must forgive what happened in your childhood. A much-needed lesson for a woman who was effectively orphaned at the age of four.

Hal Schaefer, Peggy's pianist in 1947 and a man with an impressive résumé, had fond recollections of collaborations with Lee and Barbour. "After she got a tune and liked it," he recalled, "we found what keys and tempos she'd like to do it in, and worked out a rough arrangement, then David would come in and make his contribution. It was a wonderful experience just to be with Dave and Peggy in those days. Sometimes, Peggy would just sit down in the middle of the rug, right on the floor, and just focus on some nice spiritual feeling." But Schaefer also recalled the perfectionism that was wearing Peggy down. "Sometimes she had problems with Capitol because they would want her to record something and she didn't feel she was ready."

Peggy's perfectionism had much to do with her shouldering so much responsibility in her career at such an early age. She demanded nothing less than greatness from herself, and if the musicians and technicians and managers around her weren't up to her standards, if something went wrong, it was Peggy's name on the record, or the club date.

By now she was a regular at the Capitol studios, recording songs of all kinds. Peggy Lee was creating an astoundingly eclectic collection of songs that spanned every musical style extant, from a smoky, cool Fletcher Henderson track called "Eight, Nine and Ten," to her subtly hip and just-jazzy-enough version of Arlen and Harburg's "Happiness Is a Thing Called Joe."

"Life was so happy," Peggy later wrote, "that I began to be afraid it wouldn't last. And it didn't. David was having more and more pain in his stomach. A decision had to be made about the bleeding duodenal ulcers."

In the autumn of 1947, Barbour landed in the hospital for a two-week stay; the state of his stomach ulcers—it was never established that drinking had caused them, but there's no reason to doubt it—was critical. A kidney was found to be damaged. There was internal hemorrhaging. It was touch and go.

Peggy was booked at the Palladium at the time, opening for Vaughn Monroe, a handsome, lightweight bandleader whose voice was known more for its "romantic"—that is, sentimental— tones than its musical ones. Monroe, who also played a fair trumpet, was the kind of musician who thought a band's chief obligation was to give its audience nice songs to listen to. Artistry wasn't paramount.

Dave was still in the hospital, but Peggy had to make the gig.

Dave's illness was news in the fraternity of musicians—Bing Crosby offered to babysit Nicki, although Peggy had made only a handful of appearances on his show—but Peggy had to meet all of her professional obligations. Barbour's band would have to get by with Monroe's guitarist, Bucky Pizzarelli, playing in Dave's place. They were lucky to get him.

Bucky was a carefree kid with an optimistic, smiling disposition who would have played his guitar for free. He'd survived the war and considered himself lucky to hitch back up with Monroe's band, which was really starting to make some noise. (According to some accounts, Monroe's was the most popular band in the land in 1945, when sweet sounds were in vogue.) When he found out he'd be learning Dave Barbour's guitar part, Bucky was thrilled—and a little nervous.

"I ran down to the record store and bought a 78 of 'What More Can a Woman Do?' and listened to that damned thing over and over again," he remembers now.

"We did two shows, one for the East Coast and one for the West Coast. She came in wearing a long dress, which was a new thing for those days, and she looked stunning. And she liked everything we did. We actually played the guitar part with the orchestra, and the second time we played it, for some reason they were running out of time, and we had to speed it up; apparently they'd wasted time in the middle. I had to speed it up, then slow it down.

"She was sensational. She finished up with her big hit, 'It's a Good Day,' and that was the finale, and they used Vaughn and the Mood Maids, and they all sang."

Bucky had no idea of the circumstances, of Peggy's husband's situation—that Dave, in the midst of a two-week stay in the hospital, was being given a fifty-fifty chance to live. Between gigs and radio appearances, Peggy would stay by his side at the hospital. Dave asked that she keep his mother away; he didn't need any more anxiety. Nicki would pick flowers to bring her father. Peggy doted. As he was entering the operating room for a second procedure, she was professing her love aloud. He looked up—as Peggy later told the tale for comic effect, which was clearly Dave's intent—and said, "Stop nagging me."

At one point, word had gotten out, erroneously, that Dave had died. When friends heard her singing "What More Can a Woman Do?" on the Crosby show on the night the rumor circulated, they were in despair. But in fact Dave pulled through—thanks, Peggy believed, to the power of prayer. Years later, she would recount how, on the ninth day of his hospitalization, she'd run into a doctor in the elevator, and had assumed from his dark demeanor that the worst had indeed happened. Dave had gone temporarily blind from nephritis and nurses were running to his room with a resuscitator.

"I shall never forget this," she would write in her memoir. "As I walked down the corridor crying out to God in silence, I suddenly saw a shaft of light coming from my own eyes down the length of the hall, and I knew that David was alive, and would live. I felt as though I had been lifted from the floor."

He was released three days later. The doctors had removed most of his stomach.

ELEVEN

Borderline

AFTER DAVE WAS allowed to leave the hospital, the Barbours escaped to the beaches of Mexico—a "rest cure," according to one account. But on the vacation that was supposed to relieve their pressures, they wrote a song that would ultimately accelerate all the demands. "Mañana," an ode to the laid-back south-of-the-border lifestyle they encountered, was one of her simplest, silliest songs, but it previewed the Barbours' new fascination with Latin rhythms and style. Peggy's Latin-derived music would, despite her Nordic roots, become as true to her real soul as any rhythm, jazz, or pop she would ever sing. But "Mañana" did more than announce an artistic sea change. Following its success, Peggy Lee would be serving a new set of gods, of rules, of pressures and paradigms.

It began one night when Dave was playing around with some Latin stuff on the guitar. By breakfast time, Peggy had produced a set of lyrics for the song. That the message of "Mañana" mocked the Mexican people was something she didn't see yet, and surely didn't intend. Work could be left undone, chores could wait—the lyrics weren't exactly an anticipation of political correctness. In Peg's poem, the car had no engine, the window had no panes, but who cared? "Mañana," Peg scribbled, "is soon enough for me." No doubt she wanted to believe the sentiment— but nothing about her was wired for the laid-back or lazy. She had to work, she had to sing. On the other hand, the Latin sentiment for expressing your emotions, for wearing your heart on your sleeve, suited her well: "I'm a frustrated Latin," Peggy said. "I like to show what I feel about something or somebody."

The interlude between the writing and recording of "Mañana" produced another big hit for Peggy and Dave, her first record to top the astounding two-million mark in sales. "Golden Earrings" owed nothing to jazz, blues, or anything remotely connected to the avantist in her. It was an overheated spaghetti-Western pseudo-tango written by Ray Evans and the immortal Victor Young, a melodrama of a melody heavy on cellos and schlock. "There's a story the gypsies know is true," sang Peggy, "that when your love wears golden earrings, he belongs to you."

"Frankly," she said the following summer, to *Cue* magazine, "that was a very ordinary vocal job, but Dave's arrangement and accompaniment were really out of this world." She wasn't being overly modest: It was to Dave's credit that the song captured the public, who clearly favored upbeat tunes lacquered with sentiment. The commercial viability of darker, more adventurous jazz rhythms was waning.

Two months after she'd recorded "Golden Earrings," she was back in the studio to record "Mañana." In the studio, Peggy affected a Spanish accent, accompanied by her friend Carmen Miranda's backup group on vocals. "I remember when we recorded it, how contagious the happiness was," she later recalled in *Miss Peggy Lee*. "Carmen Miranda's Brazilians—a vocal chorus—and her musicians added a lot with their effervescent Latin rhythm. The Brazilians were perfect for 'Mañana.' When we were doing what I believe was the first 'board fade' [turning down the volume on the studio recording equipment as the song nears its end], the Brazilians decided to samba out of the studio and down the street, playing and singing 'Mañana.' "

Music historians dispute her belief about the board fade; it had been used for more than a decade. But no one questioned the phenomenal impact of the song: It sold more records than any other in 1948, and minted large amounts of cash much like the mindless novelty hit "Come Onna My House," which launched Rosemary Clooney's career four years later. "Mañana" sold an astounding two and a half million records for Dave and Peggy. "Dave deserves all the credit," Peggy said. "You know, if he weren't my husband, I'd be glad to tell you he's the greatest musician and arranger in the world."

By now, thanks to her hit records and regular appearances on both the Crosby and Durante radio shows, Peggy Lee was a star, earning national plaudits. But more and more, Peggy was given to episodes of illness that seemed to have psychosomatic roots, and she'd found herself compelled to seek further spiritual guidance to get her through the tough times. She'd spent nearly every day of her quarter century on earth working to make it this far. She'd slugged it out doing farm chores, working carnivals, singing auditions, traveling through late nights on cold buses. But whatever the benefits, tensions mounted, too. An unforeseen offshoot of the success of "Mañana" was a lawsuit accusing both Lee and Barbour of plagiarism, which would soon go to trial.

Sometimes, though, the actual work reminded her of what she

loved and why she had chosen a life in music. There is no question that Peggy loved going in to work. Heading over to the studios to cut a record for Capitol was the closest she had ever come to having "a real job" with normal hours. She found herself dressing up for the sessions. Nice clothes made her feel good, and, she believed, made her singing better. She liked to think of herself as a professional.

"Everyone had the feelings that I had about making [the songs] the best they could be, and going for the best thing—all the time," she said much later, recalling the Capitol days of the forties in a 1993 interview with Ken Bloom and Bill Rudman. "We'd do a three- or four-hour session. Everybody was on time, and all business. We had our material. We were ready. These days, when people record, they're given so much time to sit around and think about what they're going to write, what they're going to do, and all of that. I've been around long enough to say this without getting my face slapped: I think that's a waste of time. I think you ought to do that thinking before you get there, and then think some more, to get a shape and a form to know where you're going before you go in to record."

Despite the prep work, there were a few unexpected developments, as was the case with the creation of the wondrous and haunting Barbour–Lee–Willard Robison "Don't Smoke in Bed," recorded in December 1947.

"Dave and I wrote that song," Lee said. "But we didn't write it all, because Willard had the title and the first line, and then he had a drink. Dear Willard. I used to lock him in a room and try to get him to work, and I'd say, 'When you get all through, I'll give you a beer,' because he had a drinking problem."

Her tolerance for Robison's foils had something to do with her fondness for his songs ("They're sort of poems set to music, little character sketches," she told her writer pal George Simon). But given her father's and husband's problems, she had also amassed a lot of experience with people who drank too much, and perhaps this gave her more sympathy for Robison. Luckily, however, Willard's drinking never compromised his considerable gifts. By any measure, Robison's words were never those of a conventional scribe; Peggy heard poems in his lyrics—with their "pastoral preachers and country concerns," in the words of author Will Friedwald.

"Don't Smoke in Bed" were the parting words of a woman leaving her husband. (They seemed to presage a personal parting that lay just a few years down the line for Peggy.) After leaving her wedding ring and a goodbye note on the dresser, she leaves an admonition: "Don't look for me. I'll get ahead. Remember, darling—don't smoke in bed."

"Don't Smoke" was a modest seller. But "Mañana" was paying for the first mink, the first Buick, and a new dream house—a large Norman French structure set on nearly an acre of fruit trees and gardens on Denslow Street in a kind of neighborhood new to the Barbours: Universal honcho Bill Goetz, Bogart and Bacall, and the Ira Gershwins lived nearby. Parties drew the likes of Spencer Tracy, Judy Garland, Oscar Levant. And Frank Sinatra.

"They say that houses reach out and claim you," Lee later wrote, "and that one did just that." It had hand-hewn beams and three fireplaces—a brick one, a black marble one, and a ceramic one. She decorated the new place with care, choosing Chinese carpets and putting up custom-sewn curtains. She painted the cabinets with "pictures of Frenchmen in red berets." Nicki's room was "white dotted Swiss with pale pink piping, white furniture trimmed with pastel colors. A canopy, curtains with ruffles. . . . Vegetable garden, jacarandas, fruit trees."

Soon after they'd decorated the place, she and Dave hit the road for a gig in Virginia. "We took Nicki along on that trip, and we had a wonderful time, but it wasn't enough to keep David on the straight and narrow. We came home to Denslow tired and troubled."

She was not specific about why they were troubled, but their worries may have been exacerbated by the "Mañana" lawsuit that had begun when a banjo player named Harry McClintock— a.k.a. Hats McKay—had surfaced to claim he'd written the melody to "Mañana" nearly thirty years earlier (in 1919, as "Midnight on the Ocean," published in 1932). In his suit against David and Peggy, McClintock asked for a million dollars in damages and an injunction against performance of the song. When the suit went to trial in New York City, Peggy decided that she and Dave should move east for the proceedings. They took a room at the Warwick Hotel. Just before the trial began, Dave disappeared for three days. Peggy's telephone calls to local hospitals and bars bore no fruit: "If anyone had seen him," she wrote, "they weren't going to tell me. He came back, almost sober, the day before the trial."

It was the contention of Peggy and Dave's lawyer, Henry Gilbert—Irving Berlin was among his other clients—that the rhythms of "Mañana" were in the public domain. McKay's odd habit of playing the banjo in the courtroom did little to endear him to the judge. The mood lightened considerably with the surprise appearance of Jimmy Durante, who showed up in the courtroom—with a piano wheeled in alongside him.

Peggy recounted the ensuing scene: "Jimmy began playing and singing his 'Laughing Song,' [he'd] tell a joke, then vamp as the audience laughed. ['The Laughing Song'] was usually notated with the words 'Ha ha ha'—exactly what Hats McKay had for the lyric to his version of 'Mañana.' Jimmy's testimony certainly bore out the public domain argument—as well as giving us all a laugh. When we took a recess, I tried to thank Jimmy, but he just shook his famous nose at me and said, 'Dat's what friends are for.'

I wanted to cry as I watched him walk down the hallway and out the door."

The key testimony came from a musicologist and radio personality named Sigmund Spaeth, who said that the samba didn't even exist when McKay claimed to have written the piece, in 1919.

The day was won. Lee and Barbour prevailed. Peggy celebrated with Deems Taylor, the president of ASCAP, at a fancy New York restaurant. Dave didn't want to accompany them; he'd been drinking.

The trial would not be the only occasion for "Mañana" and Dave's drinking to conspire to bring Peg dismay. At about the same time, Peggy later noted in her Broadway show, Dave, on a binge with Carlos Gastel, would try to sell the rights to "Mañana" for two tickets to the Rose Bowl.

By now, it was hardly a surprise that Peggy could count on a little help from her friends. She'd become a regular on Bing's show, which had found a new home on ABC, sponsored by Philco. The switch to ABC was huge news—and it shook up the business forever. "During the war," Gary Giddins explains, "Bing made a lot of transcription discs for the armed forces, and thought they sounded good enough for broadcast. So after the war he insisted on prerecording [the] Kraft [show]. NBC refused. Bing walked out on his contract, and the subsequent suit showed the contract to be illegal—the number of years involved bordered on indentured servitude.

"So he was now a free agent and every major corporation in the U.S. started bidding for his services, sending free cars and other kinds of stuff. Crosby, however, would not be moved on the issue of prerecording. NBC and CBS refused, fearing that if they permitted transcriptions, they would lose their affiliates—they thought the only attraction of network radio was that it was live. Finally, ABC . . . agreed and Bing chose Philco as the sponsor. The controversy was front-page news for several months— *Billboard* devoted an entire issue to it. . . .

"Thanks to the enormous amount of publicity, the first Philco broadcast was a huge success and ABC became the third major network—one star after another switched to it when their contracts were up. At this point, Crosby was introduced to John Mullen, who—working with Nazi blueprints he found during the invasion of Berlin—was trying to build the first tape recorder. Crosby financed him and helped put together the Ampex company and also 3M—to figure out how to make tape, which took much longer. By 1947, Crosby was the first performer with a tape-based studio, revolutionizing the entire business, and the Philco ratings climbed to the top.

"Kraft continued less successfully with other hosts. The irony is that the 'biggest story since talking pictures' was soon forgotten, as a new invention took hold: TV. Though, as many observers pointed out, TV followed the exact same trajectory as radio, beginning live and then switching reluctantly to tape."

In October 1946, the Philco show hit the airwaves, with Bob Hope as Bing's guest. Two months later, Peggy appeared, and sang "It's a Good Day." After that, she became a regular, and she was in fabulous company. Bing's guests were the best of the best—Durante, Jolson, Jack Benny, Groucho Marx, Mickey Rooney, Judy Garland, Dinah Shore, Connie Boswell. In a short piece about Peggy around this time, *Newsweek* described the circumstances that led to her hooking up with Bing: "Her staunch refusal to leave Hollywood kept her off several good radio programs. Then, last fall, Bing Crosby suddenly needed a good girl singer. He hired Peggy and got a girl who could sound as good on her own as she did in duets with him."

Over the next few years, Lee and Crosby would pair up on

"It's a Good Day" several times; the song jibed well with Crosby's philosophy of never complaining. They'd sing countless other duets, combining their extraordinary talents on any number of stylistic offerings. On one extraordinary show in 1948 they offered up a handful of Gershwin songs, duets including "'S Wonderful," "I've Got a Crush on You," "They Can't Take That Away from Me," "I Got Rhythm," and "Summertime," some featuring the singular jazz violinist Joe Venuti.

On one of his earliest shows with her, Crosby asked about her new house on Denslow and inquired about Dave's health—all very personal, all very friendly, all very gentlemanly. It seemed he was trying to calm her down. Just before airtime, she had professed her nervousness. "When you introduce me," she asked, "would you please not leave me out there on the stage alone? Would you stand where I can see your feet?" On that show, and thereafter, Bing made sure to stay within her sight—leaning on a prop, hovering somewhere nearby. "Bing was always finding ways to help give me confidence," she would write. Professionally, they were an equally good fit: Both always arrived at the studio before the others for rehearsals. "I was always impressed by his promptness, his honesty, and his modesty," she explained. "I remember him [once] saying, 'I wish I could really make something of my life.' It amazed me that he could feel so humble. I tried, in a stumbling sort of way, to tell him what the world thought of him, but I don't think I convinced him."

Both Dave and Peggy continued to be drawn to all things Latin—mambo, conga, samba. Peggy was a particular fan of the buoyancy of the people behind the music: "They make you feel like a light bulb!" she told *Metronome*. Dave was a particular fan of Afro-Cuban rhythms, of the figurative place where Latin meets jazz. A few miles off the coast of south Florida, Havana was boiling over, and its rhythms were flowing back to the States where they were mixing with the black blues-jazz rhythms of the mainland. Dave was into Perez Prado, and when he was recording without Peg, his band was playing with mambo rhythms, though not too extreme: He wanted them accessible, he said, "to people in Salt Lake City and Fargo."

But both Barbour and Lee were a little scared of the *true* new. Their sweet stuff was scoring big. "Golden Earrings" became the highest-selling piece of sheet music in the country. At one point, the ten top-selling records featured two artists with two hits each: Crosby and Lee. "Golden Earrings" was at Number Three and "Mañana" was at Five.

Swing was more or less finished. The singers were more of an attraction than the men behind them. For one thing, the cost of mounting a band, bus, and show for theaters or clubs was prohibitive for promoters, especially when people weren't dancing anymore. Bop continued its takeover of jazz, with mainstream *Life* magazine seeing fit to introduce the style in a 1948 story. Bop, it seemed, was the new standard-bearer for a generation of musicians who played for themselves, their peers, and their art—but not necessarily for audiences. To traditionalists, the increasingly unstructured sound was inaccessible, uncleaving to melody. ("It's nervous music more than exciting music" was Benny Goodman's take.) Others considered Louis, Billie, and Teddy Wilson strictly passé. The future of jazz, said the avant-garde writers, belonged to Bud Powell's piano. To Bird and Diz.

Mainstream Los Angeles still preferred the safer stuff; in February 1948, Shep Fields and his Rippling Rhythm Orchestra were rousing them at the ornate Cocoanut Grove, in the Ambassador Hotel. Buddy Rich and Helen Forrest were entertaining at the Palladium. Billy Berg's jazz club was thriving; in 1947, it had welcomed Armstrong—a maverick, but never a bopster—and the audience had embraced him. One night, Ella had sold out Berg's place on Vine. Benny Carter and Peggy were in the audience. Ella wanted to pay tribute to Benny, and called Peggy up, too. Peggy sang a Carter song called "Lonely Woman."

The Barbours wanted to continue their creative/musical explorations. But bop's social and cultural trappings were offputting to the couple. In an interview in *Metronome* with Peggy's old friend George Simon, Dave chastised the interviewer for the magazine's record reviews, which tended to favor the forward and look askance on the old: "[The reviews] almost sound like a cult. They sound as if they're afraid to admit to a little sentimentality in music. . . .

"Bop is sensational," Barbour continued, "the damnedest thing that ever happened, a terrific stride forward. But the actions of some of the cultists are too much for effect. Some of them stand and gape like idiots or stare right through you. . . . Most of these cats today can't sustain a note. It seems to me that outside of what they're doing, the bop world finds music in general a pretty abstract thing."

And for Peg, it was downright "neurotic," this stuff—that's the word she used. In the lingo of the time, when Freudspeak had entered the mainstream, "neurosis" implied imbalance, something she wanted no part of; both Peggy and Dave went out of their way to subscribe to the idea of being positive as a way of living.

"You're not being a boob or an idiot to want to like people," Barbour told Simon. "That's the way it's supposed to be. That's a positive type of thinking!"

"It would help if people loved each other more," Peg added. "When you see unloveliness in others, it's because you have some unloveliness in yourself."

In retrospect, the most remarkable thing about the story is Barbour's passion for the music, and the extensive quotes—possibly the lengthiest quoted legacy the man ever left. That he could wax so eloquent about his music, but be so much less expressive as a husband, seemed indicative of his priorities.

Not long after the interview, Peggy's other old-friend-turned-critic, Leonard Feather, gave her *Metronome* magazine's blind-fold song test, a regular feature in which musicians were asked to listen to songs and name the artists. Other than showing the extraordinary range of her musical knowledge—she correctly identified cuts by not only Artie, Billie, Bessie, Sarah, and Frank, but also Slim Gaillard doing "School Kid's Hop"—the Feather piece was significant on another important level.

To start with, in the introduction, Feather, a man of authority and influence, put on paper a thought that was often being articulated: In a time when the jazz camps were warring with the popular camps, and when the lines of demarcation were supposed to be inviolable, Lee, Feather proclaimed, could do justice to both: "In the world of popular singing, there is a very thin, vague borderline between what is considered by the pundits to be jazz singing (Bessie Smith, Louis Armstrong, Billie Holiday) and what is dismissed as mere popular singing (Dinah Shore, Perry Como, Jo Stafford). Jazz critics, even those on the Moldy Fig side who cling so tenaciously to the old, the pure and the earthy . . . contradict themselves and one another widely when it comes to singers, sometimes even vote for a Crosby or a Sinatra where you fully expected them to root for Josh White or Leadbelly.

"In the charmed circle of singers who have earned praise and respect from both sides of the fence is Peggy Lee. Everybody likes her singing because it is both jazz singing and popular singing. Everybody is happy to be able to praise her, too, because she is one of the nicest and most genuine people in show business. All of which made her the perfect choice for a vocalist to submit to the blindfold test."

The other insight came from Lee herself, when she asked Feather to delete a criticism of one of the songs because the unnamed artist was a nice guy whom she knew.

"You know, I'd never make a good critic," she said. "I just like to relax and enjoy music, but when it comes to criticizing, I'm afraid to hurt people's feelings."

Her favorite songs on Feather's playlist? Billie on "Any Old Time," Lee Wiley's work on "Easy to Love," Bessie Smith doing "Nobody Knows You When You're Down and Out," and—especially—Louis and Ella singing "You Won't Be Satisfied."

It wasn't just the music press that was now flocking to the side of America's favorite media-savvy, photogenic young love couple–songwriting duo. In larger demographic circles, the public soon learned that Dave and Peggy called each other Normer and Popper. He called her Peg O'Lee, or "the Canary." She tended the garden and sang to Nicki and fed their adopted stray collie, Banjo. The public image was one of bliss. A *Life* magazine spread showed photos of domestic happiness: Dave writing a song while Peggy gardened; Dave playing Nicki in a Ping-Pong match; Nicki giving Peggy a good-night kiss. The opening shot of the spread, though, was all business: Peggy leaning her elbow on a tower of records, one of a sea of piles of vinyl that surrounded her, accompanied by the caption "Singer Peggy Lee leans on a stack of records of her hit tune 'Mañana.' This record alone should bring in $75,000 in royalties in 1948."

The accompanying one-paragraph story notes that "Miss Lee sees as much as she possibly can of her 4-year-old daughter, Nicki. When she cannot, Nicki plays herself to sleep with one of her mother's records."

Between recording and performing on the radio and in theaters and clubs—and a television debut, on Ed Sullivan's *Toast of the Town*—Peggy Lee brought home a quarter of a million dollars in 1948. She earned $5,000 a week at the Paramount in August, the same week she appeared on Sullivan's show. The performance portended her relationship with a medium that would not always flatter her, nor showcase her to best advantage: "She looks excellent in close-up," wrote *Variety*, "although the full-length shots tend to harden her appearance. Miss Lee concentrated on ballads, which made for a high degree of audience satisfaction."

In New York, she stayed in a thirtieth-floor suite at a hotel overlooking Central Park, at $45 a night, with Dave, Nicki, Nicki's nurse, a maid, and a personal assistant. Dave was recording on his own, too: "Forever Paganini" and "Forever Nicki." In *American* magazine, one Jack Long pulled out all the stops, in a prose style that helps explain why his magazine soon went the way of gas streetlamps: "I may as well confess it publicly—I've fallen in love with a girl named Peggy Lee. Let me explain at once that I am not a hep cat, nor even a 'gone character' when it comes to jazz. I am not charged by young women who stand on a stage and swing their hips in front of a microphone. This may explain why I was a dead duck the first time I saw and listened to Peggy Lee, a girl who can sing a song better than anyone I know, and leave her hips alone."

Continuing her emphasis on her domestic bliss, Peggy told Long she was trying out a new lyric: " 'There's something about an old leather chair.' It'll be a song about the comforts of home life, and pipes and slippers and so on. . . ."

"It seems the Barbours," Long wrote, are developing "a strong taste for the fireside." There was no hint of trouble at home. One of Peggy's quotes rang true, despite all her newfound wealth: "There was a time," she said, "when I was lucky to make a dollar for an evening's singing. But I was happy then, and I could be happy doing it all over again."

Was she really longing for simpler times? Why, given everything she now had? Perhaps, despite all the public posturing, her household was not the happy place she and her publicists tried to present. By now, Peg was apparently drinking also. A few years later, a William Morris man named Val Irving would confide to a mutual friend, who requests anonymity, about having to bring Peggy two different bottles before recordings and before performances. One was always brandy.

Other musicians would speak in later years of having heard the tales of Peggy's consumption of alcohol in the late forties, but none would ever speak of seeing her out of control or debilitated by it. As for Dave? By now, it was interfering in a serious way with both the couple's marriage and their social life. Peggy was enjoying the company of musicians more and more, and enjoyed inviting the cast and crew of her radio appearances back to Denslow Street, where she'd cook for them. But, she would write in her memoir, "Dave would say, 'Get rid of these people.'"

Above all, he was not likely to heed the importunings of others. "He was a wonderful guy," trumpeter Pete Candoli, a friend of both, says now. "If he wanted to drink, he was a man. You know what I mean."

You Was

Radio's critics maintained that the medium's musical product was necessarily inferior to what consumers heard on records. With new shows airing every week, hosts and guests couldn't have the time to master complicated, more artistic arrangements; as a result, radio audiences would get simplicity or repetition or B-grade pap. But the generalization didn't always reflect reality. Not when the lineup was inarguably top-of-the-trade. And radio never got any better—in terms of music, sophistication, entertainment, cool, or daring—than the show Bing Crosby aired from San Francisco's Marine Memorial Auditorium in the summer of 1949 with guests Peggy Lee and Louis Armstrong—along with two more of the purest jazz virtuosos in the land: trombonist Jack

Teagarden and violinist Joe Venuti. By now, Bing was happily married, and at the very top of his radio game.

"Now, Ken"—he nods to announcer Ken Carpenter as the evening opens—"Miss Peggy Lee approaches." Carpenter's response: "That's what I call a slick chick."

As Peg takes the stage, Bing implores the anonymous bandleader, "Please drop a downbeat and get those boys blowing and playing and stroking and swinging."

Crosby and Lee duet on "You Was," with music by the estimable Sonny Burke and lyrics by Paul Francis Webster. (A few years later they would furnish Lee with one of the greatest jazz vocals of all time.) Warming up, seeming natural and terrifically simpatico, the two friends come together on the frothy, sweet bubble of a song with thrilling results replete with Webster's trademark rhymes (the heart is a "spherical lyrical miracle") and the coyly entrancing ungrammatical verbal hook: The question is who "the sweetest one I knew was." The answer: "I'd say you was."

As Lee walks off the stage, Bing says to Ken, "That's the nicest thing ever to come out of North Dakota."

Now enter Louis Armstrong. Side by side stand the two men responsible for making jazz rhythm accessible to a nation. "Three weeks ago," says Bing, "I got a big charge out of seeing a bright satchel-mouthed face beaming from the cover of *Time* magazine—the face of one of my best friends. Tonight I'm just poppin' with pride to give a friendly five to the most sensational horn of them all, Louis 'Satchmo' Armstrong."

Then the banter begins—a scripted dialogue, no doubt, but their few seconds of verbal riffing provide an interesting window on an extraordinary cultural time and place, a moment when mainstream white America, embodied by its first true superstar, could overlap with mainstream black culture, embodied by Louis—its undisputed king.

Bing: "It's fine as wine in the summertime to have you
with us."
Satchmo: "I'm pleasurated, pops."
Bing: "How do you get those crisp, clear, clean notes?"
Satchmo: "Every night I dip my trumpet in Did."
Bing: " 'Did'? What's that?"
Satchmo: "Did's the stuff that's already done what Does is
gonna try to Do."

Next, Teagarden and Venuti join Armstrong for a hopping ragtime–New Orleans–funeral "Panama," with Teagarden's trombone holding its own against Satchmo's trumpet. The bliss is
transporting as the pair's artistry silences bop's boosters and their
jabs at the purity and melody of more mainstream jazz. Music
could get no cooler than this.

Next, slow down for a duet by Bing and Satchmo, comes
"Lazybones," the Johnny Mercer–Hoagy Carmichael anthem,
made into a hit in the thirties by Mildred Bailey. Armstrong, befitting the times, the place—and his lifelong friendship with
Crosby—willingly plays Stepin Fetchit.

"I'll do the singing," says Bing, "if you do the mugging."

It begins with Bing addressing "Lazybones"—Armstrong.
How, Bing wants to know, "you 'spec to get your cornmeal
made?" Satchmo's somnolent reply? "I don't get no cornmeal
made," because, "morning til night" he's sleeping in "that old
shade."

When Bing closes the show, bringing his guests to the stage,
the verbal riffs reach jazzy heights. "I'd like to tilt my skimmer to
Miss Peggy Lee," says Crosby, "for buzzing up from Tinselville
to be with us tonight."

Answers Peggy, with a smile that's obvious even on the radio:
"It was a crock full of kicks for me, Bing. I really enjoyed hearing
the mellow members of the society of *hot*."

It was probably around the time of this broadcast that Bing asked Peggy Lee to dinner. Flustered and nervous, she accidentally hairsprayed her coiffure with a room deodorizer. "Knowing how prompt he was," she wrote, "I started to wash my long blond hair early. It was a fairy-tale situation. Makeup and hair finished early, I eagerly awaited the sound of the doorbell. When it finally rang, I thought, 'I'll just spray a little of this hairspray to make sure. . . .' It was sweet-scented room deodorizer! I turned all colors. Bing laughed and laughed as I tried everything, and finally ended up washing my reeking hair again." ·

At an upscale restaurant, she confided to her friend that she used to save her money to see his movies, that she never tired of watching *Mississippi*, which she first saw at the age of fourteen. "He had lost the girl and sang 'Down by the River,'" she later explained, "and I was crying, because I wanted everything to work out for him. And when I told Bing how heartbroken I was, he took me all over San Francisco, one place after another, searching for a pianist who knew that song, and sang it to me. . . . Imagine your idol singing that song to you."

There's no hint in any recountings that this was a date in the real sense; even in the next few years, as her marriage was coming apart, she was faithful to Barbour. Her relationship with Crosby would be nothing more than a friendship of the highest order. But as the years passed, Crosby would never be far from Peggy Lee; he would send notes to be waiting for her when she'd arrive in distant cities. "Once he sent me a wire," she wrote, "referring to his last appearance at the Cocoanut Grove. It seems he had 'hit the sauce' a little there; his wire said, 'Dear Peg, please pick up my laundry. I left there rather hurriedly, in 1931. Love, Bing.'"

When *Billboard* named Peggy Lee the "Nation's Number One Vocalist" for 1948, it was on the sales strength of "Mañana" and

"Golden Earrings." And suddenly the press wanted to know everything about her history.

"Even when I was a tow-headed youngster on my dad's farm, I was convinced that I was destined to some day become a singer," she told the *Chicago Sun-Times* during an engagement at the Chicago Theatre. For now, at least, the more personal confessions seem to have been silenced, along with some of her concerns about the present. Hal Schaefer, her pianist on the road in 1949, observed that stardom was not her primary concern. "If Dave was happy, she was happy."

By the end of 1949, sales of just three of her records with Dave—"It's a Good Day," "Golden Earrings," and "Mañana"— had reached four million.

On the radio, as transcriptions reveal, she was on top of her game. "Aren't You Glad You're You," which garnered an Oscar nomination for Johnny Burke and Jimmy Van Heusen, was up-swinging and affirmative. Peggy imbued it with what seemed like sincere delight and wonder. Less poppy was Ellington's "I Let a Song Go out of My Heart," rendered with more than a little Billie Holiday. Ellington's, she told one trade magazine at the time, was her favorite band. She also liked Woody Herman's boppier stuff, like "Lemon Drop." The bopsters' stylings still annoyed her, but the music was beginning to talk to her—in particular, Charlie Parker and Dizzy Gillespie's "Cubana Bop."

She was also still a huge fan of Willard Robison's, and on the radio, she and Barbour performed Robison's languid, bluesy, yet bouncing and jaunty " 'Tain't So, Honey, 'Tain't So," a jazzy tune about appreciating the good things in life. With its typically Robisonesque storyteller's opening line—"Listen, listen, children: Nothin's as bad as it seems"—Peggy goes on to admonish, "Just be thankful for the things you have got. Don't buy a house until you've paid for the lot." Lee lays back vocally on this track; she's doing her flat-weary-black-inflection thing. The whole package adds up to two minutes and twenty-four seconds of absolute cool.

Meantime, ten days later, she laid down a "standard" for Capitol—"Ghost Riders in the Sky," and it took off. On first listen now, it seems a rigid, boring exercise in cowboy hoke. But at the time, it was an established hit, and it's an important addition to her canon, for if the jazz and blues in her would always find the most evocative expression in her songs, she was forever open to any and all genres. From the start, she was a pop singer as well as a soulful chanteuse, and when she took on "Ghost Riders"—a popular anthem for sure, a huge hit for Vaughn Monroe—she brought something distinctly Peggy to it: a mysterious, idealized spirituality. Somewhere beneath the layers of overproduction lies a very tangible hint of the mystery that the legend of cowboydom had always lent to American myth—enhanced, no doubt, by a childhood spent facing an endless Western frontier expanse.

By now, Dave could no longer be relied on to perform on the road. Gastel, and Barbour's physician, told Peggy he was not "emotionally" fit to go out, as she later recalled in her book; the doctors had told her David's drinking was "out of hand." So Gastel sent her into the outback on her own. In some of the venues, things began to get as woolly as they had when she was a teenager at the old Jade Room. Gastel booked Lee into a club in Washington—a club with a chorus line of women wearing nothing but hats, and a bubble machine. On the marquee, the food was given equal billing with her name.

Even scarier at first was a trip to St. Louis. She arrived without Barbour, and the union head threw a fit: Hire Peggy, and you're supposed to get Dave, too. She called Gastel, whose response she'd never forget: "Well, you're really in trouble." Her manager of five years was basically hanging her out to dry. So Lee called the union man, one Harold Kopler, and invited him to her suite.

"If you are not satisfied after one week," she told him, "I will work for nothing." Kopler backed down.

But she felt abandoned. "At the time," she later recalled, "we were recording a lot of things, all different ways—orchestras, small groups, whatever. David wasn't well. So my manager and David just sent me out by myself. I think that was a dirty trick. They sent me out without any music. They sent me out with arrangements for 'Golden Earrings' with big strings . . . nothing fit. I had a piano player and a drummer. I got down there, and there was a society band—three tenor saxophones.

"I thought, 'What do I do now?' But it turned out well. There was a guitarist, formerly with Benny, named Mike Bryant, who just happened to call me. I said, 'Mike! How are you! And where are you?' He said, 'I'm right here in St. Louis.' I said, 'Come down here and bring the guitar.' He said, 'I sold it.' I said, 'Borrow one. And bring a bass player.'

"And so he did. He was there within an hour, and that afternoon we put together a whole show of things with a quartet, and it was a big success—and it was thrilling to do it. We could do anything we wanted. We weren't restricted in any way; so you see they did me a good turn. Threw me in the water and let me sink or swim."

The engagement was so successful that Gastel flew in to bask in her glory.

"How did you do it?" he asked.

"*I* did not do it," she said. A higher power, she implied, was involved.

"Well," Gastel said, "could you pray to help me win a football game I have a big bet on?"

"I don't pray for bets," she told him.

"If anyone makes fun of my beliefs," Peggy would later recall, speaking of this episode specifically, "I just clam up. I just want to leave a residue of hope."

That residue of hope—of belief in something that lies beyond the physical world—says a close and lifelong friend, would underlie every moment of her life, whether it was apparent to the rest of the world or not.

The St. Louis episode was a pivotal point in Peggy's career, with all of its lessons. It taught her that from here on out, she was going to have to be able to manage her affairs on her own and would be unable to count on men—for logistical support, contractual support, emotional support, or business help. In the upcoming years, as Peggy Lee gained a reputation for being a stickler for detail—to the point of being known as a control freak of the highest order in all aspects of her life—there's no question that the "St. Louis blues," as temporary as they were, had instilled new resolve in her.

From then on, Peggy called her own shots. For now it was her name on the billing, which meant that it was she who would be held accountable for every detail, successful or failed. If later years would increasingly bring notice of her insistence on perfection, it was in St. Louis where the lesson was first driven home.

On another level, the St. Louis experience was a seminal one creatively and artistically. Within the next few years, a Peggy Lee show—whether in Ciro's on the Strip, or the Copacabana or Basin Street back east, or the Sands or the Flamingo in Vegas— would be distinguished by not only her music, but the arrangement of her shows. The order of her set lists, the specific choice of her songs, would be thought out in detail, so that each show would ride its own narrative wave; her attention to this detail was such that she kept notebooks recording the playlists of virtually every show she performed. St. Louis was the first real Peggy Lee production. Without a safety net, left to her own instincts, she'd triumphed.

Peggy came home with pneumonia, setting the pattern that would emerge again and again: a performance, a lapse in health, a recovery in bed. More and more, it was the crowds she needed for support, but the resultant high would drain her until she could get her energy back up and do it all again. The new, and forever after, cycle of Peggy Lee's life had begun. As a friend would opine, some years later, her true addiction was to the sensations she would always receive from her audience's adulation.

At home, Dave's drinking was increasingly sapping her strength. One night, as they drove home, Peg saw a policeman ahead and warned her husband. "I'll catch him," was Dave's response, and he hit the gas. Barbour's problems had intensified. His behavior was growing more and more bizarre. One night, she wrote, "he talked about insects. I suggested he close the screen. I even got an exterminator. But when the man came, David wouldn't allow him to do his work. What David did was throw a book at me. He never liked me to read."

As her marriage foundered, Peggy's fortunes at Capitol were plateauing. Her few chart hits in 1949 and 1950 included duets—with Dean Martin on "You Was," with Mel Tormé on "The Old Master Painter"—and "Bali Ha'i."

"Bali Ha'i," from the Pulitzer Prize–winning Broadway show *South Pacific,* was a rendition of a popular, enduring classic that, like "Ghost Riders," may not have been the deepest thing she ever sang, but clearly struck a metaphoric chord. There was something about this anthem that had a bit of New Age priestess to it, a glimpse of a centered place that lent a triumphant tone to her musical reading of a song that has since been sung by thousands. Perhaps it was a dose of Holmesean spirituality at work, lending a subtle sense of reassurance and inspiration to this rendering—even, on some subliminal level, a sense of healing.

For all of her adult life, friends would increasingly speak of Peggy Lee's quest for something more in her life, a pilgrimage fueled by the pains and traumas of her childhood—a journey with distinctly spiritual roots. If later years would bring changes in musical tastes that challenged her interpretive skills—the advent of rock and roll most conspicuously—she would forever be able to bring a strong spirituality to songs that aspired to inspire, no matter what the nation's current musical tastes. As one of her friends late in life, radio producer Bill Rudman, offered, "Like many artists who are damaged, she found a way to use her pain and turn it into something redeeming. She really was a deep thinker, and she was very much ahead of her time in the thinking and feeling that inspired the music making. One of the ways she tried to heal herself was by healing others—and whether or not she succeeded as her own physician, she ministered to the needs of millions." Perhaps the inspiring tones of "Bali Ha'i" underlay the song's success. Or perhaps, as history suggests, it was simply a very lovely song.

By now, the jazz singing pantheon was led, year in and year out, by Sarah Vaughan, with the usual names behind her—Ella Fitzgerald, Anita O'Day. By now, Peggy was no longer considered a jazz singer. But she was enjoying constant, big bookings, and, not yet thirty, was a veteran in all ways. "I feel younger now than I did three years ago," she said to an interviewer. "Listen, my mind or yours, or anybody's, doesn't grow any gray hairs—unless we want it to."

By the early fifties, the nascent television airwaves needed live programming, and nothing sold like a pretty face—especially a "transparent North Dakota Scandinavian complexion" topped by "beautiful ash-blond hair," in the words of one smitten writer.

More and more Americans were finding out that there was a face and a body that accompanied Peggy Lee's voice. At the time, in fact, there may not have been a sexier looking, acting, or feeling woman on the American entertainment landscape. Her earliest television appearances (an unknown date on NBC's *Hour Glass,* which is described as "the first hour-long entertainment series of any kind produced for network television" by the *Complete Directory to Prime-Time Network and Cable TV Shows; Cavalcade of Stars,* on the now-extinct Dumont network; and the 1948 Sullivan appearance) may have given audiences a hint of the lady's unusual vibe: sensual and wholesome at once; gifted with a tune and comfortable as hell in front of a camera. But on May 27, 1950, Peggy Lee made a leap into a whole new league, taking part in a night that went down in television history for a number of reasons—not the least of which was that it saw the television debut of Frank Sinatra. Sinatra turned heads that night, but he didn't eclipse the full unveiling for American audiences of Miss Peggy Lee, in all her glamour, guile, and seductiveness. The camera loved her—and the feeling was mutual.

By the spring of 1950, the radio show of one of the giants of the forties was losing its luster. Bob Hope was in a rut. With Crosby still ruling, and Jack Benny's show starting to soar, and Arthur Godfrey blanketing the sound waves, Hope was running scared. It was time to consider the fledgling medium of television, then viewed by the entertainment biggies as strictly ghetto, where center stage was commanded not by performers, but by the products that were now filling the kitchens, living rooms, and laundry rooms of the two-car-garage suburban landscape. It was one thing to hear a radio man shill a phonograph (as Bing's sidekick Ken Carpenter did on the radio, pitching the Philco 1405 record player with its Dynamic Reproducer tone arm, Scratch Eliminator, and "special tone chamber"), but it was another to stare at a refrigerator. Who in their right mind would want their honed-on-radio humor to share camera time with a lamb chop lifted by Dennis James out of a meat tray?

But General Motors called Hope with an offer he couldn't refuse: a ninety-minute special promoting GM's appliance division. And they told him to name his price. When Hope asked for $50,000, they countered with $40,000, and an offer of $150,000 total for five shows. Hope bit.

The first *Star-Spangled Revue* aired on NBC on Easter 1950. For that one show, Frigidaire forked up four times what it cost the company to sponsor an entire season of Milton Berle. What they got for their money was Hope cracking wise, Douglas Fairbanks stiltedly skitting, and Dinah Shore singing nice, predictable pop. All in all, it was an evening layered in the inoffensive. It left little artistic mark on the landscape, and a whole lot of images of large, glistening white enamel appliances.

Reviews were middling. The public was accustomed to seeing Hope on a movie screen, polished and perfect. In person, where mistakes were revealed to millions and more attention was paid to the placement of the sponsor's bulbous refrigerators than of the props for skits, Hope was something of a letdown. In trying to get a feel for "what television consisted of exactly," said John Crosby in the *New York Herald Tribune*, "[Hope] never quite succeeded." The pressure was on for Hope's second installment.

So for his second canary, Hope turned to someone with a little sex appeal: Miss Peggy Lee. Next, he chose a young singer with a teen following, a guy with a voice like velvet who had never appeared on television. The kid from Hoboken: Frank Sinatra.

Peggy's work was going to be cut out for her. The show opened with several static shots of appliances. Not even the actual appliances—*drawings* of appliances. Hope followed, looking snappy and elegant in a white dinner jacket with a black bow tie and black handkerchief. He launched into a monologue centered entirely on the subject of money, and how much everyone else was making in Hollywood: "Jolson doesn't know whether to go on NBC, or buy it." It got a good laugh, but given his own salary for the show, Hope was risking planting seeds of resentment.

But he didn't hesitate to skewer the medium that was now making him rich. "I think television is wonderful. I really do. It's bringing back vaudeville to kill it at a more convenient time." Then he turned semiserious: "It takes real courage to get your feet wet in television. I'm really glad this chap decided to take the plunge. I'm thrilled to introduce Mr. Frank Sinatra."

Sinatra, astoundingly thin, balletic in his movements, and dazzling with his smile, showed no nerves about appearing on the tube. He nailed "Come Rain or Come Shine" with a suggestion of cockiness that was in equal parts annoying and appealing. His absolute composure, performing live in front of an audience whose size he couldn't begin to guess at, made it instantly obvious that he would have no problem climbing back to the top.

After the song, he and Hope traded jokes about, of course, money. By the time the curtain peeled back on Peggy Lee—"I'm glad this next gal decided to fly in from Hollywood, because her beauty and her style of singing are an asset to any production. . . . Here she is, the great Capitol recording star, Miss Peggy Lee"— serious artistic expression didn't stand a chance.

But Lee filled the screen immediately—at home, self-assured, winkingly seductive. She had turned thirty the day before, but she looked like a twenty-two-year-old with a little too much makeup. She was wearing an off-the-shoulder chiffon gown with dangling rhinestone earrings and a similarly faux-dramatic necklace. Her hair was curled tightly to her head. Her mole had been penciled in a little too prominently, hinting of stage makeup. Oddly, she was posed sitting on a bench, as if standing would be too much of a strain, as if the frail girl needed to catch her breath. Her rendition of "Bewitched, Bothered and Bewildered" was pleasant but undistinguished—at least until the final measures, when she threw in some syncopation and jazz, but too little, too late.

The rest of the evening furnished a blur of bad, overlong comedy skits. But one skit featured Peggy—and she seized it. She played a woman trying to hook Hope into marriage, singing "It's so nice to have a man around the house." But every time Hope tried to show her the floorplans for their new dream house, another one of Peg's boyfriends showed up: a veterinarian, then a baseball player. By the end, she was surrounded by a dozen suitors. The innocent implication of it all was that Peg's character collected men like knickknacks, and liked to keep them all at bay.

But while everyone else on the show was physically stilted, Peg played her courting of Hope to the hilt, caressing his chest through his shirt, stroking his face, rubbing her cheek against his. In a landscape so sterile it numbed, her obvious physicality was hard to ignore. But getting true musical art out there on the broadcast waves was going to prove to be a Sisyphean task. Many years later, a friend told Peggy Lee that the medium was too small for her. But despite her ubiquity on the small screen for the next two decades, it wasn't the size of the screen that would forever hamper her; it was that television took away the intimacy she fed on. She was giving, but she wasn't getting anything back, and without a live, intimate audience, Peggy Lee was at a distinct handicap.

In early 1950, Peggy's father surprised her by showing up in California. They had remained close emotionally, if not physically. Peggy Lee was never heard to utter a single angry syllable about Marvin Egstrom. Logic would suggest she would have been mad at her father, for marrying an abusive woman. Those who knew her well insist that she always understood his shortcomings.

Dave was in Cuba on vacation. There is no question that Marvin's unexpected appearance was welcome. But his health was failing; he had cancer, and he coughed constantly. The impetus for the visit was clear. He was not long for this world. He had left Min behind in Millarton, where the couple now lived—and he was here to catch up.

"I just had to see you," he said.

"I was so glad to see him I started to cry," Peggy remembered.

She arranged for her doctor to examine him; he told her that her father had less than a year to live. Peggy prayed for his health. Her father assured her that her brother Milford, now married, with his own electrician's business back in Jamestown, was taking good care of him. "I stressed the importance of doing exactly as the doctor ordered. He promised he would, but I'm not sure he believed me."

She introduced him to some of her musician friends: "I went about collecting them from any source I could—musicians are always good for a laugh. He enjoyed that I had a husband who loved me. He didn't know about David's problem; I didn't tell him."

She showed him her gardens, and the jacaranda trees. She asked him "if things had ever changed" with Min—had she ever relinquished her dominance over him? Nothing had changed, he confided. But Peggy knew that the fact he'd made the trip, possibly defying his wife, spoke worlds. His affection for her was obvious: "He was so proud of my success. He was glad to see that my life had apparently turned out so well."

She put her daughter in her nurse's room and her father in Nicki's pastel bedroom. One night she heard him crying, and went in.

"I'm just realizing," he said to her, "I haven't been much of a father to you."

"Don't cry," she said. "I love you. You must have done something to make me love you the way I do."

Min called the following day. He said he had to go back. "Knowing that if Min came out it would be unpleasant for us all, he was adamant about returning," Peggy recalled.

She took him to Union Station, the huge Mission Deco terminal with its cavernous waiting rooms. With the train about to leave, she put him in a wheelchair and rolled him all the way across the tiled floors, down and up the ramps and onto the train. He was laughing the whole way.

She would see him one more time, very soon after, when fate intervened to bring her home.

Home

THE NORTH DAKOTA Winter Carnival, Valley City's annual celebration of all things agrarian, helped to nurse the state's farmers
through the winters. By 1950, the carnival was in its twelfth year,
and Val City had grown. A huge new pavilion stood proudly on
the outskirts of town, home to the indoor activities of the carnival, and the entertainment aspect had grown in stature: Lawrence
Welk, of Strasberg, North Dakota, had performed a few years
back.

Peggy flew in with Dave and three musicians: pianist Hal
Schaefer, drummer Al Stoller, and Jess Bourgeois, on a night
flight from Billings, Montana, to Fargo. "One of the musicians
said she was excited to approach Fargo," said the Valley City pa-

per account: " 'She could hardly fasten her safety belt as we pre-pared to land.' "

She was met at Hector Airport late Sunday night by a clot of VIPs including Ken Kennedy and hotelier Tom Powers, who said, for the record: "Peggy was the star of the only high school nightclub in the Northwest." At a reception at the Gardner Ho-tel, Peg regaled the crowd with "Mañana," then headed out to Valley City the next day for two days of music and festivities hosted by the town that has always liked to claim her as its own. Under the banner headline "Peggy Lee Welcomed 'Home' " (and the subhead "Twelfth Annual Show Off to Good Start with 400 in Livestock Judging Event"), the Valley City *Times-Record*'s ac-count speaks glowingly of the good time had by all: "A radiant Peggy Lee returned today to Valley City, where she received a tu-multuous welcome from the homefolks who jammed the city for the opening day of the 12th annual winter show."

The inaugural parade featured no fewer than four marching bands in snazzy uniforms, filling the town with music that went on for hours. The American Legion's maroon-and-yellow forty-man band came first, followed by the college band, and the high-school band, and the Valley City Hi-Liner band.

And then came Peggy Lee, riding high on the back of a pregnant-looking convertible, bedecked in finery that was unlike anything the people in Val City were used to seeing downtown, with a white beret and a mink coat. But despite the high-Hollywood costume, there would be no prima donna attitude on this visit. No flaunting of her success. From the moment her plane touched down, by all accounts, Peggy Lee not only acted the old North Dakota girl, but reveled in her. Unbeknownst to friends and family, her marriage was on its very last legs. But this girl was the Peggy Lee of "It's a Good Day."

As the car slowly made its way down Central Avenue, little

girls ran alongside to touch it. As she waved to the throngs, the look on her face was touching: triumph and humility coming together in a particularly wistful way.

A black-and-white photo of Peggy Lee surrounded by crowds, a strikingly evocative portrait of middle America and a girl who had lived there, ran in *Look* magazine. It was credited to *Look*'s roving photographer Stanley Kubrick, who would soon forsake still photography for motion pictures.

That night, she played the first of four shows. "Before a packed auditorium at the North Dakota Winter Show," wrote the Fargo *Forum*, "Peggy Lee held a musical get-together with the folks of her old home town last night. As she sang songs for almost an hour, she continually asked her audience, 'What do you want next?'"

Despite the premier lodgings available at the Rudolph Hotel, Peggy accepted an invitation to stay at the home of her old friend Belle May Ginsberg, the piano player from KVOC, now reunited with the girl who'd left town heading westward so long ago. Peggy treated Belle the way you're supposed to treat old friends, recalls Belle's daughter. But Dave was clearly a little disconcerted at the reception held in the home of Mr. and Mrs. Herbert Stern and attended by governor Fred Aandahl.

Dave pretended to enjoy the buffet. He stood there in his gray pinstriped suit and black turtleneck, sporting a handkerchief and holding a cigarette, in front of a table laden with cakes, cookies, and pastries. He looked like a cross between Cary Grant and Rod Serling—a strikingly handsome guy, cool as hell, who was about as comfortable in a musty North Dakota parlor as Nathan Detroit at a christening.

Peggy and Belle May entertained at the piano, and then Dave—the man who had wanted to make his avant-garde music accessible even to the people in Fargo—sat at the keyboard as the governor did his best to hold his own in a duet with Peg. "I hope he's a good governor," Dave deadpanned.

"She was no celebrity," read *The Forum*'s account of the fete. "She was just a girl coming home for a visit, with a husband she wanted the folks back home to know and like. And like him they did. He's quiet, with a sly sense of humor, and he entered right into the evening's fun."

Not everyone agreed with *The Forum*'s sunny assessment of hubby Dave.

"Her husband wasn't exactly attuned to North Dakota," recalls Lois Brier, whose husband owned the Hotel Rudolph at the time. "At one time, Peggy Lee had sung in the Rudolph dining room. When she came back for the carnival, she stopped in, of course, to see Howard and everything, and when she left, apparently she was going on to Wimbledon.

"She got into a truck and her husband made a rather nasty remark about her mink coat riding in a truck. Somebody said, 'You'll probably see more mink coats riding in North Dakota, sir, than anywhere else.'

"He did not like the sticks. But she understood us."

After the final show, on Tuesday night, Peggy and Dave went separate ways. Dave and his band caught a Soo train back to Fargo to fly out the next day, while Peggy went east to visit her father. Mother Nature was not as welcoming as the homefolks had been, and the snows were heavy. The *Forum* told the tale of her visit home beneath the headline "Peggy Lee Braves Blizzard in Truck to See Father": "Valley City—Peggy Lee, following her fourth performance at the North Dakota Winter Show before a packed house Tuesday night, left in a blizzard in a farm truck driven by her brother Milford (Mel) Egstrom for the bedside of her father, ill with cancer at the home near Millarton. Milford

Egstrom explained he brought the truck for it was necessary to drive through fields to avoid drifts and the truck provided the only sure means of getting Peggy to the bedside of her father. Peggy's husband, Dave Barbour, with his quartet, was able to make a late Soo train out of Valley City after the show."

That night, on her final visit with her father, Peggy read the Twenty-third Psalm aloud. "I never understood that until now," her father said. Then, as she recounted in her memoir, he told her, "I don't want you to come back when I go. You go on and do what you're doing. Maybe folks won't understand, but *we* know, honey, and that's all that matters."

Peggy returned to Fargo to fly home. That day's *Forum* offered a final story about Peggy's visit: "Peggy Lee put on a great show," said a Valley City businessman who was with her through a series of receptions and appearances in the stock barns, homes, and restaurants, with cameras continuously flashing from the time of the arrival of the plane in Fargo late Sunday night until the farm truck rumbled out into the blizzard on Tuesday. "But where Peggy proved herself a truly great person was through her graciousness and thoughtfulness and kindness to others. She is truly humble. Her great success has not made her forget the struggle she made to get to the top. She was on her toes day and night, and tried very hard to remember each acquaintance after an absence of a dozen years."

"It was a wonderful, warm reception," Lee later wrote. "I had not realized that the people in North Dakota cared so much about their homegrown girl singer."

On April 26, 1950, seven weeks later, Marvin Egstrom died. He was seventy-four.

"Relatives were informed last night," wrote *The Forum* two days later in announcing the passing, "that Miss Lee and her husband would return for the funeral."

Actually, Peggy did not go back home. Her sister Marianne attended, with her husband.

Services were held at St. John's Lutheran Church. Marvin Egstrom was buried at Highland Home cemetery outside Jamestown, on a bluff overlooking the river, with a breathtaking view of hill, dale, rill, and river. And, winding its way along the bank of the river, a railroad track.

Peggy had enough to worry about in California. She tried to get Dave into Alcoholics Anonymous, but he refused to join the program, although Peggy mentions in her book that she was able to persuade him to "entertain the members. . . . Ironically, I later learned that some of the members thought I was the alcoholic."

The imminent demise of her marriage led Peggy to take the next logical step in her career. In the late forties, she'd been approached by MGM at least twice about film roles, but things hadn't worked out. Now, Bing got her onto the silver screen for the first time since her uncredited turns in *Stage Door Canteen* and the now-lost *The Powers Girl*. He was able to do so, she later said, in a remarkably revelatory wire-service interview, because she had finally realized that she and Dave were finished.

"One of the reasons I didn't want to do movies was that I was married," she told Bob Thomas, the Associated Press's movie critic, a few years later. "I was already involved in too many things. I knew that if I added movies to them, it might be the last straw that would break up the marriage. As it was, the marriage broke up anyway."

What she told Thomas next, though, was even more striking: In one paragraph, she offered nothing less than the key to the entire journey she'd taken, from the town hall of Nortonville to the sound stage at Paramount Pictures.

"Another reason was that I just couldn't face [the movie cameras]. Getting up there before an audience had always been torture for me. I guess I've always been shy. I always had to give myself a pep talk before I went out to sing. I said to myself that if I gave in, and didn't meet the challenge, that I wouldn't be able to do anything in life."

No doubt, Bing's presence as the star of the otherwise lackluster *Mr. Music* provided incentive enough for Peggy to meet the next challenge. It wasn't a tough one. The movie, a showbiz flick based on the hoary "Let's Put On a Show" device, featured Bing as a talented but lazy songwriter with a penchant for golf and the horses. His young assistant and romantic interest—an actress named Nancy Olson, less than half Bing's age, which was forty-seven at the time—insists he get back on track and write a musical. Spiced by a score by Johnny Burke and Jimmy Van Heusen, *Mr. Music* was character actor Richard Haydn's third directing job, and thankfully, it would be his last. By now, Bing was getting a little long in the tooth to be convincing as a rake who could attract a college kid.

The whole thing was a forgettable affair, except for one five-minute slice of High Entertainment featuring Bing, Peggy, and the world-class husband-and-wife dancing team of Marge and Gower Champion—two Los Angeles natives who by now were becoming the successors to Astaire and Rogers. To movie audiences, they seemed to float on air.

The rehearsals for the penthouse entertainment scene gave Marge Champion ample time to observe Miss Lee. The granddaughter of a London butcher, Champion had grown up two blocks from Hollywood High and spent a considerable chunk of her childhood in her father's dancing school observing the likes of Shirley Temple, the Lloyd kids, and Joan Crawford.

"It was one of the first things Gower actually staged for a movie," Marge Champion recalls, "and [Peggy] couldn't have been more agreeable about anything. But she was, I think, a very shy person—the shyness that usually comes from a kind of fear of being found out about something. I always felt that people who are really stars, they have a secret. And it was always as if she wasn't one to flaunt her sexiness, but somehow you felt that she had a deep, deep secret. She'd smile and do everything that was required of the song, but she really was gifted with stardust, and that to me is having a secret, and there's no way to get anybody to share it, but you've got it inside, and it comes through in the performance."

Marge's husband was a perfectionist of the first order, and Peggy had no trouble taking instruction from someone as determined about the details as she herself was. Another thing Marge noticed about Peggy was her careful enunciation of the lyrics. You could hear every syllable—"and you understood the meaning behind the lyric. It's not just to say the word. It's to use the eyes, or whatever you use, to make it mean something else. The meaning behind the word. The subtext."

The setting was Paul Merrick's penthouse apartment, with the requisite grand piano, and a terrace where, beyond sliding doors, the city beckons glowingly. Dozens of tuxedoed and sequined society types have gathered to hear some of the tunes from the show Paul is writing. We've just heard a nondescript ballad sung by Paul from an easy chair, to the accompaniment of an uncomfortable-looking Dave Barbour on acoustic guitar, when Peggy approaches from the crowd, wearing a black sequined off-the shoulder gown. Clothes were a fifties woman's vocabulary, and Peggy spoke volumes with this gown. Her figure filled it nicely—though there was at this point not an extra ounce of flesh on her—but her body language suggested discomfort. Her shoulders were hunched, and instead of animating her, this splendid costume, wrapped around a posture that was far less confident than she had shown on Hope's show, projected a distinct sense of unworthiness.

But now the blazered Paul shushed the crowd: "Quiet, every-body: You're about to hear Peggy Lee give one of these tunes the A treatment. Peggy and I have made a little deal here which we hope will produce something fairly electric"—and the spotlight was on her. She seized the screen, a woman at home in a party full of people, all of them well rehearsed in looking as though they were having a good time. This was the kind of party that some part of Peggy had wanted to attend for a long, long time. Back home, she liked cooking for the musicians, the radio crews. But in the coming years, she would come to enjoy—even to need—the company of the A-list, too.

As she and Bing launch into the quite engaging "Life Is So Peculiar," Dave is playing the guitar off to her side. But—symbolically, perhaps—all that is visible on camera is his left hand, fretting the chords on the neck of his guitar.

The Burke lyrics fashion light, nonsensical wordplay around a message that espouses, once again, the theme that Peggy and Bing seemed so often to have in common: Don't worry. Be happy. Despite the curveballs life throws your way, it "doesn't pay to com-plain . . . Life is so peculiar but you can't stay home and brood."

Peggy and Bing's chemistry was undeniable—not alluring or flirtatious, just pro-to-pro. Their number was followed by the dance routine choreographed by Gower Champion: the husband and wife hopping from the top of the piano, to the easy chair, to the terrace, to the edge of the terrace. Marge and Gower twirling on the awning poles, Marge's skirt billowing in perfect time. Marge and Gower skipping up the stairs and down. Gower is ath-letic beyond belief, but graceful as well—part Astaire's artistry, part Kelly's exuberance. Marge keeps perfect pace.

Other than the dance number, Peggy's duet with Bing was the highlight of the film. It seemed to promise a career that knew no limits. But Peggy Lee would never again share a movie screen with anyone even close to her own talent. Life is so peculiar, indeed.

Marge Champion remembers one more thing.

"I never, ever saw her without her eyelashes on."

In the fall of 1950, Peggy was performing in Las Vegas when a handsome action-picture actor named Robert Preston approached her after a show. He was a trained musician, gifted on several instruments, who had turned to acting in high school. After more than a dozen roles in Westerns, thrillers, and war movies, his career had seemed to peak.

He was also married, and his opening gambit was probably meant innocently enough: He'd been a pilot stationed in England during the war, he said. He'd heard her singing.

"I've got to tell you," he said, "I thought you were black. Can you imagine what a surprise it was to see this blond Scandinavian walk out when they announced you?"

A pilot. A pilot who was handsome and charming. Who understood the jazz in her. "When I first saw that face," she would later write, "I knew it meant trouble. But there was no room for cheating in my book."

Peggy continued to appear on the covers of magazines, including the October 1950 issue of *Metronome,* which coincided with her two-week stint at the Paramount, where she appeared with Dave's quartet and Harry Edison on the trumpet. On the *Metronome* cover, she smiles gorgeously next to the husband who looks handsome and snappy in jacket, tie, and French cuffs. The cause for the happiness was Dave's quartet's record, *Mambo Jambo,* a hit for Capitol.

In the *Metronome* interviews, both husband and wife spoke of their musical philosophies. They shared a love of a place where progressive sound and sentimental themes could find common ground. Barbour comes off as opinionated, cocksure, and compelling: once again, anything but shy when discussing the music. Barbour's riff, panning Stan Kenton's big band and praising the talent of jazzman Charlie Barnet, made it clear that his own tastes still lay in the progressive. (He praises Serge Koussevitzky, the Boston Symphony conductor known for his love of pushing the orchestral envelope.) But he confessed that some day he wanted a big band of his own—not to play concerts, but to make people *dance:* "I like to see people out there on the floor having a ball, and have a band that jumps," he said.

Meantime, Peggy, in a low-cut gown, was looking sexy as hell in the accompanying spread. At age thirty, she already had a few wrinkles, but they only emphasized her now classic beauty. (Not surprisingly, the article's accompanying photo made her décolletage very inviting.) For her part, Miss Lee took the time to praise the singing of Billie Holiday, the songwriting of Willard Robison, and the unashamed sentimentality of Sinatra, whose music she found refreshingly unmacho: "He has a sort of neuter gender feeling that's very appealing," she said—a startlingly enlightened thing for a wife and mother to say on the cusp of the most socially conservative decade the twentieth century would see.

"I once wrote something called 'For People Who Are Not Sentimental,' proving that everybody really is," Peggy said. "Those who don't show it very often have a great deal [more] of it in them than others, because they've shoved it down all the time."

And then, shifting into the second-person singular, she offered the magazine's readers a rare glimpse into the bashful little girl still inside her, and the journey she'd taken thus far: "It started when you were a little kid and ran eagerly to show something you had," she said of herself. "The grownups laughed at you, and if they laughed often enough you made a vow to yourself to shut the door and never let them see inside of you anymore."

On New Year's Day 1951, Peggy hooked up with a comrade in goofiness. The collaboration would be a fruitful one for the next ten years: two stars in the mainstream spotlight, but hardly mainstream themselves. Steve Allen, one of the most voraciously curious Renaissance minds in twentieth-century media, was already pushing walls, envelopes, and anything else he could find.

On her first appearance on his show, Peggy Lee, still a television novice, sang a simple, effective version of "Danny Boy," delivered on a set designed to resemble a moor. The featured guest was a manicurist from the nearby Astor Hotel: typical of Allen's anarchic, kid-in-a-candy-store approach to his medium. Anything was allowed, and his free-associative, spontaneous shtick and off-the-wall sensibility spoke worlds about the era: Cool was still allowed, odd was not shunned.

Offstage, like Peggy, Steve Allen was extremely shy. "He'd be most happy if you invited him to a party and let him play the piano," recalls Leonard Stern, a writer on the show and a lifelong friend. "That way, he wouldn't have to talk to anyone." As the lead writer on the show, Stern had an office adjoining Allen's, but when Allen had something to suggest, he'd write Stern a memo rather than walk next door.

Onstage, Allen was anything but reserved. With his hair slicked back, dressed in a short-sleeved shirt and a sweater vest, he looked like George Reeves as Clark Kent, without the muscular build. After one of Peggy's numbers, he performed a rendition of "The Sheik of Araby" by clicking his fingernails. At every point, his offhand patter bordered on the downright strange. And the second Allen turned his hand over to the frumpy workingwoman who was to manicure his nails, he was flying without a net:

"Sometimes my nails get so long," he told his sparse live studio audience, "when I make a fist, I slash my wrist." No one laughed. He was undeterred. "This is cream polish," she said, dipping his hand into a bowl. "It's always very nice to have your cream polished, I always say," Allen replied, clearly ad-libbing. This time the audience laughed, a little.

When Peg crossed the stage, she said, "Hello, Stevie," and the easy rapport between the two was unmistakable. They would never be close friends, according to Steve's wife, Jayne Meadows, but they were simpatico. Peggy would appear frequently on his show: two curious minds, shy but extraordinarily creative.

That day, her slightly swingy but mostly unadventurous performance of "Danny Boy" was competent, if a little unusual; nothing about her vibe, at this point in her career, would suggest she should be singing a weepy Celtic classic, wearing a plaid dickey buttoned to her neck, on a set that included a fake rock and, in silhouette, an anonymous bagpipe player behind her. Perhaps, on this occasion, Peggy had reason for weepiness. Dave and Peggy had now decided to part formally. The separation would be announced in April. By her own later account Dave had asked her for the divorce, telling her, "Remember, it wasn't you. It was [the] bottle."

"The escalation of my career, the move to Denslow, the endless personal appearances, recording, promotional work, must have been too much for David, and who should have understood that better than I?" she would write in *Miss Peggy Lee*. "Finally, because David loved Nicki, and I didn't want her to see him drunk, he begged me for a divorce. I agreed, broken-hearted. When I explained to Nicki that we loved her, and each other, she seemed to understand." Those who know Nicki Foster now maintain that she has never blamed her father for any untoward behavior.

Thirty years later, in her Broadway musical, in which she would narrate the events of her life to a musical score, Peg would describe this juncture of her life as one in which Dave was "in trouble with his drinking" and realizing "he's going to the bottom." In a symbolic gesture, she says, Dave took the strings off five guitars: "He is saying in effect he is through with music."

The Valley City newspaper's April dispatch changed the story slightly: "Songstress Peggy Lee, who spent her girlhood at Wimbledon, and made her first singing appearance in Valley City before skyrocketing to fame, is seeking a separation from Dave Barbour. A United Press dispatch from New York reported her saying she will take up residence in Las Vegas, Nevada, next month to obtain a friendly divorce."

One month later, the caption in the Fargo *Forum*, accompanying a photograph of a downglancing, clearly distraught Peggy, read thus: "The former Fargo girl told the court her husband had told her he no longer loved her. The blonde Peggy had charged cruelty." There is no further explanation of the cruelty; presumably, it referred to the drinking. This is the only intimation that Barbour's request had anything to do with something other than his alcoholism.

The caption accompanying the AP wire photo on May 16, 1951, injected a little humor: "Shapely Peggy Lee sang, 'He didn't love me anymore'—to a superior court judge. She had stated, reported the wire service, 'His wanting freedom caused her to lose weight and become emotionally upset.'"

They had been married for just over eight years. They would remain close friends, and Dave would be an attentive and kind father to Nicki until his death in 1965.

As her contract with Capitol came up for renewal, Peggy was worried about losing her label, too. For starters, Johnny Mercer, her champion, had ceased involvement with Capitol several years earlier. For another, according to music writer Will Friedwald, in his liner notes to a collection of Peggy's Capitol singles some years later, "Capitol was taking her for granted," which was confirmed by Alan Livingston, then a Capitol executive and later its president, who acknowledged that this was indeed the case. Livingston recalled that Lee hadn't scored any big hits for the label since "Mañana," and Capitol complacently assumed that her renewal was routine. And while Capitol's in-house magazine did feature her on its May 1951 cover, according to the April 6, 1951, issue of *Down Beat*, she had "lapsed into a rather languid vein during the past few years"—although her latest single, a rendition of Benny Carter's "Rock Me to Sleep," had "injected a spark." Lee graced the influential magazine's cover two weeks later, with the release of another single featuring "The Cannonball Express" and "That Ol' Devil," an original Barbour-Lee composition. But again, the message sent by the magazine's writer was mixed. On "The Cannonball Express" the verdict was this: "Lee is on the warpath, and she's hip: She's got a jumpin' crew under Dave Barbour's direction"—but "Devil" was judged "a vapid original" and the critic added: "Nothing happens on this one."

A little added perspective is necessary, though; it was not as if she had disappeared completely. While her hits diminished in quantity after 1949, a year in which she placed four songs on the charts (in 1950, she had two songs on the charts; in 1951, she cracked the Top Fifteen once), her peers were faring no better. Sinatra had hit a fallow patch, too, while the lighter-weight popsters like Rosemary Clooney and Frankie Laine were enjoying success. Still, she was no longer at the forefront commercially, or the cutting-edge artistically.

Now, against the backdrop of this tapestry of emotional turmoil, Peggy Lee stepped forward artistically. It was all quite evocative of a quote she had once given to George Simon: Life is "a big turmoil. To make progress, you have to make a mess." After the death of her father, the divorce from Dave, and the end of her relationship with Capitol, Peggy met the challenge and strode forward to a new place, to a new, higher ground. The world of popular music was a fractured landscape. The pop scene felt fallow and far too safe. The avant-garde insisted on cutting too dangerous an edge. The field was wide open and ready and eager for a voice that could transcend both camps—could sing of blues and dark places and complicated emotions, and could couch them in song that could enthrall the masses.

Over the next several years, the girl from the flatlands would claim a territory all to herself—not a safe place, but a shifting ground, where anything and everything was not only possible, but probable.

Lovers

THE MUSIC COMING out of the radio speaker is a snazzy, slickly orchestrated instrumental version of "It's a Good Day" as rendered by the orchestra of Russ Case, a bandleader/trumpeter whose chief claim to fame was having conducted for Perry Como in the forties. The voice of the announcer belongs to a man whose name has been lost in the mists of history, but on July 15, 1951, there is a buoyancy to his energetic tones: He has happiness to impart to a nation huddled by its Philco speakers: "Yes, it's the girlfriend, Peggy Lee, brought to you by the makers of Rexall drug products and ten thousand independent Rexall druggists. . . . You've got a date with Peggy Lee!"

Well, she was single again—why not tempt millions of American men with a radio date? When Rexall gave Peggy her own show on CBS, a few months after her divorce was final, it was no surprise to anyone. Between her guest-star turns with Crosby and Durante, she'd made dozens of radio appearances. Though the new show was at first an unadventurous fifteen minutes, it was a great listen.

If the song lists were conventional—radio wasn't the place for risk-taking—Peggy's flirty, comfortable personality was far from the run-of-the-mill, girl-next-door type. Often, as was the case on this show with guest star Benny Goodman, her come-on at the start of the broadcast was, well, definitely a come-on: "*Hell-ohh,*" she breathed, as the strains of "Good Day" waned, as though she'd just opened the door to an old friend.

"You're right there, and I'm right here, and all we're missing is a song. And in just two bars, we'll have that," she told listeners on Benny night, before launching into a standard—"If I Could Be with You"—replete with plenty of jazz flourishes. Given the circumstances, the lyrics in the second verse may have carried some extra meaning: If the narrator could spend just "one hour a night" with her man, she's "telling you true" she'd "be anything but blue."

Equally double-edged was a bittersweet "Make the Man Love Me," from the 1951 stage musical *A Tree Grows in Brooklyn*—a song (written by Arthur Schwartz and Dorothy Fields) she inexplicably never recorded, but evoked with bittersweet undertones on the air.

Lee's patter between songs was light and frothy, but when she introduced Goodman, she clearly wanted to add some gravitas. Benny's more recent fame had never equaled what he'd enjoyed with Peggy. With the death of swing and the fracturing of jazz, Benny was still a living legend, but his days of dominating the scene were over.

"It's a real thrill," she said, "for me to introduce my special guest for today. We don't get serious often on this show, but about this fellow—I guess I learned more from him than anyone else in the business. I got my first big break from him. It's my old boss, Benny Goodman!"

"Can I move right in and make myself at home?" Benny asked.

"Benny," she said, "it's your home, your band, your tune, your clarinet, your time."

Goodman was determined to serve notice that his chops hadn't waned. To make his point, he chose a Mel Powell instrumental called "Clarinade," written to show off his dexterity. At the end of the half hour, he was back for a sweet, melancholy, truly sad and soulful rendition of Gordon Jenkins's "Goodbye," which for virtually his whole career years was his sign-off song.

A few months later, Peggy was back in New York—at the Copacabana, a glittery, large, noisy club that drew A-list folk, but which was never a big favorite locale of the musicians. Unfortunately, Peggy was not herself; she seemed at loose ends, at least according to a reporter from *The New York Herald-Tribune*. She'd flown in on a red-eye and lost some luggage. The reporter described her as "nervous as a cat. Her hands tremble, she puffs incessantly on a cigarette, holds herself under control with visible effort." The writer attributed her state to "overwork. She has a schedule that would kill a coal miner." She'd risen at ten, had orange juice and coffee for breakfast, then a sandwich at the smoky rehearsal hall. Business meetings, press interviews, and other obligations led to a last-minute run-through at seven. The show ended at nine. Wound up, meeting sponsors and VIPs down on the floor, she was up all night and had scrambled eggs at a local place at five in the morning. She got to sleep at six, only to start the whole thing up again just hours later. The next day, a cinder somehow found its way into her eye, and she had to wear an eye patch all day long, until right before the show: "A murderous routine. Why does she go through with it? Well, maybe it's that $8,000 a week. Wouldn't you?"

The Copa gig included a playlist that, characteristically, spanned the musical spectrum. This was a woman not enslaved by the current *Billboard* rankings. On any given night, scattered in among the Gershwins (" 'S Wonderful") and other standards (Gerald Marks and Seymour Simons's "All of Me") were some interesting diversions, including "La Vie en Rose" and Willard Robison's "A Woman Alone with the Blues."

One night, songwriter Sonny Burke caught the Copa show. A former vibes player from Scranton, Burke had gotten his big break arranging for Jimmy Dorsey, then headed back east, where he began conducting and doing arrangements for Decca. The label, of course, was always on the lookout for new talent. Peggy's contract with Capitol was almost up. It was a fortuitous evening. When Burke, a well-known arranger for several bands, saw Peggy Lee that night in the very late night hours in one of Manhattan's most glamorous and popular nightclubs, he saw one of the purest stage expressions of sexuality that modern music had yet produced.

The Latin groove had been a mainstream of the club scene for a long time on the West Coast. Hot L.A. clubs like the Mocambo, the Troc, and Ciro's had been featuring Xavier Cugat, a Spanish bandleader so unrestrainedly expressive that he was given to leaving his podium to take gals for a spin on the dance floor. Cuban bandleader Desi Arnaz was also helping fuel Southern California's Latin vibe, and the jazz known as "Cubop" could be found around town, too.

Peggy Lee had layered conventional pop with a Latin bounce before, of course—notably with "Mañana." There was no doubting her affinity for a Latin beat. But "Lover," her first post-Dave single, took Latin to a place no one had ever dreamed. A waltz by

Richard Rodgers and Lorenz Hart first heard in the landmark film musical *Love Me Tonight,* in 1932, the song had been a nice hit for Capitol two years earlier, featuring Les Paul on guitar. Their version was sweet, something you could skate to, maybe. But Peggy heard a different song in her head. Capitol didn't. They refused to let her record it.

Her inspiration for this unique arrangement lay in a French film from 1935 called *La Bandera,* starring Jean Gabin. "He had joined the French Foreign Legion because his girlfriend had treated him badly," Lee recalled in her autobiography. "As his regiment was riding out into the desert he waved a banner to change the gait of the horses. It struck me as I was watching that it could be the change of a musical key: Raising the key would have the effect of seeming to go faster. Then the rest of the idea came: The gait of the horses resembled Latin rhythms. Then I thought, 'All I need is a song that goes with that rhythm.' "

Lee's arrangement transformed "Lover" into a frenzy-inducer. But it wasn't just the hurtling tempo or the beat of the drums that was special: The song marked the first time that Peggy used her extraordinary time to maximum heart-stopping effect. As the beat increased, growing trickier and faster, she never lost it, though she played with it mercilessly.

If there was just one thing that everyone who worked with Peggy Lee over the next forty years would agree upon, it was that her time and rhythm were as precise as anyone's who ever sang a note. It was as if she was gifted with an inner metronome that allowed her to hear the beat without fail, without flaw—a gift that would inform every level of her success in the fifties. Her answer to the conformity of the decade was a kind of rhythmic rebellion; year after year she would find new ways to play with the beat, to find it in places no one else would have dreamed of looking.

In "Lover," she made her listeners wait, coming in about a half measure after ordinary ears might have sensed that she should;

then she caught up with the rest of the band. For most of the song, she didn't sing a syllable in time with the band. She stretched and corralled the beat, playing with it like a kitten with a yarn ball—but by the end of each measure, of each chorus, of each line, she was somehow right in time. Add the gown and the brilliant blond coif, and Sonny Burke was hooked. Both he and Decca executive Milt Gabler were overpowered by what she did with the song.

Burke and Gabler asked for more than an encore; they asked for Lee's signature on a Decca contract.

"Can I record 'Lover'?" she asked.

"You come with me," Gabler said, "and you can record whatever you want."

The new collaboration would produce, over the next five years, nine singles in the Top Thirty, and the LP that many consider the greatest female jazz-vocal album of all time.

On April 28, 1952, Peggy Lee went into Liederkranz Hall, where she'd worked with Benny eight years earlier. Last time, she'd had to climb over Lou McGarity on a pile of crates. This time, the recording problems were somewhat different. The label had brought in Gordon Jenkins's complete, string-heavy orchestra. Liederkranz was acoustically ideal for sound that was, as the players said, "heavy on the mice," or strings—a direction that mainstream pop arrangements were taking at the beginning of the Eisenhower era. Producing the session was the famed Morty Palitz, a former Columbia exec whom she'd first met when she was singing at the Buttery.

Peggy wasn't looking for mice that day at Liederkranz; she had brought in eight percussionists—at her own expense. The arrangement called for each verse to ascend, as the metaphoric horses started to gallop, by a half note each time. Her voice would grow in intensity and rise in pitch with each verse.

When Peggy listened to the first takes, it was everything she'd hoped for: a wild, full-throated mambo-samba ride on a bucking bronco. But there was a problem: Her voice couldn't be heard. Liederkranz's soaring nineteenth-century space absorbed Jenkins and the percussion; Peggy had vanished. They spent three hours trying to balance the sound. Nothing worked. Back at her apartment, she burst into tears.

A few hours later, the phone rang. Palitz told her he thought they had a solution. When she got to the studio the next day, she was led away from the orchestra into an isolation booth and given earphones. They gave it another shot. The following day, it finally worked. Peggy's voice jumped off the recording: higher and faster and higher and faster and higher and faster, ending with a rushing, falling-off climax of the single word "Lo-ver," ending on a discordant note.

As one of her future lovers would observe, Peggy's performance of the song sounded like a woman achieving orgasm. She had created a headfirst anthem of sex, need, desire, and earthiness. The song sold a quarter-million records in the first two weeks. It hit Number Three. Sales eventually topped a million for her new label. Other singers were using the strings and lush orchestrations to play it safe; Peggy's "Lover" was a fast freight, hurtling.

Another notable audience member at the Copa gig was her old pal Robert Preston. The sparks that had briefly flown in Vegas were reignited. "We both had a problem," Peggy would later write, in a brief, charmingly purple passage in her book that did not actually name the man in question. The dilemma was obvious: Preston was married, but Peggy and he couldn't help themselves.

"I was really on my own now, and he came to see me at the Copa. He walked me all the way home, and we weren't even aware of the cold. The emotion between us was so strong it held us in that wonderful spell that can't bear to be broken. . . .

"He wanted to be married. I wanted to be married. He'd been separated for some time, and I had rationalized that it was all right. My divorce from David was final. Nicki fell in love with him, too. Every Tuesday night was their night out, and I was not allowed to go: the Plaza, or the Tavern on the Green. He would carry her piggyback. He took me to the races and baseball games. We went to the opening nights of *The King and I* and *My Fair Lady*. We dined at Danny's Hideaway almost every night. Then we would finish our evening with a few sets at the Embers and listen to Red Norvo.

"We drove in the country. We planned to be married in Greenwich. He bought me an antique wedding band. I'd meet him every night at the Henry Hudson Theater.

"He went back to California to ask his wife for a divorce. But he didn't get the divorce. He offered to give up everything he had ever made, but his wife told him that wasn't enough. We separated, and I went into shock."

The relationship, of course, was doomed. Preston would never leave his wife; their marriage would last until his death in 1987.

"They were mad for each other," says Phoebe Jacobs, the former publicist at Basin Street East who became a close friend of Peggy's. Jacobs's assessment is echoed by others who knew them both. It was Peggy, Jacobs says, who talked Preston into taking a role in a musical even though he'd never seriously sung on the stage. Ultimately, Preston's performance in *The Music Man*, in which he starred as the legendary con man Professor Harold Hill, earned him high accolades and was the highlight of his stage and film careers—thanks, in part, to Peggy's personal vocal coaching in preparation for his appearance on Broadway.

Lee's decision not to publish Preston's name in her memoir thirty years later suggests discretion about it all, but during their whirlwind New York romance, she was photographed with Preston in very public places. If she had any deep ambivalence about interfering in Preston's marriage—he had been married for only five or six years—she didn't show it at the time. "I was so in love with him," she wrote, "nothing mattered."

The Preston relationship, which would last on and off for years, represented one of her true loves—and one of her true friendships. That it couldn't work may have had something to do with the intensity of her devotion and commitment. This was a woman whose idea of love was all-consuming. In any and all of her meaningful relationships, she wanted control, and she needed it. Anything short of complete, mutual devotion would never be enough.

As life progressed, and she was on her own more, it was increasingly harder for her to be that woman alone.

I've never enjoyed hearing my music performed more than I have on this occasion," read the telegram Richard Rodgers sent to Peggy. More famously, he was said to moan, "Oh, my little waltz." Later, he seemed more amused. "I don't know why Peggy picked on my little song," he said, "when she could have fucked up 'Silent Night.'" For most listeners, the song was nothing short of a revelation. No one had heard anything like it. Critics weighed in from coast to coast. One said that "Lover" "achieves the highest degree of pure sensuality ever projected into a song." Another listener pretty much erased any doubt that Peggy, in her first effort without Dave, had landed smack on the cutting edge: *Down Beat* ranked "Lover" the fourth most popular record of 1952, behind Jo Stafford's "You Belong to Me" and two by Nat Cole—"Somewhere Along the Way" and "Unforgettable."

Not content to revolutionize music, Peggy had now grown so confident in her artistic muse that she began to read poetry on her radio show in 1952. On this incarnation of the show, Russ Case's orchestra had been replaced by a more talented, adventurous ensemble—the Sonny Burke Orchestra. While the intro was still "It's a Good Day," bongos were included now. It had moved forward, jazzward, coolward, about a thousand miles.

"Hello there, you . . . and you . . . and you, too," she said, opening one show, as if using a come-hither finger curl on all of us.

"Hi, Peggy," responded Bob, the straight man. "You know, we've been getting a lot of mail on your poetic introductions to songs. Have one tonight?"

"Yes, I have, Bob. This is by William Butler Yeats:

> *"The cry of a child by the roadway,*
> *The creak of a lumbering cart,*
> *Are all in your image that blossoms . . .*
> *A rose in the deeps of my heart."*

Say what? Yeats on feel-good radio? But she knew exactly what she was doing: After she finished the poem, she launched into a lovely rendition of her old standard "These Foolish Things," a composition full of similarly bittersweet images that, if slightly short of Yeats, were definitely in a comparable vein: daffodils, candlelight, silk stockings, and "the sigh of midnight trains in empty stations." But the most evocative image of these lyrics (written by Holt Marvell, Jack Stachey, and Harry Link) would echo for the rest of Peggy's days: "Oh, how the ghost of you clings./These foolish things remind me of you."

Peggy Lee loved words—lyrics, poetry, character sketches. "Lover" may have shown her way with a beat, but again and again she proved that much of her success stemmed from her appreciation of the beauties and subtleties of language. Put it all together and you have an artist now at the height of her powers, and poised to show her strength and independence.

After finishing her radio shows for the season, Peggy headed back east; she'd put together a great new band and was ready to hit the clubs again. On board were drummer Larry Bunker and three Woody Herman veterans: Joe Mondragon on bass, Pete Candoli on trumpet, and the astounding Jimmy Rowles on piano. Lee and Rowles had worked together for five months back in 1942 with Benny, each trying to push the jazz envelope as far as swing would let it go. Ten years later, they would have no restraints to overcome, and their work knew no boundaries.

A native of Spokane, the son of a woman who played jazz piano by ear, Jimmy Rowles had moved to Los Angeles to work in the jazz clubs of Central Avenue with Slim and Slam, the jazz-vaudeville act of Slim Gaillard and Slam Stewart. Later he would team up with Lester "Prez" Young, the hall-of-fame tenor-sax man who'd played with Benny Moten, Fletcher Henderson, and, in Kansas City in 1936, Count Basie. (It was Young who later opined of Jimmy Rowles, "I worked with that gray boy at Billy Berg's. You don't have to tell him anything. He always knows where you're going." Praise came no higher than the kudos of Prez.)

Rowles joined Peggy full time in 1951, and he had a great deal in common with his new chanteuse. Like her, he had a wild wit, and his musical tastes were wide-ranging. He'd had the privilege of playing keyboard for the *Ebony Concerto,* which Igor Stravinsky had written for Woody Herman's band in 1946. He would later be called, by Carmen McRae, "the guy every girl singer in her right mind would love to work with."

Lee's decision to hire Rowles as her musical director speaks worlds of her own personal tastes, for he was purely and simply a jazz man. For Rowles, Lee represented the chance to work again with Mondragon, the bass player who had also played with Herman in 1946. Another part of the lure for Jimmy was the big money she'd promised him. But of course, there was also

Peggy Lee's charm: He hadn't had anyone pay that much attention to him, he would later reminisce in an unpublished biography written by jazz writer and photographer Tad Hershorn, "in a
long, long time." So he packed up his California house and
moved his family east. While his wife and son stayed with her sister up in Massachusetts, he worked with Peggy in New York.

But they stumbled at the start. She worked the band hard, he
would recall, and paid them little—a reflection not of miserliness,
but of her lifelong insistence that she spare no expense for her
shows. She spent her money on the best arrangements, the best
clothes, the best producers. Even at eight grand per week, the
take was spread thin. And, Rowles discovered, she expected from
everyone else the extreme loyalty, perfectionism, and commitment she demanded of herself—a great idea for an artist, but annoying for a family man. If she called a rehearsal, the band was
lucky to get out by dawn. On the weekends that Rowles tried to
get away, he would write, "something would happen with Peggy"
so he couldn't. She was possessive. Worse, wrote Rowles, "she
wants someone around all the time. She hates to be alone."

So he quit. But he came back. Then quit again. And came back
again. Eventually, they found common ground. Things settled
down. They grew close. She called him "Stretch." He called her
"Sue." Says harpist Stella Castellucci, who would soon join the
band: "I think he was one of the few people who could give her a
real scolding, like a dutch uncle."

After they became buddies, Peggy and Jimmy made beautiful
music together, literally, from coast to coast. Los Angeles wasn't
playing second fiddle to New York's club scene anymore. By
now, Hollywood had become a "café town," in the words of
George Schlatter, and he would know: He managed the club of
clubs, Ciro's—the epicenter of the scene. And he, like his
patrons—Marilyn Monroe, Lana Turner, Ava Gardner, Gene
Kelly, Cary Grant, Howard Hughes, Dorothy Lamour, Martin

and Lewis, Sammy Davis, Jr.—was transfixed by the lady who came to own the room.

It was Billy Wilkerson, the former owner of a speakeasy back east (now publishing the *Hollywood Reporter*), who built Ciro's, to compete with Mocambo's and the Cocoanut Grove. To run his new club, Wilkerson hired a man named Herman Hover away from New York legend Earl Carroll, whose notorious speak had featured a naked woman in a bathtub of champagne that patrons could pay to scoop out by the glass. In Ciro's the women weren't quite nude, but the entertainment, clientele, and booze were first-class. They were all part of a brief era on Sunset Boulevard when there was one point to life, and one point only: to enjoy.

You'd drive your Caddy into the circular driveway and leave it for the valet. Just inside the door, you'd meet Johnny Oldrate, the diminutive Italian maître d': "He could knock you on your ass with either hand if he had to," Schlatter remembers now.

You'd hand your overcoat to the coat-check girl, buy a pack of Pall Malls from the cigarette girl in the short black-and-white dress—low-cut—and "long high heels and fuck-me pumps and opera hose." (It was an effective costume; Huntington Hartford married one of Ciro's cigarette girls.) Then you'd turn right and enter the room: a sea of tables to the right, up a few stairs, the stage to the right. The tablecloths were white, each with a Ciro's ashtray that Schlatter bought wholesale at three cents each so patrons wouldn't steal the silverware. Why would such elegant people steal? Because, perhaps, they were slightly out of their senses.

"Before dinner, you had two or three martinis," as Schlatter recalls. "Then you drove to the club, and you sat down. There was a two-drink minimum. Then you had dinner; usually you had a little wine. Following dinner, you usually had a little brandy. Then you had a nightcap, usually followed with one for the road. That's enough alcohol to make you inflammable. The best part was we all had a relationship with the California Highway Patrol. They wouldn't arrest you, they'd take you home. Like the night they snared Martin and Sinatra. They put the flashlight in his face, Dean started singing. They asked him to walk a line, and he said, 'Not without a net.' "

But even through the haze of spirits, Peggy's nights were something special. Start with the lighting. Somehow, with household extension cords, all under the supervision of the head busboy, Manuel, Schlatter managed to meet all of Peggy's requests—the Courvoisier, the echo chamber, not to mention the colors and dimmers. Reds, ambers, pinks. It was all part of the backlighting "to make her look great." Schlatter didn't mind; he considered Lee too creative, too compelling an act, and too nice a gal, not to grant her every wish. She was so special that each time she played the club, he would have her dressing room repainted a different color, as a favor, to surprise her.

"We *loved* Peggy," he recalls. "*Everyone* loved Peggy. Peggy was an E ticket. Remember when Disneyland started up, and there was an exclusive ticket you could buy to get you on all the great rides? The E ticket? Peggy was an E ticket. She was magical. . . . Some performers perform to a crowd. Some perform with an audience. But Peggy invited the audience into her wonderful, crazy, pastel world, with a lot of lights and a lot of cotton candy."

Sure, there was a lot of crazy. She may not always have been too reliable—one night, forty-five minutes late, she'd apologized profusely, explaining that on the way to the club, she'd seen a burning building. Her retelling of the scene was enough to make Schlatter wish he'd been there too. Another night—well, to this day Schlatter isn't sure why she did what she did. "See," he begins, "Peggy would love to talk onstage. She would come out and talk and turn the saloon into a living room. And she'd have no sense of time. She'd go on a bit. So one time we had a premiere or something happening somewhere, so the owners of the club said,

'You talk to Peggy. She'll listen to you. Tell her she has to do a short show.'

"When she came in, I said, 'Hi, Peggy—here's the thing: We have reservations. The first show must end on time.' And she gave me a pat on the cheek and said, 'Let's have a taste'—she would have a taste of Courvoisier before she went on. So the show started on time and she came out and she didn't talk that much. She did the show. Then she went right back on stage and did the same show again, without a break, top to bottom. I thought Hover was going to kill me."

Why did she repeat the show?

"I don't know. I guess she drifted off a little. Peggy wasn't too specific sometimes. All right, maybe that night we had more than a little Courvoisier."

Lee's eccentricities, notes one of her musicians at the time, extended beyond her stage behavior. One day she arrived at Ciro's having spent the afternoon hanging head-downward on a slanted board. She'd been in pain from an undiagnosed ailment in her midsection; she thought her liver might be upside down, so she was trying to turn it right side up.

Among the visitors at one show at Ciro's in 1952 was a director and Hollywood Renaissance man named Mel Ferrer. He'd met Peggy when he'd cast Dave Barbour in his thriller *Secret Fury* two years earlier. (Ferrer would eventually gain fame as Audrey Hepburn's husband, and as the director of the television show *Falcon Crest*.) At Ciro's, Ferrer saw a woman whose act, he believed, had grown slack. He thought she was singing too long and talking too much. He could tell that the musicians adored her. But he thought he could rework the image. First, he told her to change her diet. "It seemed to me," he said, "that she was too fat." He also offered a few stage directions.

"A lot of little tricks," said Ferrer of what he supplied to Lee. "One was bridging every song in her act, kind of a segue, with

Peggy talking to the audience very briefly—getting them to like her personally—and with the music in the background, changing into the key of her next song. And all in split-second timing." Ferrer also suggested that Candoli help out on the bongos. Her drummer should stand up every now and then. She should try gesturing with her hands more.

The addition of a lighting director from Columbia Pictures added additional drama and introduced Lee to an added dimension of theatricality that she would never relinquish. "Frankly, it's a commercial move," said Ferrer. "Sure, but Peggy has a kid and she needs to make money, the big money that she's capable of earning. This'll help her. Yes, I think this will really help her."

Thereafter, the Ciro's faithful enjoyed quite a late show: five saxes, three trumpets, two trombones, a bongo, Peggy, and plenty of props. For "Don't Smoke in Bed," a flower was hidden on the stage; it was Candoli's job to put down the trumpet, pick up a hidden string tied to the flower, and slowly drag the rose into the spotlight at the end of the song. (One night, when the string dragged over just one petal and left the rose in the darkness, Peggy was less than pleased.) There was also the little doll she liked to sit up on the piano, a man doll; she'd sing a love song to it. (He, too, was Candoli's responsibility, and Peggy was a little miffed the night the doll fell over.)

Pete Candoli couldn't have cared less about Lee's demanding nature. Like any jazz musician he grew sick of playing the same notes night after night after night. But with Peggy, no night was ever like the one before or after. She would set him free, then respond to the notes *he'd* played: "Nothing threw her, musically— *nothing.*" If she sang a note, Pete didn't have to worry about his answer, didn't even have to think. If he felt something, he could blast it right out, just play it, and she'd play right back off it. The whole set list was one long narrative, as carefully choreographed as the lighting and the roses. And it ended, of course, with

"Lover," which Candoli sometimes thought went on too long. Not that he didn't like it; it was just that the musicians were exhausted enough at the end of a Peggy set. And some nights, she just wouldn't stop. "She used to take some brown vitamin tablets, a handful, before the last show," he recalls. "You'd look at her eyes, they'd be shiny black. . . . Vitamins or something. She was flying. . . ."

The crowd was never ready to go home, but Candoli and company wanted to collapse. He had to towel himself off in the dressing room. But then, always, she invited him in to dissect the night and talk about what they could do differently. Candoli says he never played with anyone who respected his chops, his ideas, his opinions, as much as Lee. "She'd call me and say, 'Pete, the rhythm in this . . .' and I'd say, 'I'll take care of it,'" Candoli said, and he'd carry out her wishes.

It was worth putting up with the weird stuff. And on the road, what he never did was take advantage of the obvious opportunities. "It was inviting," Candoli says now. "But I respected her. I never went there."

There was always time to push another musical envelope. At some point, Peggy heard Ravel's *Introduction and Allegro for Harp and Chamber Orchestra,* and she decided the band needed a harp. Not a usual instrument for a pop orchestra, or a mainstay of anyone's small jazz combo. But she asked her bandmates: Anyone know a harpist? And Candoli did.

Nine years of private instruction and intensive study in New York had given Stella Castellucci a facility with harp that belied her young age. But her lineage suggested that she was also born with some talent: Her father, Louis, the son of a bandmaster back in Europe, had played the baritone horn; he'd even done a gig with John Philip Sousa.

After graduating from high school, Stella needed a job that paid real money, and joined the ABC radio orchestra. One night, when she was twenty-two, she got a call from her friend Candoli: "I'm up at Peggy Lee's house," he told her. "We're rehearsing. Peg thinks she might like a harp in the act."

Stella was stunned. No one in her musical family had ever crossed over this far. But Peggy Lee? Stella, like any young musician, loved her stuff. Stella didn't have a driver's license, so her dad drove her to Peggy's house in the family's Chevrolet station wagon. When they arrived, Peggy shook Stella's hand and put the girl so at ease that, to her horror, Stella heard herself saying, "Hi, Peg"—as if she'd known her for years.

" 'Just sit down, and come in when you want to,' Peggy told me," Castellucci recalls. "In the middle of 'I've Got You Under My Skin' I started to play. The only reason I was qualified to be in that room was because I grew up knowing all those standards—Cole Porter, Gershwin—as a very little girl. I loved that music."

When she started to play, Stella's notes didn't intrude, but they went beyond mere background. For an hour, the twenty-two-year-old harpist never stopped. "Then they broke for dinner," Castellucci remembers. "Daddy was there with me, and Peggy invited Daddy to have dinner. It was a lovely time. I noticed during dessert and coffee, Peggy was in a corner talking to Pete, and maybe Joe Mondragon. I thought, 'Oh God—I've bombed.' I knew they were talking about me. Then Peg comes over and says, 'Stella, you want to go on the road with us?' "

On the ride back home, Stella was worried that her father might not approve, but he was as delighted as his daughter. The next week, Stella Castellucci was playing jazz harp next to Peggy Lee in Vegas. They'd work together for the next ten years.

FIFTEEN

AMONG THE SEVERAL admirers attracted to Peggy Lee at Ciro's was regal, imperious Michael Curtiz, the Hungarian who'd directed *Casablanca*. Curtiz was casting a remake of Jolson's *The Jazz Singer,* the story of a Philadelphia cantor's son who can't bring himself to follow his orthodox dad's wishes for him to take over the temple. The kid's heart is in singing jazz. Worse still: The kid is in love with a shiksa nightclub singer.

For the new picture, Curtiz had Danny Thomas in the lead, but his first choice to play the singer's girl hadn't worked out. Curtiz himself had discovered the lady, and signed her to a contract, but Doris Day turned him down. She and her advisers at Warner Bros. didn't think the character fit the image of her "present standing." In other words, what would America's sweetheart be doing in a gin mill?

Then Curtiz saw Peggy Lee's act—and he was entranced. Her showmanship was as solid as her singing, and there wasn't a single song she didn't inhabit completely. She acted her lyrics. Her looks weren't too shabby, either. "If she can put into acting the emotions that she puts into singing," Curtiz told a New York tabloid, "she'll be terrific."

"Big movie career is predicted for Peggy Lee," opined *Down Beat*. The contract with Warners, it was reported, was for two pictures a year if her option was picked up, and it had a generous rider: She could make pictures for other studios, and keep working on television. "Peggy's progress from this point on should be interesting to watch," wrote one trade writer. "Much will depend on how she makes out in her *Jazz Singer* role."

The original *Jazz Singer*, the first widely successful feature film with talking sequences, had featured Al Jolson, the most widely known entertainer of the first third of the twentieth century. The remake seemed to have all of the ingredients for a rollicking success. The original film's popularity seemed a good omen, and Curtiz had, after all, directed *Casablanca*. The mix got more interesting when Peggy was officially cast as the costar, nightclub and musical singer Judy Lane.

Danny Thomas, playing the lead character, Jerry Golding, wasn't a singer of renown, but he had character and appeal. What he didn't have was jazz. An iota of it. And what Curtiz didn't have was the slightest sense of pacing or staging. His camera was lead-footed, his lighting dark. The bottom line, though, was that between the endless hours filmed in the temple and the cantor's home—furnished and shot like sets in a low-budget Roger Corman adaptation—and the stilted direction, the movie had enough obstacles to overcome without the other hurdles that kept pop-

ping up during production. Four days into filming, Harry
Warner insisted they stop shooting in Warner Color and shift to
Technicolor, because the studio was using the latter for a big pro-
duction called *Lady Fatima* and Harry didn't want *The Jazz
Singer* to be shortchanged. Whatever the reason, the film looks
overcolorized.

When the production had to shift from the temple in Philadelphia to Los Angeles, the folks in charge of location found a
similar-looking temple, but hadn't done their research: The first
temple was Reform, while the L.A. temple was orthodox. The
L.A. rabbi was apoplectic: You can't wear hats in here! While that
discussion dragged on, the crew broke for lunch: ham sandwiches. The production was banned from the place and had to
find another temple.

But the final nail in the coffin was driven during postproduction. The writer of one of the script's later drafts—approximately
the twenty-fifth—was none other than Leonard Stern, creative
talent from the Steve Allen show who was one of only three
scriptwriters actually credited. Unfortunately for Stern, the producers couldn't leave well enough alone after shooting wrapped.

Although they made only one small change to Lee's character
during postproduction, it was a killer, and it may well have helped
sink the film. Part of the original plot involved the tension between the cantor's highly religious family and the fact that his
love interest was a gentile. During the writing of the new version,
Stern had been advised to make Judy's religion ambiguous. They
wanted him to disguise Peggy Lee's waspy image.

"I said that if you don't bring up the fact she's not Jewish,"
Stern recalls, "then all the cantor is objecting to is his son's being
in show business. Now, in the fifties, any cantor with a son as successful as Jerry Golding would announce it from the pulpit."

The decision to eliminate the cross-religious tension, it struck
Stern, was bad enough. He wasn't ready for the final script

tinkering—that he'd had no part in, that he had no idea was coming, until he heard it with the rest of the audience at the premiere.

During filming, Peggy met a small-time supporting actor named Brad Dexter. He was big and muscular—a former boxer—and handsome. But he didn't have the ambition to become a leading man. He wasn't competitive, and didn't demand the spotlight; his ego was modest. "He was a real, real gentleman," bongo man Jack Costanzo recalls. "He was a very happy-go-lucky man."

Like Peggy, Dexter had been through what could be called an identity makeover; two, actually. Born Boris Velijko Milanovich, son of Serbian parents, he first became Barry Mitchell. Then John Huston cast him in a small part in *Asphalt Jungle,* and suggested he change his name to Brad Dexter. Clearly, he was flexible. "Brad," says George Schlatter, "was not burdened by the greatest intellect"—which makes him a very curious choice as a partner for Peggy. (Barbour, by all accounts, was brilliant, and Robert Preston was a sharp and witty raconteur.)

At the time she met Dexter, Peggy was also seeing one of Ciro's major lotharios, a businessman named Greg Bautzer, also sought after by the likes of Ava Gardner, Lana Turner, and Joan Crawford. Dinners with Bautzer, she later recalled, would invariably be interrupted by telephone calls from Howard Hughes. When Bautzer proposed, Lee would later write, she was taken aback, and laughed out loud. He took her response the wrong way, and that was the end of it. But it wasn't a mocking laugh: "My low-self-esteem quality came to the foreground again," she explained, and her words ring true. She didn't consider herself in the same league as Lana Turner.

Bautzer was a legend. Brad Dexter was a nice guy who wouldn't deflect any spotlights. "Well, Peggy was high maintenance," says George Schlatter. "That required a lot of attention. She was a meshugennah. You know—a pain in the ass."

It was about this time that a woman named Lillie Mae Hendricks entered Peggy's life. She was a small, energetic black woman who would be cooking and keeping house for and generally comforting Miss Peggy Lee almost until the end of her days, though Lillie Mae never actually lived in any of Peggy's houses. By all accounts, she was a sharp, witty, no-nonsense woman. On the night of Peggy's wedding to Dexter, Peggy wrote, she became "Mama Lillie Mae"—serving four hundred guests, and urging Peggy to take a little cognac to cool her out.

Peggy and Brad married on January 4, 1953, in Peggy's garden behind the Norman French mansion on Denslow Street. It was Ernest Holmes who married them—in more ways than one. After she'd been seeing Brad for a short while, it was Holmes who asked Peggy if she was going to marry him. According to her eventual retelling, this had started the machinery. At the ceremony, Peggy wore a pink taffeta dress designed by Howard Grier. Dave Barbour played the guitar at the rehearsal, and offered to play at the wedding. Peggy said it would be inappropriate. Years later, she told *Cosmopolitan* magazine that Nicki's reaction to the wedding was charmingly to the point: "Mother, let's make this one do, so that I won't get confused."

The couple headed east on the *Super Chief* for the January 13, 1953, premiere of *The Jazz Singer*. At some of the station stops, fans piled onto one of the most famous cross-country trains in history to see Peggy Lee. This had to be good for her ego. But it was probably less than thrilling for Brad Dexter. Being Peggy Lee's husband had to be a tough gig. Dexter had a career of his own, and it must have been hard for him to be in the shadows, even if he wasn't possessed of an enormous ego. What Peggy really seemed to want from the marriage was a good father figure for her daughter.

The film premiere took place at the Paramount Theater in Times Square. Peg was just as eager to see the credits as the film. She'd written three songs: "Imagine, there, in the credits, songs by Rodgers and Hart, by Cole Porter—and, by golly, me," she told the press. "When I heard about it, I flipped!"

But all Leonard Stern remembers is the disaster of the scene that the director insisted on fiddling with. At the juncture in question, Jerry and his father leave the temple, with Judy and Jerry's mother trailing behind them. As they pass by the camera, the father says to the son: "She's a very lovely girl, Jerry."

Then you hear a woman's voice—Judy's—saying, "It's been a long time since I've been to a seder." They'd made platinum-blond Peggy Lee from Dakota into a Jewish girl. "It got the biggest laugh in the theater that you might have heard in your lifetime," Stern recalls with a rueful laugh. Otherwise, little about the film evokes memories.

Note for note, the remake of *The Jazz Singer* is the least joyous movie about music ever committed to celluloid. But Lee came out almost untouched. Although her performance was sometimes on the stilted side, Curtiz took the blame, and Lee had moments where she truly seemed to jump off the screen. Her nightclub performance of "Lover" was nothing short of ecstatic: wild, sexy, unrestrained, and every bit as enticing as the live version. She was photographed leaning back in the curve of the white grand piano, nearly writhing—as if she were pinioned by invisible velvet ropes, trying to get free, but not trying terribly hard. When she idly rubbed the top of the piano with her hand and a handkerchief, it was as if she were stroking it sexually. When she reached the climax of the song, she leaned her head back, and her final, blissful, oblivious word—"*Lo-ver!*"—left little to the imagination.

Lee's nadir musically, unfortunately, was a song she wrote by herself. "This Is a Very Special Day" is a cartoon ripoff of her own "It's a Good Day." To a simple, bouncy beat, as she rides a carousel, wearing a puff-shouldered dress, Lee smiles her way through her stanzas, which seemed to have been penned in five minutes on the back of an envelope.

But her turn in Curtiz's film did offer another moment of distinction, a purely dramatic piece of poignant acting in a film largely devoid of such. Halfway through the film, when Thomas's character has temporarily defied his heart and returned to the temple, Judy Lane calls him from a producer's cocktail party in a swank Manhattan apartment, and tipsily apologizes for calling him so late at his parents' home: "If I hadn't had a drink," Judy says, slightly fuzzy, slightly ditzy, a little high, more than a little sultry, "I'd never have had the nerve to call you." It's like a scene from a different film, it's so compelling—and so believable.

As any serious dramatic actor would admit, playing drunk is difficult. Playing slightly so is even more difficult. In the wake of the film's release, *Down Beat* was kind to one of its own: "Peggy registers not only as an actress, but as a unique new screen personality."

They were less generous in appraising "This Is a Very Special Day," which they judged "passable."

Years later, Peggy would make a singular remark about this unfortunate project to an Associated Press reporter—the only true, unfiltered take on the movie that she would ever offer, at least for public consumption: "There were some lines in *The Jazz Singer* that absolutely stoned me. I couldn't get them out because I didn't believe in them."

The film left no impression whatsoever on the cinematic landscape. But it did earn Peggy a shot at a bigger auditorium than she'd ever graced: The Academy Awards ceremony of 1953 was hosted by Bob Hope, at the Pantages Theater. Johnny Mercer and Richard Whiting's ironic anthem "Hooray for Hollywood" was being played by the Motion Picture Arts and Sciences orchestra as the crowd filed in. It was the twenty-fifth anniversary of the awards. A tall, larger-than-life statue of Oscar stood stage left, dominating the scene, rising from a huge cake like the robot from a grade-B sci-fi flick.

The picture of the year was *The Greatest Show on Earth,* which beat out the color-drenched spectacle of *Moulin Rouge.* Gary Cooper won best actor for *High Noon,* besting Brando in *Viva Zapata!* and José Ferrer, Rosemary Clooney's husband, in *Moulin Rouge.*

The competition for songs was fierce, but disappointingly shallow: The only one worth not throwing back was Nicholas Brodszky and Sammy Cahn's "Because You're Mine" from the movie of that name. But the renditions of the five songs were intriguing. Nightclub entertainer Billy Daniels wrested an operatic version of "Am I in Love" from *Paleface* that was every bit as stunning as Celeste Holm's rendition of "Thumbelina," featuring her mugging to a finger puppet, which was embarrassing.

And the third live performance featured one of the oddest-looking couples ever to grace the Oscar stage. From the wings came Peg, looking silvery and svelte in her high-Decca look, holding the hand of a tall, thin, gaunt, decidedly unhappy-looking Johnny Mercer. In his tails, Mercer looked like the butler for a third-world dictator. Worse still, they'd been assigned a silly novelty piece called "Zing a Little Zong" from a Bing Crosby film called *Just for You,* written by Harry Warren and Leo Robin, in which the lyrical device is to replace all the *S*'s with *Z*'s: "When you're zittin' by the zide of me, I want to zing a little zong. . . ."

Hooray for Hollywood.

Soon Peggy Lee was screen-testing. There was talk of her playing the role of twenties torch singer Helen Morgan in a feature film. She'd also landed a part in a film that was never produced, a sort of remake of Curtiz's *Casablanca* called *Everybody Comes to Rick's*. But her personal life was offering less promise. She had a nice man by her side, but he didn't seem to play much of a part in her life, at least if a profile in the Fargo newspaper was any indication. Peg's typical day, the scribe recounted, consisted of filming from dawn to dusk, then coming home and writing a novel, painting in her studio, playing the piano, taking a "slight interruption" to help Nicki with her homework, then rehearsing her club act, and consulting with managers. That the writer never saw her writing her novel or asked her to furnish any portion or description of it raises the obvious question of whether Peggy—the girl who wanted to be liked—was pumping up her creative résumé a bit. No one doubted that she had many talents. One of the projects she told reporters about—a film adaptation of the life of Claude Debussy's mistress, for instance—was written, but never produced.

Not that she wasn't really busy. She slept for only four hours a night, she told the faithful representative of the Fargo *Forum*, and had mastered the "Thomas Edison Technique" of power napping. There was no mention of time with the husband whom Stella Castellucci found sweet, handsome, and in love with his new wife. "Nicki," adds Castellucci, "was crazy about him."

Dexter wasn't getting much work. But he was never jealous of the inevitable crowd of musicians who flocked to his wife and were drawn in. "She loved to have people around her," Castellucci says. "She did not like to be alone. . . . Ernest Holmes and his wife were frequent visitors. She really did love Ernest and his wife. It didn't matter that she was raised Lutheran. She took to

Ernest Holmes. He and his wife were always at her home as guests—lovely, elegant people."

Brad—a simple guy with simple tastes—did not seem to have much in common with his new wife. Clearly, though, he found Peggy's brand of artistic personality a little tough to handle— along with her actual performances. In the eight months of their marriage, he attended only one—at the Sands in Las Vegas. Peggy was the featured act; José Greco's dance troupe was the opener. Dexter showed up unannounced. Stella Castellucci recalls, "She was just so happy to see him, it was wonderful."

But the feeling may not have been mutual. After the show, Dexter hung out at the bar with Pete Candoli, who sensed that Brad and Peggy had had a little "scrimmage." Brad apparently felt that the Peggy he'd been living with had been a little less optimistic, buoyant, and bouncy than advertised. Pete suggested that maybe she needed a few more new tunes, some new blood in the act.

"She doesn't need any more tunes," Candoli recalls Brad saying. "She needs a fuckin' doctor."

But according to Stella Castellucci, when Peg asked for a divorce, Brad was devastated: "He begged her not to divorce him," Stella says. "I think she loved being married because she loved being in love. All of her music said so. . . . I don't think she ever got over her horrendous childhood in that respect. I think she would have been very happy living on a little house in the hill with the man she loved, but sometimes I think the art took over."

Dexter and Lee separated on September 21; the divorce was finalized on November 3. The wire-service caption to a photograph in the Fargo paper reads, "She charged cruelty and testified that the actor criticized her friends and business associates and had only worked three weeks during their marriage."

"I came to the conclusion that I loved him, but I was not in love with him," Peggy wrote, "that I was living a lie. I asked him for a divorce. When he left Denslow, we were both crying." They would remain friends, and, at one point, both Barbour and Dexter would visit her—"like something by Noel Coward," she said.

At this point, Peggy sold the Denslow Street house, temporarily moving into the New York duplex of her new agent, Tom Rockwell. Carlos Gastel had been jettisoned, leaving behind a stormy wake. Her current manager, Ed Kelly, was by all accounts an honest man beloved in the industry. He treated Lee well and faithfully for some years to come. "Carlos was pulling things behind the backs of all of his clients," Peggy told writer Gene Lees in his wonderful biography of Woody Herman, *Leader of the Band*. "I still have some forgeries of his. He forged my signature assigning some very valuable songs of mine to a publisher without my knowledge. He was supposed to be my manager, and he was my destroyer."

Now, muddying her financial waters even further, she sold the Denslow house "for a fraction of its real price," she wrote, "because David, and then Nicki, echoing what her daddy had said, told me they didn't like the house. I should have realized that [Barbour's sentiment] was just a pronouncement with more bourbon in it than common sense, but I was so shaken, I wanted to make them happy. . . . Nicki has since told me many times, 'Why did you listen to a child?' "

The answer could be divined, perhaps, in the private nickname Peggy had for her daughter: "Little Rock"—as in her bastion of strength and reliability in a time when, increasingly, she needed an anchor. "A good friend," Peggy wrote, "told me they had found David among the packing crates one night, playing [his guitar] and crying."

Brad Dexter said he'd never marry again. But he did—twice. In fact, Dexter not only landed on his feet after he parted from

Peggy, his career took off. Like so many other men in Peggy's life—Hal Schaefer, Jimmy Rowles, Frank Sinatra—he was linked with Marilyn Monroe in 1954; they were companions not lovers. He landed villainous roles in macho movies including *Run Silent, Run Deep* and *The Magnificent Seven,* in which he appeared alongside McQueen, Brynner, Bronson, and Coburn.

Dexter's most intriguing relationship was actually not with a woman but with Frank Sinatra, who cast him in *None but the Brave* and welcomed him into his entourage. One day on location at a beach in Hawaii, a riptide carried Sinatra and the producer's wife out to sea. Dexter swam out and kept them afloat until lifeguards could arrive with surfboards. Soon thereafter, Dexter became a producer in Sinatra's film company, a pal, and a confidant.

It was seven years after his divorce from Peggy that Stella saw Brad Dexter again. The two met when Stella Castellucci was spending the summer at Peggy's house and Brad was coming for dinner. Stella offered to make herself scarce, but Peg insisted she dine with them. "He'll be glad to see you," Peg said. They were having a lovely conversation, Stella recalls. "I don't think they ever realized I was sitting in the room. I was a fifth wheel. I vividly remember his saying, 'Why did you leave me, Peg? Why?'"

Peggy had no answer. Hereafter, faced with choosing between relationship and career for emotional sustenance, she would invariably choose the latter—a decision that might befuddle and confound outsiders, but certainly not her peers in show business. Perhaps a passage from the gospel (that is to say, the memoir) of Anita O'Day is worth considering: "Musical intimacy is on a completely different plane—deeper, longer-lasting, better than the steamiest sexual liaison," wrote O'Day. "Passion wears out, but the longer you work with a really rhythmical, inventive, swinging musician, the closer you become. . . . So I drank, got high, learned to cover up my feelings of pain beneath a hip, swinging-chick personality I'd carefully developed. When I went on stage and sang . . . I got the love I craved. I didn't need anyone. For me, music equaled love."

SIXTEEN

Coffee Break

LEE'S NEXT HOUSE in Los Angeles was perched high above the city, on Kimridge Avenue, in Beverly Hills: "a low-slung house on top of a hill with an Oriental look and a view of seven mountain ranges," she recalled. She bought it in 1954 for $40,000. The place revealed a different sensibility than prior Peggy home-decorating jobs. Kimridge was ornate, over the top. In her first house as a single woman she chose to surround herself with elaborate beauty.

"Nicki's room had a white marble floor, mostly covered with white fur. Her bed was gold-leafed wrought iron surrounded by clouds of yellow chiffon. The canopy was caught back with gold-leaf antique carved wooden cherubs. The white marble continued down the hall to my boudoir, which opened on a private little garden with a trickling fountain."

In Peggy's bedroom, a pale-blue velvet king-size bed sat atop a white carpeted platform surrounded by white louvered shutters, a trompe l'oeil painting on each wall, a white railing with two white urns, white curtains controlled by a button, a crystal chandelier, mirrors reflecting the chandelier, pale-green silk print Louis XIV chairs, a chaise longue. The landscaping included a pool, a Japanese garden, a large fish pond stocked with perch, goldfish, carp, and catfish, Rangoon lime trees, and a bridge over the pond to a pagoda.

The garage was converted into her studio, which, according to one journalist's account, had "been warmed over with travel posters, file cabinets, professional recording equipment, a grand piano, a tiny desk and a portable typewriter."

She threw a Japanese costume party for her housewarming. Guests included Duke Ellington and Steve Allen and Jayne Meadows.

But she didn't stay put for long.

Manhattan was hopping. At the Bandbox, both Charlie Parker's and Buddy Rich's combos were playing, to be followed by Billy Eckstine, Count Basie, and Dave Brubeck, the latter now gaining prominence as the leader of the "Cool School," a West Coast jazz sound frowned on by the bop critics. Marian McPartland was playing her remarkable jazz piano over at the Hickory House. Zoot Sims was at Le Downbeat. On the East Side, the trio headed by Red Norvo—Dave Barbour's old buddy on the vibes—was at the Embers. Mabel Mercer was at the Byline Room.

But for actor and Lee fan Don Hastings the choice was easy, and one trip to a room called La Vie en Rose paid off in a bigger way than he'd ever anticipated. One night he walked into the club, made a left turn to the bar, and got himself a drink. When he turned around, there she stood, in a strapless net gunmetal dress with something pink underneath: Miss Peggy Lee. Their eyes met. Lee gave him a slow once-over—up and down—and smiled before moving to the back of the room, toward the stage.

"My heart stopped," Don Hastings remembers today, as if it were the proverbial yesterday.

Mr. Hastings went on to a long and successful career as an actor. But he would never shake the memory of Miss Peggy Lee. Nor would he want to. He not only saw the woman up close, he saw her perform during the engagement that some would call one of the musical pinnacles of her career. She would eventually turn in more spectacular shows. She would grow as an icon. But at that moment, her music, not her stardom, was paramount, and it would never be better than at La Vie en Rose, up on East Fifty-fourth Street.

They did "Blues for Benny." They did "Hard-Hearted Hannah," with Peggy—now fully given over to using props on stage—holding a gun, and the band wearing derbies. They did "Lover." Leonard Feather, writing in *Down Beat,* was impressed. "Being very cautious about overstatement, we will only say conservatively that Peggy gave the greatest performance we have seen delivered by any singer in a Manhattan club in the last five years—and that includes everybody, male or female, from Lena Horne and Sinatra on down. . . . If you have inferred that we are overboard for Miss Lee, you are right. Peggy does for a song what Jane Russell does for a sweater. If you only know Peggy Lee from records, or radio and TV and theaters, catch her some time in an intimate nightclub like this. If you don't get a genuine thrill— Jack, you must be dead."

Peggy was not, however, met with universal acclaim. In perhaps its first glance at Peggy Lee, *The New Yorker* listed her engagement in advance under "Big and Brassy" clubs. They'd messed up the idiom. Then they messed up their blurb: "Peggy

Lee leaps, not always surefootedly, from one slippery glissando to another, a feat of daring that is generally admired in some musical circles." To be fair, however, the review ran before Peggy arrived in New York. After they'd actually seen her act, the magazine changed its tune: "Peggy Lee," wrote the anonymous reviewer, "is sighing like the wind in the willows (it sometimes rises to the intensity of a nor'easter)."

But she hadn't been able to put it all down on vinyl—not yet. None of her records had ever captured the jazz, rhythm, and sensuality. There'd been bits and pieces, there'd been hints, but no disc of vinyl had captured, in depth, in breadth, the complicated creature she'd become—until August 1953, when a lady who'd been through two bad marriages and a rocky affair, a woman who had always felt the blues, stepped up to take her rightful place, once and for all, with the rest of the pioneers.

Black Coffee, Peggy's first Decca album, broke all the molds. Leavened by a few safe strolls into brightly lit corridors, it's a dark, hip journey. This dose of black coffee didn't cure a hangover. What it did was take the edge off the dark moods that called for the next highball, but gave those same dark moods their say. You want to weep? It's cool. No, it's more than cool. We have a soundtrack for the blues in you—a collection of songs that will make the dark glow. There was no rictus grin on this canary, no bright, camera-ready fifties fakery.

It would be a few years before the war between the opposing currents of the fifties—the Eisenhower promise of suburban bliss versus the reality of those unable to afford it—really started crashing into the culture. The canvas abstractions of Pollock and Rothko, the free verse of Ginsberg and Ferlinghetti, the stream-of-consciousness novels of Jack Kerouac, hadn't yet surfaced to shout in the face of conformity and tranquilizer-induced happiness. The nation's placid surface was still fairly unruffled.

But for 1953, given the American emphasis on musical sweethearts (Doris Day on down) and repressed emotions, *Black Coffee* was pretty damned innovative. Just look at the photograph of the artist taken around this time: This was no eyelid-fluttering beauty queen; her dyed-platinum hair was cut short, severe. She was an Ayn Rand iron-willed individualist character planted comfortably in a Beat novel, the cool, brainy babe, nobody's fool. In the shot, her face was framed in three-quarter profile. She was, as usual, gazing at something off camera, her expression a smile, but only by an iota: It was a steely look, and with her black collar turned up, it was all business. There was something going on in the photographs of Peggy taken during this time. She went from looking happy and innocent to something else. Then, her life had gone from "It's a Good Day" to *Black Coffee*.

Black Coffee wasn't just about Peggy Lee. It was about Pete Candoli's trumpet and Jimmy Rowles's piano. By now, Rowles had had a talk with her after a show in Vegas. "Now listen, Sue," he said, using his private nickname for her. "We don't want a contest between the piano and you. You're the star. And they don't want to hear me fiddle around all the time you're singing." A piano man who'd grown up watching Teddy Wilson, Ellington, and Basie, Jimmy knew that the greats didn't allow the instrument to rival them as a presence. There were times when only a little or no piano were what was called for: Sometimes silence from the keyboard lets the rest of the thing fall into place.

So there was less of Jimmy Rowles, and, on *Black Coffee*, that was definitely more. The supercool trumpet of Candoli, however, laced its way all through the set, bringing this record into the jazz-vocal-album stratosphere. "We knew it was a happening record," Candoli recalls, "because, first of all, Joe Mondragon was the bass player, and Jimmy was on piano. Milt Gabler, the head of A&R at Decca, was a nice guy: 'You guys do what you want. It's your show.'"

The title song was a simple blues number already famously

recorded by Ella and Sarah, written by Burke with lyrics by Paul
Francis Webster, the immortal lyricist who would win three
Academy Awards. It wasn't written expressly for Peg, but like so
many other songs she'd hit with through the years, while others
recorded it, it really shouldn't have been performed by anyone
else: The narrator, a lonesome late-night soul who's "talkin' to the
shadows," hasn't slept "a wink," "walk[s] the floor" and
"watch[es] the door," and, to pass the time, "I drink . . . black
coffee . . . lord, how slow the moments go when all I do is
pour. . . ."

Next, after an upbeat version of Porter's "I've Got You Under
My Skin," she takes Porter's "My Heart Belongs to Daddy" on a
Latinized roller-coaster ride, replete with Candoli's muted trumpet and Rowles's piano having fun with the beat. With three
tempo changes, and the bass hammering the notes with love and
an audible sense of adventure, the band takes Porter's standard,
tears it into shreds, throws it in the air, and lets it flutter down
wherever it wants.

If your taste ran more to the blues, Peggy rendered Willard
Robison's "A Woman Alone with the Blues" as well as she ever
had. "When the World Was Young," with Johnny Mercer's lyrics,
an adaptation of Gerard Phillipe's "The Cavalier of the Boulevard," spoke of emptiness, and it seems to have lines from
Peggy's life story written all over it. She seemed especially herself,
given the recent changes in her life, when she posed the question:
"But where is the schoolgirl that used to be . . . me?"

Like "Lover," this number reached listeners far and wide. It
even found its way into a trailer on the set of *Rebel Without a
Cause,* where Natalie Wood, still a teenager, a troubled kid who'd
been Sinatra's lover as an adolescent, a girl who was having all
sorts of difficulty sorting things out, would play the song again
and again and again. They couldn't get her out of that trailer

when the cameras rolled. She couldn't get enough of that line about the disappearance of "the schoolgirl that used to be me."

Improbably, and surprisingly to the editors of *Down Beat*, Peggy finished second to Ella for Female Singer of the Year for 1953. Peggy had gone several years without even really registering in the voting. Sarah Vaughan had held the top perch for six years running, and would reclaim it soon enough. But in the year of *Black Coffee*, Peggy Lee beat her out. Sassy slipped to third. Peggy had her jazz credentials back. And Decca had its jazz singer: "Miss Lee—like Nat King Cole—is a perfect example of how to retain a jazz feeling and still make the squares love it," said *Variety*.

Far more convincing were the words of *Down Beat*'s Ralph Gleason. A jazz purist, and never a big Peggy fan, Gleason—like many others—was suddenly unable to refrain from stating the obvious: Beneath the immaculate staging and all the rest, Peggy Lee *was* a jazz singer, and the top of her game was as high as it got.

Gleason reviewed four jazz acts playing in the Venetian Room in San Francisco in the summer of 1954: Count Basie, Nat Cole, trombonist Pee Wee Hunt (coming off a record that sold three million copies), and Peggy. "Personally, I would never have figured her to be a top act [from] her performances with Goodman and her records," wrote Gleason. "But she is. She is simply sensational." It was one thing to beat out Sarah but lose to Ella. It was another to have Ralph Gleason rank you over Basie and Cole.

It's possible, of course, that the interview Gleason had done with Peggy a few weeks earlier might have swayed his judgment, for at the time, there were few men who didn't fall under the spell of the lady in one way or another. In that discussion, Gleason brought up a rumor he'd heard: that she was thinking of retiring. Apparently, she'd had a difficult, less-than-critically-acclaimed engagement recently. In her choice of words, her retort to Gleason was instructive:

"Retire! I should say not! That was a bad week. You have weeks like that along with the good ones. When you like music, what are you going to do? It's a disease."

She had never spoken of her muse as an affliction before.

Dolph Traymon had seen some aspects of the disease close up. They came with the territory where insecurity and booze were the trademarks of the great ones. As the onetime pianist for both Lee and Sinatra, Traymon would know. He wasn't in the Jimmy Rowles league, but he was a good musician, and working with Peg was one of the highlights of his life, despite his having to put up with some pretty tough love.

At La Vie en Rose during a later engagement, Dolph was on piano, fronting a six-piece band. And Lee was proving very hard to play for. But she was the Queen. "The sound of her voice—it was delicate, but it had volume, if you know what I mean," Traymon recalls now. "She could change gears just like that. She didn't depend on the band to do the work for her. She *was* the band."

"Do a good job, babe," she'd say to Dolph before the show. Even as he'd start up the music, he couldn't help noticing the effect she had on the room: "The way she walked, by the time she was at the stage she had them all hooked.

"And hot? They wanted to stampede the stage sometimes—that's how hot she was. Once she started, if the crowd wasn't quite right, she'd tamed them within seconds. If they were still too loud she'd sing softly enough to quiet them right down—softer and softer, until they'd have to shut up. And not just the crowd—the waiters. There was no serving when she was singing.

"But it's part of the package: Just because you're a star doesn't mean you're confident or secure. She wanted the affection of the audience. If you gave an introduction to her, and they're all noisy out there, and can't hear her, and she can't hear the introduction, you have to do another. And if you have to do another for her after that, that'd be a tough situation; if she doesn't do well on *that*, the next show she'll come out bombed. She liked booze. She was a heavy drinker. But it was hard not to be, if you're at the bar between sets, and you're in the mood for one, and some guy buys one for you. And another. It's a way of the lifestyle. It's a hazard of the trade."

It was also quite routine for the time. It was an era when the white suburban executive's mission on Friday was to start to drink, and the only rule was to be able to show up sober on Monday morning. To judge the drinking habits of the early Eisenhower years from the perch of the clean, sober, righteously judgmental twenty-first century makes no sense. Now add the particular appetites of the artist. And finally, heed Tallulah Bankhead's plea to J. Edgar Hoover, when she was asking him to consider the nature of the beast when he was investigating Billie Holiday: "You know that every artist has to have a little something, sir, to help give her the lift every once in a while."

No barometer of the liquid intake of the mid-fifties could be as telling as one of Peggy's most entertaining television performances: Sid Caesar's classic *Caesar's Hour* with Carl Reiner. The date was October 11, 1954: the beginning of the golden age of television and the height of the golden age of drinking. A single skit lasted the entire ninety minutes of the show. Its setting was suburban Westchester County–style fifties dreamland America. The plot: Caesar, new guy at the country club, has been tapped by pals to line up the entertainment for the annual dance. His character knows someone who knows Peggy Lee. Sure, he can book her, no problem.

As he dials the phone to reach his friend, he's idly singing "Lover." In the next scene, he manages to crash a recording session to buttonhole the star, though his pratfalls cause the glamorous singer to interrupt her mock-attempt to record "Why

Don't You Do Right?" a half dozen times. (The screwups would have caused heads to roll in real life, but she tolerated them quite graciously on camera.)

In the skit, Lee agrees to do the gig, and on the night of the fete performs a torchy "Come Rain or Come Shine" with a muted trumpet. Her hair is coiffed in the platinum Decca do, her figure by now slightly zaftig. (She would increasingly fight weight problems; the word "Rubensesque" would not be out of place describing her here.) The performance, of course, is dead-on; she gives an arch-bluesy come-on in a flouncy dress, performing as if she were on stage at La Vie en Rose.

Caesar's character, however, doesn't get to see her sing. Worried that the night might be a failure (causing him to lose social status), he's been slugging shots of whiskey since early evening. By the time Lee appears, he's hiding with a bottle in the bass fiddle case, cross-eyed and thirty sheets to the wind.

But the funniest stuff in the show wasn't Caesar's character's descent into a stupor. The laughs came from the way he played the Man with History's Worst Hangover on the next morning's commute. The flap of the train's elastic shade seemed the sound of cannon fire. Here was physical comedy at an all-star level, in an era when a man who'd gotten blindly drunk was clearly well within the norm of social behavior. Men these days were drinking themselves to death after work. (Women, on the other hand—at least a few in Hollywood—were pilling themselves to death for lack of anything to feel. It was Rosemary Clooney's fate at the time, despite a marriage that seemed fine on the surface, to descend into a pill addiction that would land her in a psych ward.)

There was drink in the clubs, drink on the tube, drink in the model suburbs, drink backstage. The middle class of America had found a promised land where the promises were all too fulfilled.

For her next theatrical effort, Peggy did a complete thematic reverse: away from dark brews and into the Disney studios. Sonny Burke was the one who called: Walt Disney was producing a feature-length cartoon about some dogs. There'd be three directors—Clyde Geronimi, Hamilton Luske, and Wilfred Jackson—and "an assembly line of animators, assistant animators, and some more animators, called in-betweeners," according to a magazine account of the process. They'd be painting thousands of pictures on cellulose acetate, to tell a classic tale of canine romance, heartbreak, and humor. All they needed were the songs. Peggy and Burke penned six of them: "La La Lu," "What Is a Baby," "The Siamese Cat Song," "He's a Tramp," "Bella Notte," and "Peace on Earth"; four more didn't make it into the movie.

Peggy and Walt, by all accounts, were simpatico from the moment she first addressed him as "Mr. Disney," and he insisted, "Walt, please." But the lasting legacy of the collaboration, she would later maintain, was her memory of Disney's creative enthusiasm and professionalism. His unfailingly upbeat approach to the daily process provided the kind of optimistic inspiration that she forever sought: "It was the first time I realized that enthusiasm is a great, great part of genius. He has enthusiasm for every part of his work. He would pose for the animators and show them different characters. He was into every corner of his work."

Being allowed full access to the Disney sound department, were she could forage for chimes and bells and all manner of sound effects to spice up her tunes, only added to the kid-in-a-candy-store memories she would have of the project—which, in truth, belonged more to Peggy than to any other single contributor to the film. She would do the voices of four characters, including two cats, a dog, and a human.

The cats, of course, have gone down in history as cultural icons. It wasn't just the coolness of Peggy's simple, silly, infectious lyrics: "We are Siamese if you please; we are Siamese if you don't please"—it was their carnivorous hunt of the goldfish (although the cats came out slightly more Westernized than originally intended; after Disney saw the scene where the cats ate the goldfish, he said they looked too "exotic," and they were redrawn).

Just as playful was her voice for the dog called Peg. "The character was originally called Mamie. But Walt didn't want to insult our First Lady." He asked Lee if she would mind if they named the dog after her.

"I thought it was quite an honor," she recalled.

Befitting the lady herself, Peggy's seductive side gained equal representation, although behind the scenes: For Peg's song, the animators asked her to lip-sync "He's a Tramp" while she casually strolled through the studio.

Her lasting legacy, though, was saving the life of the character Trusty. "In the original story, old Trusty was killed by the wagon. By this time, every character was real to me, and I started to cry. 'That's too sad, Walt. Please let him live.' "

"You need the drama!" said Walt.

"Please!"

For her efforts, Peggy was paid $3,500. At the time, she couldn't have cared less about the money: "It was the best experience in my life." Some years later, in 1988, when the video release of the film outsold *Top Gun* to the tune of some $96 million, she would have a change of heart about the cash.

SEVENTEEN

Kelly Girl

LEE'S PERFORMANCE ON the Caesar show, her ease with the Disney creative machine, her ability to emerge unsoiled from the hokey swamps of *Mr. Music* and *The Jazz Singer:* All of it suggested that Peggy Lee should have a film career. The camera loved her. Her comfort level in the limelight was extraordinary, whether she was riffing with Bing Crosby, Sid Caesar, Bob Hope, or a spaniel.

There would be more movie offers, but the trouble, she would say later, was the material coming her way. "I've had opportunities to do pictures in the past," she told one scribe, "but they were generally for the fluffy, gay musicals. I'm not against them. Some people are great in them. They're just not for me."

But when her friend Jack Webb called one day to tell her he

had a role she'd love, how could she not take it on? It was a movie about jazz, and she'd have some great numbers. But Webb warned that she wouldn't get any glamorous makeup. He was after something gritty, and too much star stuff would detract from what he was trying to do with the character.

She asked him to send the script, which was called *Pete Kelly's Blues*, the tale of a jazz cornetist with a heart of gold in a Kansas City speakeasy in the twenties. The plot involved Pete's struggle with a corrupt local politician played by Edmond O'Brien, who wanted to extort and control the band. Jack, of course, would play Pete Kelly.

Peggy's role wasn't the lead: That was Janet Leigh's, as the speak-slumming socialite who fell for the penniless jazzman. Lee's role would be only supporting, as Rose Hopkins, the corrupt pol's blowsy, alcoholic saloon-singer girlfriend. Rose could sing like a goddess, but was locked into a masochistic relationship with the politician, whose mistreatment of his lady went beyond mind games. He liked to beat her up. Rose couldn't break free because the booze had crippled her. It wasn't a "gay musical."

Peggy got the part.

Arthur Hamilton was a staff songwriter for Jack Webb's Mark VII productions on the Disney lot. Webb, as it happened, was a huge fan of jazz, of Peggy Lee and Ella Fitzgerald, and of Dixieland. At one point, so appreciative was he of Hamilton's talents that he bestowed upon him a 1951 Studebaker.

And soon it happened that young Art Hamilton found himself escorting Peggy Lee. It all began with a cool tune called "Bouquet of Blues," written by Art and sold to Miss Lee, who recorded it on the flip side of a Decca single called "Let Me Go, Lover!" The blues song was right down Peggy's alley, and Art was told one day that Miss Lee would like to meet him. He should come catch her act at Ciro's, she said. He had never been to Ciro's. "I just couldn't afford to go," Art says.

On the night in question, Art Hamilton didn't spend much time savoring the cuisine, the famous sauces, or the cocktails. He split his attention between Peggy Lee and the men in the audience. There were some five hundred of them, and Arthur noted that they all had their metaphoric mouths hanging wide open. It was like group hypnosis. He had never seen anything like it—and he told her so after the show, when she had instructed her driver to take the rest of the night off. They were sitting in his Studebaker.

"[Those men] were transfixed by that woman on the stage," Art says now, and that's what he told Peggy herself. Art found her response telling; it gave him some insight into the pressures besetting a woman who, night after night, put her soul into pleasing the crowd:

"I don't want to talk about her," said Miss Lee.

"She wanted to let her hair down and just talk," Art says. "What was left of the evening, we talked about haiku poetry." This star, now thirty-four—a good ten years older than he—wanted to go to the Hamburger Hamlet on Sunset. She always did love a burger after a gig. (Three decades later, after a Reagan White House engagement, she would hit McDonald's.)

One day Jack Webb stuck his head into Art's office. "We're going to do a movie," he told him. "A jazz movie." Webb gave Art the outline, with emphasis on the strongest character in the script: the alcoholic nightclub singer whose man beats and humiliates her until eventually she snaps, goes crazy, and ends up in an institution.

"Sounds interesting," said Art.

"Peggy Lee is playing the girl," said Webb. "She's perfect. I need you to write her a song she can sing in the mental institution."

"Man," thought young Arthur Hamilton, "this has got to be a hell of a song." So he wrote and wrote. He tried anything and everything. He wrote five songs in a week. None was right. Meantime, Peggy went off to Vegas for an engagement at the Sands. Art, the simmering flame, thought a good-luck gesture was called for. But what do you send Peggy Lee to distinguish your affection? What can you come up with that she'd even notice? Or remember? Not flowers or anything routine.

Art happened to be in the shower when it hit him: *a phrase.* He was a songwriter, right? His gift was songwriting. "I was taking a shower, and I nearly electrocuted myself with the thought: Send her a wire on Western Union that says, 'Sing a Rainbow.'" At three words, the message fit Art's budget. That night, his telephone rang at four A.M. She'd finished her last show.

"Jesus, I loved your telegram," she told Art. "Which of us is going to write the song?"

"Which song?"

"The song called 'Sing a Rainbow.'"

"Well," Art said, "you can take the title and work on it, if you want."

"No, no. It's your title, and it's your song."

Pete Kelly's Blues was a step up from *The Jazz Singer*. With Janet Leigh, O'Brien, Lee Marvin, and Martin Milner, Webb had gathered some fine talent. Ella Fitzgerald playing a speakeasy owner named Fat Annie was an additional coup. But once again, Peggy Lee was in the hands of a ham-fisted director. Jack Webb would go down as an icon, of course; Joe Friday, in Webb's *Dragnet* TV series, was a classic television character, despite (or perhaps because of) Webb's two-dimensional portrayal. Webb's talent behind the camera had some of the same stiffness. But he couldn't keep Peggy down no matter how lackluster the material.

Webb's character's narrative, as written by Michael Breen—he'd end up writing *Dragnet* a decade later—matches perfectly Jack's clunky performance, beginning with Pete Kelly's opening-scene voice-over: "If you're looking for a new way to grow old, this is the place to come: 17 Cherry Street, Kansas City," he intones. "The beer's good. The whiskey's aged—if you get here late in the day."

It hardly hurt the project that Ella sang a couple of wonderful numbers, or that Marvin, as an aging, philosophical clarinetist, single-handedly lifted some scenes right off the ground. Cinematographer Hal Rossen also knew how to light a blonde. (He'd been married, briefly, to Jean Harlow, and also shot *Singin' in the Rain* with Debbie Reynolds.) We can only assume that Rossen kept his dismay hidden as he went from filming one of the greatest musical films in history to helming one honchoed by Joe Friday.

But Rossen's camera simply fell in love with Peggy Lee and her character, Rose. From the opening shot, with Lee in a white-fur-collared coat and frosty platinum-blond hairdo, right up to her final scene in an insane asylum, Peggy is full of life. Despite being surrounded by a crew who held Ph.D.'s in overacting, she doesn't ever overdo and reveals the same try-less, achieve-more appeal she brought to her singing. Even in her handful of scenes with Webb, the cornet player with the heart of gold, she manages to seem credible.

Of course, the autobiographical dialogue didn't hurt. In their first scene, after the villain politician demands that Kelly give the washed-up chanteuse a tryout at his joint, Pete asks Rose, "Were you any good?"

"A couple of people said I was," says Rose. "They even talked about New York. But I got sick and had to go away." She slugs her shot of whiskey. "People said all I needed was a new start. But when you're thirty-five the only start you need is for home." Not incidentally, Peggy was thirty-five at the time.

When she had to play drunk, she played it perfectly: "I'll be fine," she says to Kelly, hoisting her glass. "I always start around noon. In case it gets dark early."

When she has to navigate the shoals of B dialogue—"You don't know him. He's too mean. He'd shoot craps on the Tomb of the Unknown Soldier"—she does it without prompting laughter. And when she has to lament her life's wrong turns, she slurs it all utterly convincingly: "Grab the chance when you get it—that's what I should have done. Grab it and have a little girl. What do they call it? The patter of little feet? Well, there will never be the patter of little feet in my house. Unless I was to rent some mice."

Rose's big number, in the crowded speakeasy, had taken flight from Art Hamilton's pen, and she delivers the slow, simple, fabulously effective "He Needs Me" with eyes at half-mast. Even Webb can't keep Peggy from stealing the last third of the film. In her final scene as a sane woman, Rose tries to sing, drunkenly, and the crowd boos her off stage. "Act sober and sing!" shouts the pol to Rose, and when she can't pull it off, he hits her— hard—and she rolls down the stairs. Exit Rose for the rest of the film, until Pete goes to visit her at the "Cedardale State Home for the Insane." As she sits alone, plinking a toy piano and singing to her dolly, Lee does a remarkable turn as a woman who's lost her mind; it's *Snake Pit* stuff, but way beyond what even an average actress could pull off when asked to play a chantoosie who's snapped. In a cavernous, dark room in the asylum, she sings a heartbreaking, simple, stunning little rhyme for Pete Kelly. It's called "Sing a Rainbow." When she's done, Pete Kelly asks Rose the name of her dolly.

"She has different names—one for every day," says Rose.

"Sometimes she's sad, and then her name's Deloris. But if she's happy, I call her Peggy."

The film disappeared, but Peggy Lee received an Oscar nomination for best supporting actress. She won the New York Film Critics Award and the Motion Picture Exhibitors Award. Most impressive was the vote of the people who actually filled the theaters: A poll of thirty million moviegoers gave her the New Star award. The Decca album of the soundtrack from *Pete Kelly's Blues* said "Peggy has rarely been so emotionally moving—and so convincing as a jazz singer."

But it would be Peggy Lee's last movie role.

In several subsequent interviews, she spoke of economic imperatives: "Agents would not have me do more movies," she said in one. "Then for another thing I was playing the part of an alcoholic singer and it got uncomfortably close to people assuming the part was autobiographical."

The former explanation rang true enough: She could make steady money touring and recording; her musical talent was a bankable, sure thing. Success in Hollywood relied on too many outside factors—as the producers of *The Jazz Singer*'s botching of the dialogue in postproduction made obvious. On the screen, the results were out of her control.

But the alcohol suspicion—one she expounded upon only once publicly, years later in an interview with *After Dark* magazine—rang just as true: "It was never my choice not to act again," she told the writer. Rose Hopkins, she explained, was a role she gave her "heart and soul" to: a tragic figure, an alcoholic singer who lost her mind, a woman whose "grip on life was . . . very fragile," and after the film was released, she said, "the word went out around Hollywood that *I* was Rose Hopkins, that it wasn't really acting." She heard the rumors that she was "an alcoholic, passing out at parties, waking up all over town." Pamphlets like "The Twelve Steps of Alcoholism" started appearing on her dressing tables. In effect, her performance had been so convincing that people had assumed it was an accurate reflection of her own life.

In fact, Peggy told the interviewer, it was anything but. "Sure, I drank," she said. "Maybe a little too much at times." But this was a decade when "everyone drank to be social." When the head of the L.A. Alcoholics Anonymous chapter, for whom she'd sung at benefits, called on her, she assumed it was a friendly visit, until the man began to talk about Peggy's problems. She told him *Pete Kelly's Blues* was a movie: "It wasn't *my* life."

She was not, and never had been, she said, an alcoholic. But the rumors can be deadly, so she decided to stick thereafter to her chosen industry.

One prominent figure in the industry who knew her at the time, who asked for anonymity, recalls that Peggy did have a reputation for having once been a heavy drinker, but for having grown beyond it. According to another source who knew Peggy well, any visits she might have taken to AA would have been in support of David Barbour.

By this time, according to one report, Peggy was able to command $200,000 a year on the road, a figure that accords with her $8,000-per-week Copa salary. Of course, by that math, she'd have had to be on the road at least half of the year—a trying enough schedule for any singer, a brutal one for a woman alone with a child. But Peggy and her daughter would make their hotel rooms into homes. They'd create their own world—pillows, ashtrays, pictures. If there wasn't a kitchen, and there usually wasn't, they'd turn bathrooms into kitchens and take along electric frying pans and hot plates so they could cook regular meals.

But despite efforts to normalize her taxing routine, interviews from this period convey a woman nearing exhaustion. One day, according to a profile in *Redbook*, Lee was awaiting a taxi to take her to the airport for a flight to Boston, with her musicians en route to the East Coast and her secretary en route to Chicago to get a fur out of storage, when she found herself unable to go ahead with her travel plans. She just couldn't go forward. Her doctor, she said, recommended complete rest.

Another time, she traveled to Carmel for a week of religious lectures, but was called back to work. She was rehearsing a Ciro's act and a television show. One newspaper reported that Jack Webb had "sign[ed] her for three additional films to be made by his Mark VII Productions." They were never made.

"Sometimes," she told Kirtley Baskette, *Redbook*'s writer, "I feel as if I'm on a treadmill not knowing where I'm headed, who I am or what it's all about." This admission came in the middle of a remarkably revealing portrait of a woman who still lived and worked each day as if it were her last. "She often drives herself beyond the limits of her physical and emotional strength . . . she composes short stories, paints, gardens furiously, carries on church and charity works and conscientiously mothers a twelve-year-old daughter despite tours which keep her absent from home half of each year. Recently her agent, calling to discuss $50,000 worth of advance bookings, found her on hands and knees waxing the floor."

What made Peggy run? In the *Redbook* piece, her manager, Ed Kelly, who had been with her for ten years, said, "Peggy has worked so hard and so long to be somebody that she has built up a rushing river inside her. She can't dam it now." Her sister Marianne believed that it was "because she had so little as a kid that she wants to give out so much." Asked about her own goals, Peggy answered, "To gain control of my life."

But her most interesting admission was a candid assessment of her journey thus far: "I would far rather have been Norma Egstrom with a real mother," she told the writer, "than Peggy Lee without one."

If life on Denslow had the flavor of a Noël Coward play, on Kimridge her existence took on a more surrealistic cast, as she collected male friends to keep her company—and there was never any question: She did like to have men in her life.

One was pianist Gene DiNovi, who'd accompanied her in *Lady and the Tramp* and *Pete Kelly's Blues* and during gigs back in New York. DiNovi was young and single, and he'd never been to California. "So now Peggy called up and said, 'I need you.' She made a captive out of me," he says, laughing. "I was in a monastery."

Peggy, DiNovi recalls, didn't like to leave her aerie above Los Angeles except to rehearse and perform at Ciro's. But DiNovi could come and go as he pleased in his old Jag, and then the Thunderbird, and then the Chrysler 300. Having joined the unofficial cast of live-in characters at "Casa Peggy"—a house that never lacked for life—he had his own room and a piano to write his music. And he enjoyed some of the greatest company he'd ever have.

Dave Barbour would frequently come up to see Nicki. "He was a beautiful guy," says DiNovi. "He was a great guy, he was just an alcoholic. He and Peggy had a great sort of humor together. He was always sneaking drinks." Housekeeper, cook, and confidante Lillie Mae was a frequent presence with *her* guy. "Lillie was like a character from a bad movie," DiNovi remembers, "always bustling around, making these crazy sounds. She and the guy had this repartee going. . . . It was wild."

There were also doctors, of course, although Gene wasn't ever quite sure exactly what was wrong with Peggy. Years later, she would write of heart problems that began to manifest themselves after *Pete Kelly's Blues*. All DiNovi knew was that doctors would visit and become regulars. "She had doctors who'd come up there, like the guy who was experimenting with cures for arthritis. She had him wrapped around her finger, you know? She'd tell him what to prescribe."

Wildest of all the crew was Jimmy Marino: physicist, childhood polio victim, visionary, failed entrepreneur, all-around genius, and all-around character. Jimmy Marino, went the story, had worked with J. Robert Oppenheimer on the Manhattan Project. He knew Albert Einstein personally. He also knew music. It was at a show at the Fairmont in San Francisco when he first introduced himself to Peggy. Thereafter he took her up on her invitation to live at Kimridge.

"He was short, muscular, olive-skinned, and he wore big rimmed glasses," Stella Castellucci recalls. "A nice head of hair. He wasn't what you'd call good-looking at all. Very pleasant-looking, though, and very enthusiastic about everyone and everything. And extremely nice to me. . . . Anyone who needed a home, she'd take them in. Sometimes, you couldn't get away."

Marino's polio had left him with a withered left arm; he stood no taller than he had as a twelve-year-old. "I was able to discuss my theory about color and sound waves with him," Peggy would recall in her autobiography. At the time, she wrote, one of her creative pipe dreams had arisen from a musical project, never spoken of before or since, that reflected her growing curiosity in exploring intellectual and musical boundaries. It involved singing a song in front of a chemically treated film screen so that, as the sound waves hit the screen, they would produce different colors.

This all got Peggy thinking that "color and sound waves might be used as a healing device. Jimmy was working on the H-bomb at Cal Tech, and he actually took my idea to Einstein, who, I was told, thought it had merit. He was even scheduled to come to dinner." Einstein never did dine at Kimridge, but Marino came back from one visit with Einstein carrying a book autographed by the man himself: "To my favorite girl singer."

By the time DiNovi met Marino, he'd also lost his right hand, apparently in an accident involving a machine he'd devised to process uranium. "But it didn't keep him from shifting his Corvette," Gene recalls. Something of a car guy himself, Gene would tool around in his T-Bird—when it was running. "I'll never forget the day I got it to the top of the hill, but it died. So Jimmy and I open the hood, and there's Jimmy on one side looking under the hood, and me on the other. Here's this so-called fancy piano player, and this fancy scientist, and neither of us have a clue. We both break up. Neither of us know what's going on. I say, 'Jimmy, you're supposed to be so smart.' He says, 'Gene, you're supposed to be so smart.' And neither of us can figure out a car." (Another time, Gene recalls, when he was driving his Jaguar, it had just labored up the hill, overheating, "and Lillie Mae's guy is driving this Model T, or Model A, and he's giving me grief because his old car has no trouble getting up the hill.")

DiNovi was astounded by the depths of Jimmy Marino's brain. "We'd sit there at night in Peggy's room, me on the floor on one side, Jimmy on the other, and the two of them would talk about all these far-out ideas. She just had this wonderful, inquiring mind, and Jimmy was so brilliant. The guy was such a simpatico character. He was like a Glenn Gould of science, if you know what I mean."

For DiNovi, the whole thing was something of a vacation in paradise. Stella would come up and they'd jam. Dave would arrive to visit Nicki, and Nicki and Jimmy and Gene would go down the hill to catch a movie. The band would rehearse during the day, with occasional breaks: One day, Peggy took them all to see *Pete Kelly's Blues,* much to the stunned amazement of the crowd.

At Ciro's, they'd spin an intriguing repertoire, from "The Siamese Cat Song"—with the musicians doing cat voices—to "Lover" and her other standards. DiNovi was in awe of the lady, musically. Like Nat King Cole, she had a way of making any song accessible. "She was able to fit the mainstream with the jazz feeling, at a time when things were getting commercial, and people loved it."

Sometimes, DiNovi recalls, when she'd feel a little down, or a little lonely, she'd open a can of Van Camp's beans. "It was her comfort food. It reminded her of the good things of her childhood."

One day Peggy and Gene were writing a couple of songs for Jim Backus's Mr. Magoo character—"Three Cheers for Mr. Magoo" and "Mr. Magoo Does the Cha Cha Cha"—and Backus came up for a rehearsal. "He looked like he'd been in a fight," recalls DiNovi. "He said, 'Look at me.' I said, 'What happened?' He said, 'There's this new kid on the set, and the script called for us to scuffle, and he really got into it.' " The set where all the trouble transpired, as it happened, was *Rebel Without a Cause*. The guy was James Dean.

They cut the record, with Backus doing the voice. Years later, DiNovi recalls, Peggy had neglected to sign any contracts for the songs; as DiNovi remembers she never saw a dime. Business was never her strong point. It wasn't for lack of smarts; more concerned with managing the immediate priorities—getting the musicians taken care of, choreographing her shows—she just tended to overlook the details of the business.

DiNovi also vividly recalls a few eccentricities: "She'd take arrangements she didn't like or need and paper the garage with them. She had a manuscripted garage." But she never, ever stopped taking the music seriously. "Music was the real place for her. That's the psychology of the accompanist and the singer. You can't be any more intimate without sexuality than with an accompanist. It's sort of a musical love affair that goes on. It's just a different kind of intimacy. Some time later, when I was accompanying Dinah Shore, she wanted to pay me for ten weeks of work and keep me around all year. There's a musical thing that

goes on that's a very strong thing. It's different with piano players. They're not looking at us for the other things that the other
men failed to do. . . ."

DiNovi's memories of his sabbatical in the monastery on Kimridge Avenue are of a happy woman, comfortable with herself,
upbeat of disposition, clean and sober and altogether delightful
to be around. But after several months, DiNovi figured it was
time to cut loose and head back east, to the real world, to the action. Back in New York, it was not unusual for him to get a late-
night call from Peggy asking him to give her a few notes for an
arrangement, something special that only he could provide. He
welcomed the calls.

Some years after that, when DiNovi was working with Lena
Horne, he discovered that Lena had been infatuated with a
strange little guy who'd briefly shown up in her life. A physicist
with a withered arm.

EIGHTEEN

High on a Hill

A DISPATCH FROM Peggy's Kimridge home penned by Associated Press film writer Bob Thomas at the time paints a vivid picture of a haven for good times, good music, and the fellowship that the singer so obviously couldn't be without: "The living room of Peggy Lee's hilltop home was rocking. The pianist was pounding out a rhythm. The guitarist and bass fiddle player strummed furiously; the drummer and bongo artist assaulted their instruments. Leaning against the piano and moaning in throaty tones was Peggy herself, dressed plainly in a yellow smock but glamorous with her tightly combed platinum hair. First she delivered 'Swing Low, Sweet Chariot' as it has never been swung before. She followed with a frantic version of 'Do I Love You?' After a half hour of this, she called a halt for sandwiches and iced tea and collapsed in a chair. 'This is awfully hard work.'"

For a brief time, after Marino and DiNovi, Peg welcomed the frequent visits of another musician. Bobby Darin's legendary curiosity, his versatility, his need to seek more and more and more from life described a personality that fit Peggy's well. He was a frequent visitor for a brief time, and their friendship was intense. In her autobiography, Lee limits her description of the relationship to the words "We became close."

One of the most intriguing artistic avenues that Peggy Lee pursued at the time was the writing of the theme song for a truly camp movie, which she performed on a truly hokey television show—and managed to transcend the aesthetic limitations with ease.

Johnny Guitar was a B Western starring Joan Crawford that, in retrospect, seems more suited to John Waters. But Lee counted the lyrics of the title song, written with Victor Young's music, as among the best she'd ever written, and certainly no one who saw her perform it could dispute the authenticity of the emotion.

She even made it work on television, on the *Colgate Comedy Hour,* where she had several tough acts to follow, including Abbott and Costello. Peggy suddenly appeared from the shadows, wandering a darkened stage meant to resemble a Western set, despite the fact that the horizon at the back was lit up as if an atomic bomb had just been detonated; the whole thing suggested nothing so much as a postapocalyptic landscape. The choreography called for Peggy to stroke a guitar that, for some reason, was mounted on the wall of a shack. The cardboard setup didn't diminish her delivery, which was slow, sultry, evocative. And never once did her eyes meet the camera, as she reminisced for her lost strummer—clearly Dave Barbour:

There was never a man like my Johnny,
Like the one they call Johnny Guitar.

A moment later, she was back on stage in a completely different incarnation, in a beaded dress she had hidden beneath her Western garb, to perform a brass-heavy, bongoed "Bewitched, Bothered and Bewildered." She still hadn't learned how to swing her body in the rhythm—but this time, replacing the grand piano she stroked in *The Jazz Singer*, the lucky prop was a scarf, and she finished by spiking it for emphasis. She tortured the handkerchief as the applause died down, and then confided, almost bashfully, "Thank you, ladies and gentlemen. I'm so glad you liked that. You make me very happy." She sounded very much as if she meant it.

Experience suggested that marriage and Peggy Lee were not ever going to get along. She'd tried it with a man whose alcoholism defied a stable union. Pressured by her spiritual adviser to find another husband for Nicki's sake, she'd tried it with an actor she didn't love. Neither relationship had worked.

On the other hand, there was nothing to suggest that her emotional needs were lessening, and maybe this explains what happened at Ciro's one night. There was a knock on the dressing-room door, and her bongo friend Jack Costanzo introduced her to an actor. When the man blurted that he'd been in love with her for ten years, Peggy told him to have a seat and asked if he'd like to have a drink with her. She was always a sucker for a line.

Dewey Martin accepted the invitation. Ten years before, he had sat in the audience in San Francisco, entranced by the songs of Peggy Lee. It was a salve for what he'd been through then: a terrible war. Dewey Martin was a pilot.

Now he found himself actually sitting by her side. The first thing he explained to her was his bleached hair. It was for a role. "*You* know," he said.

"I know," said the platinum lady, and she gave him her phone number.

Dewey Martin—independent, moody, strong, and handsome—had gone through his share of ups and downs after climbing out of the cockpit in the South Pacific. Steady film work hadn't delivered rewards. After scoring a couple of decent roles in forgettable pictures—including a cowboy turn in *Big Sky*—he'd earned a contract with MGM, where he'd appeared in eight movies in four years. He'd also married a model, but that marriage hadn't worked. A role in a picture filming in Rome had led to some nomadic wanderings in Spain. At the time he met Peggy Lee, he was a man perhaps looking for the missing piece of the puzzle.

According to an uncredited article written at the time, when Dewey called Peggy, she was painting the house, and asked him to call back. He didn't. So she sent him a note: "What happened to you?" He called again. Within a few months, they were seeing only each other. Within a few more months, he was calling her every night from a small town in Utah where he was filming a TV show. Ultimately, he proposed to her.

"I remember seeing him in the audience at Ciro's," Stella Castellucci recalls. "And at the time, she was so vulnerable. Very alone."

They married in April 1956 amid a flurry of comic mishaps that suggested, from the start, another misstep for Lee. They decided to tie the knot in Palm Springs; he'd fly in from Utah. When a storm grounded his chartered plane, he borrowed one to fly himself, but he couldn't find the Los Angeles airport. He flew down through the clouds to Burbank, where they got their license minutes before the bureau closed. On April 28, 1956, she became Mrs. Dewey Martin.

In public they did the things newlyweds do: They stood on line at Disneyland. They visited the San Diego Zoo. They went to Tijuana, to see the bull that Dewey's famed matador friend had named for Peggy. They lived in Peggy's house. Martin later told an interviewer that he bought the house from her—the man should own the home.

Apparently, the man should own the woman, too. Martin confessed to the writer that he knew his wife would "probably" always sing, but "she knows she never has to work another day if she doesn't want to." This was a noble, fifties-steeped attitude. But anyone who had any real understanding of Peggy Lee would have a hard time ever entertaining it.

The wedding night wasn't a stunner, according to Peggy's later account to Stella Castellucci: They had gone to a friend's home in Palm Springs to celebrate. In their hotel, she brought out cocktails and hors d'oeuvres. According to a story she would later tell a close friend, he was watching TV. There was a Robert Preston movie on the television, and, mindful of her affection for Preston, he flipped the tray over and struck her.

Lee's Decca LP *Dream Street,* issued two months after her marriage, contained some of her best jazz stylings, although it would never get the recognition it deserved. "For *Dream Street,*" she said in an interview, "I picked tunes I had really wanted to do for a long time. I felt a need in myself to do material that would be different for me." And different it was, featuring fine examples of her jazz, her pop, her blues, her ballads, and her Latin. She opened with one of the most moving, weird, dark, spooky numbers she ever sang: the spoken-word "Midnight." The song took us to a blighted emotional neighborhood, "where old dreams are traded for new: I know where they're bought, I know where they're sold. . . ."

"The dark, moody side," says Stella Castellucci, who played on *Dream Street,* "was where Peggy lived . . . in her heart and soul."

A bouncy cocktail-jazz riff called "What's New" featured Rowles and Castellucci. Then there was "You're Blasé," a wonderfully sardonic thing by a couple of unknown writers that she seemed to have chosen just to reflect her current darkness: "You're deep, just like a chasm; you've no enthusiasm. You're tired and uninspired. You're blasé."

Two of the most powerful numbers harkened to times when things had seemed simpler. The classic Arlen-Harburg plaint "Last Night When We Were Young" is a killer, and not just because she always seemed to be able to channel every bluesy feeling Harold Arlen ever wrote. At thirty-five, already in the midst of a third bad marriage, she was perhaps beginning to wonder, in the mood of the song, where things had gone wrong.

Her reprise of the old Benny hit "My Old Flame" was a surprise and a delight—far superior to the syrupy version she'd recorded for Benny a decade ago.

But the dark, strange undertones of *Dream Street* further muddied the water when it came to classifying the woman who was now firmly planted in the pop-singing pantheon: What kind of singer *was* she? Did she belong in the jazz polls? And what kind of *person* was she? Playing drunks and singing about hanging out in lost neighborhoods with people looking for love in all the wrong places?

Unquestioned was her talent, although sometimes there were suggestions that it was this very quality that was holding her back. "Musically she's too good for her own good," wrote *Down Beat* critic George Hoefer in the story that was coverlined "Peggy Lee: Too Good for Her Own Good":

She has been too successful in several areas to win acceptance in the jazz world, and not quite commercial enough to attain the pinnacle of fame awarded to lesser stars by an undiscriminating mass public. There is something original about Peggy, a something that has not been clearly defined. Peggy has given jazz performances on records that mark her [as] the greatest white female jazz singer since Mildred Bailey.

By late 1956, the Martin-Lee household was no longer a welcoming place for stray geniuses, players, or pals. The house now featured a sign above the doorway that read GET LOST, MAN, GET LOST. Dewey wanted no crowds: "All that's changed," he said. "Our home is for us, our family, and our friends."

Martin's jealousy of every musician he saw by his wife's side further underscored the inappropriateness of the pairing. He just didn't get the dynamic she was accustomed to. A break from the antisocial route came, however, in December 1957 at a Christmas Eve party at which the couple entertained forty of their friends in the mirror-walled living room overlooking the pool surrounded by Japanese landscaping. As described in the newspaper account, the evening took on the patina of a Broadway play whose first act might hint at a surprise ending later on: Over drinks, Martin announced that they'd all play a game called "Don't Trust Your Husband."

He then led her on a scavenger hunt around the house, from books to records, as the party followed along. The final treasure was a small box beneath the tree with a poem in it professing Martin's love to his wife. She cried in front of the guests.

Peggy Lee's public profile had never been higher, but her act had definitely hit a stale patch. She was a frequent headliner at the Sands but critics found her spark to be dimming. It wasn't that she had stopped trying: Band members recall her paying more attention to details, from her dress to her personal grooming; if the stage was close to the crowd, she'd use a Q-tip with Vaseline to make sure that her nostrils were clean.

On piano, Peggy was now backed by a legend. Lou Levy, "the Good Gray Fox," had worked with all the great bandleaders, from Georgie Auld to Cootie Williams, Charlie Christian, Count Basie, Woody Herman, Zoot Sims, Stan Getz. Before it was all over, after stints with vocalists from Anita O'Day to Tony Bennett and Frank Sinatra (on "My Way"), Levy would joke that he'd worked with every singer but Pavarotti.

He was not only a gifted accompanist, he was a great keyboard man in his own right. It was no surprise that he and Lee were a good fit. He was handsome, he was smart, and he was gentlemanly. His relationship with Peggy, some players thought, transcended their work on stage. "One time," Mundell Lowe, Peggy's guitarist for many years, recalls, "we had to change planes in Chicago. They were both in the sauce a little bit—you know, you're on a plane after a great engagement, you have a drink—and in the terminal, there was a gate for a flight to Puerto Rico. Peggy said, 'Lou, let's go to Puerto Rico and get married.' He says, 'Okay.' They were heading toward the gate when we grabbed them and said, 'You can't do that, you idiots.' "

Levy had brought a new bass player on board in Vegas, an old pal he'd worked with in Georgie Auld's group. Max Bennett enjoyed more than the jazz, he enjoyed the rituals of showbiz life—the hugs, the words of assurance—and the get-togethers afterward; it was a community. He loved playing with Peggy Lee, though they had their share of tough moments. He once confronted her about nit-picking during a rehearsal when she knew the band was on a deadline to pick up their tickets to get out of town after a show and get back to their families. If they didn't get the tickets that day, they'd be screwed. When she kept them, Bennett called her on it. She gave it right back. There was some of the diva to her, sure—"But if she liked the way you played, you could do no wrong," Bennett says now. "She was definitely on your side. Yes, sometimes she could go beyond perfectionism unnecessarily. But it was never, 'I know more than you do.' She just would get into something and worry it to death."

But the upsides, Bennett recalls, were a joy: They'd hang out after a show (when they didn't have to leave town), catch a late late show at another club, have parties in her room—nothing crazy, just family—"and all would be forgiven."

Today, Stella Castellucci emphasizes the family aspect of her association with Lee. She loved the hugging and support before each show, and there were other benefits, too. "Peggy made a lima bean casserole with sour cream and mustard. I'd never had anything like it. I loved it. So one of the engagements we were working, we were holding hands and kissing before the show, and I started saying, for no reason, 'Lima beans.' That became our break-a-leg ritual. She'd look at me and say, 'Lima beans.' "

Stella was in awe not only of Peggy's voice, but of her song writing chops. Though it had been a while since Peggy had had a hit with original lyrics, the words for "The Siamese Cat Song" alone spoke of a muse that Castellucci marveled at. "Peg could write a [song] on a dime," Stella says. "She could write a complete lyric in a few minutes. All she needed was an idea and a melody. She was a born lyricist, and a born jazz singer. I don't know where the purists all get this, why they all have this attitude about jazz. I mean, *Black Coffee*? What more proof do you need?"

Not all of Peggy's musicians were thrilled about having to hang out with her all day and night in Vegas. Jack Costanzo's bongos were a key ingredient of the show, but he was more of a free spirit than Lee liked in a musician. "She liked to take ownership of people," says Costanzo. "She wanted us all to hang after the show. But I wanted to do stuff on my own. She disliked that I wouldn't mix with her and the band. But I had my own life. I was young, I swung as much as I could."

Costanzo's frustration over Peggy's insistence on control of her band would be echoed by musicians and managers for many years to come. For Lee, the band was family, and the family stayed together. Sometimes wives would be excluded from tours—not only because she wanted the band's devotion to be directed solely toward her, but because this family was sacrosanct. It was from the family of her musicians that Peggy increasingly and ultimately sustained her truest love.

"I would say that with Peggy the performance came first. And then everything else came after." This last reference was to men. "If I'd been her boyfriend, I think it would have been tough. I don't believe when it came to romance she was extremely . . . well, I always got the feeling that Peggy wouldn't be extremely affectionate.

"I would say that Peggy Lee was a sad girl, and the happiness she had in life was her music. She had dysfunctional marriages, for whatever reason. I think she was truly a sad person . . . and the music made her very happy. And, of course, when it came to music—writing it as well as performing it—she was just a genius."

By early 1957, Peggy's obligation to Decca had run out. It had been a satisfactory relationship; she had delivered her share of hits, but creatively she had stagnated, and Decca, according to writer Will Friedwald, "was in decline at the time." Capitol hadn't slipped any, though. "It was regarded," says Friedwald, "as the finest record company in the world."

Lee's return to Capitol for the next fifteen years was prompted by reasons never fully understood, but there is no doubt that two men had an influence. One was a producer named Dave Cavanaugh, with whom Peggy had developed a friendship. The other was her new neighbor up on the hill.

When Peggy and her daughter first moved into the Kimridge Avenue house, their home was isolated, at the end of a street, backing on a canyon. Feeling isolated and afraid of snakes, Peggy and her daughter once surrounded the whole house with a coarse rope laid on the ground, because they'd heard that snakes wouldn't slither over it. But soon new homes were popping up around them. One belonged to Capitol recording artist Frank Sinatra, her old friend. "There have been very few men in our business who have affected me so deeply I can't express myself," Lee wrote in her memoir. "Frank is one of them. Frank invited me many times to his house for dinners or parties or movies in his theater. We also shared quiet talks and funny jokes...and planned a whole album together. It was totally his concept."

Despite Lee's words, there is actually some dispute about whether *The Man I Love*, the first Peggy Lee album produced after her renewed association with Capitol in July 1957, was actually Sinatra's idea. But there is no doubting his contributions to the record, which he produced and which stands as one of the landmarks of her career. Nelson Riddle's orchestra, which backed Peggy, was conducted by Sinatra. The charts were Sinatra's. The choice of songs was Sinatra's. The album-cover art featured a misty-eyed Peggy looking over the shoulder of a man (Dewey Martin) hugging her; it was Sinatra who suggested that Lee have menthol sprayed in her eyes to give them an appropriately misty look during the photo session.

Wondering whether Peggy and Frank's complicated but at times intimate friendship added a special dimension to their work together would be strictly conjecture. But no one disputes the depth of their relationship, which went beyond their being sexual lovers, as they seem to have been now and then. The timing of their liaisons is not clear. "He was smitten by her artistry and talent," Peggy's close friend Phoebe Jacobs recalls. "There was a sameness about them. I do know that he came on to her many times when they were neighbors." The details of their affair—the length, the frequency—have rarely been spoken of, and were certainly never discussed by either Lee or Sinatra. But few who knew them both would dispute that their personalities meshed on many levels.

To start with, they shared a trait that was unusual in the record business in its first few decades. According to Will Friedwald, "Sinatra was one of the first recording artists who took control of his own destiny—planning arrangements, picking songs, having an active hand in everything. It used to be just the A&R people at the labels who would say, 'This is what you're singing today.' Sinatra was the first real example of a singer who had the presumption to decide what to sing. And Peggy was the first female singer to follow Sinatra in that regard."

As producer Ken Bloom points out, both were perched at the top, besieged by wannabes and wanters. "They could relate," says Bloom, "because each of them knew what the other was going through. They were on an equal level. They were sort of the same person, really, except one was female and the other male."

"What we have here is Primal Masculine and Primal Feminine—yin-yang to the max," says Bill Rudman, Bloom's partner in producing one of Peggy's last great records, *Love Held Lightly*. "And what deepens it is that Sinatra *also* had real vulnerability and Peggy *also* had real toughness—all of which helped make their performances so rich. No wonder they were a mutual admiration society. They lived the whole blessed continuum of sexual energy."

For most of their lives, no matter what else was going on, Lee and Sinatra would remain true friends. In later years, when Lee needed work, Sinatra would help find it. When she was hospitalized two decades later in New Orleans, Sinatra sent a plane to bring her home. To aid her recuperation, he had air-conditioning installed in her home. When she needed him in any way, he was always there. They were lovers only briefly, but their friendship was enduring.

At times, Sinatra's commitment to the family took on added dimensions, like the night he brought a Vegas girl to the house and left her with the teenaged Nicki and a friend while he spoke to Peggy in another room. Upon returning to discover that his date had supplied some champagne to the girls, Sinatra lost his temper over the cavalier behavior of the woman.

The Sinatra patina to Peggy's first disc in her second Capitol era was about as golden an endorsement as any project could get, but *The Man I Love* was not Peggy Lee's best album. But two of her signature songs are worth the price of admission alone. The first, fortunately, was the first cut on the first side, Gershwin's "The Man I Love." After a chokingly gossamer-string set of flourishes to kick it off, Lee delivers this ballad perfectly, heart-swellingly. The flutes, the strings, the over-orchestration do everything they can to oversell the sentiment. She defies them all.

But this album would forever be known for a song unlike any other she would ever sing, a tale that would ultimately represent the unfulfilled dream of her life. Like the other purely autobiographical song that would eventually bring Lee her first Grammy, "The Folks Who Live on the Hill" seemed to have been written for Peggy alone. Unlike "Is That All There Is?," however, this song did not speak of harsh, cynical reality, but of its opposite. It was a sentimental, affecting dream that seems to symbolize the longing of a generation for the comforts of hearth and home.

"The Folks Who Live on the Hill," with lyrics by Oscar Hammerstein, II, and music by Jerome Kern, could have come off as corny in an average singer's hands—or, perhaps, in the hands of a woman who had actually found the peace and long-standing marital tranquillity the song describes. The lyrics, chronicling the stages of a marriage, tell the story of a woman who never seems to have wanted more than her husband and their home on the hill. Peggy, driven by ambitions that may have overpowered her hopes for such security, suffuses the lyrics with longing; she caresses the words so carefully and delicately that she seems to be reaching out to touch the hopes and dreams of the couple whose journey she follows. Nelson Riddle's strings, though sometimes on the saccharine side (especially for contemporary listeners), here enhance rather than overdramatize the essential emotions. The end result is a fairy tale that seems to distill the long-gone dreams of a generation, replete with all of the ingredients for domestic happiness: a house "on a hilltop high," that "two can fill." An "added wing," a few changes here and there, "as any family will." But none of the alterations to their dream cottage matter a whit, held up against her ultimate dream: for she and her loving spouse to "always" be known as the "Folks Who Live on the Hill."

It would forever be one of her favorite songs. "For all of that glamour," Stella says now, "she was very happy to be sitting by her fireplace, preferably barefoot, or cooking a pot of lima beans, or gardening." This is the voice we hear in "The Folks Who Live on the Hill."

Phoebe Jacobs had first met Peggy in Phoebe's role as publicist, assistant, boundless energizer, and general doyenne of Manhattan's music-entertainment milieu. Years later, as an acknowledged observer of the New York jazz scene of the fifties, Phoebe would count her relationship with Peggy as one of her life's highlights. The two were introduced in 1957 when the latter was doing television specials, and Phoebe could not help but be stunned by Peggy's energy. The woman she saw on the Revlon set was energetic, healthy, and charismatic, seeming to enjoy the track she'd chosen: a fast one.

"She had the specials, she was doing club work, she was

recording—it would have been physically impossible unless she was one hundred percent. And man, this lady would party. You know—after things were over, you had to have wine. That's where she and Sinatra were exactly alike: If you got through at three in the morning, you could be falling asleep in a chair, but you had to stay there with them. You couldn't leave."

If they shared some obvious character traits, Frank and Peggy were definitely dissimilar in their approach to their art—as wonderfully evidenced by her appearance, a few months after the release of the album, to sing a duet with Frank on Sinatra's television show in late 1957.

At the time, Sinatra had seized a corner of the television airwaves for himself. His weekly guest list included the very best talent in the business: Lena, Dinah, Ella, Bing, Satchmo, Sammy, Dean, Elvis. The music was invariably cool, but Sinatra always tried to be cooler than the guest; it was all about him, and the tunes tended to suffer. When he was belting with the guys, he usually managed to come out on top. Opposite some of the women, though, it was hard to ignore how far out of his league he was wandering.

One week, when Dinah Shore was at his side, she giggled her way through a medley of "A Foggy Day in London Town," "I've Got You Under My Skin," and "All of Me." She laughed her approval as Frank, who was having trouble reading the lyrics, interjected punch lines. They had such a fun time, with Sinatra dragging on a cigarette, that the viewer felt privy to a late-night living-room jam around a piano. Dinah's confidence was unmistakable, but she willingly relinquished the dominant role to Frank.

On another show, Lena Horne seized her moment, wresting the attention away from her host as they traded snatches of song. When Horne, with her Cheshire-cat grin, segued into her classic "Stormy Weather," she stole the show. They were two heavyweight champions trading punches. Horne was a force of nature, even on the small screen; but together, she and Sinatra generated no heat.

When Ella had her turn, she was just Ella: sensational, if a little nervous and absurdly intimidated. The admiration between her and Sinatra seemed real, and mutual, as they made their way through "Can't We Be Friends?" (in which he mockingly praised Pearl Bailey, Dinah, and Lena). Ella played it as called for. In a duet with Frank on "Moonlight in Vermont," she was grooving, eyes closed. But one somehow got the feeling that despite her brilliance, she was never quite immersed in what it was she was singing.

Now it was Peggy's turn. At the top, Frank appeared in the foreground, well lighted, with Peggy behind him on a small stage, draped in shadows. She seemed posed, frozen, like a music-box doll not yet wound up. Uncharacteristically, Frank tried to be serious in his introduction; he wasn't even smiling as he intoned, "Ladies and gentlemen, one of my favorite people, an all-time great singer, here she is, a swingin' gal and a swingin' tune—Miss Peggy Lee."

Right on cue, the lights went up, and Peggy unfroze, parting the veil on the front of her skirt to step down as if descending the staircase of a royal palace. Seated next to Sinatra, her sexuality seemed a physical presence—maybe too much so. Her tight décolletage looked slightly painful, and at times she appeared a near-caricature. When the loose patter started, she didn't seem to want to join in.

"What do you say we segue into a pretty song?" asked Frank.

"I'm all for it," answered Peggy, absently.

Whereupon Frank threw in the kind of ad-lib that had made Dinah and Ella giggle: "I must say, you're *awfully* agreeable." At this, Peggy turned away with a half smile. She would not play the game. Her attitude seemed to suggest that she didn't care about his ratpack cool. She was not on board to give the big man his required sexual salute. *She* was on camera, and she was starting to sing a song, and this was her church. So he'd better stand back and be respectful. She responded with a look of chastisement that was truly astonishing: He'd been rebuked.

Yet once they started up "Nice Work If You Can Get It," backed by nothing but snare, piano, and bass, she lightened up, and their flirtatious interplay was suddenly fabulous. Once she was singing, and singing as well as she ever would on television, she let her hair down—at least figuratively. Her actual hairstyle was a tight, short platinum helmet. Maybe that had something to do with her initial frostiness; it looked as if you couldn't have parted her hair with a chisel.

Only with the final lines of the song—"Nice work if you can get it, and if you get it, won't you show me how"—did she allow herself, now that she'd nailed it, to snap out of the role and turn to stare at him, wide-eyed. In this bout, there was a clear winner, and it was not even close. She'd wiped the stage with him.

For all her fluorescence on the tube, though, her over-orchestrated Sinatra album had not brought her the hit record she'd been seeking for such a very long time.

Things Are Swingin'

DEWEY MARTIN'S SIGN on Peggy Lee's mansion on Kimridge Avenue in Beverly Hills still exhorted visitors to stay away. But down in the city, far below the glittering hills, somewhere on a nondescript reach of Western Avenue, another sign hung above another doorway. It announced the name of a bar, and it welcomed the establishment's motley crew of customers. The actual name of the place is lost to history, but this much we know: the patrons weren't lured by reputation or snob appeal. To these people, the name on the matchbook didn't have to be "Ciro's." These patrons hadn't shown up to steal the silverware—unless they really needed it. They went to have a drink, or three, and hear some music, though the place didn't even always have music.

On this night, the band featured Max Bennett and Nino

Tempo, musicians well respected by their peers around town. Tempo was a handsome jazz tenor saxist. At age seven, after clarinet lessons with the master, he'd sung with Benny Goodman. But when he'd first heard Charlie Parker, Tempo had immediately switched to sax. On this night, he'd called a couple of players he knew to ask them to sit in on a random gig. When Max Bennett showed up with his bass, he had to have asked himself, "What the hell am I *doing* here?"

But he knew the answer. He was doing something he loved: playing music, something he usually did in a different kind of venue with none other than Miss Peggy Lee. And he was having a good time, despite the fact that no one was even paying much attention. This place was so far removed from the frippery up the hill that when a Hispanic guy came in off the street with a song and asked to sit in, the band let him take the microphone.

"What do you want to sing?" Nino asked.

The kid laid it out for them. It was a simple, funky tune: no key change, a good bass line. A soulful, catchy rhythm. Bennett liked it, and not just because the bass line was the heart of the thing. He liked it because he instantly heard someone else singing it. He knew he had to get this song into Peggy's hands.

Together, a few days later, Bennett and Peggy found the sheet music for "Fever," written by Johnny Davenport and Ed Cooley, recorded two years earlier by its third credited co-writer, Little Willie John.

Little Willie was "a stone genius," said the immortal jazz vocalist Jimmy Scott. Willie was all of five feet tall, and all of seventeen years old, when he'd hit with an album called *All Around the World*. But it wasn't the title song ("If grits ain't groceries, eggs ain't poultry, and Mona Lisa was a man"), but a tune with a shorter title that attracted attention. "Fever," laden with horns, gospel voices, electric guitar, was always a crowd-pleaser when he hit the road, with a young soul singer named James Brown as his opening act. Little Willie, whose penchant for packing heat landed him in some trouble, would be dead of a heart attack in prison by the time James Brown hit it big. But he might have heard Peggy Lee sing "Fever" a couple thousand times in the joint, if he had a radio.

Peggy loved the song. But Max and Lou wouldn't be around to record it; they had to hit the road with Ella Fitzgerald. One night in Palm Springs, Peggy had told her musicians that she was quitting touring for a while. Max had an idea why. "She was married to Dewey Martin," he remembers, "and he knocked her around a bit, and she decided not to work live for obvious reasons." Peggy didn't tell Bennett face-to-face about any mistreatment; she was apparently protective of her man. But Bennett was not alone in believing that, at home, these were trying times for Peggy.

So Max and Lou hit the road with Ella. Peggy went into the studio, and the sessions produced an album called *Things Are Swingin'*, with "Fever" issued as a separate single. "Capitol felt certain repertoire was meant for singles and not for albums," said Cy Godfrey, who would later become Lee's attorney. "Peggy had what were considered 'rock hits' in this time period, and her albums at the time stayed with the adult pop-singer image. The kids bought the single of 'Fever,' and their parents bought the album."

The album was titled for a pleasant enough major-keyed bounce of a thing—half jazz, half pop—that owed to Porter, to Mercer, and to her own lyrics, whose rhymes were identifiable as a genre all their own: Things were swingin'; birds were singin'; bells were ringin'. She couples "what the blues is" with "ones and twoses"—" 'cause where love is you can always find a rhyme, and where love is things are swinging all the time. . . ."

As a whole, *Things Are Swingin'* was a slick product with a heart of soul just dying to break out. The arranger was the versatile Jack Marshall, formerly a jazz guitarist in Billy May's band. While Peggy herself was largely in charge at most of her sessions, her collaboration here with Marshall suggests that this time out he might have exerted a bit more control. The horns tried to swing, but too much so; they stepped on the beat too heavily, lending a forced quality to the entire platter; the cumulative effect was not cool, but just dying to be.

Nearly every song, every lyric, testified to the grand, symmetrical beauty of love, when in fact all was not quite right: The wipe-the-slate-clean revolution of the sixties was beginning to telegraph itself with the Beat movement. Kerouac ruled the literary landscape, and jazz was pushing itself to extraordinary places, as Miles Davis's *Live at the Blackhawk,* recorded in the San Francisco nightspot, attested.

In many ways, Peggy's album was too safe, too easy—but very accessible. "Alright, Okay, You Win" was buoyantly hip. She managed to make the slight "It's a Wonderful World" listenable, if only for her spot-on vocals. "Ridin' High," a Cole Porter tune, was filled with similarly shallow sentiment. The song that surprises, though, is one for which she wrote both the music—as simple as simple can be, a couple of smiling chord changes, is all—and the lyrics. It was called "It's a Good, Good Night," and it served as a sort of thematic bookend to her "It's a Good Day" of more than a decade earlier. This sequel appeared not in the dawn of Lee's optimism, but, after two and a half marriages, in her midafternoon. Yet she brought humor, and some character, to the effort. "Hear ye, hear ye, ring the bell 'cause all is well," she proclaimed in an intro, before setting down her lyric of buoyant optimism: "Got a feeling I can't lose, and it's nothing like the blues. . . ."

It was convincing enough if all you asked of your happiness was that it be the kind represented by, say, the chorus of a musical comedy. But something about Peggy's voice and interpretation—

a slight caution, a slight resignation—now suggested that this starry, cartoon version of happiness was not attainable.

In the end, though, one thing unified *Things Are Swingin'*: Peggy's voice was transcendently smooth. From the first measure ("It's a wonderful world," with the word "world" trailing off to encompass about five different feelings) to the last, she had reached a place where no musical syllable was allowed to pass without being convincing and accounted for. Even for listeners grown accustomed to her pitch, her time, her tone, her edges of velvet—even as she rode the placid waves of this somnolent cultural current—her voice on *Swingin'* is extraordinary.

More convincing and captivating than anything on the album was "Fever," the sexiest song that Peggy Lee—or maybe anyone— ever sang.

She had definitely seen room for improvement in Little Willie's version. His arrangements were over the top; this cut begged for elegant spareness and distillation. Lee also had some fun messing with the lyrics and added some of her own, hipping the thing up with Beatspeak that flirted with parody: Captain Smith and Pocahontas had a "very mad affair." When her "daddy" wants to kill him, it's "Daddy-O, don't you dare." When Romeo puts his arms around Juliet, it's "Julie, baby, you're my flame. You give me fever."

The basic chart for the song was Jack Marshall's, and he would win the Grammy for the song's arrangement, although, according to Max Bennett, it was "obviously rearranged by Peggy and the musicians." It was Peggy's idea to cut out the guitar and use just a string bass, Jack Mondragon; a drummer, Shelly Manne; and a finger-snap, furnished by Howard Roberts, the guitarist whose guitar had been shelved. It was likely Manne's idea to use his fingers on the snare and tom-tom to accompany his perfect bass drum. Legend has it that additional finger-snapping may have been overdubbed, but there's no question whose fingers would do the snapping for the rest of her career, and in the sultriest, coolest fashion imagineable: Miss Peggy Lee's.

The sparseness of the sound—the drum and bass sounding equally Beat as they share the beat; they could just as easily have been backing a Ginsberg poetry reading somewhere in the Village—allowed Lee's delivery to attain a degree of hip that no popular singer had ever come close to. Lee's version of "Fever" drew on both the darkness of "Why Don't You Do Right?" and the knowing weariness of "Black Coffee" to produce a singular anthem for mainstream pop-music listeners who had some beatnik buried beneath their suburban facades. What's most astounding, perhaps, about this single was that it was recorded and sung by the woman who, at the same time, was giving us the decidedly restrained and over-orchestrated offerings on *Things Are Swingin'*. There could be no more telling testament to Lee's versatility as a jazz-pop singer than the conjunction of these two records.

As a gesture of ultimate cool, the finger-snap would soon be embedded in the culture (see the finger-snapping routines of the Jets street gang in the 1961 Jerome Robbins–Robert Wise film of *West Side Story,* for starters). But no one would ever wield a finger-snap like this one. Lest anyone doubt that Lee's snap was now a paramount part of the lady's image, check out the *George Gobel Show* from 1958 in which Lee sings the song alone on stage—surrounded by a dozen disembodied arms snapping their fingers.

Not only did Peggy not win the Grammy, she never even got credit for the lyrics she'd inserted, despite the fact that they appear on the sheet music. ("Watch your copyrights!" she would later write of this oversight.)

It wasn't just the record-buying public that was grateful. Some of the more old-school critics, taking delight in the song's defi-

ance of the rock craze, celebrated its "rise to a position usually reserved for baying vocal groups and splay-legged caveboys," in the
words of *Melody Maker*. "The final key to the success of 'Fever'
[is] its lyrics," wrote the magazine, "with their suggestion that
the great lovers of history not only felt the sting of teenage passion . . . but spoke of it in the teenage vernacular. A rose by any
other name would still be a gas. It's good to know that Romeo
and Juliet had parent trouble, too. . . .

" 'Fever'. . . combines strong jazz qualities with a number of
proven Hit Parade ingredients. Peggy Lee works to the absolute
minimum of accompaniment: one bass, one percussionist, and
two or three finger-snappers. The result is novel and extraordinarily compulsive. With such a sparse backing her singing is utterly exposed, to a degree that only a handful of popular singers
in this world could survive. [Nat Cole did it in the similar "Calypso Blues."] The subtle inflections of each phrase, the way she
raps out the title word, the conversational, almost mocking way
in which she tells her story: these things are the result of a
planned artistry which seldom glimpses that pot of gold at the
end of the Top Twenty rainbow."

Critics from the jazz trades were hoping against hope that the
rock-and-roll fever was abating; they anticipated the chaos it could
cause. They sadly envisioned the demise of the American Songbook. Peggy echoed the sentiments in an interview at the time
"Fever" was released. "I get around this country a great deal," she
said, "and find that most of the people—even the teenagers—are
longing for good popular music today. Rock 'n' roll is fading; the
ballads, the fine jazz, the melodious standards—which have never
died—are being played and sung more and more. And the bands,
along with first-rate singers, can give these to us."

In February 1958, nearing the top of her game in terms of showmanship, Peggy hit the Copa again, with great fanfare. It was not

the most intimate of clubs—"Entertainment on a mass-production basis," sniffed *The New Yorker*. But if the reviews are to be believed, she overcame this particular circle of nightclub-excess hell: "If there's nothing like a dame, there's also nothing quite like an in-person version of Miss Lee, who's gorgeously coiffed and gowned," wrote *Variety*. "The phrasing, the articulation, the authentic charm, and the sincerity show all the way through, finally to encase the audience in an indefinable aura; they know they've been had, by a singer who sneaks up on them without their being aware of it. There's hardly anyone in the business more artful, that way and in others, than Miss Lee. Significantly, she avoids current songs like the Asian flu"—with the exception, of course, of "Fever."

She was billed as "The New Peggy Lee"—a concession to the coming wave of rock and roll—and she sported a new hairdo, billed as "the chrysanthemum cut." Add the excess of the wardrobe—a $15,000 champagne-colored mink coat, and fashions crafted by Princess Mariosa and Don Loper—and you have a hell of a theatrical presentation.

Add Joe Harnell, the new pianist, and you have a hell of a musical show. An arranger to the stars, including Lena, Judy, and Pearl, Harnell had been a student of Nadia Boulanger's in Paris, of Aaron Copland's at Tanglewood. Multiple talents, multiple Grammys.

Some nights Harnell and the other musicians followed Peggy back to the suite for late-night cool-outs. The high times were very high: "She would entertain us by doing an impression of what chickens would do when it rained on the farm. They would stand in the rain and drown: The water would fall into their nostrils. She'd stand up straight, with this funny expression on her face, and fall forward onto the floor"—onto the carpeted floor of the Sherry Netherland. There were moments sublime—the whole gang in song, starting with Peggy doing a Bach partita, and the rest of them taking it in whatever direction the mood commanded.

Once, after too many drinks had been consumed, Dewey Martin—a handsome guy, Joe thought—came out of the bedroom and told them to take their act somewhere else: "Hey, Peg, would you let these guys go and let's get some sleep?" As Harnell recalls, she threw an ashtray at him, and he struck her. As the altercation ensued, Joe remembers dropping his eyes to the carpet. "He was volatile as hell," Joe recalled. "But it seemed she was baiting him. Her taste in men was not very good. With the exception of the marriage with Dave . . . the choices she was making were not very healthy. I think there was some morbid appeal to dominating these guys."

Another incident stuck in Harnell's mind. Many years later, as he told the tale, he emphasized that his affection for her was eternal. Her complicated moods, her dualities, were all part of what made her the greatest musician he had ever worked with, and one of his dearest friends. "But there was one time when we came back to the house . . . it was two or three in the morning. She woke Nicki up and asked her to make sandwiches *right now*. It was brutal. That was the nature of her ability to change from the absolute pinnacle of beauty and love and kindness and flowers into a very difficult, demanding person."

By now Joe Harnell was more than an accompanist and sometime musical director. He was also a middle-of-the-night-telephone-call receiver. But after she'd divorced Dewey, he almost became something more. One night she offered to take him further. He'd been in the same situation with Garland—"another wounded bird."

"I took Peggy home one night, put my arms around her to give her a hug goodbye, and her mouth touched mine. I was terrorized. Terrorized in the sense of like, 'What if this was to happen, like I think she wants it to happen?' " At this point, in the retelling, Joe Harnell laughs a small laugh. "I think I would have been deceased a long time ago. She would devour people like me. I literally ran from Peggy when the potential for a more serious thing was present."

They did not align their lips, they did not kiss, and nothing was ever said of it.

In late May 1958, the nation's disc jockeys assembled in Miami Beach, and Peggy joined the George Shearing Quintet to entertain at the Ambassador Hotel. The resultant album could be considered one of the best live jazz albums of the era—if indeed it had been live. There is serious question about that among music historians.

No one could question that the record is *lively*. Their version of "I Lost My Sugar in Salt Lake City"—as incongruous a song title as ever existed—was sublime. On "Do I Love You?" it's hard to believe that jazz piano or jazz vocals could ever reach higher heights. Nor can we question the authenticity of her look that night: sexy and classic, all at once, as she leaned casually on Shearing's black grand piano, her physique hourglassed into a stunning white gown, the décolletage cut just low enough, a single strand of pearls encircling her neck.

But the music? There's no way of knowing. According to Will Friedwald, in his liner notes for a later Capitol CD reissue, "within days of the convention, [the musicians and producer Dave Cavanaugh] were at work transforming the event into an album."

Further forensic research by Friedwald and other musicologists provides ample evidence that this was a studio record—which takes nothing away from the quality, but must put an asterisk on the whole thing. (Shearing, whose friendship with Peggy dates to her days with Dave Barbour, declined to comment for this book.)

On July 15, 1958, Peggy and Dewey filed separation papers. On September 1 they officially divorced. She charged cruelty. According to the Associated Press, "Miss Lee charged that Martin was moody and jealous and upset her prior to singing engagements."

The UPI dispatch stated that Miss Lee, thirty-five (still!), testified that Martin, also thirty-five, was "extremely jealous and making her friends so unwelcome at their home that they stopped calling." She waived alimony.

Years later, one of her musicians and friends, Jay Leonhart, would offer an assessment of Peggy's plight with marriage: "She couldn't live with husbands and still drink and fuck and have fun. She was such a star that marriage wasn't important. She had a relationship with the world! She had men lined up around the block. They probably proved impractical. She'd have to stop performing."

In an interview years later, Lee waxed pensive for a moment on the subject of the failed marriages, comparing them to costume parties. "But the . . . unfortunate men I had the costume party for would immediately become Mr. Lee. It bothered me that it took their pride away. . . . You know, adulation can be a terrible thing."

No one knew this better than Benny Goodman. He'd been in Belgium when he started getting calls from nightclub impresario Ralph Watkins, who'd opened a little club called Basin Street East on East Forty-ninth Street in the former gymnasium of the Shelton Towers Hotel.

Watkins had been persistent. So Benny came home and took him up on his offer to headline the new establishment, which was small but comfortable, unpretentious but elegant. To get from the stage to the dressing room you had to pass through the liquor room, the pantry, and the kitchen. But the place had a good vibe.

Benny was packing them in at Basin Street East by 1958, right around the time Texaco lined him up to host an acclaimed jazz-themed variety show called *Swing into Spring,* starring Ella and Jo Stafford. In 1959, they asked him to host another. He called his old canary. His first offer of remuneration was, of course, next to nothing.

"Benny, I'm not going to work for that!" Peggy protested.

"Well, you worked for that with the band," he said.

"Sixteen years ago," she replied.

They settled on a fee, and Goodman brought in André Previn, Ella Fitzgerald, and Lionel Hampton. The artistry was hypnotic. A sixty-minute network television show devoted to nothing but great jazz today would be rare indeed, but between Previn's solos, Hampton's dancing vibes, and Peg's and Ella's vocals, it was a concert for the ages—even with Texaco's big-finned infomercials mucking up the pace.

One moment on the show is worth singling out: when Peggy is singing the hell out of "When a Woman Loves a Man," and Ella is off-camera, Peggy sings, "Tell her she's a fool and she'll say, 'Yes, I know,' " we hear (but don't see) Ella say "*Uh*-huh!" Ella's respect for Lee is obvious.

Swing into Spring wasn't just an example of Goodman's enduring artistry. It was also a night when his cold heart—"The guy who pissed ice," one of Peggy's friends would later call him—arrived in full freeze: The cast was crowded in the corridor about to go on. This was live television. Ella was wearing a dress with a lot of beads on it. "You're not going to wear that thing, are you?" said Benny. Whereupon Ella broke into tears. Previn and Peggy had to calm her. By the time the show began, she was cool. They all were.

It was during the rehearsals that Benny told Peggy he'd found a room that was perfect for her: Basin Street East.

Peggy's first Basin Street engagement came in March 1960—a winter nearly as harsh as the one that would follow, with its February blizzard. The appearance featured the first New York marquee appearance of her official new moniker: *Miss* Peggy Lee.

"It looks better on a marquee," she explained years later, "and it sounds better phonetically when someone announces it for a show. Walter Winchell was very critical about it at first. Actually, it's just part of the name."

She was being paid $12,500 per week, and by all accounts, "the Marilyn Monroe of the chanteuses," as one scribe called her, earned every penny.

"The svelte blonde thrush," said *Variety,* "is more in her element here than she was at the Copacabana in her last New York date. This is strictly a music room and what comes out of Miss Lee's pipes is strictly music. . . . Her work here is bound to get talked up around town, which will keep the captain at his post directing the heavy load of traffic."

"The sign on the wall said 'Occupation by more than 340 persons is illegal and unlawful,'" reported the *New York Journal-American,* "but last night Basin Street East was crowded to the very edge of illegality. In all her yesterdays, Peggy was never better than last night. Only a superlative artist could sell out a club the size of Basin Street East on such a raw, snowy night. . . . Peggy's phrasing is crisp, her diction faultless, every song a delight. She uses her hands constantly; their action becomes part of and enhances her routine. She's magnetic and exciting, and exhibits rare stage presence. Everyone loved her last night, and their affection was not misplaced."

"Rarely has there been a more carefully prepared and tastefully executed nightclub act," was *Down Beat*'s assessment. "Over the years, Peggy has acquired a great deal of stage presence for in-person appearances of this type. She seems to be calmer and more in control of the situation on a nightclub floor than in front of a television camera."

Lee shattered all of Benny's attendance records at Basin Street.

Ralph Watkins would later say that if Benny built Basin Street, Peggy made it a home. But if she was earning her pay, she was spending it, too. As Leonard Feather wrote, "She had the whole bandstand rebuilt to provide her with a more effective entrance-way; had the orchestra enlarged from five to thirteen men . . . and the electrician had to follow more than 130 lighting cues in a 35-minute show." The lighting was the work of specialist Hugo Granata, flown in from Los Angeles especially for the engagement.

No asterisk was needed on the Capitol album released in July 1960, *Pretty Eyes,* conducted and arranged by the immortal trumpeter Billy May, Dave Barbour's buddy from the early forties. It contained at least a half dozen true Peggy Lee keepers. "If I had to pick someone for a desert island arranger," Peggy told Will Friedwald for his book *Sinatra! The Song Is You,* "it would be Billy, because he can write every style for brass or strings or for large or for small, and he writes with such humor as well as beauty."

The album-cover photograph depicts a sultry Peg wearing a platinum French twist, dangly diamond earrings, false eyelashes, and lacquered lips. But the detail that counts here is her smile: It's half of one, and it looks like the expression of someone who's just heard someone's tale of the blues, and her look answers, "Yeah, tell me about it, I know, I've been there. But don't worry about it—it's still worth the trip."

The cover also features the legend "Music arranged and conducted by Billy May," and in a time when album notes seldom deigned to mention musicians, May's name signifies the treasure within. Billy May, among other things, was known for a sense of humor—in life, and in music; his arrangements smiled. Unlike Nelson Riddle's sentimental stuff, May used his strings the way a chef uses spices: You hardly know they're there. They never get in the way, but they make the whole thing cook.

In his drinking days, May liked his bottle. And he loved his job. "I always felt," he told Friedwald, "that most people who wanted to be musicians probably got stuck working in a garage or something, so those of us who were lucky enough to do what we loved should at least have some fun with it."

The sense of fun, the unmistakable glee at doing the work, only begins to tell the tale here. The tone of Lee's voice on "It Could Happen to You" (Johnny Burke–Jimmy Van Heusen) makes it clear she's smiling as she sings. But it's "Too Close for Comfort" and "In Other Words"—later known as "Fly Me to the Moon"—that find a way, thanks to May's arrangements, to infuse songs of romance with feelings of jazz. Standing alone, however, in terms of quality is the last cut on the disc: "Because I Love Him So," with music by Milt Raskin and lyrics by Lee herself. Raskin was a pianist with a perfect Peggy résumé: Wingy Manone's band in 1937, the Famous Door in '38, then Krupa and Tommy Dorsey.

Peggy's lyrics are right-on bluesy, but with an added fillip when she goes irreverently casual on us: "Oh, I don't know . . . because I love him so. . . ."

She ends with a big blues belt, but what stays with a true Lee listener when this gem of a record is over is that odd little slice of spoken/sung conversation—"Oh, I don't know"—stuck into the middle of the song. It's *real.* The phrase would never make it into any anthology of lyrics—the definitive anthology, *Reading Lyrics,* written by Robert Kimball and Robert Gottlieb and published by Pantheon in 2000, includes no fewer than six Lee lyrics nestled amid the masters—but it was as characteristically Peggy as any lyric she'd ever write.

She was officially single again. In New York, Robert Preston had been starring in *The Music Man* at the Majestic, so she may not have been lacking for company there. But back in Los Angeles, she was free to play the field. Her neighbors Jayne Meadows and Steve Allen served as unintentional matchmakers this time. It was only natural that they would ask their newly single pal to a party. At Jayne and Steve's parties, Peggy was not the center of attention, nor did she seem to want to be. In a guest's home, she was invariably shy; she would do her best to melt into the background. Jayne Meadows had marveled at Peggy's singing through the years. But beyond that, she was fascinated by the *acting* in Lee's act. Jayne's own theatrical skill was well established and when she saw Peggy sing, she saw a wonderful actress. She figured that the sexiness wasn't real; it was all theater, camouflaging what was perhaps insecurity or extreme self-consciousness. Lee's whole stage construct—the minimal movement and the downcast eyes, the little thing she did with her mouth—was calculated, she thought. Meadows also noticed that Lee's eyes—the windows to the soul—never seemed to have any expression. They didn't let you in.

Today, Jayne Meadows offers the opinion that it was Peggy's laid-back effect that kept the public from putting her in the ultimate pantheon of greats: "I think that she was—of course it's a square saying this—but I think she was too cool," Meadows says. "She was the coolest thing I ever saw in my life. If I had to play Lady Macbeth in the sleepwalking scene, I would maybe visualize Peggy.

"Peggy would sit in a room at a party, and when she talked, everything was cool. I think there has to be some fear there—and I don't understand why, when you've got that talent and that face."

Jayne and Peggy weren't particularly simpatico on a personal level. Peggy loved soap operas, an addiction that Jayne did not share. One night Jayne took a table for a charity ball, and among her guests were Peggy and a friend who was a soap star. Peggy's fascination with the woman, the whole evening long, struck Jayne as strange. It was as if she was identifying not with the person, but with the character she played. It was almost childlike. Jayne was made slightly uncomfortable by Peggy's capacity to be drawn to a medium that played out life in such an exaggeratedly dramatic fashion.

Jayne herself was certifiably brainy; after nights of partying from club to club back in the fifties, she'd still be able to memorize a script in a matter of days. Producers called her "the IBM machine." She was perhaps not as cerebral as her husband—no one in entertainment was—but hers was a life of the mind. Jayne was talkative, expressive, extroverted, opinionated; next to her, Peggy seemed shy, quiet, even slow. It was as if she was a beat behind.

Despite her beauty, as Peggy sat in a corner of the living room, Jayne felt no jealousy; Steve didn't find Peggy attractive. Peggy was just not Steve's type of girl. On the show, Steve told his wife, she sometimes seemed childlike—charming, but childlike.

But as one of Steve and Jayne's regular guests, Peggy was a perfect fit, in all ways. Steve's producer, Bill Harbach, was a handsome man, with a face that looked as if it had been smiling into soft winds and pastel sunsets all his days on earth—which he more or less had. He was working on editing a Crosby special with Johnny Mercer at the time of his introduction to Miss Lee. Billy had a lot of things going for him: innate charm, innate goodness, a remarkably carefree demeanor. He knew popular music, and even more about lyrics: He was the Choate-educated son of Otto Harbach, the classic American lyricist.

Peggy Lee and Billy Harbach were like members of the same club: Both had a fondness for being around brilliant, artistic people. They also shared jokes on the phone late at night. Peggy's favorite? "Hey, Bill: A mother comes into her son's room, outraged, and says to the kid, 'I found a condom on the patio.' The kid says, 'Mommy, what's a patio?' "

Peggy also loved to tell show-business stories, like the one about the time Erroll Garner dropped into Louis Armstrong's dressing room in Cleveland: "What's new, Satchmo?" Armstrong's answer: "White folks still in the lead."

She *loved* that. She loved tales of the business. She loved everything about the business. She and Harbach also loved hitting the clubs. Billy took a certain amount of satisfaction in the evening an old friend pulled him aside and, in stunned disbelief and admiration, said, "What are you doing with Peggy Lee?"

One night in August 1960, Peg asked Billy if he could come by and catch her second show at Ciro's, which started at 1:00 A.M. He couldn't; he was on his way to the studio to edit a Crosby special. But he said he'd blow his car horn as he drove down Sunset. "If you hear someone honking, it's me saying, 'Good luck.' "

On his way to work, he stopped at Ciro's and wrote out a note that said, "Ow-OOOOO-ga," and had it sent backstage to Peggy.

He called her the next day. From then on, their password was "Ow-OOOOO-ga."

Soon after, he went home with her one night. But all they did was listen to music. Their favorite was Ray Charles singing "Just for a Thrill." For weeks they played it, and lay in each other's arms until dawn. Harbach was comfortable, because this was a pace he could understand. It was all about friendship—at least until, finally, it was not, and they were lovers. The affair was short-lived. But the friendship endured for forty more years.

"She wasn't an animal," Phoebe Jacobs recalled. "To be really sexual, you have to be an animal. She reeked sexuality, but . . .

they would start out by being friends. Some women could meet a guy and flip for him. Peggy wouldn't do it that way. You were her friend first. You had something in common with her. It wasn't across a crowded room, suddenly, bang!"

Rainy Nights in London Town

ALTHOUGH SOME CRITICS found the television medium too sterile for Peggy Lee, an appearance in late 1959 proved not only her suitability for it, but also the fact that, done well, television could be unbeatable. The variety show, as practiced by the pros, was not yet an also-ran forum for mediocre entertainers. At this point, the talent was first rate, the energy enormous, and the music jazzed. *The Bing Crosby Show*, on which Lee appeared, was arguably the single greatest musical-variety show that ever aired, featuring nothing less than the Mount Rushmore of popular singing at the end of the era when pop-jazz ruled the land.

Start with music by Sammy Cahn and Jimmy Van Heusen. Add a roster of musicians led by the brilliant Brit, George Shearing, and pianists Paul Smith and Joe Bushkin, a player with swing in his blood who had worked with Billie Holiday, Tommy Dorsey, and Benny Goodman. Finally, bring on three more musical guests accompanying Bing: Louis Armstrong, Frank Sinatra, and Peggy Lee. The sum total? An hour of astounding talent, all caught in a crosscurrent between the old and not really so staid, and the pulls of the blossoming counterculture whose influences could no longer be ignored.

When Bing sang, "I'm feeling like Aristotle Onassis 'cause I've got my rose-colored glasses, everything is rosy now," it seemed a fun little lyric, but it spoke to the larger question of the day: whether the optimistic glow of the fifties might be fading in the shadow of missile crises, fallout shelters, and the Beats. Kerouac's *On the Road*—the now legendary Benzedrine-fueled account of cross-country wanderings—had soared through the literary landscape. America was celebrating its more libertine impulses.

Bing's show tried to have it both ways: lampooning the Beats, but tacitly acknowledging the fustiness of the older generation. The show's art direction veered from hilariously ugly to the avant-garde. Abstract canvases plastered all over the sets suggested the overlap of the traditional with the modern, and the abstract element showed up even in the advertising: A dancing chorus of no fewer than eight guys and gals was on hand, with Florence Henderson leading the pack. The dancers performed against a backdrop of abstract-expressionist murals, pushing— via song and dance—the 1960 Oldsmobile with its Quadri-Balanced Ride and Vibra-Tuned Body Mountings: "We've got rocket engines. Smooth as sippin' sassafras." The choreography for the Olds routines alone would put half of today's modern Broadway musicals to shame.

But the true art was in the huge musical talent crammed onto a very small screen. There was Frank, cigarette in place, singing "Willow, Weep for Me." There was Armstrong doing "Mack the Knife," horns swinging behind him. And then there was Peggy, wearing a skintight gown, harps in the background, doing "Baubles, Bangles and Beads" as she glanced away from the camera, flirting nonstop with the viewing audience.

Afterward, awaiting her arrival onstage, Bing and Frank dissected her number:

> *Bing:* "Wasn't that delicious, Frank?"
> *Frank:* "Beautiful."
> *Bing (smiling):* "Very baubly, bangly and beady."
> *Frank:* "She do cast a spell."
> *Bing:* "She do, indeed."

Now Peg joined the boys. When she got out on stage, Frank, in a voice laden with double entendre, said that her song had given him "an idea." Peg flirted right back: "Hearing you sing gives me an idea, too," she said to Frank, grabbing at his lapels.

Musically, for the traditionalists, there were flights within flights, medleys within medleys: Peg doing "Up a Lazy River," Armstrong blowing "Pale Moon Shinin'," Sinatra bopping through "If I Could Be with You." Peg and Bing floated through "High Society," and soon it all blended together in a wave whose undertow swept viewers along like a dream.

But there was also something else going on, on another level: a nod to jazz, to true jazz, and a plea to Americans not to obliterate the beat, which the all-stars addressed in distinct ways, all entertaining. The first was a Bing-Peggy comic sketch-duet about a couple of society swells turning their noses up at the beatniks. She's in a white fur wrap, he in tails, as obviously pot-stoned beatniks splay around them surrounded by mock-modern art. All of it was meant as satire; Bing and Peggy were as much the butt of the joke as the beatniks whose hygiene they mocked, in the Van Heusen lyrics of "Too Neat to Be a Beatnik, Too Round to Be a Square."

But there was something else going on in this formal-wear duet of a little Van Heusen ditty: Bing the square was singing from the heart, but Peggy probably wasn't. It was easy to believe that Bing disapproved of the beatniks and their free-form poetry, the weird abstract art of Pollock and his abstract-expressionist painting fraternity, and the squawkings of the avant-garde jazz musicians. But Peggy, playing a square with her nose turned up at such innovative expression now infiltrating mainstream culture? Highly unlikely. As a British writer of the time, Patrick Catling, put it: To satirize something you have to first understand it. Here, while Bing is trashing the Beats, the woman on his arm seemed to be very much in on the joke, because, in her musical and artistic heart of hearts, no one better understood—and appreciated—the cutting edge.

Now, very briefly—all too briefly—another man entered Peg's life and left it. His name was George Capri. She never wrote of him. She never spoke of him. But in late 1959, when she was appearing at the Riviera in Las Vegas, the gossips took notice: "Before Peggy Lee planed back to the coast, she and her current admirer, Las Vegas hotelman George Capri, cozily clinked champagne glasses at the Arpeggio."

And a few months later: "While Peggy Lee was in New York, George Capri of the Las Vegas Flamingo visited her three times, and the whisper around Las Vegas is that this romance is serious." It was.

According to Stella Castellucci, he was a "great love. . . . She really fell hard for this guy, as did he for her. They became engaged." Capri had already made plans to move out to Peggy's place.

Unlike every other man in her life until now, Capri wasn't in the music business—not as an entertainer, producer, or actor. He was, by the few accounts available, a businessman. In a parallel universe, perhaps, she married him—a straightforward guy who was neither a threat to her own stardom nor tangled in other relationships. Perhaps, in that other universe, she moved forward into a satisfying final act with a companion who truly appreciated her. But in this universe, one snowy December day, Capri was on his way to New York on business on a United flight. The DC-8 jet collided over Staten Island with a TWA plane, a Constellation.

The TWA plane plummeted to the ground, killing all on board. The United jet, its right wing crippled, limped down to the ground. The pilot tried to keep aloft until he could crash-land in Prospect Park, but he came up short. The jet slammed into the Park Slope section of Brooklyn, instantly killing everyone on board except a young boy who was thrown into a snowbank. He would die several hours later, but not until he'd given a quote to the press. As they came down through the snowstorm, he said, the city had looked like a snow globe.

Seven weeks later, in a blizzard, Peggy Lee took the stage at Basin Street for her famed February performance. Across the cold river, down on Sterling Place in Brooklyn, pieces of the United jet were still being salvaged. The wrapped Christmas presents that had fallen from the plane had long since been collected.

"She was heartbroken," recalls Castellucci, but if Capri's death had devastated Peggy, it went unnoticed by everyone from the trades. "It is pretty tough to match her in any department," opined *Billboard;* "if ever a performer 'owned' a club and its audience, it's Peggy Lee at Basin Street East." The higher-end rags, like *The New Yorker* (where the writers, apparently, were above treatment by an editor's pencil): "She is a pair of honed skates evolving fast figures on a pond of glare ice, leaping into the air and descending with a vehemence that scatters little jets of frosty crystals." Presumably, that meant the guy liked her.

Peggy's pianist Joe Harnell remembered the Basin Street engagement that winter, of course; he knew it was a landmark. Capitol was recording for a live album, the crowds were aglitter. Part of the thrill, naturally, was Peggy's musicality; there were nights when her command of the place and the jazz sense to her songs was so astounding that he says he literally almost fell off the piano stool. He had never played for someone who could tell a story in sound with such clarity and mood. Peggy Lee was amazing to him: She'd do something huge and swingy—a full-blown "Lover," for instance—and with the final note, as the place was going insane—people shooting to their feet, the applause a waterfall of sound—in the middle of this chaos, with no prompting from Joe, she'd start the next song: a different key, a different note, a different rhythm.

"How do you know where the hell to come in?" Joe asked one time.

"It's no big deal," she said. "Don't make it into something great. I can just do it."

If he played a chord that had an extra note, or a tone too grave, or anything not quite appropriate to her musical vocabulary, she'd raise a finger—only her forefinger—just an inch or two. No one could see it but Joe. And he would never do that again.

Harnell recalls how she'd choose and arrange the songs to tell a story—a romantic story, of course, and with several acts: Boy finds girl, boy wants girl, boy marries girl, loses girl, finds another girl, finally comes back to the original girl; the whole story is in the titles and lyrics, one after another. There was a true wisdom on display about relationships—and Harnell knew well where it came from, for he was privy to all sides of her life.

Her set list now included a medley of songs by one Ray Charles. "Yes Indeed!" was a rousing, swinging Peggy Lee show-stopper, at a time when Charles's stuff was still largely unknown to the pop world. "What she did for Ray Charles!" says Phoebe Jacobs. "He could not work in a New York nightclub because of his drug record. She does this medley, and she becomes the first pop artist to recognize rock and roll—real rock and roll—as what it really was: an important thing on the music scene. The kids were playing Ray Charles, and she told me, 'I know I can do it right. This man deserves recognition and respect.' She was the first pop artist to revere Ray Charles."

Now at the age of forty-one, at the time of her highest art and perhaps her most avid search for lasting affection, Peggy crossed the pond and fell into the arms of a British writer named Patrick Skene Catling, a man every bit as talented—and complicated—as she. His would be a brief chapter in Peggy Lee's epic story, but no other relationship would be as starkly instructive in the lessons of balancing an artist's life.

It all began with her arrival in England. From the start, and not surprisingly, the British—always on the cutting edge of popular music—had loved her work. In 1961, with the coming murmurs from Liverpool not yet audible, Londoners loved to hear mainstream American pop. That year, the Pigalle club alone would be hosting the likes of Tony Bennett, Patti Page, and Steve Lawrence and Eydie Gorme, and, for three weeks in July and August, Miss Peggy Lee.

Riding the crest of her Basin Street triumph, Peggy found a most receptive public in London. Her songs ranged from "Fever" to "I'm Gonna Go Fishin'," from "Just for a Thrill" to "Lover." Dressed in white, with platinum hair to match, she riveted the Pigalle so completely that in the quiet moments of the ballads, in the silences, not a sound was to be heard from the audience. It was no surprise that the press would be appreciative. Nor, considering the principals involved, was it unpredictable that one particular journalist's appreciation of Peggy's talents would extend above and beyond the call of professional duty. As a feature writer for *Punch*, the irreverent and stylishly satirical journal of life in the Empire, Catling stood out from the rest of the Fleet Street showbiz hacks. Add his considerable writing talent and his screen-test looks, and throw in his rakish demeanor and his passions for jazz, liquor, and beautiful women—well, how could their meeting have turned out otherwise?

It's not as if welcoming Patrick Catling, who was five years younger than she, into her bed within a few days of meeting him put Peggy in undistinguished company. After all—according to his wonderfully readable autobiography, *Better Than Working*—this was a man who not too many years earlier had received the affectionate kisses of Jane Russell on the evening of the day he first interviewed the movie star.

Born in 1925, Catling was the son of a correspondent for Reuters who once published a novel after unsolicitedly seeking the advice of H. G. Wells. (Wells answered with a letter of his own, which would stay in the Catling family until Patrick sold it in the seventies to pay an electricity bill.) Young Patrick became a writer after his father advised him that not only was writing a viable way to pass the time, it paid better than working. But he found his lifelong passion on the day when, as an eleven-year-old, his father brought him a 78 of Duke Ellington's "Jubilee Stomp."

Catling's family soon moved to the States, crossing on a Cunard liner on which the kid spent his time listening to Fats Waller songs on a windup gramophone. They set up shop in the exclusive WASP bedroom enclave of Bronxville, New York, in Westchester County, a place of privilege where fathers routinely bestowed fancy cars upon their teenage sons and cocktails flowed in torrents behind the draped windows of Tudor-style lairs.

Young Catling found his way to some other lairs, too—the ones on Fifty-second Street, where he caught Billie Holiday at the Onyx, and at the Hickory House, bandleader Joe Marsala grew so fond of the kid that he presented him with some studio outtakes of Marsala playing with Jack Teagarden. Back in B-ville, as the kids called it, he had an affair with his mother's thirty-six-year-old best friend.

Next stop was the Royal Air Force. Stationed in the Bahamas, Catling hooked up with the exiled duke of Windsor in a golf-course bar after the duke had driven his Cadillac convertible on the fairways. But it was back in Toronto in 1943 where he caught Benny Goodman's band and was smitten from afar by the blond girl singing that most un-Benny-like blues number, "Why Don't You Do Right?" He played the song again and again on juke-boxes across the city. It was more than jazz, this song, he thought; it was drama. In Nassau, Catling got married at age nineteen to the gorgeous twenty-one-year-old blond daughter of a British foreign correspondent; the marriage lasted less than a year.

After the war, he landed a job on the staff of the Baltimore *Sun* and married again, which didn't stop him from enjoying Ms. Russell's company after a night spent at the Frolic Club, in the wilds of Baltimore, listening to Johnnie Sparrow and His Golden Arrows. A subsequent sabbatical in Los Angeles to write Jane Russell's biography had its own set of highlights: Catling drank with Robert Mitchum at the Hangover Club, listened to Joe Bushkin, and tolerated Mitchum's bebop jokes ("Two bopsters walk past a church. Suddenly, the bell falls from the tower and clangs on the sidewalk. 'Jesus!' says the first cat. 'What was that?' 'C sharp,' says the second"). He lunched with Marilyn Monroe, although, surprisingly, nothing developed between them.

He covered the Korean War. He befriended the president of Costa Rica. But Catling never strayed far from jazz. In Baltimore in 1955, watching an emaciated Billie Holiday at a tiny club, he was stunned when, after singing "Strange Fruit," Holiday walked to his table, kissed him, and sat down to share a bottle of gin. The following year, now posted in London, he drank regularly at 10 Downing Street with Prime Minister Anthony Eden, partied with Evelyn Waugh, drank with Kingsley Amis, lunched with Vivien Leigh.

Separated from his wife, he met Peggy Lee one day in London in July 1961 with a group of other reporters. As the champagne flowed, he asked Miss Lee if he might have a private interview. They held it in a splendid, luxurious suite in the Dorchester Hotel previously occupied by Taylor and Burton.

Thereafter, each day, Catling enjoyed an afternoon drink at his usual spot, then repaired to Peggy's dressing room, where she enjoyed her usual prestage doses of brandy. He watched each show from a table near the stage and joined her at her hotel after the last performance for late-night murmurs. As he got to know her, Patrick Catling came to admire a great deal about this lady. And he sensed the constant struggle within her between the professional and the pleasure-lover.

When her London engagement was over, Peggy asked Patrick to accompany her to Monaco, where she was to perform for Princess Grace's charity. Technically he was her translator. They engaged more in pleasure than in work in the Hotel de Paris, although the quarters were less splendid: They met not in her bedroom, but the translator's.

When she invited him to move back with her to her home in Los Angeles, Patrick readily accepted the invitation and set up shop on Kimridge Avenue. The Japanese garden, the pool, the Cadillac reminded him of his previous posting in Lotusland, although the furnishings were different. Whereas Jane Russell favored purple dressing rooms, and five dozen shoes, and a pool shaped like a harp, Peggy's place was more modest, if elegant in a very specific, fantastic way—the marble, the deep rugs, the chandeliers, the pastels. Some of the plantings in the garden were plastic, but then this *was* Los Angeles. As a devotee of Evelyn Waugh's brilliant satire of Angelean life, *The Loved One*, Catling expected no more. Or less.

Catling soon came to realize that Peggy at home bore little relation to Miss Peggy Lee. The performer's stylings promised glamour, star-studded nights out, the high life in every respect. But they dined each evening on the same steak and salad and drank the same red wine. They did not often leave the house, and when they did, she donned a dark wig. She had no social life to speak of, despite having a wide range of friends. Her most regular visitor was a doctor who injected her daily with a vitamin shot that, Catling noticed, made her feel very good.

Catling didn't care that he'd moved into a monastery. He spent hours listening to his favorite Peggy Lee music performed by Peggy Lee. He heard her sing like Lady Day as the sun went down. But he was confused. Never particularly fond of the grindstone himself, Catling nonetheless found the indolence up on Kimridge a little numbing. Despite the ample bookshelves, she never read. She didn't paint. She didn't seem to be doing any creating of any kind. So Catling began to do some research to drum up freelance work on his own. Just for something to do. Then one day he discovered that Peggy had been doing a little research, too: on exactly how one obtains a Mexican wedding. For her and Patrick. She had apparently informed several friends and acquaintances of their intentions. Just not Patrick.

"But I'm still married," said Patrick. "Technically."

"You can get a divorce in Juarez, and we can get married on the same day. A Mexican divorce-wedding."

Whereupon, in short order, Patrick Catling left the Peggy Lee household and flew to New York, alone and free. A few years later, he moved to Ireland, exiled himself in the country, met a woman, and fell in love—for real. To this day, they remain happily together.

Joe Harnell had decided to move on by now—but not, he recalls, before he'd arranged for a successor, so as not to leave Peggy in the lurch. "When I left, it was on the condition that, with her per-mission, I get someone to replace me. I got Quincy Jones."

Phoebe Jacobs recalls it a little differently. She remembers that her daughter Suzy and Peggy's daughter, Nicki, had been listen-ing at the time to a song called "Swanee River Rock," by Quincy Jones, and Peggy had liked it. When Peggy discovered that Jones had arranged some of Ray Charles's stuff, she decided she wanted to have him do some of her own arranging. "So I called him in Europe," Jacobs says, "and said, 'I'm working with Miss Peggy Lee, and she wants the arranger who works with Ray Charles. I found out it was you. Would you be willing to come back to America?' " He was.

"They were very compatible from the start," Phoebe says. "I think Peggy would have liked to have been, more than anything else, black. Peggy sang more like a black lady than she did a white lady."

A typical day for Quincy Jones, the precocious fourteen-year-old trumpeter growing up in Seattle, would begin with playing Sousa marches and polkas at school, followed by a gig at a Seattle tennis club wearing a white cardigan playing "Room Full of Roses" for the all-white membership as they dined. Then he'd change into a different costume for a date at a club like the Rock-ing Chair or the Black and Tan, playing blues for strippers and comedians, then go on to the Elks Club to play bebop till dawn.

Later, in New York, the first charts he'd paid for were stock arrangements of a number from a Disney film: "The Siamese Cat Song." When he finally met its creator, he was not surprised to find Lee a very independent lady; she had ridden the big-band buses and trains, where the girl had to hold her own. On Hamp's bus, Quincy remembered, it was forbidden even to carry the canary's bags. Any canary who came off a bus having learned to carry her own load already had the spirit she needed to make it big.

"I think she had genius," Jones says now. "The genius to understand how to confine yourself, to contain yourself. If you have to use that stupid word, she had *feeling*. Sensation. Believing. Attachment to the thing."

That Peg and Quincy became a good match romantically, well, this surprised no one who knew them. To start with, he was an unabashed lover of women—"a big dog. And, *please,* man!—you're working, you're around each other, and chemistry either happens or it doesn't," he says. "And sometimes if it's not happening, working brings it about."

He'd always tried to be cautious about work affairs, but Peggy broke down his boundaries. "We loved each other," he says. "We did. We had a relationship, you know? A strong relationship. Details? Details are details, you know."

"I don't believe in that, man," Jones says of kiss-and-tell revelations.

"Having known their association, and knowing both of them, I would say this," Phoebe Jacobs recalls. "This was such a unique relationship, it was so special, that he wanted to keep it to himself. 'Phoebe,' he told me, 'there are some things you want to keep in your heart.' He adored her. He just adored her."

Though his gigs with Peggy were good for Jones professionally, success came with a literal price. Jones's mother had turned him in to the IRS in an attempt to keep him from the reach of "sinful devil's music." The government agents, who had trouble tracking him down, did finally score: The IRS office, as it happened, had a view of the marquee of Basin Street East, where he was playing with Peggy. So Jones took his medicine.

For Peggy, Quincy was compatible. He had a mind as well as a talent, and a spirit. Like Peggy, "Q" was a jazz artist, but also pragmatic and practical: He'd found a way to make his muse marketable. He was also handsome—and risk-free. There was no way they were going to feel compelled to formalize anything. That was what Lee seemed to want now.

"She once told me," Stella Castellucci recalls, " 'I just can't live without the Man.' " And the best way to live with the Man, when your own true universe revolves around yourself and your art, is in brief, intense couplings.

Perhaps her personal relationship with Jones clouded her judgment, but their professional collaboration was something of a musical misfire from the start: Quincy's brassy, commercial-feeling orchestrations couldn't easily coexist with Peggy's adventurous musical soul. Whatever the reasons, Q's first album with Peggy—*If You Go,* released in the fall of 1961—was somewhat devoid of true *feeling*.

Jones's sentimental arrangements were simply over the top; it was as if he'd put a rococo frame on an Impressionist painting. Lee gave the classic "As Times Goes By" a "misty treatment, slow and sensual," in the words of Will Friedwald. But while her delivery is poignant, it was obscured by veils of strings; it was as if her voice were trying to take flight but, encumbered by the strings, unable to truly soar. Johnny Burke and Jimmy Van Heusen's lovely "Here's That Rainy Day" was nearly drowned in frilly flutes. Hoagy Carmichael's "I Get Along Without You Very Well" was notable largely for its solo by Benny Carter, one of the great alto sax players of all time.

If *If You Go* had been nothing but Peg dueling and mating with Carter's sax in front of a small combo, it could have been a great record. But Jones seemed to be making more of a movie soundtrack filled with strings and flutes than a Peggy Lee album, and while such ornamentation was de rigueur in a lot of pop stuff of the time, it didn't quite suit Peggy.

The most memorable legacy of this LP was a behind-the-scenes moment. One day, in the studio, during a break in rehearsals, one of the string players played something innocuous—

to Quincy, anyway. It was a German-sounding oom-pah-pah thing, a tuba riff, but on the violin. As Jones recalls it, Peggy went into a rage. The music somehow reminded her of her step-mother.

"Fire them all," she said, meaning the string section.

"All of them?"

"All of them."

Quincy did as she said. The entire string section had to walk. The bitch of it was his having to rewrite the whole piece for French horns and flutes. But to Q, it was worth it, because "the woman was an artist, period," he says, telling the story of what Nadia Boulanger said to him once in Paris: "A person's music can never be more or less than they are as a human being—it starts with the person first."

Peggy returned to Basin Street in November 1961, with Quincy conducting. Ray Charles caught some of the shows. "I was the one who invited Ray Charles in the first time," Phoebe says. "I invited him to the second show and he came in with an entourage. It was our habit to invite people for breakfast, and Peggy didn't want to invite everybody up to the apartment, so I said, 'Let's go to the Backstreet,' where they had great pizzas. It was like three blocks from Basin Street. It was on Second Avenue and Fiftieth Street. They sat and they ate pizzas together, because when she did the medley, he was so adoring and wonderful. He was like a little kid."

As usual at Basin Street, Phoebe was an ardent admirer of her artistry—watching Lee's every nuance, studying the woman who sometimes she wished to be herself. No one studied Peggy as closely as Phoebe.

It was at her November 1961 gig, at the end of a very long year, when Peggy collapsed on stage in the middle of a late performance. This was no psychosomatic intrusion. "She passed out on the stage," guitarist Mundell Lowe recalls. "Several of us put her on the chaise longue, and the medics came in, and they took her to the hospital."

"That night, she told me she had a pain in her ribs," Phoebe recalls. "It was the second show. I said, 'Maybe your bra is too tight.' Then I felt her body. This woman had a 103 temperature. I said something to the boss. 'Oh, she's had too much brandy,' he said. I called her a doctor. I asked him to come over, unbeknownst to her. All he did was hold her hands and he could tell she was burning up. He called the ambulance. Three days before Thanksgiving.

"The second or third day that she was in the hospital," Jacobs recalls, "the doctor told me, 'I think you'd better call her sister and bring Nicki in. It's touch and go. It's critical.' The next day was Thanksgiving. Peggy was in an oxygen tent. She said, 'Is it Thanksgiving yet?' and I said, 'No, it's tomorrow.' Then she motioned for me to bend down, and she said, 'I want you to go to the Carnegie Deli, or the Stage, and I want you to order the works, and have it brought here for the staff. Everybody here has to work tomorrow, and I want them to have Thanksgiving. I want cranberries and stuffing and sweet potato.' She couldn't have any."

Lee was diagnosed with double pneumonia. Her left lung had been damaged—in later accounts, she'd say that doctors contemplated removing it. Up until the seventies, she would often be accompanied by a breathing apparatus nicknamed Charlie to provide doses of pure oxygen to compensate for the damaged lung.

"After that, her fortitude as far as performing is concerned was cut down to an hour," Mundell Lowe recalls. "She could do an hour, then she ran out of steam. It was part of the pressure she was going through at the time. I remember her saying to me once that a publisher had sold all the rights of the things she did with Dave. So by now she was running after the money monkey. And not having a husband to lean on, it's tough.

"But I have to tell you something else about that engagement. They took her to the hospital, and I had a note from her later: 'You were never paid for the Basin Street job.' I said, 'No—being with you and knowing you're okay is payment enough. I love you.' But she insisted on paying me."

Back in Los Angeles, for a time, the Kimridge house hosted a new guest, and if there were whispers about the black guy staying with the white chick up on the hill, no one ever mentioned it out loud. But one snapshot makes it clear that this was no run-of-the-mill boarder. Lounging on a couch, Peggy and Quincy seemed a couple in love.

If Jones was the Queen's king, Phoebe Jacobs, back east, was her lady-in-waiting, and she came to know every aspect of Peggy's personality. "Miss Lee" was what Phoebe called her; it was a sign of respect and love. "I'd get to the club at ten in the morning," Jacobs recalls. "When she'd come to New York it was like something I could never imagine, I had ten telephone lines and they'd all light up at one time with people wanting to make reservations. I thought if I heard the word 'reservation' one more time I'd punch someone.

"But when you get through with work, where do you go? Could I go anyplace better than Basin Street East to hear Peggy Lee? So I go home, I change my clothes, and I go back. And after one show, a dream comes true. Miss Lee says, 'We're going to have breakfast together.' So I go have three cups of strong coffee, and I go to the Waldorf Towers with Miss Lee, and Judy Garland is going, and Sammy Davis, Jr., is going, and Art Carney, and Jackie Gleason. I was out of my mind with joy. But when it came to four o'clock in the morning, I couldn't keep my eyes open, so

I snuck out and I came home. I took the limousine she kept downstairs to take whoever needed to go someplace.

"I don't know if it was an hour or a half hour later, I open my eyes and Peggy is standing over me. So I figure I'm dead. I figure I'm laid out, and she's in the funeral parlor. I said, 'Peggy, where am I?' She said, 'Dummy, you're in bed. Why did you leave?' So I said, 'I'm tired. I'm sick.' She said, 'You are going to get dressed and you are coming with me. Just throw a coat over your nightgown.'

"When I got to her suite, she made breakfast for everyone, eggs and champagne. She could cook you a frankfurter in beer and it would taste great; she was a brilliant creator of instant dishes. Balzac said something about how people who are really full-blown human beings have a supersensitive ability to taste and smell and hear. She was creative in everything she did, and always good at it.

"So then she says to everybody, 'You're going to have to excuse me, I'm going to put this child in the tub.' She knew she'd fix me up if she gave me a bubble bath. She had Henry Kaiser's apartment that year—three beds, three baths. She said, 'You're not coming out until you're feeling better.' That was Peggy. She was a generous host."

The late nights that stretched until dawn were too numerous to count. So common was the sight of Peggy crossing empty streets in the wee hours, Phoebe says, that the Con Ed guys came to know her personally. "When I'd cross Lexington Avenue with her at three in the morning, the guys in the sewers were coming up on the ladder: 'Hi, Peggy doll.' She'd stand and talk to them. She was unreal. 'Hi, Peg, how ya doin', baby?' She'd stop and talk. One guy told her he was having a baby. She remembered his name. She was unbelievable."

It wasn't just the workmen who came to know Peggy. The pigeons on Lexington Avenue were part of the gang. She'd feed them with rolls from the club. One day Phoebe had forgotten the rolls.

"What have you got in your pocketbook?" asked Miss Lee.

"Peppermint Life Savers."

Peggy chewed up the candy in her mouth, then sprinkled it for the birds, who devoured the delicacies.

Perhaps the most enduring testament to the brilliance of Peggy's nights at Basin Street are the countless people—whether friends, musicians, or random fans—who, forty years later, can recall with crystal clarity the details of a night they caught her at Ralph Watkins's place in the early sixties: a song, a gown, the smoke. The way that her energy would sweep the room, and the room's energy would sweep right back to her.

Years later, in a general discussion of her live performing style, she seemed to be talking of no engagement in her life so much as Basin Street:

"I do not pretend that in the beginning I could gauge an audience," Lee said. It was something that came "with practice, with work." The work, she said, was considerable. The song would have to be pondered in depth for its meaning, so that the delivery could be special. And yes, the hair and the gowns, she said, were part of the formula—"side-effects." There was always a moment of trying to collect a quiet about her before she stepped into the lights. She'd do her best to erase any thought of celebrities or friends in the audience.

But after that, she said, "the music takes charge." The audience, the band, and the singer "become one, like a circle."

It was as if, she confided, she became a different person: "I'm really two people. I'm not even me when I'm out there."

PART III

Angels on Your Pillow

The Best Is Yet to Come

PEGGY LEE'S CATCHY, bluesy, swingy-as-hell 1961 single of Sy Oliver's "Yes Indeed!" was already engraved on American memories when Ed Sullivan's show featured a clip of a cute, flirty Peggy on a visit to a crowded ward in a veterans' hospital. Sullivan, wooden as usual, bantered with her before she began. She just smiled, then mentioned she was going to open with "I Love Being Here with You." "With me?" said Ed. "With you," she answered, "—and with them."

Then she nodded at the hundreds of young men surrounding her, in wheelchairs, on foot, in beds, and it was hard not to believe her: Peggy Lee was surrounded by a sea of soldiers—and presumably, some pilots among them. Wearing a casual blouse, her hair only softly coiffed, looking realer than she had in decades, she began to sing, and before long, the young men on their gurneys were banging on the walls in rhythm. What had started out as a staged moment had quickly evolved into a rocking, jazzy free-for-all. The ward could have been at Basin Street.

When the film clip was over, we were back onstage live at the Sullivan show where Ed intoned: "Ladies and gentlemen, she really *killed* them"—a verb that Ed was not prone to using.

Before she recorded her next album for Capitol, Lee did a one-night show in New York, where, uncharacteristically, she was not the headliner. In May 1962, Peggy made an unusual appearance, at a birthday party in front of seventeen thousand people at Madison Square Garden along with Jack Benny and Maria Callas and Ella Fitzgerald and her buddy Jimmy Durante. It was a Democratic Party fund-raiser, and it was JFK's birthday. And everyone knew how much Jack liked a blonde.

Peg's performance that night has long been forgotten. The act that followed, as another blonde took the stage, bathed in Peggy's own customized light, stole the show. It was Marilyn Monroe's most historic performance, and it was her last. Singing "Happy Birthday" to JFK—wearing a Jean Louis gown that Adlai Stevenson would describe as "skin and beads," an outfit that would fetch $1.2 million at Christie's in 1999—Monroe left an indelible impression on the crowd, which included Jack, Bobby, Ethel, Rose, Pat, and Eunice. But not Jackie. "That performance . . . belittled the entire presidency," said Jeanne Martin, Dean Martin's wife.

In retrospect, it was somewhat fitting that the two blondes, Norma Jean and Norma Deloris, were booked side by side. They had much in common; an account of a dinner party attended by Monroe at about that time mentions one diner's remark about Monroe to another guest: "She's had a sad and lonely life and she has no self-confidence at all."

But Peggy Lee wasn't entirely without confidence at this point, at least as a performer. With her next two records for Capitol, she certainly proved that. With the immortal Benny Carter doing most of the arranging, *Sugar 'n' Spice* and *Mink Jazz*, her next two LP offerings for Capitol, were full of nuance and longing, style and substance. Neither album strayed far from the jazz in her, a commodity that would soon be harder and harder to find in her albums as rock began its reign.

On *Sugar 'n' Spice,* Cy Coleman and Carolyn Leigh's "The Best Is Yet to Come" featured so many wonderful hooks that it was virtually impossible to forget the tune after the first listening. "See See Rider" was infectiously bluesy, a brilliant version of a traditional song (and the last good rendition before rock and rollers Mitch Ryder and the Detroit Wheels had their way with it, reducing it to simplistic). On Harold Arlen and Ted Koehler's "When the Sun Comes Out," soothed by head-nodding horns, Peggy's performance spanned the blues of both the old generation and the new.

Mink Jazz, the next record, was a true triumph. Despite the overwrought glamour of the cover art, what lies inside the jacket is Peggy Lee pared down to her musical best. The musicians included her pal Lou Levy on piano, Jack Sheldon on trumpet, Max Bennett on bass, and flute-jazz pioneer Harry Klee—all conducted by Benny Carter and Max Bennett. From the opening flights of Sheldon's trumpet on "It's a Big Wide Wonderful World" to her cool warblings on Bennie Golson's "Whisper Not," this is Lee's last true jazz-feeling album for twenty-five years. Arlen and Koehler's "As Long as I Live," all of two minutes long, was pure Peggy—with trumpet, flute, and piano all jamming expertly. Three seconds longer was a jazzed version of Jerome Kern and Dorothy Fields's "I Won't Dance."

Mink Jazz spent nine weeks on the *Billboard* pop charts. "Peggy Lee has that remarkable ability," raved *Cash Box* maga-

zine, "to really communicate with her audiences . . . superb listening enjoyment throughout."

The early 1960s were a watershed for Peggy Lee, in every aspect
of her life. Her daughter, Nicki, married in 1963. (She was twenty
years old.) Peggy sold the house up on Kimridge Avenue and
moved to the penthouse of a new apartment building. She was
alone after her string of affairs with Jones, Harbach, Capri, and
Catling. But her musical marriages from this period were strictly
made in heaven. She was on the verge of partnering with two of
the greatest songwriters of modern times, as well as one of the
era's finest drummers. All were rock-solid, deep, sustaining relationships that would last for years.

But she did give marriage one more try—though it was a halfhearted effort at best. He was a bongo player she met in Vegas—a
good one, too, according to Jack Costanzo. They met in the first
week of February 1964. Within days, the wire services reported
that Lee was to wed "Argentinian-born bandsman Jack del Rio."
Two weeks later, they married.

"She called me from Vegas," Phoebe Jacobs recalls, "and said,
'Come right now. I'm getting married. You have to be my maid of
honor.' I said, 'Peg, what are you getting married for? Shack up,
put on a wig, go into a motel with the guy. Have an affair.' But
no, she was very proper. And she was in love with love."

"He was a very handsome man," says Stella Castellucci. "Very
pleasant. They married in her yard. Just close friends attended.
We met him on the night they were married. She invited my
mother, father, sister, and brothers. I think there were maybe
forty people. . . . Here's this big good-looking hunk of a Latin
fellow. Extremely sociable. Talked to everybody. He and my father had quite a conversation about music and so forth. Perfectly
pleasant guy. She had this lovely little private reception in her liv-

ing room, and a lovely little buffet dinner. They had their wedding night in their home."

In later years, Peggy would hint to one of her musicians that the union was never consummated and that, suspecting that her husband wasn't even Latin, she didn't let him into the marriage bed. A few years later, she explained more to a friend: "I married him because I thought I was going to die at the time" (presumably from one or another not-serious illness).

"Apparently," says the friend, "they'd run off into the desert for a couple of days, and Peggy was always ladylike, so she thought the right thing to do was to marry him."

"When he carried me across the threshold, into my house," Peggy told her pal, "he said, 'I want to thank you for giving me all of this.' And I thought to myself, '*Uh*-oh.' " They were officially divorced nine months later.

At this point, with Peggy having struck out four times in marriage but having peaked at the top of the nightclub world—in a couple of years, she'd soon be commanding $50,000 a month for her final Basin Street engagement—it's a good time to pose another question: Was she unlucky in love and extraordinarily lucky in her music because music was what she truly cared about? For she always wanted romance but ultimately chose the fame—even with the negatives; the lifelong impulse to distance herself from her childhood was the strongest drive of her life, and the fantasy of being a singer is what kept her going. In the final analysis, romantic happiness was secondary to finding, in fame, a safe remove from the unhappiness of her youth.

Lee's next album for Capitol, *I'm a Woman*, left true jazz behind, but opened up a new creative door. The album was uneven, though not without several highlights (notably a louche, bluesy "Come Rain or Come Shine"). Yet fortune smiled on its title cut, a rocking, uptempo story of a strong-willed supergirl who could party all night and do chores in the morning. It was written by two men named Jerry Leiber and Mike Stoller. And for better or worse, it gave Lee a much-needed hit. Better, because of her taste for fine gowns, good hotels, the best lighting and the best arrangements, and, always, the best musicians. Worse, because it began to take her down a path toward rock and roll that she should have avoided, but ultimately couldn't.

Musically, 1963 would forever be known for the British invasion. From here on in, anyone hoping to keep a foothold in the popular-music world would have to stick at least a tentative toe into the rock-and-roll realm. Stateside, at least, this meant being able to sing loudly, and with a bit of rhythm and blues and an exuberance bordering on the raucous. One of the surest ways for an artist to guarantee she was in sync with the genre was to sing a Leiber and Stoller song.

Two ordinary white kids who met in their teens in Los Angeles, Leiber and Stoller shared a true love of R&B, and instantly began to churn out one of the most memorable canons in songwriting history. In 1953, "Hound Dog" hit big with Big Mama Thornton. Elvis covered it three years later—and his version sat at Number One for eleven weeks. That record has yet to be broken.

The team followed up with classic after classic: "Poison Ivy," "Charlie Brown," "Yakkety-Yak," "Riot in Cell Block No. 9." But Jerry Leiber's lyrics weren't all as simplistic as this selection suggests; after all, he'd been a philosophy major in college. And Stoller didn't only lay down sax-laden rock; in his teens, he was writing formal quartets. In other words, Jerry and Mike weren't just masters of chart-topping, race-defying rock and roll. They were capable of tunes of remarkable depth, soul, and beauty, including "Save the Last Dance for Me" and one haunting hit that stands among the best popular songs ever written: "On Broadway."

In retrospect, Lee's pairing with the duo for "I'm a Woman" seems like a no-brainer. But as it happened, this triumph was something of a fluke: "We sent her a demo of 'I'm a Woman' that Jerry and I cut in the Brill Building, in an interior studio," Mike Stoller recalls. "We sent it to [producer] Dave Cavanaugh at Capitol—and we never heard a word about it. Early the next year there was an article in *The New Yorker* about Peggy Lee at Basin Street East. The band was being conducted by Benny Carter, and the article said she was a 'knockout,' and it said, especially, you gotta hear her sing 'I'm a Woman.'

"Well, we thought, 'You can't copyright a title, so maybe it's someone else's song.' So I went to Basin Street on a freezing cold February, ice on the street, and I went in, and sure enough, it's our song. I went back with trepidation to meet her. I'd never seen her—this is *Peggy Lee*. She was very kind, and she said, 'It's very nice to meet you, it's a good song, it works really well.' "

So Stoller called Cavanaugh, who told him they planned to record the number just as she had done it in the club, with piano and bass drum. "I said, 'Couldn't we get a trumpet and an alto sax?' " says Stoller. Cavanaugh conceded that a couple more instruments wouldn't hurt. "So we went to the Capitol studios in New York, and actually, we produced the record. I did the horn arrangement, conducted by Benny Carter. And after that, Cavanaugh never called. Never said a word."

Years later, Stoller called pianist Mike Melvoin, the pianist for the session. "We got to talking," Stoller recalls, "and I mentioned how strange it was that Cavanaugh had never called. 'Don't you know about that?' Mike said. 'Peggy came in and said, "Here's a stack of demos. See if you like anything." I picked it out of the stack.' "

I'm a Woman, despite its flaws, was arguably Peggy's best album for more than a decade. Despite the breathlessly double-entendred liner notes ("There used to be a phenomenon in the music business known as an all-girl orchestra. Peggy Lee is an all-girl girl, and oh, how she is orchestrated!"), the title cut is actually Jerry Leiber's feminist anthem. Lee's take, despite its commercial success, was largely unadventurous. That "I'm a Woman" rocks is not in dispute. That its lyrics, which describe an independent superwoman (who could do the housework, grease the car, feed the baby, put on her makeup, do the shopping and still have time to kiss her man and give him "the shivering fits"), fit the singer to a tee, of this there's no question. But where was the Peggy who could play with a beat, swing some jazz into her every lyric? On the other hand, the sense of humor that underlies this female manifesto is undeniable, and is its strength. Perhaps the song owes part of its success to the legions of women who, long before other female singers were trumpeting themselves as feminists, knew that Peggy Lee was the woman best qualified to sing for them.

"She sang it too straight," Jerry Leiber says. "It *killed* me when she did that. I don't know *why* she did that. She could always be funky. Also, she sang the fucker dead on the beat. I wondered, 'Why would she do that? Did she join a new church?' That turned me around. I had always felt she was one of the funkiest white women in the world."

The single received a Grammy nomination—her seventh, coming on the heels of the prior year's *Live at Basin Street East*, even though that "live" album was cut largely in a studio; only after her death would a recording of an actual live show be released. That time she had lost to Garland's live Carnegie Hall recording. This time she lost to Ella.

Leiber and Stoller would serve Lee well, but it was another new relationship that would keep her grounded in the music that she loved. Grady Tate would provide the backbeat, both literally and metaphorically, for the rest of her career—and the talented drummer came to her at the recommendation of Quincy Jones.

Tate had a singular style. Born and raised in North Carolina, he was—like Peggy—an artist with no formal training. But he had a world of jazz inside him. No one would ever know Peggy Lee as well as Grady Tate did. For starters, they kept the same hours. "As a kid, I wouldn't sleep," Tate says. "I still don't. I'd get out of my bed and hook up my mom and dad's Victrola as soon as I was old enough to figure out how to operate it. I'd listen to Louis. I'd listen to the big bands. Turned them down low and listened all night."

After college, Tate married and moved to Washington, where he accompanied a saxophonist friend to an audition with keyboard heavyweight Wild Bill Davis, "godfather of jazz organ." Fueled by a couple of drinks, Tate asked to sit in. As he puts it now, something inside of him leaped out. "I got up there and I played, and my whole soul just enveloped me. It came from within. I was just one piece of soul. I didn't know who I was or what I was doing, but that soul took me through something that impressed Bill enough to call me the next morning."

Three years later, Tate was playing with Les Spann, and not long after, with Quincy. Then came Peggy. Backing her in her last shows at Basin Street in 1965, he found himself stunned. He had never heard or seen anything like her. Tate is not given to overanalysis. He likes to let his art do his talking. Asked about Lee, he supplies a quick take: "We played. She liked me. She *loved* me. I loved *her*. She loved me because I listened so intently to what she was doing. And what she was saying. And how she was saying it. And what was demanded of that particular moment. And it worked. It *worked*."

Back in Los Angeles, Peggy—who loved gardening and ornate landscaping—found that she hated her penthouse, even though her daughter, Nicki, and Nicki's new husband, Dick Foster, were living with her. "I was absolutely paranoid about living there—

up on the thirteenth floor, open all around, alone after everyone had gone home for the day," she later recalled. And so she tried a novel approach to get evicted.

According to her book, she'd put on loud parties to break the lease. "At some point," she writes, "we put on a recording of 'Pass Me By,' which Cy Coleman had just finished scoring. We played it at full volume and marched down the hall, into the elevator, continuing to march in place, outside into the lobby, around the lobby, back into the elevator, and back upstairs to the penthouse. . . . Unfortunately, the landlord didn't break the lease; he loved the excitement." No doubt because the drum major one night was Cary Grant.

Peggy had first met Grant back in the fifties when she was performing in Vegas at the Flamingo. Grant introduced himself and asked her to supper. In *Miss Peggy Lee,* she recalls having to miss the date because she wasn't "feeling well"; if that account is accurate, she must have been near death to stand up Mr. Grant. Years later, in an interview, he explained the motives for his backstage call: "A very sensible move on my part. I had always admired her talent. A most remarkable singer. She knows what every musician is doing. How many singers stand up in front of an orchestra and don't know what's going on? When you go to see Peggy, you know what you're going to see, and it's marvelous."

At Basin Street a few years later, the handsomest man in the history of cinema tried again: He called and asked for her help in getting a table at the club. She accommodated him, and Grant ended up sitting next to Quincy Jones and Ray Charles. Lee and Grant even fed the pigeons peppermints one night. Cary and Peggy remained close friends from there on out—close friends at the very least. Visits to Peggy's home stretched late into the night. Grant would soon marry actress Dyan Cannon. But clearly, Peggy Lee attracted an extraordinary pantheon of gentlemen.

As bands like the Stones and the Kinks mounted their own musical revolutions, Peggy was not alone in finding herself unable to adapt. *Pass Me By,* her first Capitol album in 1965, had a most unfortunate title. It featured a clunky version of "A Hard Day's Night"; on the other hand, the title track (written by Cy Coleman and Carolyn Leigh) did become a top twenty hit on the adult-contemporary chart. For true Lee aficionados, thirsting for the artist beneath the lacquer, 1965 offered up a dollop of pure Peggy. If you were lucky enough to be watching Ed Sullivan on Sunday night, April 4, you were treated to four of the most deliriously cool minutes of a very cool lady's life.

The success was due not only to Lee's genius, but to the song, Sy Oliver's "Yes Indeed!" and two young men named Bill Medley and Bobby Hatfield, otherwise known as the Righteous Brothers. Their Sullivan show rendition of "Yes Indeed!" with Peggy was off the charts. The three crowded around one mike—Peggy doing her best to monopolize it, the boys backing off in deference—but even Peggy could sense something special in these white boys who had an awful lot of soul to their sound. Against all odds, the trio soon had the Sullivan crowd clapping in rhythm. And at the end of the song, no one wanted to stop: "One more!" shouted Peggy, and the "brothers" were happy to comply.

In May 1965, Lee moved again, with Nicki and her husband and her first grandson, David, into a large one-story place on Tower Grove Road in Beverly Hills. Nicki Foster had by now become an artist herself—a painter of enough renown to have several shows of her own. Their new home, naturally, was aesthetically exceptional: "a beautiful new house surrounded by spectacular pine trees," Lee wrote. "There was a profusion of geraniums, wild strawberries, and some lovely rock-garden plants strategically placed around the two [swimming] pools—the larger pool washing over the rocks to the wading pool."

Further beautifying the landscape was Cary Grant. He would sit by Nicki's son David's crib and even later told a friend that that experience influenced his decision to have a child of his own.

Nicki Foster and her husband would soon move into their own home. A few years later, Nicki would move to Idaho. The move would be interpreted for years as an "estrangement" between mother and daughter, a characterization that Nicki, according to friends, has strongly disputed. Nicki and Dick Foster gave Peggy three grandchildren: David, Holly, and Michael.

On December 12, 1965, Dave Barbour died of "massive internal bleeding from natural causes." He was fifty-three. According to Gary Giddins, Bing Crosby's biographer, Frank Sinatra took care of all of Barbour's final medical expenses. In her own book, Lee maintains that she and Barbour had been thinking of getting back together. He'd been sober for thirteen years. Others dispute that account.

Dave Barbour's death signified a great deal for Lee. He was the one man—other than her father—whom she had ever truly loved. He had helped sustain her over the years; he emotionally supported her even after their divorce. He'd helped see her through emotional thickets, and the professional challenges of adapting her craft to a swiftly changing marketplace. Peggy had lost a true friend.

Perhaps the fates sensed her need for another one, for in 1965, she began an entirely different kind of relationship—arguably the most successful relationship of her life. For the next thirty-six years, Peggy would have a buddy. But you wouldn't have known it from their first few meetings. Peggy and her new hairdresser started out on rocky footing.

"I was not impressed—she was always late," Kathy Levy, née

Mahana, now says. "I would go to do her hair, and she wouldn't be there. At that time, I was traveling with the Bennys—Jack and Mary—and I did Mary Benny's hair. She was my big thing. I couldn't keep her waiting. Mary'd taken me under her wing when I was nineteen. So if Peggy wasn't on time, I'd just leave. Peggy didn't care for that much. But she started being more on time.

"So the time came for our first plane flight together. At that time, it was hip to go to an astrologer, and mine had told me not to fly the next morning. So I loped into Peggy's dressing room and said, 'I can't fly tomorrow morning. I can meet you there the next day.'

"She froze. She gave me this steady stare in the mirror. Then she said, 'Let's get one thing straight: I'm the star, and you don't forget that.' I said, 'Uh, okay, I'll be there.'

"So she tortured me for a few more months. And then we were in New York, staying in Gordon MacRae's town house on Sutton Place, and I came down with infectious hepatitis. Her wardrobe girl told me, 'Don't tell her you're sick!' But a doctor came to see her, and he examined me, and pulled down my lower lip, and said, 'Hepatitis.' And I had to be quarantined up on the top floor of the house. No one was supposed to be near me. But one day she come bounding up those steps singing, 'Have a banana, Kathy,' and brought me a banana. Then she flew me home—first class. And then she hired me full time. She knew she had me—I was broke."

The friendship quickly blossomed; Kathy found out it was real after she began to fall for Lou Levy, Peggy's "Gray Fox" (so called for his prematurely gray hair). He'd accompanied Sarah Vaughan, Ella Fitzgerald, and Anita O'Day before hooking up with Peggy—musically and romantically. (Peggy and Lou's affair had been about as brief as an affair could get, Kathy Levy says: They slept together once.)

But Peg's psychological bond with Lou was as strong as her relationships with all of her long-term pianists would always be. When Kathy Mahana and Lou Levy began to get serious, she was warned by the wardrobe girl: "Stay away from Lou Levy." Lou and Kathy tried to hide their budding love as best they could. But before long, it was impossible. On plane flights, Lou was passing notes up to Kathy in first class. And to Kathy's relief, Peggy happily resigned herself to the reality.

"When she decided Lou and I were an item," Levy says, "she and I looked at each other. And we just knew that we were too good friends to let it bother either of us."

Over the years, by all accounts, there would be few people who could overrule Miss Peggy Lee. Kathy Levy was definitely one. "She was afraid of me because I had a worse temper than she did. She respected me because I had figured out a system to deal with her: I would just stop talking to her, and she couldn't stand it. She fired me once. I quit six times." And always came back.

As Kathy Levy recalls, in the mid-sixties, life with Peggy meant a lot of laughing, and a communal friendship that felt like family. Like the night in a motel on the road when a musician performed the first (unofficial) wedding of Lou and Kathy, with Kathy wearing Peggy's slip as a bridal veil.

Or the day Phoebe Jacobs showed up unannounced at the motel in Cherry Hill, New Jersey, with a doctor to examine Peggy. The musician with whom Peggy was having a brief fling literally had to hide beneath Peggy's bed while the doctor examined her. Or the night in Vegas in the mid-sixties when Lee's show had been a hit, and they were gathered in Peggy's dressing room. Peggy had donned a fur coat and was about to leave. "So Grady [Tate] came strolling in, his own smooth self. We'd just finished the show. Peggy was about to leave the dressing room. He poured them both a drink, and he said, 'Let's toast.' So Grady says, citing an old hillbilly song, 'I don't care if it rains or freezes, as long as I got my plastic Jesus.'

"Well, Peggy had been pretty involved with Science of Mind, and at this point, she pours her whole drink over Grady's head. We all froze in fear. She didn't move. He stared at her. Then he picked up his drink, and poured it over her head—onto the fur— she had ice in her eyelashes. I could hardly breathe. I was about to go into cardiac arrest. Then they both broke out laughing."

Yes, Kathy says, at the time, the booze was flowing, but only because even now, in her mid-forties, Peggy was still scared as hell about going on stage: "When I was first on the road with her, she was so frigging nervous she'd get plastered in a show, and we had to get the hook to get her off."

But Levy's overriding conclusion about her best friend? "I always thought I was the wind under her sails," Levy says, "when it turns out it was the other way around.

"She really was the funniest person I ever met—not just joke-funny, but seeing the humor in reality, in everyday lives. In herself. One of the first things I remember was when she was in the bathtub—when you're a hairdresser, when you see someone with wet hair, you see them for real—she was in the tub, and I was looking through some pictures, and there was Jack del Rio. She says, 'Oh, that was one of my speed bumps.' "

Kathy Levy would become so close to Lee over the next thirty years that when they were apart, they'd talk nightly on the phone—half the time, Levy says, both of them falling out of bed laughing at the stories they'd share. It seems only natural, then, to ask of one of the few people who knew the Norma inside Peg why she was never again able to sustain a true romantic relationship.

"Because [by the mid-sixties]," says Levy, "she didn't want to, for starters. That part of her life was over. She realized during that time that it was not in the cards for her. For one thing, she hated going out, unless it was for work. Work is all she did. . . . Peggy was capable of falling in love—but only if somebody loved *her*, not 'Miss Peggy Lee.' Although it was hard to separate them at times, there were definitely two of them. I knew them both well."

It was the high life on the road. But in the studio, Peggy had hit a relatively fallow patch. While she did put nine songs on the adult contemporary charts from 1964 to 1967, singers like Barbra Streisand, Aretha Franklin, and Dionne Warwick were now more prominent on the national scene. Albums like *Big Spender*, although it did crack the album chart, and *Extra Special!*, a Capitol compilation of material mostly previously released, were nothing special. In her defense, few singers of her era were still in the limelight. The core record-buying public was now half Peggy's age and was missing most of her stuff—and that was too bad, because, on occasion, some of the blues purists were losing out on some treats.

For at the same time Muddy Waters and B. B. King were introducing their acid-addled legions to true blues, the blues junkies could have found on *Big Spender* a tune she'd recorded eight years earlier, a tune that had understandably been ignored. (It was the B side on the 45 of "Fever.") "You Don't Know" was pure, undiluted, twelve-bar blues: slow, soulful, low-down, and gorgeous. The lyrics were as simple as blues ever got—and remarkably similar to the original "Fever" lyrics: "You don't know how much I love you / You don't know how much I care / You don't know how much I need you / Without your love I can't bear."

But she took them to a deep-down place this time. If Capitol's Peggy offerings of the time were top-heavy with tunes that appealed to "adult-contemporary audiences," there was certainly no shame in this. It's just that "You Don't Know" revealed that the lady's soul was still in place, and it didn't surface nearly enough in the rest of her "adult" fare.

Television increased her reliance on mainstream middle-aged pop. She was doing as much television as ever, but the camera no longer loved her quite as much. She'd gained considerable weight. A Sullivan appearance of October 1, 1967, revealed a strangely different lady than the one of a year before. Her chin was longer. Her nose had a vaguely different shape. Her cheeks had been pulled tighter.

In person, Lee was still a major-league attraction, if a slightly larger one: "Plump and unbecomingly coiffed, but still glamorous," said an anonymous reviewer of a Copa gig in 1967. And in certain venues, the perfect nitery entertainer was still drawing as in the days of old.

In February 1963, Miss Peggy Lee had made her first appearance at Irv Cowan's Diplomat Hotel in Miami—"a South Florida Gold Coast poshery," whose other acts included Judy Garland and Maurice Chevalier. The Diplomat's Café Crystal was a perfect venue for Lee, and she became close friends with Cowan, who, for the rest of her life, would appreciate her gifts and neuroses. Lee would return often to the Diplomat, and the south Florida crowd was a perfect one for her blend of high cosmetics and popular melody.

In 1967, *Variety* noted, "Miss Lee looks really good onstage, if slightly heavier than last time around. She is working very easily on some fine charts . . . and is in full control as she styles her way through the show with something less than the voice of old."

Her lyric-writing talent, though, needed no face-lifts; she was regaining some poetry in her words. A quote she gave an interviewer some years later may provide a key to the rejuvenation of her songwriting skills: "Sophie Tucker once said you had to have your heart broken at least once in order to sing a love song. In fact, I used to almost resent that. But I've found out that she was right. Of course, you don't go around looking for those kinds of experiences. But I've often wondered why so many great singers have had a lot of grief and pain in their lives—Mildred Bailey, Billie Holiday, Judy Garland . . . I'm sure there are many more. Maybe it's because the soul needs to be pressed down or heated up in a flame, tested in some way in order to promote future growth."

"The Shining Sea," with music by Johnny Mandel, conducted by Quincy Jones, gave us some of her best lyrics ever. The song would be used in the very fine comic film *The Russians Are Coming! The Russians Are Coming!,* directed by Norman Jewison. The tale behind her creation of the song's lyrics provides one of the best illustrations ever of Peggy Lee's ability to interpret the mood of a piece of music—not just with her singing, but her words and images. If anyone ever had doubts that Lee was in touch with every stratum of song, the tale behind the creation of "The Shining Sea" would dispel them.

Mandel had told Peggy nothing about his intentions. She didn't even know he was scoring a movie. He had just asked for some words to a melody. When she heard his music, she penned a poem. She spoke of a "shining sea," where an unnamed man with "strong, brown hands"—to those in the know, the hands belonged to Quincy—"gathered seashells there for me."

These lyrics intuited exactly what was necessary for Mandel's purposes, and when Mandel read what she had written, he was stunned. "I didn't tell her anything about the song," Mandel recalls now. "I didn't tell her what it was for. What she did is write a lyric description of what was happening on the screen at the same time the song was playing. I said, 'Peggy, how did you do this?' She said, 'What?' I said, 'You don't know this, but it's for a movie. Are you busy tonight? Let's go to the director's guild, they're screening it.' When the scene came on and she saw this boy and girl walking along the beach, her mouth fell open. 'How did I do that?' "

By September 1968, with more of a body, a huskier, mellower voice, and no man by her side, Peggy Lee needed—now more than ever—a commercial hit. And her old guitarist from Basin Street, Mundell Lowe, delivered it—literally.

Seven years earlier, Lowe had seen Peggy collapse on stage at Basin Street. He had helped her to the dressing room and watched her being taken away in an ambulance. He had no idea that he would be coming to her rescue at least one more time.

TWENTY-TWO

All There Was

THE SCENE WAS a bar on West Forty-eighth—Jimmy and Andy's, downstairs from the legendary A&R Studios, founded by Phil Ramone. Jimmy was the owner. Andy was the cat who lounged in the window. Mundell Lowe was the guy at the bar after a show at the Copa when Leiber and Stoller, also in attendance, pressed a disc into his hand. It was a strange song, they conceded. But could he get it to Peggy?

As Lowe recalls it, he took it up to her suite at the Waldorf Towers. "She listened to it a few times," Lowe says. "She thought it was a little negative." At some point, her feelings apparently changed, perhaps when she realized that the song's lyrics seemed to have been taken straight from her own life. Leiber's lyrics must have seemed eerily familiar, the moments of sorrow and joy—

including, remarkably, the narrator's memory of her house burning down as a child. And of a trip to the circus. And of a lost love. The chorus was the killer:

> *Is that all there is?*
> *Is that all there is?*
> *If that's all there is, my friends*
> *Then let's keep dancing*
> *Let's break out the booze and have a ball*
> *If that's all there is. . . .*

Soon thereafter, Leiber was summoned to Lee's suite at the Waldorf Towers.

"I rode up, like, thirty-six floors"—actually, probably thirty-seven, to her favorite Waldorf Towers digs, 37F—"and I was claustrophobic," Leiber recalls. "It felt like an hour. She'd gone up between sets, and the suite was crowded with people. But Peggy was holding the disc, and she said to me, 'If you give this to anybody else it's your life. This is mine. This is the story of my life.'"

In retrospect, it was a fortuitous match—a woman searching for creative footing in a shifting cultural swamp, and two veteran songwriters in search of a new way to express their talents after two decades of spectacular collaboration. Having sold their Red Bird label, Jerry and Mike were looking for a new direction, and in "Is That All There Is?" they found one. The song was sui generis.

"It was inspired by a Thomas Mann novella called *Disillusionment*," Leiber says, as he sits by Stoller's side in Leiber's Los Angeles beach house over the course of a long afternoon of memories. "I was very touched by it," Leiber continues. "This story starts off with an old man sitting on a bench in the piazza, and not too far away from him a younger guy is sitting there, and

he's complaining about all sorts of things in his life . . . disillusionment. And the old man is speaking from another point of
view: 'If you think *you've* seen the blues. . . .'

"It just appealed to me. . . . I thought, 'I wonder. Can I translate this long short-story idea into song form?' Because I'd been
thinking for a long time, and Mike had too, very similar things
about enlarging our scope, our parameters as writers."

"He showed these vignettes to me," recalls Mike Stoller, "and I
said, 'These are wonderful. I love this.' I set them to music, pretty
much the same, virtually the same for each one."

The music was as haunting as the lyrics: Stoller wove a simple,
sentimental tune to back up the different pictorial scenes that
Leiber had created. That was as far as they'd gotten when they
got a call from the manager of an English singer named Georgia
Brown, who was finishing up a long stint starring in *Oliver*. She
was looking for new material for a TV special and liked the song.
"But it needs a refrain," she said.

"So we grasped at something we'd been working on for something else," Stoller recalls. "It had some lines like, 'They all wear
coats with the very same lining. . . .'

"She said, 'That's it—it's perfect!'" Stoller remembers. "'I'm
going to do it on the show,' and they left, and we looked at each
other and said, . . . 'This doesn't make any fucking sense.' So I
said, 'I'm going to work on an idea. Some music that I think will
fit the music with the spoken verses.'"

And here something happened that had never happened to
them before, nor would it ever happen again. "The next day,"
Stoller remembers, "I called [Jerry] and I said, 'I got the music.'
He said, 'Wait, I've got a lyric.' I said, 'Can I come over? I love
this music. I'd like to play it for you because I really think I got
it.' Jerry said, 'I would prefer, since this is a lyric piece, to give
you the lyric first.'

"I don't win too many arguments," Stoller says, "but I won

that one. I played the music for him. He said, 'Play it again.' I thought he just wanted to hear it to get it into his head. But instead he recited and sang the lyric—and we didn't have to change one syllable."

"Every syllable fit every note," Leiber says. "It was perfect—the one time in fifty-five years."

"I do know she thought it was written for her," says Leiber of Lee's reaction. "She just said, " 'This is me, this is my story, do you understand?' And that's when she fell in love with the two of us. She never was really that friendly prior to this.

"But I thought I had written such a universal lyric that anyone who read it would think, 'That's my story.' I had no specific artist in mind. What was in my head was Kurt Weill's wife, Lotte Lenya, because the whole thing has that sort of color of German. . . . I heard a singer around the time called Clair Waldoff, who was with the Berliner Ensemble. But I was also thinking how unrealistic that is . . . we're not going to get a record company to back something like that."

Before Peggy saw the lyric, they had approached Marlene Dietrich, who seemed more interested in talking about a visit with the Kennedys at Hyannisport than about the song.

"She was like a teenager," Leiber recalls. "Then she serves us a couple of little dried-out hors d'oeuvres . . . and she's got this reputation for being a master chef? And then finally, after about forty-five minutes, she said, 'Well, boys, I hear you have a lovely song for me. Will you play it?' "

Dietrich listened to the remarkable narrative, with its final musing:

> *I know what you must be saying to yourselves:*
> *If that's the way she feels about it*
> *Then why doesn't she just end it all?*
> *Oh no, not me. I'm in no hurry for the final disappointment*

'Cause I know just as well as I'm standing here talking to
*   you*
That when that final moment comes
And I'm breathing my last breath
I know what I'll be saying to myself:
"Is that all there is?"

"Then," Leiber recalls, "Dietrich said, 'Boys, I tell you that's a very lovely song but I must ask you something: Have you ever seen me perform in person?' I said, 'To tell you the truth, I haven't.' She said, 'I'm glad you didn't lie to me. Because if you had seen me in person you'd know that that song is who I am. Not what I do.' "

"Then we sat down and said, 'Let's send it to Streisand,' " Stoller adds. "She's an actress and she can sing. But I heard that her manager failed to show it to her because he didn't think it was commercial."

"And that was partially right," Leiber says. "Led Zeppelin was the kind of band that had hits at that point. 'Is That All There Is?' could have been cut in 1929. He probably didn't show it to her. We didn't hear from her for weeks.

"So we thought, 'You know what, let's send it to Peggy. She's not an actress, but she's one bitch . . . of a singer.' "

"Good thing you finished the sentence," Stoller observes.

After the Waldorf meeting, the deal was struck. Then the boys visited Peggy's new house in Los Angeles on Tower Grove. That day, she played them a record she'd been listening to a lot—Randy Newman's first album. It was a good sign, Leiber thought; Jerry was such a fan of Newman's that he wanted him to arrange Peggy's song. In retrospect, there couldn't have been a better choice. Right out of the gate, Randy Newman had shown himself to be a songwriter with a singular gift for musical poetry that spoke as much of melancholy and regret as joy and celebration.

Peggy Lee herself was not only looking for a modern musical direction; she was at sea personally. That year she was playing the Riviera in Vegas, and Peter Levinson, a young publicist for the John Springer agency, had just been assigned to her. Levinson, a classical jazz fan of the first order, would go on to write definitive biographies of Harry James and Nelson Riddle.

He remembers the night of his first meeting with Peggy Lee well. He'd just caught Harry James and Frank Sinatra at Caesar's, and returned to catch Peggy's second show. The Riviera was overly air-conditioned to the point of frigidity. It might have been only a joke, he recalls, but the opening act's bassist was playing with mittens on. Peggy was gaining weight now, and the cold was intended to counteract the heating effect of the lights.

"After I watched the second show from the wings, she said, 'You want to hang out?' I went up to her room, and we talked. There are no lights on in the room. Right below the suite is the sign that says 'Riviera.' And the light kept going on and off, this red light, it was like a whorehouse."

According to Levinson, Peggy made an invitation of an obviously sexual nature. "I said, 'Uh, Peggy, I just got in from New York tonight,' and I begged off. There was nothing sexual laid on me after that. I didn't do it that night because, well, she didn't appeal to me. That kind of thing can hurt if you're going to have to deal with someone professionally."

One month later, on January 24, 1969, Lee went into the studio with Leiber and Stoller to record their very odd, half-sung, half-spoken composition. It promised to be a marathon. The team had been known to put an artist through fifty takes in a session.

As Leiber recalls, "Peggy said, 'I'm only going to do three

takes. Don't ask me to do any more.' Now I know who she is. She's a pain in the ass anyway. She's very difficult. She's very autocratic."

"I'm reminded," Stoller interjects, "of a comment that Zoot Sims supposedly said of Stan Getz: 'Stan's a great bunch of guys.' "

"I loved her," Leiber answers him. "I even loved her big ass."

"She had much narrower hips at that time," Stoller offers.

"I thought," Leiber answers, "she was gorgeous the whole time—until she died, okay?"

Peggy took her place in the studio. She was in good spirits, and she'd arrived with further spirits of her own. "I did see her with a fifth of brandy the day we recorded the song," Leiber says. "I remember her walking over to a ledge that was in the studio, and casually putting it on the ledge. But we never saw her drinking.

"So we started. We were up to seven or eight or ten or twelve takes. Then she said, 'I told you—I'll do a couple more' . . . and I thought, 'Oh shit, we don't have it yet.' We were sitting there, the two of us, waiting for her to throw in the towel or whatever. We really liked what she was doing when she hit a good phrase."

What Leiber didn't like was a slight alteration Peggy made to the lyrics. Instead of saying, "I'm in no hurry for that final disappointment," she sang, "I'm not ready for that final disappointment." It was a seemingly trivial semantic change at the time—but, as we'll see, it was anything but.

Peggy did not throw in the towel. In fact, she seemed to be gaining momentum as the session continued. "I think she had a belt around fifteen, sixteen, seventeen," Leiber says, "because she started to get a little mischievous. It sort of became, 'Now, *watch* it, baby.' And then I thought, 'We're cool; she's talking like a chick does . . . when you know you're going to get laid.' You know you're home.

"So it's getting better and better and better," Leiber continues, "then all of a sudden, on take thirty-six, we hit a take where I would say, take for take, outside Big Mama's 'Hound Dog,' it's the greatest single take we've ever had—"

"The greatest *performance* we've ever had—"

"—in the fifty-five years we've been making records. We both looked at each other like, 'Man, we never expected this.' How good it feels! So we said, 'Peg, come on in.' She came in, sat down, and said, 'Yeah. That's it.'

"So I said to the guy recording it, the guy on the tape, 'Play it, man,' and we sit back, ready to bathe in the glory. He pushes the button and nothing happens.

"You remember the Pranksters? Ken Kesey's Merry Pranksters? This guy was one of the Pranksters. He's the engineer. He was very coherent and very straight and very literate, but there's no sound. *No sound.* He says, 'I don't know what happened, Jerry.' I thought, 'We are going to have a heart attack. Not me—*we.*' It wasn't on tape! It was not recorded!"

Leiber's voice is rising in the retelling. Stoller is shaking his head. "He didn't push the record button on the greatest tape I ever heard! Killing the kid would have been too kind. But she didn't say a thing. I said, 'We need one more take.' She said, 'Okay,' and did one more take."

And then something happened on the thirty-seventh time around—something that hadn't happened on the first thirty-six. Perhaps it was fatigue. But this time, something was slightly different: "She did something on that take on the refrain that was especially good, out of nowhere," Leiber recalls. "She had a kind of melancholy sound, that very wispy kind of sound she can get in her throat. In the end, the final take was very good. It was real good. It just didn't approach take thirty-six."

"And when we were finished," Stoller says, "she invited us all to the Windjammer for dinner."

"I couldn't believe it," Leiber says. "I would have pulled out a penknife and cut the heart out of the engineer . . . but she just said, 'We have a take, right? Are we finished? Let's go have dinner.' She was completely unpredictable."

Take 37 was only one part of the song that would be released. There would be doctoring, and mixing, and finessing. "The next day, or the day after," Stoller says, "we took the tracks to Wally Heider's studio, on Cahuenga, and started piecing together spoken words from all the various takes. Fortunately there was good separation [from the instruments], because she'd been in a booth. So we could take the lines and live-line them in to where they would fit. The spoken words were taken from two or more tracks."

So, the $64,000 question: Is the song about triumph or resignation?

"It's up to the receiver of the song, the listener," Stoller says, "to describe it as a downer or an upper. It depends on how you choose to hear it. But the key is in the refrain: 'If that's all there is, let's break out the booze and have a great time.' "

"The key to it is in the redemption," Leiber claims. "The key is 'I know what you're thinking,' and this is where Peggy blew it. I'll tell you why exactly. She sings, '*I'm not ready* for that final disappointment.' But the line is, '*I'm in no hurry* for that final disappointment,' which is the joke: Who the fuck *is* in a hurry for that final disappointment? The point is, after all of this gut-wrenching and breast-beating, this daunting story, someone says, 'You want to know something? I'd still rather truck it on out. I'm in no hurry.' It's a joke, man! It's a joke! But 'I'm not ready' makes it sound like she will be, at some point."

The composers had no particular hopes for their strange composition. "We never thought it could be a hit at the time," says Stoller, "because it just wasn't happening. Grand Funk Railroad was happening." Adds Leiber: "It had no backbeat." On top of which, he adds, Capitol wanted to drop Peggy (a fact later confirmed by a Capitol exec named Brian Panella, who soon became her manager: "Candidly," he confirms, "they weren't crazy about it").

The song was not immediately released. But, according to Peter Levinson, Capitol, hoping to promote some younger artists, approached the producers of *The Joey Bishop Show* about booking some of their acts. As Stoller recalls it, "Capitol went to Peggy and said, 'Will you do *The Joey Bishop Show*?' and she said, 'Yeah, if you release that record.'"

So they pressed up fifteen hundred records, and she went on Bishop, and after she had finished singing the strange and haunting song, the telephones started ringing. It was a runaway hit.

At the time, producer Dave Cavanaugh, who'd been with Peggy for nearly a decade at Capitol, was no longer in such a prominent position at the label, according to Brian Panella. "There were still a lot of people who wanted to hear Tony, Peggy, Ella. And while Peggy was the consummate artist—she'd had decades of success, and if she had failures, she'd always come back—the new kids at the labels in those days had a different outlook. Here's this forty-eight-, forty-nine-year-old lady, while the Beatles and the Beach Boys and the Steve Miller Band are generating numbers that no one has ever seen!

"So she had to get their attention. And when 'Is That All There Is?' hit, it created a maelstrom. Capitol did not give it the strongest push."

"She had an awful lot of courage," Leiber says. "'Balls' might be closer. Because she hadn't had a hit in a long, long time."

"That song, to me, was Peggy Lee," says Jack Costanzo, her longtime bongo player. "If you wanted to say, 'What was the one song she ever did that identifies her?' that's the song. . . . I would say that Peggy Lee was a sad girl, and the happiness she had in life was her music. She had dysfunctional marriages, for whatever reason. I think she was truly a sad person . . . and the music made her very happy. And she was a genius. And that song was her."

How to explain the huge, entirely unanticipated success of "Is That All There Is?" Because the song had more in common with late-sixties America than first met the ear. For the legions of the young who adopted the Fillmore East and Fillmore West as their cathedrals, revolution wasn't the only musical drawing card. Kids also responded to songs that expressed their sense of disillusionment. Enter forty-nine-year-old Peggy Lee with a song whose lyrics—not so different from those being penned by the Joni Mitchells of the day—seemed to perfectly express the ambiguities of the time . . . and you have a hit.

Popular reaction was divided. Some Americans wrote letters to editors of newspapers voicing dismay at the song's pessimism and resignation, qualities that had worried Lee from her first listening. "Lee thought for months about her interpretation," wrote *The Christian Science Monitor*. " 'Being a very positive person, I didn't want to sing anything that was negative,' she said. 'My approach was positive, and now I'd say that 85 percent of my listeners regard the song as being on the positive side.' "

Peggy Lee was still considered a top-flight act by hotel magnate Kirk Kerkorian, who counted himself a special fan. In July 1969, he was completing his thirty-floor International Hotel in Las Vegas, which would become the world's largest resort hotel. (The swimming pool was the second largest man-made body of water in the state of Nevada, surpassed only by the lake being held back by the Hoover Dam.) Still under construction, the place opened in July with two high-profile performers. In the Showroom Internationale, Barbra Streisand—billed as "The Most Exciting Star in the World"—was earning $125,000 a week. But the room was huge, and word of mouth was not good.

Appearing in the smaller Casino Theater was Miss Peggy Lee, who had reportedly signed a million-dollar two-year contract with the place.

"I felt that Barbra wasn't 'into it,'" pianist Artie Butler, soon to be a Lee friend and collaborator, later told one Streisand biographer. "I don't think live performing was her strong point. Peggy Lee was performing downstairs in the lounge. And after Barbra's show, I remember everybody getting up and going to see Peggy Lee. Now, *she* got standing ovations. There, you're talking about a live performer."

"[Streisand's] performance," wrote Streisand biographer Dan Lamond, "had been finely calculated, but that magic rapport which Sinatra and Tony Bennett and Peggy Lee can establish with their audiences never really got going for Barbra.

"One of the critics wrote she could pick up some pointers from Peggy Lee. The next night [Barbra] went to listen to Peggy Lee."

"I'll tell you what happened," Mike Stoller says. "This is the story I heard from someone who claims he was sitting with Barbra in the small room: Barbra wanted to hear Peggy. Barbra came in with [her manager] Marty Erlichman and this unnamed other person, and Peggy was singing 'Is That All There Is?' and Barbra turned to Marty and said, 'Why don't I get songs like that?' Well, we'd sent it to him, and either he'd heard it and decided it wasn't right, or because it came from Leiber and Stoller, he didn't bother to open it, figuring it wouldn't be a song for her."

Behind the scenes, according to Brian Panella, there was a ruffle going on between the two singers: Peggy had asked that the hotel put a "tent card"—a small promotional ad—and an accompanying record in every room of the hotel. "Streisand wanted every one taken out.

"So in her act, Peggy killed. But Peggy made known how angry she was with the hotel, and made such a stink about it that after that the talent buyers in Vegas didn't want to touch her."

TWENTY-THREE

Grand Tour

ROCK HAD SEISMICALLY altered the landscape. The American Songbook was out of style, the victim of a cultural revolution. And Peggy was free to go in any and all directions, as she had always wanted to do—but what was out there for a woman of her age and experience? Talent no longer seemed a requirement for success. For the first time, the songs that were the big commercial hits were being recorded by mediocre—at best—musicians. The center had shifted. A woman trained never to throw away a note could get lost at sea.

Peggy couldn't rest on the old hits. So her only option was to try to translate some of the new songs for her audience. The results were uneven. Held up against the classics of the generation she was still performing so proudly, the new pop now sprinkled into her act and albums seemed lightweight and sentimental, but without any meaningful, heartfelt, *earned* sentiment to back them up. "By the Time I Get to Phoenix," "Raindrops Keep Fallin' on My Head," "Help Me Make It Through the Night," "(I Want to) Make It with You" simply don't stand the test of time, in Peggy's hands or anyone else's, when compared to the great American Songbook. For the most part, whether musically or lyrically, they just didn't give her enough to work with.

James Taylor's "Don't Let Me Be Lonely Tonight" was an exception. In 1986 Atlantic included it in a bountiful compilation called *Atlantic Jazz Singers,* in which Peggy found herself in the company of Joe Turner, Ruth Brown, Ray Charles, and Aretha Franklin. Ahmet Ertegun himself was the executive producer. Leonard Feather's liner notes praised the "very slow tempo [that sets] a half-whispered mood that is recognizably Peggy Lee in the first measure."

But Sly Stone's "Everyday People"? Don't even ask. And as lovely as George Harrison's "Something" was when rendered by Harrison, no matter who took it on, this song belonged to the ex-Beatle and needed the power of his own journey behind it to lift it off the ground. In Harrison's hands, it was a magical mystery tour to a place of true beauty. In Peggy's, it was a pleasant song, and forgettable.

"But why should she want to adapt?" asks Johnny Mandel now. "She was a tonal treasure. There was nobody like her. She was a very warm, intelligent woman who was also very intuitive. . . . She gave her own stamp to the music. So why adapt? When you've embraced the ultimate in sophistication in music, with Arlen, with the early Porter, with Berlin and Kern, why should she make the change?"

But adapt is what Peggy Lee tried—as best she could—to do. Mixing popular songs with her classic repertoire, she continued to draw crowds in every city, selling out her engagements from Vegas to the Royal Albert Hall. In London, a *Times* writer noted, "It is not only that she looks the age of Bardot—just over 30— but more importantly, she sounds young, too. She has this enchanting manner of whispering, half-teasing the words of a song, and employs her jazz training in the superb manner of handling a lyric. How much shrill-voiced young pop singers of today could learn from her. Or perhaps they could not, because it is her background that bred what we hear today. . . . I would like to hear her again backed by a really good band in a more sympathetic surrounding. Her London fans, however, would obviously support her anywhere. She was rapturously received."

On Lee's 1969 album, *Natural Woman,* the modern stuff outweighed the classics, and the results were mixed. To the Peggy fans, it was a triumph, as *High Fidelity* magazine's review attests: "Peggy Lee can work with any vocal fashion and flatter it without betraying herself. What other white singer, for instance, can get into Ray Charles material on his terms as well as her own? As usual, Miss Lee takes over once she decides to, singing market hits with more natural instinct than any other of our classic pop singers, including Frank Sinatra."

But while it was true that other classic pop singers like Frank and Tony Bennett and Mel Tormé were having similar difficulties rendering the modern stuff, Peggy's difficulties with the genre seemed somehow more profound; unlike the men, she was innately musically capable of tackling every emotion, every beat, every style. Perhaps it was too much to expect of her, to invest even the slightest of popular songs with true Lee dimension. A swingy "Lean on Me," cowritten with Mundell Lowe, came to life, but it was the exception. Even Billie Holiday's "Don't Explain" sounded forced and overproduced.

But in person, she could still work magic with the most painfully pedestrian stuff. If Peggy could animate "Spinning

Wheel," a white-bread hit for the safe, second-generation ensemble of the band Blood, Sweat and Tears, she could breathe life into anything. Recordings had never been her raison d'être anyway. "Peggy Lee" was the name on the records, but "Miss Peggy Lee" was the name outside the clubs where she had so successfully held court. And now Miss Peggy Lee found her next great club: the Empire Room at the Waldorf-Astoria.

She would open there on April 7, 1969, to considerable fanfare, with a mix of standards and pop—and "Is That All There Is?" The song's earliest public performance, prior to *The Joey Bishop Show* or its release as a single, came at a large party she threw just before leaving for New York that year. As the single played on the stereo, again and again, she told a journalist, "I've lived the whole thing—the fire, circus, marriage, all of it." That North Dakota childhood, she said, was "like a century ago."

Up on Tower Grove that day, the open bar was "leaking pretty good." Lillie Mae circulated with "yum-yum trays." Carmen McRae and Johnny Mandel were in the crowd. The sofa was "twice as long as Broadway." Nortonville was nowhere to be seen. More intriguing to the correspondent from *Cue* was Lee's looseleaf notebook, which included "the programs for Chicago and New York, with alternate selections," along with lyrics for all the numbers; a page of dietary reminders ("No, No, Never" for truly naughty foods); an itemization, almost to the last lipstick, of the wardrobe and accessories that would fill Lee's twenty or more pieces of luggage; memos to management ("Important, Please Note: Need organ, timpani"); and rosters of musicians in the cities where she would be performing (Chicago, New York, Miami, Las Vegas). Everything was organized to the nth degree.

Said Lou Levy that day, "We do it the hard way. We may spend $15,000 on new arrangements alone and maybe a total of $35,000 before we even hit the road."

Peggy opened in New York for a black-tie crowd. Eighteen

musicians provided a near-orchestral backing. They included Lou Levy, guitarist Lowe, and Tate.

"It was one of the most prestigious rooms in the city," Brian Panella says. "It wasn't built as a showroom, but lo and behold, when Peggy was in the Empire Room, she was embraced. She always had an eloquence that spoke to the New York image. But the room was lacking accoutrements—a limited-size stage, no lovely chandelier."

Mundell Lowe recalls: "The room wasn't that grand. The Waldorf was geared for the chicken-raisers from South Carolina. . . . But, man, was she on her game. She had them. Peggy always had a way of directing the traffic right up to the stage and into the palm of her hand, you know what I mean? She had an intense look that would turn the men into Jell-O. I don't think the women liked it, but that was their problem. And at the Waldorf she was at the top of her game. It was so well rehearsed, we had it down to every movement of her hand."

She had found her footing in a storied home base that, for several years, she could truly call her own. The only smudge on the mirror, according to a close friend, was the oddest of moments one night during that first engagement: For the first time anyone can recall, a frustrated, snippy side of Peg peeked through the gauze. Gay-press music critic Freeman Gunter, one of her best friends for the rest of her life, would never forget it. His aunt and uncle were in town, and he took them to the show. And they caught Peggy in a very strange moment when she seemed to lapse out of her upbeat persona, and a dark side emerged:

"Now I don't know if this is drugs, Valium, cognac, or what, but she just got *weird*. She baited the audience. She bullied the audience." She sang "The Short Song," a fifteen-second ditty she'd composed to break the mood in a show if something wasn't right: "I don't know what it was, but as long as it's gone, it's all right."

"Then she recovered," recalls Gunter, "and went on with the show. My aunt and uncle were in from the Midwest, and they thought, 'She's hip, and we're not getting this.' Well, I'm hip, and I wasn't getting it either."

According to Brian Panella, Peggy was having financial troubles as the new decade began. "Peggy had a major tax problem," he says now. "Uncle Sam was about to put a lien on her house." Her lavish spending habits were beginning to outrun her income. There was one bit of good news, though: "Is That All There Is?" had been nominated for a Grammy. But given that she'd been nominated eight times before and never won one, she could hardly get her hopes up.

TWENTY-FOUR

Diplomacy

LET PEGGY'S VOICE soothe the ruffled political waters. That was the idea. Well, part of the idea. Mostly, the thought was to get someone into the East Room of the Nixon White House to entertain Georges Pompidou, the president of France, and his wife on extraordinarily short notice. Someone was needed to put an elegant veneer on a night meant to bring some calm amid a complicated political roil. Miss Peggy Lee seemed ideal.

Usually, the State Department and the White House took months to line up live entertainers. But there was a complication in February 1970: Pompidou had just agreed to sell a hundred and ten Mirage fighter jets to a young man named Muammar al-Quaddafi in Libya. Pompidou had, on the other hand, refused to sell fifty Mirages to Israel. Pompidou's eight-day state visit to the

United States would inspire vocal demonstrations in several large cities, including San Francisco and New York. As the day of Pompidou's dinner approached, State's list of potential entertainers grew ever shorter. Jewish singers wanted no part of the performance. A week before the dinner, recalls Lee's publicist Peter Levinson, his agency got the call. Could she sing for the Nixons and Pompidous? "Is That All There Is?" was a hit in France. It felt like a good fit. Peggy was thrilled.

On the surface, the stars should have been aligned: Emboldened by her biggest hit, she looked great that night, even somewhat conservative, with one long loop of pearls and a long-sleeved black dress. But she'd somehow lost her underpinnings.

The affair began with a few words from Nixon. "Our artist tonight, Miss Peggy Lee, comes from the heartland of America. . . . From the farm in North Dakota she went to Hollywood, and then to New York, and then finally to the pinnacle of success in the musical world. An indication of her success is that she's sold more than ten million records, and they're still selling. She has many other capabilities. She's an artist, she writes poetry, she's a sculptor, and she's a diplomat . . . because one of her very best selling records is entitled *Big Spender*, [and] she's not singing that tonight."

She started with "Almost Like Being in Love," with a frenzied up-tempo backed by Grady's fierce drums; the horns cooked, the band was wildly in a hurry to get this squarest of rooms cooking. But the applause was decidedly muted for what was one of her best renditions of that classic ever. Then, for a time, the headliner became the Peggy of old, with a sensational "Watch What Happens," and her medley of "Some Day My Prince Will Come" and "The Most Beautiful Man in the World."

According to Levinson, when she came off after her first bows, she slugged a stiff drink; she wasn't happy. He recalls: "She gave me this look of exasperation: *'God.'* The music was too sophisticated for that audience, and she knew it."

Tate recalls the evening with bittersweet memories. "Peggy didn't drink as much as people said she drank. There was a thing where she wanted to be almost incoherent at times, but that was one of her crips, one of the things she depended on when all else fails. . . . She wanted to be mysterious. And out of it."

It was a strange night, then?

"She ended up very strange," Tate responds, "to herself, and to everybody."

Levinson recalls, "The makeup lady says to me, horrified, 'You can't believe how much cognac she just had.' Now the audience is kind of shifting around, and she's on the stage, and I see the cognac had hit her."

The first indication of something amiss was her patented Peggy patter, a violation of presidential decorum that forbade speaking to the president or his guest. But patter she did: "I want to thank you so very much for making me feel so very welcome here," she said, with an overdose of breathy sultriness. "Do you realize I've tried to be here a number of times? And, uh . . . it's a very kind of wonderfully warm feeling, and Mr. President and Mrs. Nixon . . . you have a lovely house."

Stranger still were her unusual cadences, subtexts, unpredictable non sequiturs. "I'm very fond of poetry . . . among other *things*," she confided in an odd Mae West accent apparently meant to seem ironic. It brought no laugh from the crowd. And her next bit came completely out of left field:

"One of my favorite humorous verses is by [the Lithuanian-born Academy Award–nominated screenwriter and humorist/poet] Samuel Hoffenstein from his book *Pencil in the Air* and it's very short. And it goes like this:

> *"Everywhere I go*
> I *go,* too.
> *And spoil* ever-*thang."*

This self-deprecating downer representation of the insecure little girl inside her drew sparse, confused laughter. But Peggy seemed undeterred.

"You know, that poem keeps me in line now and then," she continued. "There's another written by Princess Grace when she was fourteen years old, and I think she wrote rather profoundly." Now Lee lapsed into a little-girl voice:

> *"I hate to see the sun go down*
> *And squeeze itself into the ground*
> *'Cuz some warm night it might get stuck*
> *And in the mornin' not get up.*

"Isn't that divine? Do you like her poem? I love it. I really wish she'd kept on writing, but I know she's happier now [giggle]. You know, more serious poetry isn't that well accepted. In fact, to quote one writer, 'To publish a book of verse is like dropping a rose petal down the Grand Canyon and waiting for the echo. . . . And I know. I wrote a book of verse and I dropped it into the Grand Canyon."

The crowd knew it was supposed to laugh, and it did. Sort of. But most of her black humor dropped into the void. If there was one song that could salvage this sinking ship, it was surely her recent hit. But even her rendition of "Is That All There Is?" was, from the start, inappropriately and uncomfortably intimate.

Her spoken opening phrase, uttered in a near whisper, was "I remember when I was a little girl, our house caught on fire—and it did, Mr. Nixon." Her mind was somewhere else during the song. And after a respectful spatter of applause, she got even weirder. "Well, I don't want to sing good night right now, if you don't mind. Do you?" She ignored the halfhearted clapping and kept on, speeding into a further meltdown.

"You've all been to Disneyland, I presume," she started in.

"No? Well, you must go. I am going to be Tinker Bell someday."

Here she paused, and, lapsing into a scolding voice, actually chided the audience.

"I don't think *any* of you have been to Disneyland. Don't you know what Tinker Bell does? She hits that peanut-butter jar and flies over the Matterhorn. I think she's about seventy-five. So that's my next job." She then launched into "Fever"—but not a routine rendition, a "Fever" delivered as if she had one. For, about a third of the way through the song, she started to free-associate:

"Fe-vah! Fe-vah! I boin. I boin? I burn. I bin. Oh, look out for the Indians. . . . Fever! What a lovely way to learn. . . . You know what you learn? You learn not to kiss chickens. You know why? Ask me why. [Here someone in the audience had the presence of mind to ask, "Why?"] Because they have such funny lips." And at this point she made a cringeworthy imitation of kissing a chicken, noisily.

The headline of the *Chicago Daily News* was "Peggy 'Bombs' at White House Fete":

> WASHINGTON—Singer Peggy Lee's sexy routine "misfired" at the diplomatically sensitive White House dinner for French president Georges Pompidou, a source close to President Nixon admitted Saturday. The misfire is officially viewed as such an international booboo that U.S. protocol chief Emil (Bus) Mosbacher is expected to take it up with the White House when he finishes escorting the French visitors around the country. The buxom blond Miss Lee would have wowed 'em in Las Vegas, but went over like a lead balloon at what had been billed as one of the most glittering soirees of the Nixons' social calendar.

"It was a disaster," a French journalist said. "But fortunately most of the visitors couldn't understand those terrible jokes. America has much better to offer."

"I really don't wish to discuss it," Lee told *The New York Times*. "Those reports were totally inaccurate, and therefore deserve no comment. If I'm sexy, I can't help it."

The antidote for a lousy performance in front of a stiff crowd lay just up the coast, in a venue where she could turn to the music she loved for solace. But she didn't find it in the Empire Room, where she'd been booked for a return engagement three weeks after the White House appearance. She found it in her suite after her shows, after the veneer of the pop singer was scrubbed off and the jazz singer came back out, to "put the pots on," as Grady Tate puts it now.

"The real shows," he says, began after the shows in the theaters and nightclubs had ended. When she came down after a performance, the show was just beginning. She'd be revved up with all the things that had hit her head. All the juices were flowing. . . . That's when the shows began—going over things she *really* wanted to do. Things she had always loved doing, and hadn't done on stage. The routine was a joy for her musicians: They'd go back to their own rooms, clean up, and assemble in Miss Lee's grand digs, and jam the night away.

"There were some performances you wouldn't believe," Tate remembers. "One night Lou Levy was just playing some changes and things, and I heard this voice, and the song that she was singing, whatever it was, she sounded more like Billie Holiday than Billie ever sounded. She could do Holiday and you'd go, '*What?* Oh *man.*' And when you looked at her you saw Billie— really, she became Billie. She always became whatever she was doing. When she sang 'Why Don't You Do Right?' she'd become a nasty little evil bitch." Here Tate paused, smiling. "She could sing her butt off, man."

In April 1970, Peggy was out in Los Angeles when Brian Panella called her with the news: She'd finally won her first Grammy, for Best Contemporary Female Vocal Performance.

"At first," Panella recalls, "she thought I was kidding. Then she was incredulous. Then she flipped. Whooping and hollering."

The roster of winners spoke worlds about how unusual it was for Peggy Lee to have been appreciated that year. With few exceptions, the music that distinguished the field in 1969, according to the Grammy judges, belonged to sensibilities that could not have been further out of touch with Peggy's. The Fifth Dimension's "Aquarius / Let the Sun Shine In" was the record of the year. Crosby, Stills & Nash won the title of best new pop artist. Harry Nilsson won as best male vocalist for "Everybody's Talkin'."

Even in the categories still vaguely in touch with the roots of American music, the winners were a pale lot: In jazz, Wes Montgomery's hardly jazzy "Willow Weep for Me" took a statue. In rhythm and blues for a group, the Isley Brothers' "It's Your Thing" was about as bluesy as a candy cane; its mindless rhythm veered perilously close to bad disco.

Lee's triumph was a ringing vindication of her determination to get "Is That All There Is?" released, and Panella, who was now her manager, was delighted for her.

On July 7, at the personal invitation of Louis Armstrong's widow—"I knew how Louis felt about Peggy, so I asked her if she would sing," Lucilla Armstrong later wrote in her autobiography— Peggy returned to the world of jazz, at least to the world where *true* jazz still mattered. It was a somber occasion. On that day, Peggy sang the Lord's Prayer at Louis Armstrong's funeral at Corona Congregational Church, in the borough of Queens in

New York City—"in a voice so soft and solemn," read the *New York Times* account, "it was momentarily lost in the distant rumble of a jet taking off from LaGuardia Airport."

Five hundred mourners packed the church, "plying cardboard fans." Another two thousand assembled behind barricades outside. Ella Fitzgerald attended, but did not sing.

"The burial service," said the *Times*, "was disrupted by souvenir hunters who tried to break off pieces of the floral wreaths even before the coffin was lowered into a vault." If Louis was listening, there's no doubt he was pleased; it was the King of Jazz who had always understood the perfection of Peggy's instrument. "Man, if you can't swing quarter notes, you ain't going to swing," Satchmo once said. "Peggy can swing quarter notes and all the rest—behind the beat, on the beat, in front of the beat."

Brian Panella, who had left Capitol when Peggy Lee asked him to be her manager, had to find a way to get her back to Vegas. She was still with the William Morris agency, but felt that Morris wasn't doing her justice.

"She tells me to tell Morris where to go," Panella remembers. "Now, Morris's guys were excellent guys. I'd established a relationship with [Morris executive] Sam Weisbord, then number two at Morris. He says to me, 'Look, she's burned bridges.' I say, 'What's it going to take to get her back into Vegas?' He says, 'I don't see how we can do it.' "

Panella pressed. She'll even fill in at the last moment if someone falls through, he said. Of course, he hadn't run this by Peggy. But a few months later another performer canceled at the Frontier, and Peggy came in. With literally three days to promote and prepare, she threw a show together. "She put her creative cap on—and blew them away. Tore the place up."

Variety gushed: "Elegantly gowned distaff has never sounded better in her many Vegas outings. Her once shy, uncertain stage presence has evaporated, and she has peaked as a pleasant song-seller. Between-tune patter spotlights Miss Lee as a low-pressure comedienne, a quality which perfectly fits her distinctive tones in a well-balanced selection of standards and freshies."

"She did two weeks of amazing business," Panella says, "and they asked her to stay on for two more."

Some of the most extravagant shows of the time, though, were now held in Lee's dramatic Tower Grove home, perched high above a ravine. Her parties were as meticulously planned as her set lists and shows. Take the clown party, with "the garden covered with tents and peanut vendors, and everyone came dressed as clowns."

Equally memorable was the New Year's Eve bash of the same year. The guest list was astonishing, and again the budget wasn't a concern.

"She flew in the Fifth Dimension to her house by helicopter," recalls her friend Irv Cowan, owner of the Diplomat Hotel in Miami. "It was a remarkable party, pretty much an all-nighter. She had helium tanks, and Cary Grant was there, and he'd take a suck of the helium and recite his famous lines—'Darling, darling'—in his helium voice. It was the crème de la crème.

"There was no telling who you'd see up there at the house," says Cowan. "I remember she had a party for my wife and myself [in an earlier year], and my wife invited Judy Garland. Judy said, 'No one has invited me to a Hollywood party for five years. Can I bring Rock?' My wife was not a singer and there she was, singing between Peggy Lee and Judy Garland."

As Peggy increasingly surrounded herself with stars, it was hard not to wonder whether the surface illusion had begun to replace the woman.

"She would give parties for people, and whether it was out of friendship, or just respect—there's a fine line there, in show business," Cowan says. "They want to be friends with each other, but in some ways, the competition is just too fierce.

"She did have great difficulties with her long-term relationships. You could see it from family to friends."

And you could see it with Brian Panella. Now in the sole employ of an increasingly demanding Peggy, he needed to re-create some heat. As he recalls it, he hooked her up with a financial analyst who had dissuaded the IRS from taking any action, and put her into investments that were sound, including a couple of downtown L.A. apartment buildings.

Panella figured he'd scored big when he arranged to have Peggy share top billing at the Westbury Music Fair in Long Island with one of the top acts in the country, comedian Don Rickles. It turned out that Rickles had loved her stuff forever. "One of my desires as a young man," he told Panella, "was to be on stage with Peggy Lee."

But it was not one of Peggy's greatest desires to share the stage with "a club comic." "But this is the Number One nightclub act in the country!" Panella told her. "Sinatra doesn't feel demeaned when he works with Rickles." She changed her mind.

A frigid cold front had swept the New York metropolitan area. Panella puts it at nine degrees above—about as cold as the lady herself on that occasion. When they drove in, Panella says, and she saw the marquee—"A Man and a Woman: Mister Don Rickles and Miss Peggy Lee"—she was less than pleased, even though she'd vetted it all beforehand.

Panella visited Rickles's room, where the comic was eating a pregame meal, and introduced himself, whereupon Rickles, assuming Panella was Italian, stood up, whipped the tablecloth off the table, wrapped it around Panella's shoulders, and pretended to cut Panella's hair.

But back in Lee's dressing room, the vibe was slightly different. Peggy insisted Panella walk back out into the parking lot in the freezing cold to read the marquee and write down exactly what it said. He quit on the spot, but told her he'd see her through the show. "The entire venue was sold out," Panella recalls. "They set every attendance record in the history of the theater. In attendance are some people from Morris, including Abe Lastfogel"—the legendary, revered Morris CEO who had joined the agency in 1912. The son of an animal-skinner who had fled the Ukraine in 1889, Lastfogel was now eighty-three years old.

Panella: "She goes out and tears the place up."

Afterward, Panella remembers, she kept Lastfogel and the other Morris execs waiting. When she let them in, she turned to Panella and said, "You're fired." Panella walked into the costume room and punched the wall, breaking his hand.

"She took three years off my life," Panella says now—smiling ruefully. But he holds no grudges: "Her childhood was horrific. Here's a girl who, at seventeen, is the only girl on the bus. She has one dress. Her earliest memories are of having to take care of herself. The harsh lesson she always took with her was, 'If you don't have the capacity to survive and do it by yourself, take care of yourself, you're screwed.'

"I don't think she ever totally trusted another man in her life after her father. I think her greatest love was Dave Barbour, and musically they were terrific together. His alcoholism was a disaster, and take the alcohol out, maybe it would have worked.

"But after that I think she kept looking to find foibles and weaknesses in men to prove herself right. And that factored into her life: to prove herself right, maybe she made choices that hurt her."

Peggy Lee's final album for Capitol was as good an example of her continuing artistic confusion as anything she did around this time. Its poignant title, *Norma Deloris Egstrom from Jamestown, North Dakota,* might have been a cry from some part of herself to keep the old flame alive. Her conductor was the estimable New York native Artie Butler, a pianist and arranger whose highly diversified musical portfolio includes the likes of Louis Armstrong, Joe Cocker, Barry Manilow, and Dionne Warwick.

"I used to cut school to go watch her rehearse at the Copa and Basin Street," Butler remembers. "I'd be watching the orchestra—and then all of a sudden she would start to sing, and the magic happened. She'd drop her voice on the music, and I'd see the eye in the middle of the storm. It was this sound that had such a mystique to it . . . a breathy, wispy voice, almost as if some spiritual thing is showing up. She wouldn't sing with a lot of strut. She just knew where to make things bounce. If she were a guy, she'd have been Mr. Cool."

The album's most poignant low spots were two of the most enduring and endearing songs from the time, and her attempts to lend them her brand of pathos were, on the face of it, understandable: Leon Russell's "A Song for You" and Karen Carpenter's "Superstar" might have seemed tailor-made for Lee. But she'd underestimated how important the singular voices of the respective creators were to their two songs.

By now, Lee's fifty-two-year-old voice was no longer full, and she allowed herself to be wrapped in arrangements that tried their best to hide her waning force. "Superstar" started out slowly, pushing the poignancy, unraveling in belted choruses on which she uncharacteristically went flat. (And no wonder: Belting had never been her forte.) The louder she sang, the more she lost the center. On "A Song for You," a ballad that begged for simplicity, she and Butler tried too hard to add some swing that wasn't appropriate.

But when she stuck to her strengths, she could still score, and she did just that on three great cuts: "Just for a Thrill" was arguably the best version of this classic that she would ever sing: slow, fluid, heartfelt. And a blues song called "Razor," written by one Jack Schechtman, was full of all of the plaintiveness that she'd always been able to bring to the blues. The last song on her final Capitol album was the touching "I'll Be Seeing You." Although she would close most of her shows with this number as the years went on, it's difficult to believe she ever did it as well as she did it on *Norma Deloris Egstrom from Jamestown, North Dakota*. It was as if she was bidding the golden age adieu, admitting that the time had come to move on. Butler's arrangement is the definitive one of a song that defined the lady.

"I conducted for her at Central Park that year, doing the Schaefer Jazz Festival," he says. "Five thousand people—jammed. There I was, this Jewish piano player from Flatbush, conducting an orchestra in Central Park! With French horns and harps! And when she sang 'I'll Be Seeing You,' I couldn't get through it without choking up.

"I think about some of the artists I've worked with. Everyone calls them artists, but very few are artists. Peggy was one of them. Even in the failing years, near the end, the integrity was never compromised. Her sense of phrasing, the delivery. I remember one time we were discussing a singer, listening to a record. And how the singer did all the vocal calisthenics. Someone said to Peggy, 'What do you think of her?' Peggy said, 'She sure gives them their money's worth—she sings two albums for the price of one.' "

Lee would not record another album for two years, but she continued to work like a dog on the road—from Cowan's Diplomat in Miami to the Concord (California) Jazz Festival to a Ramada Inn in St. Louis—and, of course, on television. In 1973, when Quincy Jones thought the time was long overdue to give Duke

Ellington a national celebration, the show was televised by CBS from the Shubert Theater, and, with one exception, Quincy's lineup was all black: Count Basie, Ray Charles, Miles Davis, Billy Eckstine, Sarah Vaughan, Aretha Franklin, Roberta Flack—and Peggy. She was not the token white, of course; it was Duke who'd first called Lee the Queen: "I consider her as great a musician as Frank Sinatra, who in that world is king," Ellington once said.

Lee's highest visibility remained her shows at the Empire Room, and in that year, her faithful saw a transformed lady. She had lost dozens of pounds in three months—on a regimen, she said, that included reclining regularly to keep her blood from flowing to her tissues, which apparently absorbed fluid in an unusual way. She told one reporter she had once gained three pounds by standing still for three hours. Thereafter, while she would change the details of her diets, she would increasingly take the advice to lie down, whenever and wherever possible, very seriously.

To her pal Freeman Gunter, the Waldorf shows were almost as intriguing as his visits to her suite afterward. "To me, the voice was topaz and toasted almonds," Gunter says now. "A dry, strangely compelling thing. Unprepossessing, yes, but pure genius. Peggy was so aware of the dynamics of intimacy—even in a room as big as the Empire Room—that she could sing a song thirty different ways. She could sing it belting and extroverted, or so quiet it sounded like a voice-over, like the thoughts were in your own mind, as if she wasn't even moving her lips. And she did this work every night. She didn't just go out there and hope to get lucky. She was driven. Maybe Peggy was crazy as hell, but that comes with the territory. Maybe your focus is different when you're a genius."

Beneath all of the makeup and hair falls, Freeman Gunter found her entrancing, sincere and innocent. He was charmed by the sardine sandwiches she'd serve on brown bread with onions and butter, by the hot dogs boiled in champagne. And he saw the disarming sense of humor in the lady herself. Like the night she called and sang him a few bits from a parody of a Broadway show she'd written that day. "It began with her belting—she could really belt if she wanted to—but she didn't like to sing that way because she didn't want her voice to sound thin, or hard. So she began, 'It's Coming! It's Coming! It's Coming! *It's Broooaaadwaaay!!'*—and then she'd launch into the ballad. It was hilarious."

In 1974, Lee's search for the album alchemy that would convince the public of her ability to adapt to modern sounds led to a collaboration with the champion of seventies light pop. It was not a highly publicized fact that Paul McCartney wanted the Beatles to record "Till There Was You" because he'd heard Peggy do it on *Latin ala Lee,* her 1960 Capitol album. Nor that Peggy was one of the first American singers to cover a Beatles song on vinyl (her less than inspiring version of "A Hard Day's Night" in 1965).

Her rendition of "The Long and Winding Road," though, in 1970, furnished a better match of sensibilities. And when she played the Royal Albert Hall that year, she asked McCartney and his wife Linda to dinner at the Dorchester. Befitting a man with manners, he brought a gift. It was a song he'd written with Linda called "Let's Love." In July 1974, with Paul producing, they recorded it at the Record Plant in Los Angeles. Afterward, they met the press—Paul in a black satin shirt, Peggy looking trim in a tan suit.

McCartney and Lee stood side by side as they bantered for the press.

"I was a fan of yours before you knew about me, Peggy," McCartney said. "Yeah, I used to have records of Peggy. I've been a fan of hers for a long time, you know. And she came to London and she invited us for dinner over at her hotel. So I thought, 'I'm going along to dinner. Well, I'm either gonna take a bottle of champagne or a song. . . . ' "

"I'd rather have a song anytime," Peggy said. "I can always get some champagne, but it would be very difficult to get a Paul McCartney song—written especially for me."

"So I took a song along and Peggy said, 'Great. Let's do it.' And really that's all there is to it."

"I was delighted, naturally," said Peggy. And, playfully referring to Paul's wife, still seeing herself as a sensual woman, she couldn't keep herself from adding, "And Linda didn't mind."

"Let's Love" was the title track of Peggy Lee's fortieth album—her first for Atlantic—and the whole thing was as airy and lightweight as the flute notes that counterpointed her voice, notes meant to denote a butterfly flitting through the piece. Even at his pop-lite worst, McCartney was incapable of turning out a truly bad song, and "Let's Love" was the type of cut that grew on a listener. It had just enough hooks to bring you back for more.

Unfortunately, the rest of the album was not impressive. On a chorus-backed faux-gospel hymn written by Melissa Manchester called "He Is the One," Lee resists her better impulses and belts out some choruses. A funked-up wah-wah thing called "Easy Evil" was anything but easy to listen to. James Taylor's "Don't Let Me Be Lonely Tonight" was precious beyond words. Worst of all, and quite incongruously, Lee went funkier still, backed by big horns, on Irving Berlin's "Always."

On the positive side, producer and musician Dave Grusin had recently written the title song for the remarkable Oscar-nominated film *The Heart Is a Lonely Hunter*. Grusin's simple melody was a tear-jerker, and Lee's lyrics were simple and lovely. ("For someone who needed me, I'd be a necessity.") Other than the McCartney song, it's the only song on the album she seems to want to belong to, and belong she does: She reaches down for every nuance she still possesses. It's a truly beautiful song.

Years later, her guitarist John Chiodini, a veteran composer who would be among the band of sidemen who would soon help bring her back to the peak of her powers, would shake his head in amazement at the lady's lyrics in this song.

"It's really poetry," says Chiodini. "Because the one line is the whole paragraph, isn't it? You get emotional just thinking about it."

But by now, some of the critics in Manhattan were finding less than poetry at the Waldorf. Heavyweight jazz critic Gary Giddins, writing in *The Village Voice,* was particularly disappointed when he paid a visit. This was of particular concern. Giddins had first heard Lee when he was a college student in Iowa. One night, during a decidedly stoned late-night listen, someone had put a Benny Goodman album on the turntable, and Giddins found himself confused: How could he not have known Billie Holiday had sung with Goodman? When told it was Peggy Lee he was hearing, Giddins was impressed: "This woman comes out of the frozen Dakotas," Giddins says now, "with a childhood from *Oliver Twist,* and she has an ear for Billie Holiday?"

By 1974, Giddins was less than impressed with a show he'd reviewed. "Peggy is a performer pickled in aspic," he wrote in the *Voice.* "[She] enters a phrase like a balsa glider riding a breeze. Only sometimes the breeze is a misjudged gust which sends her sailing flat or sharp or somewhere in the great uncharted middle. Peggy sells sex, but like an untouchable apparition. Her breathy voice quivers like the lips of a goldfish. Anita O'Day is sex, riding the rhythm as relentlessly as Calamity Jane. Anita's audience titters, not unafraid that she will suddenly tell them to fuck off. Peggy is staged and drained of soul. . . ."

Years later, Giddins would come to regret the harshness of his prose; after the last New York club date of Peggy's life, two decades later, this master of the genre would pen a review that would more than make up for the darts he'd thrown this time around.

But Giddins wasn't alone in 1974 in his distaste for this incarnation of Peggy. "For years critics have employed a hirsute hyperbole when discussing Peggy Lee, declaiming about her 'soul' and her warm, provocative performances. To criticize her is to deface the Statue of Liberty," wrote the reviewer David Tipmore. "Rarely does anyone address how disinterested and selfish a performer she can be. Watching Miss Lee sing the R&B hit 'You Make Me Feel Brand New' demonstrated this remoteness: The soul of the song was supplied not by warm singing or acting, but by the red gels and the bleached back-up trio. At the end of the show, the audience stood politely and gave Peggy Lee a standing ovation. It was as cool and controlled a standing ovation as I've ever seen—even considering the regal surroundings.

"Economics aside, ignoring the need to expand artistically, the audience wants the old Peggy Lee back. So do I. I want 'My Old Flame.' "

The old Peggy hadn't gone anywhere; the flame still burned, very low and very deep down, if you looked hard enough. The press, still eager for insight, found her increasingly eager to give it. While most of her interviews from this time dwell on her health, there were some insights sprinkled amid the dirge of viruses, operations, and other infirmities. For the Fargo *Forum*, she offered up a wonderfully evocative image for the musical journey she was taking through the changing times: "It's like a wheat harvester, forever moving forward, retaining the good and shedding the bad."

After one show, the writer for *After Dark* sat at her bedside for hours, and she began to talk candidly about her life, men, and career. Never again would she be as revealing in print, or as real.

"I guess I needn't have gotten married as often as I did," she said. She was simply "looking for a father for my daughter." David Barbour, she said, was the man she'd truly loved—on top of which, "It's hard when a man and a woman are in the same line of work. I was more successful, and that's hard for a man to take."

Is there any one special man in her life? No, she concedes. She could lie, of course, "but lies about love are the saddest lies of all." She goes on to lament her station: "I miss being in love. . . . But perhaps you can't have both. I tried, but it never works."

For a short time, her soul mate became a man named Robert Richards, with whom she was never involved romantically. Richards was originally attracted by more than Peggy Lee's musical chops. He was a professional artist, fluid with brush and pencil, but he found that while Lee was technically an amateur at this craft, her paintings and drawings were the real thing; there was a feel to them, a particular aesthetic. Painting might be a parlor hobby, he thought, like her privately published book of poetry, but there was no denying the talent. Her artistic sense, he came to see, transcended its more obvious boundaries.

By 1974, Richards and Lee were good enough friends for Richards to be on Peggy's Christmas card list. "I love you madly" was her salutation. But in early 1975, Richards had not yet been paid for his latest Peggy Lee posters, and contractors on the project were pressing for their pay. Peggy told him to contact an assistant. He did. "It's common practice," the assistant told Richards, "for her to keep people waiting forever for their money. She's usually out of it anyway. You'll be lucky if you ever get paid."

Richards, though, suspected that something she'd told him at the time rang true: "She once said to me, and this is an exact quote, 'There's never been one day in my life I haven't had to worry about money.'"

That year, Lee gave Robert Richards a birthday sketch, signed from one of her cats. It was not about him, though. It was about her own birthday, and she'd drawn a woman hanging a sheet on the line, with a smiling sun, and a smiling cat, and a dog, accompanied by a Paul Simon lyric:

"Yesterday it was my birthday. I hung another year on the line. I should be depressed, my life is a mess, but I'm having a GOOD TIME."

This, of course, brings to mind one of her more memorable quotes: "To make progress, you have to make a mess." That's what Peggy had told her critic pal George Simon so many years ago. By her own admission, she had the mess. Now came the progress.

TWENTY-FIVE

Mirrors

On a July day in 1975, Peggy Lee was totally, completely, utterly alone—in a sound booth in the A&M studios in Hollywood. "Peggy would get into her own space, literally and figuratively—which is the only way she could do the songs," says Johnny Mandel. "She put her mind into a certain place, a place where she was with only herself, in order to make this thing happen—the total antithesis of Sinatra, who hated singing in a booth. Peggy liked it."

At the time, Mandel himself was outside the glass, with more than Peggy to worry about: He was conducting the orchestra, dozens of musicians, playing everything from tubas to banjos, who were taking a complicated journey through some unique material written by Jerry Leiber and Mike Stoller.

Leiber was pacing out in the hallway. He'd been kicked out of the session by Peggy. Or had kicked himself out—or both: They were two stubborn, combustible artists with two different visions for a collection of songs that were nothing short of visionary. The album would be called *Mirrors*—if they ever managed to finish it.

"It was hilarious," says Kathy Levy. "At some point, she just said, 'Out!' He said, 'I'm leaving!' Now he's pacing up and down the hallway, singing the songs himself. She just took command. She was incredible."

By now, Levy was a lot more than a hairdresser, friend, and late-night telephone pal. She handled situations. But she didn't have to handle this one; she knew Jerry and Peggy would work it out.

"During that period, recording and rehearsing *Mirrors,* Peggy went through periods where she wouldn't speak to Jerry," Stoller says. "And then would switch to where she couldn't stand me."

"She always needed a target," says Leiber, with a smile. And how could he not smile? That Lee had agreed to put her name to this highly creative but thematically bizarre material speaks worlds of her courage and artistry, especially given the likely commercial payoff.

Mandel had already had several productive sessions with Peggy at home, going over the songs, the pace of the lyrics, and other aspects of the album. As always, Mandel found her a joy to work with at home: "She was comfortable there. She'd voice whatever opinions she wanted, although she was more held-in than a lot of singers in that way."

Mandel was the perfect choice to arrange and conduct this distinctly unusual set of songs, poems, and melodic strangeness. Peggy was the perfect mainstream artist to keep Leiber and Stoller from straying right off the edge—which is clearly what they had set out to do. How else to explain a song called "Let's

Bring Back World War One"? (No way, said Peggy.) Or what about the tango called "Humphrey Bogart," with the lyrics, "Come on and Humphrey me, push me against the wall / Come and Bogart me just like you did Bacall"?

"She wouldn't do that one, either," Mandel says. "She said, 'I can't sing that. They're friends of mine.' I think we did a gay version of it, where it's even funnier, with some guy singing, 'If you'd only come down off your TV screen and be mean to me, I think I'd die.' "

The songs that actually made it onto the record were nearly as weird and wonderful as the discards. A collection of Leiber and Stoller compositions from different eras, an amalgam of every musical style she'd ever attempted, *Mirrors* featured dark songs, short songs, spacy songs, sexy songs, and songs about love—from the G- to the X-rated.

Gone were attempts at pop. After breaking down a wall with "Is That All There Is?" the boys were now trying to prod her into completely unexplored territory.

"When we started conceiving *Mirrors*," Stoller says, "it was when Peggy was going to be dropped from Capitol. We had hoped to use these songs in an album for Capitol with 'Is That All There Is?' and that should have been the album title. We wanted to go right in [after the single was released]. But I guess she wasn't ready for that final disappointment. So it got done on A&M, who signed her on our behalf—as in, 'We don't want her unless you guarantee you're going to do the album. We don't want to deal with her.' They'd heard she was trouble.

"So now all these years after 'Is That All There Is?' she was ready to work with us again. This was January, February, March of 1975. We played what we had for Gil Friesen at A&M, and he said, 'I don't know if it's commercial or not, but they're all good.' "

With a very few exceptions, the songs are great. But they came a decade late, or a decade early. A mid-sixties album, full of this kind inspired lunacy, done by Peggy at her peak, would have stood the world on its head. In 1975, daring wasn't the thing to be; the project didn't stand a chance at the time. But *Mirrors* stands as one of the most remarkable examples of what the wildly converging emotions beneath Peggy Lee's surface could do when given full, adventurous flight. The first cut—"I'm Ready to Begin Again"—was written for *The Madwoman of Chaillot*. But on this record, it sounded distinctly as if it had been written for the madwoman of Bel Air. A dark, spooky, druggy haze envelops the song, an odd character study written in oom-pah minor, coming from a place where Joel Grey meets Kurt Weill:

> *When my teeth are at rest in a glass by my bed and my hair*
> *lies somewhere in a drawer*
> *Then the world doesn't seem like a very nice place, not a*
> *very nice place anymore . . .*
> *But I put in my teeth and I put on my hair and a strange*
> *thing occurs when I do*
> *All my teeth start to feel like my very own teeth and my*
> *hair like my very own, too.*

If there was a singer out there who was doing more cosmetic reinvention every day than Peggy Lee, she hadn't revealed herself yet; "I'm Ready to Begin Again" was a refreshing dose of Peggy being self-mocking. But there was no irony on the second song, though, and thankfully: "Some Cats Know" was one of the best tunes she would ever lay down, a licentious, vampy tune. The music was major-keyed blues, replete with jazz-solo frills, but it paled next to Peggy's come-on; the words were coming straight from Peggy's heart, or somewhere a little lower. And the feline metaphor was the crowning touch:

Some cats know
You can tell by the touchin'
They don't come on a huffin and a puffin
And a grabbin and a clutchin
Some cats know how to take it nice and slow . . .
Some cats know how to make the golden honey flow
But if a cat don't know, a cat don't know.

Straight sex isn't the only kind of sex on this record, either. Leiber gave her a brief one-minute monologue to chew on, a poetic pensée in kink, all spoken to a tango background:

Oh, the Tango is done with a thin black moustache—a wide
scarlet sash, black boots and a whip
Oh, the tango is done with sea-faring trash . . . fresh off
the ship
Oh, the tango is done with a dangerous dance, a
treacherous step
And if one should trip, your frail body breaks with a snap
and a twist
And a gold watch slips onto a thick-tattooed wrist
And a gray merchant ship turns black in the sun as it heaves
to the east when the tango is done.

But the two songs that make this record unforgettable had been written by Mike Stoller decades earlier, when he was still a teenager, for a quartet of winds, including clarinet and bassoon. The first, a pure opium dream, is called "Little White Ship," a tune that would have been very much at home on the Stones' dark answer to the Beatles' *Sgt. Pepper, Their Satanic Majesties Request.* Stoller takes the melody down as many strange alleys as Leiber takes his words, which describe a spooky trip across a metaphoric River Styx in a bed—a vessel that's very familiar to a singer who would famously be known for retreating to her own boudoir to evade the pressures of the outside world: "Clean beds and pillows . . . a little white ship to sail the dark of the night in . . . clean bed and pillows / come aboard, all aboard."

But for flat-out bizarre—and flat-out autobiography—the coup de grâce was "The Case of MJ," a morbid, catchy, creepy tune about a little girl named Mary Jane whose father has gone away: a little girl who, the lyrics imply, is going to be punished for being very bad. The spoken interjections are meant to be a voice that represents, of all things, a psychoanalyst: the one kind of doctor that Peggy Lee could never abide.

> *Mary Jane can go out and play*
> *Mary Jane's been a good girl today*
> *She ate all her peas*
> *She said thank you and please*
> *And she didn't mess up her pretty white dress . . .*
> *(How old were you when your father went away?)*
> *Mary Jane tried to run away*
> *Mary Jane has been naughty today*
> *She won't eat her peas. She won't say thank you or please*
> *And she's made a mess of her pretty white dress.*
> *(How old were you when your father went away?)*

"I helped that song along," Mandel says, "by having done movies of this kind. . . . I got real off-kilter and weird and unbalanced—from a child's perspective, not an adult's. It was menacing, on the edge, psychotic . . . like she did in *Pete Kelly's Blues.*"

In some ways, *Mirrors* was an exercise in self-indulgence, but it represented an artistic triumph in an otherwise often arid decade. For obvious reasons, the label wasn't entirely behind the product. Peter Levinson, who had left Lee by then, fielded a call at the time from an exec at the label: "Would you please take Peggy Lee off our hands? We don't think the record is very good, and we're not spending a lot of money on it, and she's raising hell."

"At the time," says Stoller, "she was off booze, and she was into Transcendental Meditation . . . anyway, one day at the studio she was really angry about something, very angry, and it wasn't directed at Jerry or me that day, I think it was directed very generally. So she says, 'I'm going to meditate.' She went out for twenty minutes. We were fixing a piano part. She came back after twenty minutes, and she was madder than a hornet—she was madder than when she left. She probably spent the time thinking about who she should kill."

"During that time we were doing a lot of TM," Kathy Levy says, "and we'd make everybody stop while we meditated. It was hilarious."

On balance, though, Jerry Leiber thinks Peggy's performance was a triumph. "Part of the experience in hearing her sing those songs was not only the singing and acting, which I think she does a superb job on . . . but strangely enough, I think those songs lend themselves to the timbre of her voice. It's something that goes beyond interpretation . . . it's the extra thing that creates the atmosphere that draws you in."

He's right. On *Mirrors,* there's a relaxed quality to Peggy's voice, in all ranges, no matter what the tempo; it's as if she's not trying to do anything but converse, as straightforwardly as possible given Leiber's unusual, evocative poetry. And, of course, the themes—a beaten child, a woman putting on her face each day to face the world anew—were hardly a stretch.

"When she recorded it, she really lived that record," Kathy Levy says now. "She really, really lived it. I can't hear her voice on it now without crying."

The album would not be released until November 1975. In the meantime, it was one thing to do Leiber and Stoller's unusual orchestrations in the studio. It was another to do them in a club. In August, Peggy was booked into the Flamingo Hotel in Las Vegas, to open on August 28, when a last-second offer came from the International. Elvis Presley had been taken ill. Could she fill in for a night? In Kerkorian's big room?

"She'd played the lounge there while Streisand was in the big room, and it had pissed her off, so she wanted to play that room," Kathy Levy says. "But she did not know the new stuff like the back of her hand. So it was a disaster. People were telling her, 'You can do it, Peg.' So she went on, and did the first half, and it was horrible. I mean, people are going to see Elvis, and they get *Mirrors*?

"One of the managers of the club was saying, 'She's dying. We've got to get her out of here.' So I said to him, 'Okay, take out an ad in every newspaper tomorrow saying, "Peggy Lee: Thank You for Subbing for Elvis."' He agreed. Then he went into her dressing room. Then I hear, *'Kathy!'* I go in, and she's sitting on the chaise, and she looked incredulous. She looked at me, and she said, 'This gentleman thinks we shouldn't do a second show. What do *you* think?'

"I looked at her and said, 'Get your purse.' I already had a limo to take us back to the other hotel. She looked at me for a second, turned around, got her purse, and we left. The next day, the ad was everywhere."

How, Levy is asked, did you get her to obey?

"We had a deal," she says. "I didn't offer my opinion unless she asked for it. If she asked for it, I gave her the whole truth, and nothing but the truth. And she'd listen."

Maybe the meditation really was cooling her out; an interview from this time with the *Chicago Daily News*, from her "gold and ivory" suite in Chicago's Palmer House, offered tantalizing hints that Peggy was growing a little more self-aware. Surrounded by dozens and dozens of roses, she discussed TM for the first time. "I never really planned to talk about that publicly, but it seems to have slipped out." TM, she said, made her feel "quiet inside, and that's a lovely experience." On top of which, she found meditation "creative. Some wonderful ideas have developed that way."

In fact, so at peace was Peggy that, on this occasion, she expounded on a potpourri of subjects, all in distinctly reflective mode—in particular, her daughter. She concedes that she'd had difficulty raising Nicki on her own while she was working and traveling, "especially during the period of her life when she had to go to school and I couldn't take her with me." After praising Nicki's talent as an artist, she admits that her daughter's expertise "so intimidated me that I stopped painting altogether." But currently, she said, they'd begun to paint together.

Most refreshing of all was her utterance, over the 2 P.M. breakfast in her princessly quarters, of how surreal the life she'd adopted truly was. "Most people live in reality," she said. "In houses with families and three meals a day, and ordinary schedules—and they dream of a fantasy world. Performers like me live in a fantasy world of costumes and curtains and lights, and we dream of—and seek—reality."

Two months after she'd smudged the mirrors in Vegas, Lee returned to the Empire Room. By now, she had the *Mirrors* material down, and mixed in some of the Leiber and Stoller numbers with the more conventional fare in a set that packed twenty songs into seventy minutes. On stage, she gave the *Mirrors* part of the show a brief intro: "It reflects people, their experience, memories, happiness, sadness, and takes you on a cruise—a voyage of the mind." Then she segued into "Tango," with its highly un-Waldorfean catalog of whips, tattoos, and black boots.

Of course, New York being New York, the sophisticated critics loved this new artistic twist. "Lee delivers meaningfully," said

Variety. According to *Cue*, "The songs, with their modal harmonies and introspective lyrics, are a vast departure from past Lee offerings, but they still fit in the Peggy Lee style. . . . Peggy Lee could have invented the word 'subtle.' Her phrasing is still clear, her voice romantic and unmistakable. The title of one new song says she's 'Ready to Begin Again.' Nonsense. She never stopped."

The *Times'* John S. Wilson praised "Johnny Guitar," although he was less impressed with her "atmospheric settings": "They may occasionally be ponderous."

By now, the Waldorf staging and choreography and lighting were nothing short of miraculous: A lyric about the moon would bring a lighting change so subtle it would barely be noticed—one of no fewer than thirty lighting changes in a single song. Audiences fell into the mood of the lyric without ever realizing they had been lured.

In the dressing room, things were just as carefully choreographed. "You wouldn't see her before the show," Freeman Gunter recalls. "She'd be getting ready. She wore incredible makeup when she worked, and her face really was a work of art. She looked ageless, and beautiful—a little grotesque in person, sometimes—but it was a face made for the stage. On stage, in lights, she looked amazing. And in a hotel bedroom at night, in the glow of the pink bulbs, which she put in all the lights, she looked amazing. . . .

In later years, Lee would be unashamed about having had extensive cosmetic surgery through the years, according to friends. Her rationale was sound: Audiences wanted to see the Miss Peggy Lee they expected to see, and Miss Peggy Lee is what she'd give them—as they pictured her, as they wanted her to be.

"She'd had lots of plastic surgery. Of course, she loved doctors, she loved having stuff done to her. She had gamma globulin shots every day at the Waldorf. A doctor would come up and give her these shots; she loved procedures. She loved that kind of thing. She'd go to hospitals to have tests. Endocrinologists would be working on her.

"One time there was a piece of dust on a photograph of her, and a friend of mine wiped it off and said, 'Don't let Peggy see that—she'll make an appointment with her doctor.'"

One year later, Peggy Lee's collaboration with the Waldorf came to an unseemly end. The divorce began innocently enough. Her first week into the gig, John S. Wilson was more enthused than he'd been in years: "Peggy Lee's annual appearances . . . are always somewhat of an adventure. There have been times when her performances there have been brilliant and others, such as the last two, when, because of material, orchestrations, or battles with the sound system, she has been surprisingly ineffective. This year is one of her good years—one of her very best, in fact. Everything—sound, orchestrations, programming, her voice—is under control and in balance. Looking slimmer and more relaxed than she has in several years, she is singing songs that, for the most part, do not pretend to be anything but good songs, songs that ride easily and smoothly on the low, throaty, shimmering tones of her voice. . . . Overall, this is a polished performance that avoids some of the heavy mannerisms she has tripped over in the past."

It was significant choice of words, considering the next turn of events. Four days after the review, on October 20, she either fell outside the elevator on the floor of her suite, or she didn't. She either cracked her ribs and fractured her pelvis in the fall, or she didn't. A lawsuit filed six years later said that she did.

Robert Richards, who was with her at the time, remembers a fall, but not a fall that could have hurt her: "It was before the second show. We started down the hallway together. Before she gets to the elevator, her heel gets caught on the hem of her dress. [The hall] has a carpet. She falls on me, I fall to one knee. She never hits the ground. She says, 'I'm fine.' She does the show. Now, there's an ashtray near the elevator with white sand on it. After the show, we go back up, and a journalist says, 'Oh, I stumbled there, too.' He said that when he got off the elevator, there was sand and he'd slipped."

Then, on the night before her final Waldorf show, on October 23, 1976, Lee received word that William Morris, which had represented her for more than twenty years, was thinking of dropping her. That night, in a fit of pique, she whipped off a telegram from her dressing room to the agency:

> DEAR NAT LEFKOWITZ AND ALL MEMBERS CONCERNED OF THE WILLIAM MORRIS AGENCY: THIS IS TO INFORM YOU THAT I WAS DELIGHTED TO HEAR THAT YOU IN-TEND TO RELEASE ME FROM MY PRESENT CONTRACT WITH YOU FOLLOWING THE WALDORF ENGAGEMENT. SINCE YOU HAVE BEEN COMPENSATED BY ME FOR MANY YEARS, IT SEEMS FITTING THAT I SHOULD DIS-MISS YOU, AND ALSO FITTING THAT I SHOULD DO SO WITH PLEASURE. IT ALSO SEEMS FITTING THAT AFTER TWENTY-SOME YEARS YOU MIGHT FEEL SOME GRATI-TUDE. I WOULD LIKE TO FIND SOME GRATITUDE FOR YOU, BUT I CAN'T QUITE FIND A REASON. RESPECT-FULLY YOURS, PEGGY LEE.

Peggy was not having a good week. Her performance the next night was not her most impressive, as a bootlegged CD indicates. She began "Is That All There Is?" normally enough—then, tiring of the song, turned to shtick: "When it was all over, I said to my-self . . . *Where's the fire department?*"

Then to the circus: "And when it was all over, I said, *Where are the peanuts?*"

"I'm getting tired of this song," she said in an aside, "—and that goes for Leiber and Stoller, too."

Finally, she inserted a punch line in the verse in which "I fell in love with the most wonderful boy in the word . . . we were so very much in love . . . then one day he died on me."

The crowd laughed too loudly.

"Well, it's time," she announced at the end of the show. "And I don't know quite how to thank you. I thought I knew how, and then I found I don't know—just that you mean a lot to me. And I'm very grateful for everything you've done. I don't plan to come back here. And I want to remember you . . . but I'll be thinking about you . . . in my rose garden."

A voice from the crowd: "Some of us will find you!"

"Well, look for me in St. John's Hospital."

"Why?"

"Because that's where I'm playing next week."

Four months later, she slipped and fell again, this time on a waxed floor at home. Two months later, she entered St. John's Hospital in Santa Monica for treatment of complications from the two falls. She wouldn't perform on stage for five months. She wouldn't regain her artistic footing for a few more years yet.

TWENTY-SIX

Piano Players

PEGGY LEE'S DEPARTURE from the Waldorf room that had served her so well signaled the beginning of a time when she separated from more than a storied venue; for the next few years, she was a woman at sea. Her live performances continued to enthrall the faithful, but her bold attempt at pushing the artistic envelope with *Mirrors* had not given her the breakout she sought. She'd been without a major commercial success for years. Now in her mid-fifties, Lee had no steady male companionship. "She'd talk about her 'boyfriends,'" Grady Tate recalls. "I'd say, 'Get out of here—you don't have any boyfriends.'" In interviews, Peggy increasingly referred to the traumas of her childhood, in effect using her public as a personal audience to exorcize her demons when a significant other—or therapy, which she staunchly opposed—might have provided a more appropriate setting for discussing the childhood conflicts that clearly still plagued her. Her spirituality at this time, say friends, had never been stronger, and sculpting and painting were a part of her daily routine, but the peace all of this might have offered seemed to elude her.

Several incidents during the next few years paint a portrait of a woman struggling with growing old gracefully, of a woman who had lost touch with her center. But one in particular serves as the boldest, starkest portrait of the Miss Peggy Lee who was letting both herself and her audience down. It was an eerily accurate replay of the scene in *Pete Kelly's Blues,* when her character had been shouted off the stage. At the Venetian Room in the Fairmont Hotel in San Francisco in 1977, recalls one witness, Peggy was way off her game and appeared somewhat disoriented: "At one point her pearls broke. She was stumbling around the stage trying to pick them up. And this guy in the audience stands up and says, 'You used to be the American Dream. What happened?' "

The answer seemed obvious: For a woman who had consciously chosen her art, and its attendant fame, as her lifelong companion, the absence of the national adulation left a void that she was struggling to fill.

"Her days were miserable," Grady Tate says. "She only came to life, man, when she was preparing for that stage and she hit it."

The results were still critically acclaimed. In particular, a weeklong engagement at the Music Hall in Detroit in April 1978 with Count Basie was a huge success—on stage, anyway. The backstage performances, though, told a different story.

The Music Hall gig had promised to be a singular engagement, for it would put her on stage for the first time with one of the musicians whose jazz had tempted her to flee the desolate prairie in the first place. Tom Cassidy, one of her managers, got $25,000 for Basie and $25,000 for Peggy for a week's work: very good coin indeed. The shows would consist of Basie's band doing forty-five minutes, and Peggy coming out to do forty-five more minutes with the band.

"It was a huge success," Cassidy recalls—for the audience, anyway. But there were troubles they didn't see. "She would sort of pass out occasionally and collapse," he says, "and have to be dragged off during rehearsals." Cassidy emphasizes that there was no sign of substance abuse; she would simply hit a wall. The opening night was sensational. The following nights were fine. It was the rehearsals that were trying: Peggy would reach a state of exhaustion and declare the day done.

"From this date," Cassidy says, "we got the largest offer we ever got in the history of the agency: ten theaters, $50,000 a date: Cleveland, Buffalo, Wolf Trap in Washington. It was a huge offer. Half a million to be split between them."

It never happened.

"Basie said, 'Are you fucking nuts?'" Cassidy recalls. "'I'm not doing one more date with that lady.'"

On a trip to Australia in the spring of 1979, Peggy's reviews were stellar, recalls Irving Arthur, who also managed her briefly, but "she was a control freak in every way." Arthur was not inexperienced in handling female singers. In 1961, Arthur had seen a young singer at a club called the Bon Soir in Greenwich Village and signed Barbra Streisand to her first representation contract.

"Peggy told me I couldn't bring my wife," Arthur remembers of their sold-out two-week engagement Down Under. "'This is business,' she said. I'm thinking, 'I don't want anything to do with her, if that's the way she is.' But we went. It was always like that, with any guy: She didn't ever want the wife around. Then when we got there, she worked the crew and musicians so hard that they never got a chance to see the sights."

Arthur's frustration at Peg's refusal to countenance the presence of other women echoes a recurrent theme of the time. Lee could be threatened by other women, a flaw born of nothing so much as the lifelong insecurity that had fueled her rise from the start: She wanted to be the most beautiful and the most talented, and having other women around could unsettle her.

The Aussie engagement was a spectacular success. As in England, and later in Japan, audiences could never get enough of her: "The fact that Lee had waited so long in her career before touring Australia," said *Variety*, "had made some skeptical. . . . But the skeptics were surprised by a Peggy Lee who was every bit the showperson they knew her to be from recordings, films, etc. Despite the house and its notoriously bad acoustics, Lee succeeded in giving one of the best shows the concert hall has seen."

Like so many Peggy acquaintances, Arthur was the recipient of many 3 A.M. telephone calls. "It's just that control element," Arthur says now. "The thing I always found so amazing about her was that we'd go to a job, and I'd have to wheel her in. Then all of a sudden, I don't know where the energy came from, a breath of life would come into her, and she'd be singing, and I'd think, 'My God, this isn't the woman I was with a moment ago.' "

Robert Richards had not lost interest in Lee's talents as a painter. He believed it was time Peggy had her own designer fabric label. His Japanese friend Shigeru Okada, of the centuries-old Mitsukoshi department store chain, thought so, too. The Japanese were in the midst of a love affair with American aesthetics in the seventies. Mitsukoshi had a Tiffany's in Tokyo now; anything Western was marketable, and Peggy's eclectic sensibility—not just her artwork, but her whole package—was elegant in a vaguely Asian way. Richards ran his idea by Lee: Your illustrations are perfect for the Japanese, he told her. This could be a very lucrative project. She was enthusiastic, and invited him out to the house on Tower Road. Come stay with me: We'll design a pattern, we'll get the deal done.

In Los Angeles, Richards's work routine with Lee centered largely around Peggy's cold bedroom, with its marble table at the foot of the bed. "She pretty much stayed in bed," Richards recalls. "Her journeys to other parts of the house were rare. I'd be sitting there in front of a little marble table in her bedroom, the cold rising off the marble. If you put your hands on it, your hand would be frozen." Richards also recalls another bedroom accessory: the silver shoebox on the bed—"full of pills . . . Valiums."

More distressing, Richards says, was the way she'd keep staff waiting until late Friday night for their paychecks, which featured her distinctive tiny signature, so small it could have been a hamster's. How does one explain a woman who otherwise lived for the bold stroke and grand gesture writing in such a diminutive style? Because she was afraid to give of herself, Richards thought. It was the signature of Norma, insecure and scared.

"She had no one to help her," Richards remembers, "no one to trust. Your heart went out to her. She had no one to take care of her in any way, shape or form. I think she was terrified. She was a lonely woman bouncing off the walls. She and her daughter talked often on the phone, but Nicki was not around."

"Nicki did have a troubled relationship with her mother," says Kathy Levy, "which is too bad, because they're both pretty terrific people. I had to make a choice because Peggy signed the checks."

The day arrived to strike the business deal that had prompted Richards's visit. Peggy was to host three representatives of Mitsukoshi Limited, founded in 1673, including the president himself, Shigeru Okada. She sketched out the dining table in an intricate drawing, including not just the seating of the guests, but the silverware, down to the butter knives. In the margins of the sketch she wrote the menu: salmon mousse, Belgian endive salad, veal piccata fettuccine, petits pois with pearl onions, Viennese torte—and the drink list, which included chablis, rosé, cognac, champagne, and sake. She also noted the floral arrangements, and the service schedule: "Cocktails—on arrival, 6 p.m. Quiche—soon after. Dinner—7:30."

The guests were on time. And then, recalls Richards, "Out she comes from the bedroom, walks ten feet—and faints to the floor." Richards helped her up, and they all helped put her on the couch. Richards was not surprised. "She was so sedentary. And those diet shakes—her interpretation of the diet shakes was that they would take off weight. She'd drink five or six a day—in addition to eating. And the nerves, the stress, and kaboom! No wonder she was fainting."

The rest of the evening went well. Okada said he looked forward to receiving their proposals and sketches. Over the next week, Richards and Peggy put together a portfolio: drawings of rooms with peach sheets and peach curtains printed in a delicate white pattern designed by Peggy. Peggy sent off the package. Okada sent a letter from Japan: He was pleased, he said, and he would show the designs to his partners. He looked forward to seeing Peggy and Richards in Paris in June: They were invited to a gala at Versailles. The engraved invitations were spectacular.

But within days of receiving the letter, Peggy started getting antsy. Why haven't we heard? Cool out, Richards told her. But she started making calls to Japan; Richards overheard one, in which Peggy was telling someone—Okada's translator, he presumed—that she had other people interested. If he wasn't ready to commit, "then send the designs back." Within a few days, the portfolio arrived. When Richards opened it, he was appalled to see that some of his sketches were stuck together. He peeled them apart and saw that his signatures had been obliterated with white nail polish.

Livid, Richards confronted Lee: "Why did you erase my signature?"

"Because, Robert," she answered, "it's not your work they're interested in."

He could not contain himself: "If Benny Goodman had acted that way," he said, "you'd still be a fucking waitress in Fargo, North Dakota."

They patched things up. Richards could not find it in himself to stay angry at Peggy for long; the snippy side wasn't the only facet he saw of the woman. She gave him a book called *The Letters of the Scattered Brotherhood,* an unusual volume of writings that had been compiled in 1948 from several years of submissions to a magazine called *The Churchmen.* Perhaps she'd first seen it through Ernest Holmes. The authors were unnamed so that their messages would not be colored by ego.

The book seemed to offer a very curious and intriguing glimpse into Peggy Lee's psyche. From the first page to the last, the volume preaches, in chapter after chapter, of the need for the individual to sublimate all emotion in order to find inner peace. "Emotion," reads one letter, "is as wild and unpredictable as the weather, and must be faced and dominated. No wonder the ancients called it the devil, for at times it will run away with you, weaken your resolve, loosen your armor and plunge you into hell." Here's another: "In human relations, refrain from the luxury of emotional storms of resentment and 'righteous' indignation. There is no righteousness in emotional violence." And another: "Be not troubled too much by the hobgoblins of the imagination, that is a useless burden. Reality is enough to bear without adding the unreality."

It's all a most curious manifesto for a woman who—even if her stage persona was restrained and minimal—always showed her emotions and was eternally unafraid to spill her all, conversationally and musically, to her crowds. If her public performing style was designed to hold something back, she nonetheless communicated her needs in full; minimal or not, she had to give out enough of herself to establish the relationship with her audience—her family. A true Peggy Lee ballad was laden with affect; when she sang of a broken heart, she was showing you the heartbreak. When she was singing of a good day, she was giving you her joy and optimism.

So when the Brotherhood preaches in one letter, quite simply, *"Silence is your role,"* the directive goes counter to everything that had transformed Norma Egstrom into Miss Peggy Lee.

And perhaps that was the point: Peggy was frustrated and unfulfilled. She was looking for a way back to a serenity she had never really possessed. Kathy Levy says Peggy's priorities were shifting. "She got much, much more involved in spirituality. She was more interested by then in developing herself spiritually, and looking at the world around her, and appreciating it. And she did."

It took extreme coaxing, Richards recalls, to get Peggy to accompany him to a Peter Allen show one night at the Roxy. Richards and Allen were old friends. The show was sold out every night. Allen asked Richards to bring Peggy. She'd recorded a couple of Peter's songs. He'd love to see her.

But on the night they attended, when Allen's assistant came out to meet them before the show, the assistant matter-of-factly mentioned that Peter would like to say from the stage that Peggy was in the audience. "I didn't come here to be exploited," Peggy replied. "You will not introduce me."

The assistant returned a moment later to explain that Peter hadn't meant to offend. Of course, they wouldn't introduce her.

The Roxy filled up, including a full complement of Hollywood types, and Allen introduced them all, from Raquel Welch to Britt Ekland. Then, come encore time, Allen did a remarkably generous thing. He said, "I'm going to sing 'Quiet, There's a Lady on Stage.' People usually think I sing that for Judy Garland. But tonight, I'm going to sing it to someone else instead. She knows who she is.' "

Relieved to have a second chance, grateful for Allen's class, Peggy rose. "And the room rose, table by table, to give her a standing ovation," recalls Richards. "I felt so good for her."

It only stood to reason that if Peggy Lee was going to find a way to get back into a creative groove, to pen some real poetry again and sing from the heart, she'd need the help of someone who had as much musical history as she did. Someone who understood the same rhythms, the same melodies, the same longings.

The problem, of course, was that finding a window back into the heritage of popular jazz had become problematic for any of the true veterans. Jazz had long ago decided to follow its own defiant path. But one jazz pianist had stayed the course for all of these decades, and thus Lee's finest accomplishment during this otherwise problematic era came about because a giant from the golden age reached out. And this time, for a change, the collaborator was a woman.

They would produce a song that hardly stunned the music world; it was just a small, pretty thing, really, a lovely piece that anchored a small, interesting album that, in retrospect, represented the first small scene in the final act of Peggy Lee's life: the journey back to her art, her family, and herself.

The place was called the Hickory House, at 144 West Fifty-second Street in New York City. It was a steakhouse, with sawdust on the floor. But for many years it had been the home of a jazz pianist without parallel. If jazz was a style that mingled a million influences, then Marian McPartland was jazz itself. A native of a village near Slough, Buckinghamshire, England, she had trained classically. During the Second World War, while playing USO shows in France and Belgium, she'd met Chicago jazz cornetist Jimmy McPartland, a Bix Beiderbecke protégé, and married him at war's end.

It was Dave Brubeck who had called McPartland one of the three greatest jazz pianists of all time. No one could argue that then; no one can argue it now. There she was in 1958, standing on the brownstone stoop in "A Great Day in Harlem," Art Kane's amazing photo for *Esquire,* flanked by Coleman Hawkins, Thelonious Monk, Sonny Rollins, and fifty-three other jazz musicians: planted securely among her peers. Only her self-deprecating demeanor kept McPartland's public profile from becoming commensurate with her singular talent. She never deigned to act like the giant she'd become.

"I was never very good," she says now, "at pushing my stuff."

Among her "stuff" was a tune McPartland had written in the sixties, without lyrics, which she called "Afterglow." It was written in one night, during a time when she was separated from her husband. She'd been seeing another man, and one evening, at a show, McPartland had spotted this special new guy, gone straight back to her apartment, and, within a half hour, written the wistful, striking melody.

One night in 1977, she decided she knew who she wanted to record it. At the time, she and Jimmy were performing in the main room of a hotel somewhere near Orlando, Florida—smack in the land of Disney. "The club was called the Village Lounge," McPartland recalls. "I'm amazed that Disney allowed this room to be what it was: a beautiful little jazz room. They'd bring in good musicians." Peggy was playing a theater nearby.

McPartland had known Lee since she and Jimmy had crossed paths with Peggy and Dave in Chicago in the forties. McPartland had never forgotten the night she caught Peggy at Basin Street: "I heard her sing [Johnny Burke and Jimmy Van Heusen's] 'Here's That Rainy Day.' It was the first time I'd ever heard it. That was the version I always think of when I play it. I rushed out to learn it, or take it off someone else's record. Some things you're absolutely riveted by, and all these years later I remember it so well."

Over the later years, the two exchanged Christmas cards—Peggy and her cat sending salutations. McPartland thought it all rather poignant. She occasionally tried to get Lee to appear on her radio show on National Public Radio, *Piano Jazz*, where she drew the crème de la crème of jazz.

McPartland had never stopped to consider whether Peggy fit the definition of "jazz singer." Jazz, McPartland knew, was more of a feeling than a style. "God, we've had so many arguments through the years about what jazz is," she says now. "I remember being in the Hickory House, talking about someone's music, people saying, 'That's jazz, that's not jazz.' I think each person brings to a performance their own feeling. I didn't think about whether it's jazz or not jazz. It's Peggy Lee.

"That's what's so great about it," she says. "Everybody does their own thing. Peggy could sing 'Folks Who Live on the Hill,' and Sarah probably did, and Billie. But they all could sing that song, and each one could be different. I have heard them all at different times. I liked Billie, but I didn't have that adoration that a lot of people have. For that style of singing, to me, Peggy is tops."

McPartland, a veteran of the big-band scene, knew that Peggy had actually managed to grow as a performer during her time with Benny Goodman—a man whom McPartland had toured with and could not abide. "He was an asshole," McPartland says. "I always thought he had a part missing—he didn't have any sympathy or understanding for other people."

Before she approached Peggy with "Afterglow" in Florida, McPartland caught one of Lee's rehearsals, and marveled at the meticulousness—her elegant dress, the precision of the lighting cues, the cassette recorder she'd listen to afterward to hone the performance: "Her every move was choreographed with lights to match. She watched everything, and everything had to be just the way she had it. Every wave of the hand was choreographed." After one show, Marian and Jimmy went upstairs to visit Peggy.

"It was like an audience with the pope," McPartland recalls. "She was in bed, in this satin nightgown, what I could see of it, and satin sheets, and a room filled with flowers. Jimmy and I came in and Jimmy kissed her hand, and all that shit. In fact, I don't remember ever seeing her when she wasn't perfectly put together—here she is even in bed, and her hair is done. . . . She played the role, in life. That was her. In order to be that way, someone has to be somewhat narcissistic, I suppose, but in terms of being a real person, she was always nice, approachable, and friendly.

"And at that time I asked her if she would listen to this song of mine. Her piano player said, 'Make a cassette of it, just the bare melody, and I'll play it for her.' That's exactly what happened."

Lee loved it, and penned a perfect metaphor for the wistfulness of McPartland's melody: embers of a waning fire still warm her— "in the days of our love."

The single, poetic line—"In the days of our love"—was not only one of the tightest, most evocative literary phrases she had ever produced; the entire piece more or less exactly mirrored the emotions of the dummy lyric McPartland had written in her head while composing the melody.

It was suggested to McPartland that Peggy's later years hid insecurity and unrealized romantic longings; that Lee's inability to find true happiness had made her songs all the more vivid.

"I would say that's a very good assessment," McPartland says. "That . . . would give her the quality that made her sing a song like the one we did so beautifully. That was what she was thinking or wishing. . . . Peggy—all of us musicians—I think we're so lucky to be able to put out our emotions musically, like me with the piano, Peggy with her [singing]. Really, she probably would have been a lot more unhappy if she was just a woman who didn't have a talent. This way she was able to thrill audiences, and at the same time, be living some of her emotions."

These days, Marian McPartland's bond with Peggy Lee goes beyond their common roots, their time with Benny, their true love of jazz.

"They don't carry my radio show in New York City anymore," she says, "but they have it twice a week in Fargo."

The new Peggy Lee album was called *Close Enough for Love*, and it was released by DRG records in 1979. Lee was recording with just a handful of musicians, including the old pro Max Bennett on bass. The combo setting had always been Lee's strength; its sparseness of sound had always suited her restrained style. Twenty years earlier, her softness suggested a power never unleashed. Now, with her more limited range, Lee's hushed deliveries served to emphasize the mood of a very quiet, reflective, soulful record. For the first time in years, this was a real Peggy Lee album that sounded as if she had stopped trying to satisfy anyone's musical tastes but her own. Absent were the current popsters. In their place—with only a misstep or two—were good, timeless songs.

The McPartland-Lee collaboration was simply beautiful. Her old pal Art Hamilton's "Rain Sometimes" evoked strains, both melodic and lyrical, of her true glory days, when she and Hamilton had brought *Pete Kelly* to its greatest musical heights. Most surprising was a cover of Cole Porter's "Just One of Those Things," arranged with an alarming disco bounce. On first listen, it seemed a dangerously leisure-suited version of a classic. But with subsequent listenings, something happens, something involving the number's underpinnings of swing, blues, pop, jazz. The small detail that held it together was a very cool guitar lick, filling in the background all the way through.

The musician responsible was a guy named John Chiodini, an exiled New Yorker whom Bennett had called into the studio to sit in on the recording of the Porter tune. A couple of guitarists had already played on some of the tracks, but they couldn't make it on the day "Just One of Those Things" was recorded.

The Porter arrangement that Chiodini first heard in the studio seemed caught between the past and present. "But I didn't want to seem too forward," Chiodini says, "so I suggested to Max on the side, 'I have an idea: a little background riff, a blues-rock thing that could underlie the whole thing, keep it rolling.'"

Peggy listened. Chiodini played his repeating riff—hitting the notes fast, choppily, each one a little jackhammer thrust that might have been on a cut produced by Brian Eno or David Byrne. For sure, the licks represented something new for Lee. And she had always had an ear for something new and interesting and unconventional.

Chiodini's minor-keyed staccato blues refrain transformed a song that never should have been updated into something quite listenable. For John Chiodini, this was the start of a long, strange, wonderful collaboration. Within three months, while rehearsing a band to promote the album on the road and on television, Lee asked for the guitarist from the Porter recording. Chiodini leaped at the chance, and stayed by her side for the rest of her life. To this day, he is stunned at his luck.

"She was like the first real woman's rights activist in music," he says. "There's so many songs. 'I'm a Woman' is obvious, but what about 'Black Coffee'? What about 'It's a Good Day'? That's her! And the way she sings it, you really know it *is* a good day. When you listen to those records, you're listening to her and Dave Barbour. That's what you're hearing. And so I became part of that."

At the time, Chiodini's arrival simply filled a need. Only in retrospect does it come into true focus. Lee's artistic salvation had truly begun. She still had Grady Tate to link her with the golden age. And now a new breed of musicians would begin to gather around her, younger men who not only heard the music and played the music with love for its true roots, but loved her the way sons and lovers love: with tolerance, with understanding, with joy.

After the release of *Close Enough for Love*, Peggy Lee bought her final house—a French Regency villa perched in the hills of Bel Air, with a view of the ocean, and surrounded by roses. On a clear day, Catalina Island beckoned from the sun-splashed Pacific. The home on Bellagio Road was five thousand square feet, with a pool. Its elegant touches included an alabaster fireplace in the master bedroom and a library. Soon a man named José Prado would join Lillie Mae Hendricks as a valued staff household member here.

Behind the unpretentious front door lay a two-story foyer with a winding staircase. But the first piece of furniture that greeted any visitor was a grand piano. This keyboard would make some beautiful music. And the first man to do it justice was a pianist who would help take Peggy Lee in yet another new direction. Over the next four years, they would create a tremendous work of art that would epitomize all that the lady was—for worse, and for better.

TWENTY-SEVEN

One-Woman Show

THE VENUE WAS a theater in the tony suburb of Birmingham, Michigan—a few short miles north of the city where two years earlier Basie had rejected her, but metaphoric light-years from desolate Detroit. Lee had been booked into the Birmingham Theater to perform *Side by Side by Sondheim*, in which she'd be working with an English pianist/songwriter named Paul Horner, whom she'd just met.

On the first day of rehearsals, Horner was sitting at the piano, up on an elevated rostrum six steps off the stage, fiddling with a tune of his own, when he heard the sound of shoes running up the steps. Turning, he was surprised to see Peggy Lee's face—he'd already noticed the motorized wheelchair on the stairway, a legacy of her falls a few years earlier. And here she was jogging up the steps.

"You wrote that?" said Peggy. Horner, flattered, acknowledged that he had. "Can I write some lyrics for it?" she said. She didn't have to ask twice.

Paul Horner didn't know that Peggy had been thinking of telling her life story in a Broadway show. Peggy didn't know that a few years back, on his first night in New York, with only $200 to his name despite his extensive musical résumé, Paul Horner had been facing the prospect of having to clean people's apartments for a living. Still, he'd blown a considerable part of his savings on a seat at the Empire Room at the Waldorf to catch her act.

Now she was standing at his side, beginning one of the most significant musical collaborations of her life. Before it ended, it produced some thirty songs, a canon that included several keepers and some outright classics. Half of them have never been heard by the public. The public is much the poorer for it.

Before long, as rehearsals for *Sondheim* progressed, Lee and Horner became consumed by the work of spinning their own tunes. Lee's attention to the Sondheim material, Horner recalls, seemed less than thorough. One morning she came in for a rehearsal and found herself unable to remember lyrics that she should have been able to master easily.

"What's the matter?" Horner asked.

"I don't know," she said. "I had this memorized last night."

When Horner suggested she put the sheet music on his piano, and lean on it whenever she needed to, she acquiesced. Forty years after her days with Lloyd Collins, she was leaning on a piano again. Within a few days, during another run-through, Peggy said something that Paul Horner would never forget.

"I was walking up the stairs, and she was riding down on the motorized chair," Horner recalls. "She stopped the chair and said breathlessly, 'Paul, we're writing something that's going to keep us for the rest of our lives.' "

When they returned to Los Angeles—Paul to an apartment, Peg to her new home—they resumed serious collaboration. Three or four times a week, whenever he was summoned, Horner would travel to Lee's "peach palace." Sometimes he had to take three different buses to reach it, a trip that could take as long as two and a half hours each way. Lee knew Horner didn't drive, but he never mentioned his circuitous route. He didn't complain: She was treating him as an equal, and he was playing her perfectly tuned Steinway grand.

Some nights, she'd call and ask just for his company. Lillie Mae, José, and butler Bernard Lafferty didn't live in. (Some time later, Peggy would encourage her friend Doris Duke to hire Lafferty. After Duke had changed her will to name him coexecutor of her estate, Lafferty was removed from that position after her death when a New York judge found that he was squandering her estate.) Horner would cook popcorn and bring it into her sanctum, and they'd work on their songs. He wondered at her indolence; she never seemed to exercise. But he reveled in her company. They were making progress on more than two dozen songs by now.

Other nights, they'd simply talk on the phone. She'd ask him for a joke. Or she'd tell him one: "Did you hear about the man with five penises? He went out and bought a pair of pants that fit him like a glove."

And she'd laugh, Horner remembers, like Santa Claus.

One night in 1981, Horner was invited to a party at Peg's house: a birthday party for Irv Cowan. The guests included Peter Allen, Marilyn McCoo, Steve and Eydie, and Doris Duke. Horner gladly blew off a hotel-lobby gig to attend the party, where he took his customary seat at her piano. He was playing some background music when Peggy's friend television producer Frank Ralston asked to hear some of the tunes that Peggy and he were working up for a show. They didn't have to be asked twice. With Peggy reclining on her chaise, microphone in hand, wearing something "flowing and diaphanous," as Horner recalls it, they offered up a frothy sample of their show: "Clown Party," a tune based on a party she'd given. The clichéd imagery couldn't dampen the pleasant tune. "The crowd was very generous," Horner recalls. "They asked for more. We ended up doing the whole thing. It was like a scene out of a Hollywood movie."

Between songs, Paul would scamper halfway up the stairs and narrate the action to the crowd: the story of Peg's life, scene by scene. Then he'd scamper back down to play the next song. "When you do the movie," Horner told the crowd, "have June Allyson be Peggy and Van Johnson be me."

He got a good laugh. So did some of the songs. "I'm Fine," a Homeric catalog of Peggy's injuries set to a simple tango, bordered refreshingly on a parody of her history of ailments, which include a crushed disk in her "low back," another that might "grow back." Her lighthearted summation of her lifelong battle with an ailing body? "And if I weren't so healthy I'd be dead."

Not all of the fare was comic. She and Horner had written the mandatory song about the evil stepmother, but she managed to avoid self-pity by couching the narrative in the third person; the device called for a woman to question a little girl about her dolly's broken arm: Did somebody do you harm? And that something in her eye? If she holds the girl, she offers, "It will help you if you cry."

In several songs lay the promise that Peggy's self-examination would be mature and reflective. The haunting "Mirrors and Marble," which took its imagery from her spacious, well-appointed bathroom in the Bellagio house, was nothing less than a stunning revelation, the musings of a woman who lived alone in a palace and found no joy in it. Horner's simple, almost frighteningly melancholic melody was matched in intensity by Lee's lyrics, which speak of "mirrors and marble and spigots of gold." It's the mirrors that haunt her, the mirrors that show her "millions and millions of me." Equally distressing is her view from without, to the Pacific Ocean below: "No one was standing there, sharing with me."

The musical gem, not surprisingly, was a railroad tune, "Riding on the Rails." Horner's chords slouched and shrugged in resignation; on this train, there was no optimism, no hope of finding prosperity. Lee's narrator was a failed tycoon, going nowhere. That she'd chosen to use her railroad song not to wax nostalgic but to comment on the human condition was a revelation. And the song was a killer.

Set in "those grand good times of ties and tails," the singer is a former tycoon riding the boxcars after his fortune has gone south. Now he rides for free, but that brings him little solace: "Never thought I'd see a bum the likes of me."

The final song predictably trumpeted spiritual triumph, wholesale optimism, and the victory of hope and faith. But despite its layers of clichés, it was hard not to be caught up in "There's More"; after fifty years, if anyone had earned the right to anticipate a higher ground, it was Peggy Lee. Her Shangri-la is a place she glimpses "behind the clouds"—a place whose mystical peace keeps birds aflight: "We don't fall off the earth when we sail away from shore" No. "There is more."

The evening's script called for a happy ending, too: Cowan and his wife said they'd try to get it produced. Danny Thomas volunteered funds. They had a show.

Horner got a $2,000 advance to work on the score. Soon, the collaboration had become a friendship he cherished. And professionally, his work continued to reach greater heights than he could have imagined. One Sunday night Peggy asked along another guest for dinner: It was none other than Mel Powell. Horner played all of the songs they'd written, while Powell sang along with Peg. Their recital included a song she would sing in the beginning of the second act, after her divorce from Dave. Lyrically, it wasn't her best, and it began with a spoken prelude: "I guess I was losing all the men in my life. David said, 'Peg, remember, it wasn't another woman. It was another bottle.'"

By August 1982, it was time to get real investors. The Cowans scheduled a party at Peg's place. In attendance were potential backers, most prominently Zev Bufman, the owner of the Miami Heat basketball team and a renowned producer of *Joseph and the Amazing Technicolor Dreamcoat.* Writer Bill Luce, who had won accolades for his script for *The Belle of Amherst,* summoned by Bufman, was in the party. There was a little star power, too: Liz Taylor was a not disinterested observer. She had entered into a partnership with Bufman and formed the Liz Taylor Theater Company.

At dinner, Luce recalls, "Peg presided at the head of the table. To her right was Zev. I sat next to him, with Elizabeth Taylor on my right. During dinner, Elizabeth regaled us with hilarious stories about the filming of *The Night of the Iguana.* She passed around the dazzling diamond ring that Richard Burton had given her. Elizabeth was very upbeat. Everyone was enjoying her— everyone but Peg. I realized she was very unhappy and unable to hide it. She was being totally ignored by her guests. All eyes and ears were under the spell of Cleopatra.

"I thought it strange to have a score before there was even a book. With an unnecessary microphone in hand, Peg took her place on a chaise and we sat in an intimate semicircle of chairs facing her. Unfortunately, Elizabeth ended up in a chair next to Peg. Her choice of seating couldn't have been worse. The performance ensued, but with no energy or color. It was bland. I felt it was

Peg's depressed mood that was sabotaging the performance. During one of her songs, a waiter from the catering service unwisely crossed behind Peg and asked Elizabeth if she wanted another drink.

"Peg was furious. 'Don't serve when I'm performing!' she barked. Then she mumbled something about getting him fired. Back to the score, with feathers ruffled, she launched into a ballad. Seconds into it, Elizabeth reached for a cigarette and Zev innocently lit it for her. Peg slammed down the mike on the chaise and since we were surrounded by large speakers, there was an explosive boom. We all jumped. Peg heaved herself up from the chaise, saying, 'I can't sing when somebody's blowing smoke in my face.'

"She stamped into her bedroom, which opened onto the living room, and slammed the door. We sat stunned. Elizabeth was cool; she put out the cigarette and looked straight ahead. Others sat staring at the floor. I watched Zev. He heaved a sigh and murmured, 'Well, I guess I'd better go in.' He disappeared into her room and in a short time, Peg emerged with him, took her place on the chaise, and said in a rather mollified way, 'I forget where I was.' Paul supplied the intro, and she started singing again. Minutes later, between songs, Elizabeth tried to ease the tension, holding out her hand with the immense diamond. 'Would you like to wear this for luck?' she joked, as if to say, 'Let's be friends.' Peggy didn't look at her. She seemed grim. 'No thanks,' she replied, 'I might break it.' Afterwards, people seemed to be feigning favorable reactions. Peg's display of temper had embarrassed them. Some had flown across the country with expectations for more than this strange evening had provided."

It was about this time that Peggy told Horner that she wanted the songs to go through her own music company. Fine, Horner wrote back—but no decisions can be made unless we make them jointly. After this, their relationship began to frost over, and Horner began to suspect she was becoming jealous of the attention his songs were getting.

The original idea called for different actresses to play Peggy at various stages in her life, with Peggy herself appearing only at the end. The word Horner heard was that Luce had written a terrific script. But Lee had a problem: "She always wanted to play herself," Cowan recalls. "We thought, to make it more realistic, there should be two or three Peggy Lees."

By now Peggy's old friend Cy Coleman, the legendary pianist and composer (*Sweet Charity*) had entered the picture. Upon his arrival, the show began to change shape, from a cast of characters playing in a linear narrative to a one-woman show.

"Part of the reason for Cy to step into someone's show," Cowan says, "was that he was somehow going to participate in the music. She had promised him something to do with the score. Whether it was creative royalties, whatever their deal was, I don't know. I didn't ask. He was certainly a worthy addition."

An artistic tension was emerging. Peg's instinct, Horner says, was to have the thing be original. But friends—and backers—were recommending that she frontload it with her hits. It's what people want and expect from Peggy Lee. It was like what Joe Harnell used to tell her: You gotta give them the old stuff.

And the story was morphing from a dramatic play into a straight bio with hints of victimhood, beatings, and Dave's alcoholism ("Dave was one sad clown"). "The thing didn't have any real meat," Cowan recalls. "Or the things people are interested in."

Production meetings were held in Lee's bedroom. One night, a theater manager Coleman had brought in questioned the wisdom of mounting a song called "One Beating a Day." He called it "Dickensian." She answered, "It's my life."

And while she wasn't ill at the time, Horner felt an implicit threat hovering in the frigid air of the glamorous bedroom suite:

that adversity in this production might send her into further ill health. "I think she used illness as a protection," Horner says. "She'd sit in bed, and all these people were putting money into the show, and they figured they'd better handle her with kid gloves. Irv said to me, 'You're frightened to tell her what you think because you're afraid she'll have a heart attack.'"

Down at the courthouse, Peg was fighting another battle. The Waldorf Hotel–Johnson Wax lawsuit arising from her two falls in 1976 had finally come to trial. She flew Freeman Gunter to Los Angeles. He stayed with some friends, and on his day on the stand, testified not that he'd seen the first fall, just that he'd seen sand on the floor at the spot in front of the elevator. "The lawyer said, 'Miss Lee claims she incurred damages, but she has continued to get good reviews.' I said, 'A performer of Miss Lee's talent and experience can find subtle nuances and shadings to make up for a loss of physical vigor.' She was just eating it up."

Lee alleged that because of the fall, she experienced a variety of health problems: hearing loss, nerve disorders, head injury. Robert Richards didn't hold the lawsuit against Peggy Lee; he thought he understood the motivation: "It was a difficult time for her financially. The expenses were bigger than the income. No one was paying attention to anything."

But Richards refused to testify for Lee in the suit. She would eventually reach a settlement with the hotel.

On one level, *Peg* seemed to be developing into an unhealthy exercise in ego, although shows featuring performers reviewing their lives were in vogue. Lena Horne had recently triumphed with such an evening, and in the years that followed, these shows would become a symbol of having made it to the top of the profession. Perhaps there was something beyond narcissism at work. By this stage in Peggy Lee's life, even the severest critic had to admit that her growing quest to broaden her intellectual horizons, to push the spiritual envelope—to use the most hackneyed of phrases, to *grow*—reflected an authentic part of her personality.

In a profile of Peggy Lee in *Los Angeles* magazine, the writer seemed wildly optimistic: The backers' $3 million was producing a work unlike anything "in musical history." The workshops in New York, he noted, would be held in the same space where *Dreamgirls* had been nurtured. Dave Barbour's part, Peggy suggested, might be played by Dustin Hoffman. Colleen Dewhurst or Maureen Stapleton, she said, would be perfect for Min.

By July 1983, Horner says, Coleman had helped persuade Peggy to turn the production into a much more conventional one-woman show. Lena Horne had had a long run, doing little but transplanting her nightclub act to the stage. Lena was a wondrous talent, but on stage, her affect was unapproachable soul; Peggy was nothing if not accessible. Throw in original material, a narrative, and the formula seemed promising—especially if Peggy laid it all out there, unvarnished.

"Writing the show," she told a *Chicago Tribune* writer, "I really had to confront my past. The truth is one of the things I promised myself it would be, because I knew it wouldn't be fair to write a fairy tale." She told the reporter that she had tried to write a book about her life, but "stopped because it became so dark and violent." (It would be nearly a decade later that she would publish her memoir, *Miss Peggy Lee*.) Somehow, she said, the show seemed to be "doing itself." She described going to see a lady before she started to work on *Peg* who she said "was quite psychic. I knew this because she was able to read my past without knowing anything about it.

"Finally she said, 'Look what's happened from all this, look what you've accomplished! You're like a lily in the mud.' And that's the story of *Peg*. The people are out there. I know they are."

Paul Horner was finding himself shut out. In workshop rehearsals, he felt slighted. "Irv himself told me she tried to have my name taken off the show," Horner recalls. "I do remember," says Cowan, "that she didn't want to give him credit, which was ludicrous."

Yet Horner couldn't help but give in to her when Lee turned on the charm. If Peggy asked him to hold her hand while she called the vet for her sick Lhasa apso, Paul couldn't help but oblige, though he'd begun to see that she had at least two personalities. "I thought, 'Who is this woman in that bedroom, and who is this woman outside of it?' One time, I heard her swear. I had never heard her swear. Bill Luce said, 'Have you ever seen anyone possessed by a demon?' It's the old thing," Horner says now. "The abused becomes the abuser. . . . The lady was like my sister, my best friend. I'd lay down and die for her. The other one, I wouldn't approach without a crucifix."

Still Horner's allegiance was unyielding. She'd insulted him, she'd wanted to control ownership of their songs. But he felt he'd discovered a true compatriot in the land of art, and for Horner, the music was all. "One thing Peggy was true to, and would always respond to, was the music," he says. "One night there was a production meeting. We were supposed to have a new song about when David and she broke up, and we needed an opening song for the show. It was a tiresome meeting, we were all trying to move things along, and at the end, one of the producers was leaving, and I started to play on the piano. She knew I was playing the theme for her breakup with Dave, and she practically pushed the man out the door and rushed over to the piano to hear it. When I got home, there was a message on my machine: 'I love your new song, and I love you.'"

But the songs were slowly changing, and not necessarily for the better. The stepmother song had morphed from the poignant dialogue with an abused little girl into a very odd Latin-flavored tune, designed for laughs but crying out for pity. It would be preceded by an offstage voice asking "Norma" if she was "gonna sleep all day?" It's 4 A.M. and the stepmother is irked by the little girl's singing—so peeved she asks for "that strap. . . ." The samba-beat chorus tells of "one beating a day"—for eleven years.

Some of the music emerging now bore little resemblance to the previous material. "In the end," says Cowan, "you have to wonder how much of the music was a true collaboration with [Horner], and how much was her overpowering him. She was a forceful woman when it came to music."

She was just as determined when it came to her old friend Cy Coleman, the Broadway lyricist and composer. Coleman had just done her the hugest of favors, although at the time it didn't seem that way. He'd brought a piano player named Mike Renzi on board, from the orchestra of the Lena show, which had included Grady Tate; Tate was now also on board for *Peg*.

"Cy's forte was Broadway," says Renzi now. "He'd had a lot of successful shows. . . . She recruited him, and he decided he'd give her creative input. They were such good friends anyway, right? So we're rehearsing at Minskoff Studios, me and Grady, no bass. Well, she'd never done a Broadway thing in her life, and she's fighting Cy all the way. Cy is saying, 'Peggy, I'm telling you—I know this is what we should do.' And then she would listen, and she would say, 'Yeah—but no.' One day he got so fed up he walked out on her. He said goodbye, and left! They made up a few days later, but basically she was trying to deal with something she didn't know anything about.

"Everyone warned her, by the way, about the show. It was a very good show, but it got ridiculous, all that stuff about the beatings, and the depression. You can allude to it, but she was trying to make it funny. It was not."

In September 1983, the backers held a press conference at the

Beverly Hills Hotel. Zev Bufman spoke of "a side of Peggy Lee no one has seen before—so private, so womanly, so intimate, so open." Miss Lee could easily go to Broadway "with two suitcases of her hits and sing for two hours and a half," he remarked. "Instead, she'll appear in a brand new American musical" featuring twenty-three new songs.

Lee appeared in a pajama suit of chiffon and a wide-brimmed hat. She had lost some weight. She was on top of her game, genuinely excited.

"This is one of the happiest days of my life," she told the reporters.

And why was she mounting a first-person tale?

"My shyness has sort of left me. I want to get out and live life to the fullest."

For the press, she and Horner performed three songs: the ragtime piano piece, a tune about Dave, and a blues song.

"The voice," reports the AP man, "was sultry and insinuating as ever, but the songs seemed to emerge from deep within her."

In New York, at Bufman's request, Luce volunteered to help Peggy find lodgings, and after meeting her at the Hotel Surrey, spent a rocky day hopping from hotel to hotel looking for suitably fancy digs.

"I showed up at the Surrey," Luce recalls. "The elevator doors opened and out she came in a red chiffon pajama suit, a red picture hat, and high-heeled red shoes. A big peony nestled on the hat. Large sunglasses covered half her face. The day before, she'd been in a wheelchair. She took one look at me and became very irritated. It was a hot, humid day and I was wearing a T-shirt, Levi's, and sneakers. As we got into the limo, she said, 'You realize, don't you, that I'm upset with how you're dressed? It doesn't go with me.'"

The Pierre and the Helmsley Palace didn't have suitable suites.

She settled on the River Tower, where her suite included a white baby grand piano.

By night, the theater was the cavernous Lunt-Fontanne, a storied palace with a legacy of glory. It had started life in 1910 as the Globe but was ultimately renamed for the "royal couple" of American theater, Alfred Lunt and Lynn Fontanne—Peggy's co-performers in *Stage Door Canteen*. Since then the hall had played host to John Gielgud and Richard Burton, even the original four-year run of *The Sound of Music*. The most recent productions, both Zev Bufman's, had enjoyed less success. Staged by the Elizabeth Taylor Company, *Private Lives* starred Taylor and ran for only five nights. It was to be followed by Cicely Tyson starring in *The Corn Is Green*, but Tyson withdrew, citing the poor quality of the production.

The ghosts didn't bother Peggy. But she found Taylor's old dressing room too small, although it had been featured in *Architectural Digest* in all of its lavender glory, replete with lavender mohair rugs and lavender towels. Peggy wanted something peach. She also wanted a bathtub. She chose a room on the third floor, even though she couldn't easily climb stairs. And so the producers built her an elevator; they had to tear out chunks of the back of the theater, letting in the Fargoesque winter wind. Guitarist Bucky Pizzarelli rehearsed on some days with a winter coat on.

Pizzarelli and bassist Jay Leonhart shared a dressing room a couple of doors down from Peggy's. "It was all peach rugs," says Pizzarelli. "Gorgeous. We figured that with the new elevator they had, it must have cost five thousand dollars a trip."

Despite all the physical alterations, major problems were left unaddressed. "We did about three weeks of previews, and every day, Peg and Cy would change things," Pizzarelli recalls. "But she didn't spend enough time on the fine-tuning," bassist Jay Leonhart says: "A show like that is almost a vanity project, it's gotta be perfect, and in the end, she didn't have the energy for the rewriting it needed." While Horner's songs were increasingly sacrificed for Coleman's Broadway orchestrations, the narrative of Lee's life was never honed.

The final version of *Peg* called for only Peggy to play Peggy— apparently at her own insistence. Various musicians would provide the voices of the other characters. But musicians of the caliber of Leonhart, Renzi, and Pizzarelli want to concentrate on their notes. "I hated what I had to say," Leonhart recalls. "And they never had me recite my lines in front of people until the dress rehearsal."

Peg opened two weeks before Christmas—with the song "Fever." Even with Grady Tate's tom-tomming doing its best to energize the crowd, the number felt inappropriate in the theater, and signaled that the evening would be, despite the hype, more of a glorified Peggy Lee revue than a conventional night of theater.

The next song was a Horner-Lee original, an anthem called "Soul," which Horner had hoped to make swing; instead, this arrangement fairly cried out for angels rising on wires. It's actually a very pretty number, and she imbued it with the requisite spirituality, but it would have been happier in a church. And if any doubt remained about whether the show would get off the ground, it vanished with Lee's first spoken words, as she kicked off the journey through her life—in the "roaring twenties" when bathtubs were filled with gin, and "the bull and the bear were riding the wind." The rhymes smack of the easiest couplets available, from "cash" and "crash" to "the late days of spring," when the world was gifted with "a child who could sing."

Broadway audiences are accustomed to hearing dialogue written by the best in the business. Leonhart's concerns were well founded: A simplistic narrative was not going cut it, even if some of the original songs distinguished themselves—and some of them did, although the railroad song had now become an upbeat anthem called "Daddy Was a Railroad Man." But it was catchy, punctuated by the beat of a man pounding rails.

Lee couldn't resist harping on all of the chores that had burdened her childhood, of course, but she and Horner had turned the episode into a bouncy thing called "That's How I Learned to Sing the Blues." But "Mirrors and Marble" was gone. Several of her classics were sprinkled throughout the evening, but she seemed to lack the voice or the energy to bring them to life. The "Basin Street" chapter of her life inexplicably featured none of Ray Charles's stuff, or any of her jazz classics, but Coleman's own "Big Spender" was on the agenda. It was a big Broadway number, but it didn't belong here.

On top of which, Lee spent much of the show reclining. This was fine back in the bedroom on Bellagio; in front of a few thousand ticket-buyers, it was deadening. *Peg* included no movement at all to speak of. It wasn't as if she was infirm; at the time, she was slightly overweight, but she could move easily.

Her treatment of Dave Barbour, in a song called "I Never Knew Why," absolved herself of any and all blame: Where she used to "blame myself and my career," the doctors, we learn, assure her, "he had that problem a long time ago."

"I think the thing wrong with the show," Bucky Pizzarelli says now, "was it was all about herself, you know. She came out smelling like a rose in that show. If she had put a little grease in there, something raunchy, to match Dave's woes, you know, I think she should have done that."

And still: Over the two hours, it was hard not to get caught up in the journey, as sappy as it often was, and there was the pleasure of hearing Peggy Lee sing. But if there weren't enough theatergoers in town who had a personal interest in her story, *Peg* wouldn't stand a chance. If, at the height of the Christmas season, people didn't have a taste for child-beating set to music, the show was doomed—which, of course, it was.

The initial reviews were not kind.

"Dressed in a flowing gown of white and silver, her head crowned by a halo of glitter, Peggy Lee takes to the stage of the Lunt-Fontanne like a high priestess ascending an altar," Frank Rich wrote in *The New York Times*. "And *Peg*, the 'musical autobiography' that Miss Lee has brought to Broadway, is nothing if not a religious rite. In this evening of song and chat, one of our premier pop singers presents herself as a spiritual icon. There is some entertainment in *Peg*, not to mention some striking musicianship, but the show is most likely to excite those who are evangelistically devoted to both Peggy Lee and God—ideally in that order."

Rich went on: "In addition to sacrificing introspection for inspirational homilies ('God has never let me down'), the star regards her personal history from an omniscient and self-deifying perspective." He likened the set to that of a mediocre talk show. And while he was generous enough about her music—"Though Miss Lee's voice is a small instrument, it is usually sure in pitch. Her rhythmic attack can't be beat"—his summation was accurate: "For those who respect Peggy Lee as a vocalist but who don't worship her as a public personality, *Peg* may seem bizarre."

On the other hand, he did single out "Daddy Was a Railroad Man" for praise.

Peggy's private reaction to the closing of her show veered from resigned to angry to deeply hurt. She was seen sobbing backstage at the Lunt-Fontanne. It wasn't just a rejection of her play; it was a rejection of her life.

"If my life was depressing, that's too bad," she told one interviewer. "I tried to make it funny. But it wasn't funny when I lived it."

But another quote, which could have been read as innocuous,

quietly suggested the significance of this episode in her life: "Self-pity is a waste of time," she told a second interviewer. "I decided the best thing to do was to go back to work."

Broadway's rejection of her life story—of this version of her life, anyway—represented both a nadir and a renewal for Lee. Perhaps the public therapy had done some good. In the coming years, talk of her tough childhood and other trials and travails would appear less and less frequently in interviews. Her subsequent public reflections came not entirely without the accompaniment of fine whines, but increasing measures of self-realization now balanced the perceived victimhood. Years later, with the publication of her autobiography *Miss Peggy Lee*, she would tell the story again without benefit of coauthor or ghostwriter. While she would leave a great many stones unturned—and recite chapter and verse of beatings, illnesses, and misfortunes—the tone she would choose for her final monologue with her public would be refreshingly buoyant. Her thank-yous, her appreciations, and her celebrations would far outweigh her blamings, her excoriations, and her woe-is-me's. If *Miss Peggy Lee* isn't the deepest reflection ever penned by an entertainer, it's a great read.

The evidence that she was able to put the show behind her, and quickly, was obvious to those who knew her. Freeman Gunter arranged for a friend of his, Allen Bardin, a fan from the South, to get an audience with the lady herself in the days immediately following the closing of the show. Bardin had gotten a ticket to the show, journeyed north—and arrived in town after the closing.

The original invitation had been for tea. But when Holly answered the door at River Tower, Gunter recalls, she said they couldn't come in unless they agreed to stay for dinner.

"The place was painted this glowing peachy-pink, and the lighting was soft," Allen Bardin recalls. "She looked fabulous—not at all weird like some of the photos. Her platinum hair was pulled back in a chignon, and she was wearing a flowing open-at-the-back jersey caftanlike creation and a terrific pair of silver and turquoise earrings. Of course, the long eyelashes and lipstick were works of art. Her little Lhasa apso was doing an imitation of an old wig thrown on the floor.

"*Peg* was hardy discussed," Bardin says. "She'd just accepted another engagement, and her focus was on that. Over dinner, she served something she called Jade Salad, and when she ate a roll, and the crumbs were now all over the famous lips, she didn't lick them off. She excused herself, and a few minutes later, the famous lips were back in place."

After dinner, Bardin found himself alone in the living room with Peggy; she was stretched on a sofa, reading a magazine: "All of a sudden, she looked up at me with those amazing eyes, shadowed by lashes, and I thought, 'She is still an inviting, sensuous woman.' I recall how beautiful her skin was . . . dewy, like a teenager's, and hypnotic, sea-green eyes. I was there for three hours, and when I left, she took my hand warmly, with both of hers, and thanked me for 'keeping the torch burning.' I remember when we walked down the hall leaving her place, she stuck her head out the door and smiled and waved at us.

"Hell, I was just some young guy from Dixie who worked in a shop at the time. She could have been not so nice and I wouldn't have cared, but my impression was that she was a warm and generous person underneath all the glamour."

Freeman Gunter recalls one other detail of the furnishings in her apartment that night: On Peggy's coffee table sat the current issue of *New York* magazine—the one containing John Simon's review of *Peg*, "which was cruel," as Gunter recalls, "with a vicious personal attack on Peggy's looks, plastic surgery, et cetera. I remarked that I had thrown my copy out in fury. She laughed most heartily and said, 'He's entitled to his opinion. And I forgive him.' "

For some more unqualified critical admiration, Lee now turned to the faithful in England, this time with a small band, on a tour of medium-sized venues in middle-class burgs. If they weren't exactly charming little villages, they were safely removed from the carnivorous jungles of Broadway. From the seaside town of Eastbourne to Cardiff, in Wales, she now had a chance to cool out, musically and mentally. After shows in auditoriums with names like St. David's Hall, lines of greeters that lasted an hour or more gave her a psychological lift. Playing with her new band gave her a melodic one.

"I've just started doing concerts with the small group only," she told one Brit interviewer, "and I like it a lot, because it's so free. We can do different numbers, and they know the music so well that it's just a great pleasure."

The music they knew wasn't modern pop, either. The new combo was distinctly rooted in jazz: Grady Tate on drums, Mike Renzi on piano, Jay Leonhart on bass. When she was asked by one journalist to name her favorite musicians, she cited her new band.

Upon her return to the States, in a discussion with *Interview* magazine, she sounded sincere when she spoke of a renewal, of a "whole rejuvenation process." Her health was good, and her breathing machine, "Charlie," was no longer needed. She was excited about her life, an outlook that went behind simple positive thinking: "It's more than thinking—it's knowing." The time had come, she said, to do "a lot of things I wanted to do."

One key to her new attitude, she said, was the one-on-one relationship she'd felt with her audiences in England and Wales, where even though the crowds ranged as high as three thousand, "it seemed like we were in a living room together."

Apparently, the renewal involved a new perspective on her past as well, for in this interview she seemed for the first time to offer up a different version of her evil stepmother—a perspective that had changed, she said, with her writing of the Broadway show. She now felt sorry for the woman. She felt true "compassion," because "if hers had been my lot in life, to feel that way and to inflict physical and mental violence on someone, I wouldn't want to be alive."

Just as compelling was her response to a question about a trip she'd taken in 1975 to North Dakota to accept an honorary doctorate from North Dakota State University: She cited the railroads back home—or the absence of them. Not only had they torn up the tracks, she said, "I don't know what they did with the various depots, and that made me a little sad because I couldn't find where I was."

That same limbo, she said, mirrored her own existence at the time: She'd like to tend her roses in Los Angeles, but she couldn't risk damaging the fingernails she needed for the New York side of her life. Most of the time, she said, "I'm on an airplane."

But no matter where she found herself now, it was a place where, finally, she was looking forward—more at rest with her past than she'd ever been, and ready to begin again.

Hip Angel

MIKE RENZI RECALLS the roses. And the view of the ocean. And the almost enchanted feel of the sun-washed California day, up on Bellagio Road. Renzi would play countless dates with Peggy in the later days of her life, in countless cities. But the day that is still foremost in his mind was the first day of rehearsals for a gig in the Westwood Playhouse, exactly one year after the curtain closed on *Peg*.

"There was a day I'll never forget," Renzi says. "You could see all the way to the Pacific that day. The view was just unbelievable. A servant [José Prado] was serving me and Grady drinks—Peggy wasn't drinking—and we just talked great talk, and sang great songs. That was a magical day. It really was."

For John Chiodini, the guitarist who'd hooked up with the

gang on the recordings of her last album in 1979, his first visit to the house on Bellagio Road was a keeper, too. For one thing, he was delighted to discover that Lee had diligently kept records of all the arrangements of all of her songs through the years. Her record-keeping made his job much easier as he later assumed the role of musical director.

But equally delightful was the Peggy Lee production at home. "She'd show us kinescopes of when she was really young and every band she had," Chiodini recalls. "There was André Previn, and Bucky, and Max—all her bands were always a who's who of jazzmen. On the wall of her bedroom were all these books. Great library. That's one thing we really got off on—talking. She was into Science of Mind, and she could talk on many, many subjects. I studied physics, and it's still a hobby, and one day we were talking, and she said, 'So, do you really understand that Einstein stuff?' I said I don't know if anybody really understands it; I like to try. Then she says, 'Go over there and get that book.' It's a book about Einstein. I open it up: 'To Peggy Lee, my favorite singer.'

"Then we'd be talking about spiritual things, and poems about Tibet. It's just so easy to see the superficial stuff about Peggy— she never hid anything. She was right out front. But to really dig down and see who she was, she was amazing."

The Westwood was a small theater, with five hundred seats. She sold out every show. "It was immediately clear," wrote Leonard Feather in the *Los Angeles Times,* "that all the elements had fallen into place. The theater is just small enough to enable her to establish a rapport, even with fans in the back row. . . . Peggy Lee works too seldom in the city where she has lived for so many years. Her presence in the right place, with the right repertoire and musicians, is a needed reminder that she is still one of a kind."

Peggy's publicist for the Westwood show was a woman named

Deborah Kelman, who would go on to work with Carol Burnett. By day, Kelman found Lee distant. The woman was definitely setting herself apart. She was accessible for interviews, but she wasn't simpatico. And the plastic-surgery scars made it tough on photographers. But by night, Kelman was moved: "Her performances were . . . quite incredible. Night after night, she was moving. She was intimate."

One week into the gig, Renzi had to go back to New York and had to be replaced. This was, of course, no small thing. From Lou Levy to Paul Horner to Mike Renzi, Peggy's pianists had always been more than pianists. They'd been among the most important men in her life, the men entrusted with translating her feelings, with matching her moods, with filling in the spaces—both musically and personally.

Following Renzi's departure, she used three other pianists in three nights, and canned them all. Chiodini came to the rescue. His friend Emil Palame was doing a gig at Nucleus Nuance, the jazz club owned by Herbie Hancock. One night, Palame remembers now, he took a phone call at the club at 1:30 in the morning. It was Chiodini: "How would you like to work with Peggy Lee tomorrow night?"

Chiodini was at Palame's place an hour later, with the guitar book for all twenty-eight songs. They rehearsed till 5 A.M. Then there was a meeting with Grady at eleven the next morning, and finally an audition for Peggy that afternoon. Wearing a pink sweater, looking fetching as hell, she walked into the room, all business, and asked him to play a small guitar bit from "The Folks Who Live on the Hill."

Twelve minutes into the session, she said, "I'll see you tonight."

For the next nine years, up to her final performance, Peggy and Emil would be paired on all of her Western gigs. Musically, they were a perfect fit. Palame, a native of Buffalo, New York, was just thirty years old, but his heart was in the music of the big bands. "I was out of step, in a way, because I knew that era of music really well," Palame says. "She looked at me as a contemporary, not as a young kid. I knew the genre. It was something important in our relationship."

And it was a relationship, with all of the now-familiar elements. If the cluster of luminaries with the boldface names who sought her out in years past reflected the essence of the woman back then, her new colleagues' affection represented an attraction to something different about her. It was a good twenty years since Peggy Lee had been at the top of her particular universe; these men weren't drawn to glamour, prestige, or the opportunity to appear in gossip-page photographs. But attracted they were.

"We talked about a lot of spiritual things," Palame says. "She was always interested in spiritual levels of living, and we related on that level, and we tried to make that happen when we played. It was an unspoken intention. . . . You couldn't just *do* a Peggy Lee gig. She could tell if you were right there in the moment or not. That was the best part of working with her. She was always right there. She was not singing a version of a song from ten or twenty years ago. You had to be there right then. Because she could feel the connection beyond the music, and she had to know you were there."

The jazz singer was coming back, and her musicians deserved a great deal of the credit.

To start with, Mike Renzi was nothing less than "the best she ever had," says Jay Leonhart.

"She could be a bitch—but they all can," Renzi says. "The champions won't tolerate it not being right. They know they're there for a reason. But she was so good, man. She had a built-in metronome. She had a pulse. [It] was just ridiculous, her timing was so good—she could be elastic with it, and never drop a beat—*never* drop a beat. She had ears of life, you know what I mean?

"Like one night, I played a chord, and I put a different note in it, on 'I Got It Bad,' and she looked at me. When it was over, she calls me in. 'I want that every time,' she says. 'It did something for me.' I said, 'I don't remember it.' She says, 'Find it before tomorrow night.' I found it."

"When Renzi came with the band," Grady says now, "it added a totally different dimension. All the pianists she had were just adorable people, but Mike added something to it that had not been there before. He added a little challenge. He gave her a little challenge every night: 'You can really hear? Let me see if you can really hear, here,' and he'd play something, and she would look around with one of those smirks. . . .

"Sure, we had arguments, we had fights. Her loves always tested her. It was to keep her sharp, 'cause we made her angry. She would go on that stage and tear it up. But if everything was just all lovey-dovey and correct and nobody did anything she didn't like, there was no spark. When she started stamping her feet, for us, it was like, 'Okay—come on, baby.'

"She was our love. She really was our love. We enjoyed going to work, because it wasn't work. It was a mosaic. It was creative. It was defiant. It was good. Raunchy. Then you'd see the soft side of her.

"She was a crazy lady, though. She was crazy. Totally fucking insane." And this was never more obvious than in one of her rehearsals for an Atlantic City gig in 1984.

"When I first joined her band," John Chiodini says now, "guys would tell me, 'Whatever you do, don't let her get into a vortex, 'cause if she gets into a vortex, you don't know what's going to happen, okay?' Of course, I didn't know what a vortex was until I learned firsthand. A vortex was when things would start going wrong at a rehearsal, and uh-oh . . . she'd spin right out of control.

"So when we were rehearsing for this Atlantic City thing, the lighting guy, way the hell up there, he was shining the wrong light on her. She starts yelling, but he doesn't know she's yelling at him. He's way up there, talking to someone else, and Peggy works herself into it, you know? I hear her say, 'You know, my doctor said if I get into this situation and it gets out of balance, then my inner ear . . .' And then she raises her voice and says, 'and then, I could get my heart like this . . .' and she's miming palpitations.

"So now, by the time the guy up in the rafters realizes what's happening—like, 'Who the hell is screaming down there?'—he's looking down and Peggy's pointing up at him. At this point she's at the end of her rap, and she's screaming. I'll never forget it. I remember exactly what she says. She says, '. . . and when I die, I'm gonna make sure it was your fault, and you're going to be charged with Murder One!' She was being serious. I mean, she'd become the mother of God, really.

"And the guy is like, 'What? What's happening?' Then people come up on stage and try and calm her down. And Mike lays down some shit on the piano, like vortex music, strange shit . . . like a soundtrack, like the *Twilight Zone*."

"She was notoriously affected by loud sounds," Leonhart recalls. "She'd go into that vertigo. Half of it was psychosomatic, of course. She would externalize. If something was going wrong, she'd find someone to pounce on, to blame."

From *The Letters of the Scattered Brotherhood:* "The nature of the human animal is subject to suggestion. The mind is moved by noises, cold, heat, stupidities, a letter, the disloyalty of a friend. But when the mind is made up, all these challenges can be divinely met; you are not defenseless."

Peggy needed to brush up on her book.

"The anger, the energy—that saps you," says Chiodini. "Yeah, sometimes before the show I'd come this close to killing her. There'd be twenty-three hours of hell in one day—but then that one hour, and it was magic. Hey, I've played for people where the twenty-three hours was nice, and then the one-hour show wasn't good. I'll take Peggy every time. But nobody did more for popular music than she did."

"The only time I think she ever got mad at *me* was when I called her 'Grandma,' after her daughter had had a child," Jay Leonhart says now. "She was furious: 'Don't call me Grandma!' She kind of took it the wrong way. But later on, when I started performing by myself, when I was doing my songs and people were wondering what I was doing"—Leonhart's own lyrics in his act are playful, funny, and goofy—"she'd come into my audience and roar. And I will never forget another thing she once told me, not ever: 'Don't ever stop writing. Don't ever stop singing.' I'd gotten some reviews like, 'Why is he singing? What's he trying to prove?' and she never stopped encouraging me: 'Don't stop!' That was so important to me."

It was about this time that Peggy gave a quote to a *New York Times* reporter that's worth revisiting. The question had been about growing older. "I don't like marking time," she said. "I like to think of everything as now. Haven't the scientists more or less proven that's true?" Ten years later, a physicist at Columbia would turn the scientific world on its ear with his popular tome *The Elegant Universe*, which made the strongest case yet for the "string theory" model of the universe—a model that attempts to reconcile the age-old rift between her old pal Einstein's relativity theory and the postulates of quantum physics. String theory has gained credibility with each reexamination of its revolutionary hypothesis—and among other things, string theory postulates that the configuration of the universe does not require the passage of time as we perceive it. Simplified greatly: Time and space are things we need in order to experience the universe; the universe doesn't need them at all.

As she turned sixty-five, the age at which most folks retire, Peggy had found a philosophical fountain of youth.

By now, it was obvious that, unlike Ella and Lena and the women who could belt, Peggy was not going to flourish in the big halls. She needed a New York room, and she hadn't played one since the Waldorf, a decade ago. More than anything, she needed an audience to come to her.

Her last great room was an intimate club called the Ballroom, in Manhattan's Chelsea neighborhood, suggested by her agent, Irving Arthur. It was the last place she'd call her own. In 1985, before her first show, her demands, as usual, were a little over the top. The Ballroom's owner, Greg Dawson, had to build a ramp to the stage for the wheelchair she now preferred to use in public. She wanted a new sound system, explaining that she could react to a bad sound system by fainting on stage. She got it all.

"Rolls-Royces and limousines jammed the street, and lines formed again," Lee wrote in her book, conjuring a fitting image, if perhaps a slightly imaginary one. According to James Gavin's book *Intimate Nights,* the first time Dawson heard her rehearse, he was worried: "I nearly died," he said. "She sounded terrible. I thought, 'She's lost it. This is going to be a disaster.' "

But Gavin, an astute chronicler of New York's nightclub scene, described Lee's debut as anything but a failure.

"One had to overlook her ghoulish appearance: She wore a white Cleopatra wig and huge dark jeweled glasses and dressed in white satin with marabou feathers, and other costumes ill-suited to her amorphous figure. [But] on her best nights, Lee was still capable of giving an object lesson in jazz-inspired pop singing, binding phrases with a subtle rhythmic pulse, and coloring lyrics from a palette that had grown almost infinite through the years."

John Wilson of the *Times* put it all a little more succinctly, and more generously: "She looked like a hip angel, and she sang like one."

Whitney Balliett, writing in *The New Yorker*, puts us right there: "She wears a close-fitting helmet covered with glass beads, huge round tinted glasses, an egg-sized amethyst ring, a heavy rope of pearls, and various silk robes and gowns. All that can be seen of her beautiful face is the tip of her nose; the famous mole drifting on the alabaster sea of her right cheek; her mouth, and her resplendent chin. The total effect is of antimacassars and gingerbread. The contrast between this encrusted beauty and the simon-pure voice is startling. The voice slowly subsumes her image, and by the end of the show has enveloped us."

TWENTY-NINE

I Won't Dance

IT's A JAZZ town, but the stage at the Fairmont in New Orleans didn't evoke the fondest of memories for Peggy. In her first appearance in New Orleans in 1971, she'd had to cut her gig short, and she was hospitalized with pneumonia when she got back home. This time around, it would be even worse. After decades of maladies that ran from strange to serious—she'd had three angioplasties, but didn't speak of them—Peggy's body finally caught up with her and delivered a dose of the real thing. Not a knockout. But a blow.

By now she traveled not only with her medication for her diabetes, but also nitroglycerine and a device to trace her heartbeat. The final night of the performance in New Orleans, feeling chest pains, she canceled her second show to rest up for her trip to

Washington. But the next morning, feeling an irregular heartbeat, she called a doctor. From the phone in her suite, a surgeon named Tom Oelsner listened to her heartbeat. He told her to come in to the hospital.

"I was down in New Orleans," she later recalled in a wire-service interview in 1986, "and as Redd Foxx would say, 'Here comes the big one!' It was quite a shocking experience to find myself in the ambulance on the way to the hospital. I thought I was on my way to the White House. I was too serious to come home. They had to operate quickly."

Her memoir paints a frantic picture. As Nicki and Holly flew in, Lee was prepped for surgery: "I was just lying there like a rag doll full of pain. . . . I had no sense of fear, just fatigue . . . and love. The clock was running."

Before the surgery, a couple of comical Peggy moments lightened the scene. First, she asked the nurse to not remove her nail polish or eyelashes. But the kicker came just before they wheeled her into the operating arena.

"I went to see her at the hospital," recalls Chiodini, who was musical director of the band. "We'd heard that she had a heart attack. We went to the hospital, and we saw her before she went into surgery. We had finished the engagement, and all the guys are saying, 'Are we going home? What's happening here? The thing's over. We have to go home. We need our plane tickets and our checks.'

"I said, 'Well, I'll try to get them.' Nicki had them. And I had to tell Nicki, 'If you don't release them, these people are still on the clock, you know?' So Nicki gave me the checks and the tickets and they all left.

"So I went to see Peggy in, like, an emergency-room thing, and they put her on the gurney through the double doors, they're wheeling her in. I'm with Emil, and she's lying there, and she sees me and she beckons me. So I bend down to listen to her. It was a scary moment. I didn't know her condition. Now she's going to tell me something. What? Do I ease her mind? Everything was racing through my head. So I heard what she said, and I just stood up and Emil said, 'What'd she say?'

"I looked at him and said, 'She asked me, "Who authorized you to pass out the checks?"'

"Then they wheeled her away."

The note of sympathy from Ronald Reagan was nice. The mail was overwhelming. "I have four boxes of mail I saved from when she was having her heart surgery in New Orleans," Phoebe Jacobs says. "I had the radio station in New Orleans announce to send cards to Miss Lee, because all these people were trying to see her."

Two weeks after the surgery, the doctors had to go back into Lee's chest to drain an infected incision. A third surgery followed, for the same procedure. Lee didn't leave the hospital until mid-November, when she was moved to a hospital in Los Angeles.

Frank Sinatra sent his private plane to bring her home.

Pianist Michael Feinstein—never a regular accompanist, but a fan of her music—has often asked himself about Peggy and her illnesses.

"She had so many operations," he says. "And she was so connected to the philosophy of Science of Mind, which is, basically, that thoughts and beliefs create reality. She was so deeply principled, and yet she endured more illnesses and operations, I often wonder if Science of Mind kept her healthy, or if she used the principles to manifest illness for the sake of attention and ego."

To Jay Leonhart, it was no surprise that her health was truly failing. He'd expected it for years. "First, she'd been a big drinker. That never works out well. *Never.* She was overweight. And she didn't have anyone by her side all that time. It would have been one thing if she had a guy she loved saying, 'Okay, we're going to go to a spa, both lose twenty-five pounds, stop drinking' . . . someone who cared, someone who would say, 'How's it going this week?'

"I think she thought she didn't need that steady man by her side," Leonhart continues. "She had all the men she needed. She had me, even though I didn't have an affair with her, but I was there. She had men all over. She was such a star, marriage wasn't important. She had a relationship with the world. She had men lined up around the block. Marriage just probably proved impractical."

In April 1986, Peggy and her boys went back into the Westwood Playhouse. Peggy looked relaxed, and, in a photograph in the Los Angeles *Daily News,* quite glamorous—entirely different from the lady who had appeared in Atlantic City two years earlier.

The months of recovery and the gestures of friends like Sinatra had restored her. She looked like the old Peggy Lee. In the interview with the *Daily News,* she reflected on the surgery, and on the work schedule that had contributed to her problems: "I don't have one of those indicators that say, 'You're tired; sit down.'" She sounded like a woman who had actually learned a few things. "One of the things that I noticed, both at the hospital in New Orleans and at St. John's here, was the love—the honest, no-fake love that these people had."

When the writer steered her into a discussion of the controversial musical flap on Capitol Hill, where Tipper Gore was trying to rein in rock music's more outrageous lyrics, Lee admitted to hoping that the efforts of the "Washington Wives" bore some fruit. She couldn't abide the thought that the negative themes she perceived in rock would "pass on a dark set of values to the next generation."

It was the positivist and optimist in her talking now: "I've enjoyed my life. Not all of it. But in retrospect, I can see that I learned from it. Growing by learning, that's what we have to leave with our young people."

A few months after the sellout shows at the Westwood, Peggy returned to the Ballroom, where, for the next four years, despite the presence of such other heavyweights as Eartha Kitt and the eternal Blossom Dearie, Peggy owned the place. She was drawing not only the old faithful, but the new breed of camp followers upon whom it was beginning to dawn that the caricature in the wheelchair had the chops to back it up.

"She was beyond old, seemingly held together by laminate and scarabs," wrote *New York Times* editor Rob Hoerburger years later. "We laughed because we couldn't decide what was more ludicrous: that she looked like a retired bordello matron, or that we were paying money we didn't really have to watch. But pay we did, picking up recruits along the way, most of whom figured they'd be witnesses to a musical wheelchair accident. One year she was rolled out festooned in feathers. Another time, when she was in the midst of a freighted reminiscence of the blues legend Leadbelly, one of us showered the room in guffaws clearly audible to Lee herself. Everybody else in the room gasped, except Lee, who giggled right back. It began to dawn on us that maybe she had been in on the joke all along."

It had been forty-five years since Peggy had earned the praise of the Manhattan critics who'd seen her take over the late shows at the Terrace Room with Benny, and once again it was the late shows at the Ballroom in which the band came alive and Peggy could channel the Peggy of old.

By now, Mike Renzi had found his ideal canary, style-wise. He'd never been a busy keyboard man—"it's more about colors, you know? If you can picture that—she sings the words, and my job is to come up with the colors to couch them in." It's not that he couldn't have gone all virtuoso on her if he'd wanted to. The true reward of playing for Peggy Lee was knowing how to do a lot of with a little: the thing of hers that Quincy Jones called her genius. And knowing how to play off her eccentricities.

"Mike had her down," Chiodini says. "He knew how to handle her."

The only real downside for her new family of musicians was Lee's insistence on playing on into the night—and heading for the dawn. They were family men, they had other gigs, they had their own recordings to play on—and the woman who paid their checks showed no signs of ever wanting to get off the stage.

"I'd call Mike 'the Terrorist' at the Ballroom," Chiodini says. "Because she'd want to do two full shows every night, because that's what the contract called for. She'd insist on doing two full shows. I'd say, 'Peggy, you can do one set of songs on the first, then the others on the second.' But she'd say, 'No, they want two full shows.'

"So we'd be there till after two, and Renzi would lose it. They'd be giving her standing ovations, bringing her back for encores, and Mike was like, 'No more! No more! You're going to kill her!' He was terrorizing the crowd. He'd just leave the stage to end the show."

But for the most part, Renzi was fond of her eccentricities. "I come into the dressing room at the Ballroom one night, and she said, 'Hi, darling,'" Renzi recalls. "And she's hitting her forehead with one of those little rubber hammers doctors use to check your reflexes: Bong! Bong! I say, 'What are you doing?' She says, 'I'm finding the nerve node to stop this twitch in my eye.' She's got one eye totally made up, and the other isn't made up yet, so it's this really funny effect. Then: 'Bingo! I got it! My eye's perfect now.'"

What Chiodini recalls most fondly of the Ballroom days is Peggy's bond with the band, and the certainty that, through all of it, the evening would bring a couple of moments of the kind of music they'd lived for all of their lives. If there was a day baseball game on television, they'd watch it in one of their apartments. Then they'd rehearse, and she'd drive them typically nuts. "Then that night we'd do, say, 'Watch What Happens,' and we'd look at each other, shaking our heads at how amazing it was, and say, 'Oh, okay. *That's* how that goes.' Like, that's the *ultimate interpretation* of that song.

"See, in the end, she really *got the lyric*. When she picked out a song to sing, you knew what the words meant. She used the lights, right? Well, she used everything the same way—lyrics, staging, whatever, and she was in the center of it all.

"It was the simplest thing in the world. Because the place for her in the orchestration, it was carved out: All things under *her*, and around *her*, and on top of *her*. That was Peggy Lee."

In 1987, the year of Peggy Lee's sixty-seventh birthday, and not long after she suffered a serious fall at Caesars Palace, she and Emil Palame composed her last truly memorable song: "Circle in the Sky."

"It was after rehearsal one afternoon," Palame says. "I started playing something. The theme from the song. Right away, she started writing the lyrics. She came out with a poem."

Her words were quiet and basic and mystical: "I drew a circle in the sky," inside which she writes two words—"You" and "I"—as the wind "rushes by . . ." and still, "our love remains." If the words are simple, the image is a haunting one, and there is no underestimating the power she felt in the scene she'd conjured: The woman herself, seeking more, reaching up to a celestial canvas, and sketching the simplest of forms, diaphanous, ethereal, eternal. The poem's minimalism is its power; her sense of having arrived at a new plateau is entirely convincing.

"She felt so close to what it said," Emil Palame says now. "She was always interested in spiritual levels of living . . . and she was so strong. She'd been through a lot; she was an incredibly strong person."

Her lyrics found a fitting partner in Palame's melody: minor-keyed at the start of each phrase, with an uplift at each end. It was quiet, it was peaceful, it was inspirational—and it worked.

"It all happened really fast," Palame recalls. "We got through two verses. She didn't have an idea of what to do with the chorus. At midnight I got this phone call. She didn't say hello. She didn't say anything. She just sang, 'Forever, forever, I loved you, forever.' She was singing the melody for the bridge. I went right to the piano, and we wrote that chorus."

For many of her acts from then on, "Circle in the Sky" would be her penultimate offering of the evening, blending right into the beginning of "I'll Be Seeing You."

The two songs provided a fitting Peggy Lee coda. A song that spoke of a love that was "stronger than a star," coupled with a song that was a poetic goodbye to the family that her audience had always been—with the implicit promise to return—all of it offering shades of her sign-off thirty years earlier on the radio, when she'd sounded so forlorn to let the audience go.

The circle now wasn't just a lyric in an anthem; in many ways, the inarguably spiritual underpinnings of her delivery of this song represented the full circle she'd described in her lifetime. Now, at the end of her recording career, she was delivering not just the blues she knew so well, but a newer message: one of completion, and assuredness, and understanding.

The spiritual tones of the near-hymn "There Is More" from her Broadway show had tried to do the same but had been obscured by the production, by the setting, by the stirring but slightly obvious lyrics. But in "Circle in the Sky," she had found a way to speak of the quiet center inside her, in a way that allowed her to share it with any listener. It is, by any measure, a moving song, delivered by a woman who was finally coming to rest.

It had been nearly a decade since she'd cut the album *Close Enough for Love*. With Peggy's success in the small rooms, she was back on her feet artistically, if not literally. The fall had left her in a wheelchair, and it wasn't just a prop now. Still, she had no interest in quitting. She wanted to keep singing. In retrospect, the solution was obvious: If she had spent so much time living the blues, why hadn't she been singing them for so long?

Fittingly, one of the oldest forms of music in the land, the same rhythms that she'd intuited through every step of her strange, glorious life, came to her artistic rescue during the closing acts of her career. Of the three albums Lee recorded in the late eighties, two were all of the blues, and they were among her greatest triumphs. That they have been largely forgotten has nothing to do with their art. Her magic may never have been greater than during this particular encore.

It was Chiodini who encouraged her to do an album devoted entirely to the blues, for the Musicmasters label. It had been a quarter of a century since she'd dedicated herself to the blues, and that had been a different time, a different place, a different feel. In 1962, when she'd recorded the album *Blues Cross Country* with Quincy Jones, she'd been on top of the world; the blues couldn't touch her. Now she knew what they meant.

Miss Peggy Lee Sings the Blues was not entirely a labor of love. Peggy still occasionally played the diva, driving everyone crazy. At one point, in rehearsal in the Manhattan studio, she decided the catered food wasn't to her liking. She was fond of hamburgers now. She sent a driver to New Jersey for a hamburger.

"But when she gets down to sing? Forget about it," says Chiodini. "Roll tape, and it's amazing. So what do you do? Get her another hamburger."

Some of the work was routine—perfectly enjoyable, bluesy for sure, but undistinguished. On an otherwise sure-footed "Kansas City," she tried to do too much and wandered out of her range, especially on high notes. On a couple of songs she forgot the lifelong dictum that less is more, especially when it comes to the blues; trills and forced emotion come up short.

But when she kept to the handful of notes that the blues asked for, she soared. "God Bless the Child" made no effort to be Billie; it was silky, and when Lee reached to bend the notes, they responded. "See See Rider" swung nicely, thanks to Chiodini's solos. It segued into a jazz jam before getting back to the blues. On "Basin Street Blues," out of nowhere, she started reaching for a few high notes—and nailed them. "You Don't Know," the blues single from 1958, was the blowsiest, most beaten-down version she'd ever done.

"Down in the Valley" was traditionally a cowboy song. She'd recorded it once before—in 1946, forty-two years earlier. This time she took some liberties with the lyrics. The accepted words of the opening verse are "hear the wind blow." Not in Peggy's version: "Down on the levee, the levee so low, late in the evening, hear the train blow. Hear the train blow, lord, hear the train blow. Late in the evening, hear the train blow."

Peggy Lee's muse—with help from her best band in years—had brought the lady home. "Peggy Lee has never been closely identified with the blues," wrote John S. Wilson in *The New York Times*. "But the sorrowing sense that pervades much of the blues has become an increasingly prominent part of her style, even when her song is not blues. This collection is a mixture of true 12-bar blues and blues-like songs that Miss Lee delivers in a laid-back manner that gives off sly, wry sprinkles. She is supported brilliantly by a group that is built around the infallible trio of

Mike Renzi on piano, Jay Leonhart on bass and Grady Tate on drums, and includes John Chiodini, who contributes guitar solos that are the high points of the set."

Miss Peggy Lee Sings the Blues earned Peggy Lee her penultimate Grammy nomination.

In February 1988, two visitors to the Ballroom didn't need to be enticed by reviews or drawn in by word of mouth; they took it upon themselves to insert themselves into Peggy's life: by jumping into her limo—with the most honorable intentions.

Bill Rudman and Ken Bloom knew music's golden age as well as anyone alive. In the last four years, the old friends had produced three highly acclaimed albums by none other than Maxine Sullivan—the original "Loch Lomond" minimalist whom Peggy had so often cited as one of her earliest influences. (One of the records had earned a Grammy nomination.) With a British jazz pianist named Keith Ingham directing a small band, Bloom and Rudman's Sullivan sides were triumphs of not only jazz, but technology: their post-recording mixing had gone a long way toward making Sullivan sound like the singer she'd been years before.

Now Rudman, a radio producer, and Bloom, a New York City writer, had an even more ambitious project in mind. Edward Jablonski, the biographer of Harold Arlen, had been cataloging Arlen's papers after the composer's death in 1986 and had come across a gold mine: a number of Arlen "trunk songs," sheet music and acetate rolls of songs written by the master himself that had never been recorded. Jablonski, a fan of Rudman and Bloom's work on the Sullivan records, approached them with the mother lode. They were understandably thrilled. The catalog was a treasure: dozens of unrecorded Arlen songs spanning his career.

The first step was to find the right singer.

"We literally went to Tower Records one night and went

through the entire rack of female singers, A to Z," Rudman recalls. "And when we were done, we looked at each other. 'Peggy Lee,' I said. 'Peggy Lee,' Ken said."

Ingham was thrilled as well. A native of London, born in 1942, and a widely respected keyboard vet, Ingham had been raised on a steady diet of Fats Waller and Art Tatum as a child. And he was a huge Lee fan.

The next step was to secure the cooperation of Miss Lee—as somehow they knew they should call her. And so they caught her at the Ballroom. And despite the cosmetic caricature of the woman in the wheelchair, the performance confirmed their judgment. Her style now suited Arlen's simple, effective emotions. "It was all instinctual," says Bloom. "But she knew what she was doing."

So did Rudman and Bloom. Knowing that she'd be traveling by wheelchair to her limo after the show, they figured they could beat Peggy to the car.

"She could walk, but she chose not to," Bloom says. "It was like Lionel Barrymore at the end—they said he was too sick to walk, but he just decided he'd walked enough in his life. Besides, by then she'd had every part of herself replaced. She'd earned the right. So after they wheeled her to the car, Bill and I jumped into the limo with her—me in one door, him in another."

The kidnapping didn't faze Lee. She was intrigued. And when they outlined their project, she was further intrigued. They sent their final Maxine Sullivan record (*Together: Maxine Sullivan Sings the Music of Jule Styne*, released posthumously) to Peggy, and were encouraged by her response: "You really understand that voice."

She invited them out to California.

"She met us in the foyer," Bloom recalls of that April afternoon. "She was wearing a white chiffon muumuuish thing, spilling out of it. She said, 'Shall we get down to business?' The house was all beige with carpeting so deep that you literally saw your footprints in it. The walls were completely covered in paintings that I believe Nicki painted, mainly of roses, and maybe a clown painting that Peggy did.

"The living room was very sparse. When you walked through it, you got the feeling that no one had been through it in a long time. It was a two-story house, but she said she hadn't been upstairs in a decade or something. There was no reason to. There were Peggy Lee roses outside, and a lap pool that probably no one had ever done a lap in."

Ingham sat down at the piano, and Rudman sang the tunes, sitting by Peggy's side on a couch.

By the time they'd run through each song once, Peggy was hooked.

"Do you know how hard it is," she said, "to find songs of this quality?"

They knew. Their portfolio of Arlen songs was a treasure trove. A Yip Harburg collaboration from a 1937 Broadway show called *Hooray for What!* A Mercer collaboration written for but deleted from the movie *Blues in the Night,* a Martin Charnin collaboration from an unproduced Broadway show called *Softly.* Two songs Arlen had written with Truman Capote for the 1954 show *House of Flowers,* Capote's musical about a couple of Haitian brothels, which had enjoyed a five-month run starring Pearl Bailey, and which had been lauded more for Arlen's score than Capote's story.

There were a couple of splendid blues efforts, including a song Arlen had written for a tribute TV special in 1961 called "Happy with the Blues." Arlen had asked Peggy Lee to write the lyrics for what would have been the title song of the show, but it was cut before the broadcast. She had, but she'd ultimately been unhappy with her words. Now she'd get a chance to give them another try.

On two more trips to the coast, the group began to rehearse the music, which Ingham had arranged. But they also spent time in her bedroom. After she'd put on her makeup, wig, and dark glasses—her face was puffy from cortisone shots for various ailments—she'd receive them in the sanctum, and begin to tell jokes—"really obscene jokes," Bloom recalls. "She was sort of like a little kid, mischievously telling these jokes."

She made her guests comfortable, to a degree, but Bloom sensed that Lee expected a certain deference. He found himself rehearsing what he'd say to her in his head, lest a seemingly off-hand remark be interpreted wrongly. Of course, neither of Lee's collaborators thought it odd that they mostly hung out in the bedroom. Or that she was always dressed to the nines in bed. "I always thought the bed was just another form of theatricality," Rudman says. "It was her salon."

"She had an image to uphold," says Bloom now. "The dichotomy, I think, was between that girl in North Dakota who she never stopped being, and Miss Peggy Lee, whom she invented and became. During her whole life, there were both elements working. Tallulah Bankhead and Katharine Hepburn and Bette Midler become clichés of themselves; they never let the curtain down. They became that person to the nth degree. But once I asked her if Norma Deloris Egstrom was still there in her. She said yes. I think that was the whole thing about Peggy Lee. The dichotomy between the two."

Before she went into the studio with Rudman, Bloom, and Ingham, Peggy had been booked for an engagement she'd been anticipating for a long, long time. Ronald Reagan was giving a dinner for François Mitterrand at the White House. Could she perform? Better yet, could she join them for dinner? These were thirty people, at four tables, including Mitterrand, Jerry Lewis, and Jacques Cousteau. Peggy dined with George Schultz, Oscar de la Renta, and Rudolf Nureyev. Her granddaughter Holly was by her side.

The menu: salmon roses with avocado and caviar on Melba toast; medallion of lamb romaine; squash and carrots; mesclun salad with raspberry vinegar dressing; Hubbard's bleu and herbal Capri cheese; pears in almond milk. The libations: Ferrari-Carano chardonnay, Heitz Cellars cabernet sauvignon, and Mumm brut champagne.

In between the dinner and the concert, she went with her granddaughter to the bathroom. Peggy later recalled asking one of the attendees, "Can you believe we're in the White House, performing for Ronald Reagan? Can you believe they wanted me to sing?"

Afterward Peggy and Holly visited the Lincoln Memorial—but not before visiting McDonald's in a car driven by the Secret Service.

They recorded the Arlen tunes in the last week of August. "She arrived scrupulously prepared," Rudman recalls. By and large, Lee was the essence of professionalism. Only one artistic fit asterisked the recording, according to a musician on the scene, during which pianist Ingham retreated to a closet until the squall had passed over. But otherwise, Lee was agreeable to most of Ingham's arrangements. The band was half Peggy's regulars—Chiodini, Tate, Leonhart—and half Ingham's choices. And as they recorded the songs, without further incident, Rudman realized how right they had been to build the album around Peggy Lee.

"It was as if she'd finally come home," he remembers. "Her voice came from this quiet place, and she was the essence of Peggy Lee. She took in the energy of the musicians, of the art, and she was totally present in each moment.

"When we sent her the rough mix, she asked for more percussion and trombone, and she was absolutely right about that,"

Rudman says. "We did that, and spent much, much time working on a final mix that would showcase her most effectively. And this album—whatever its flaws—put her out there emotionally in a way she hadn't been in a long, long time. I'm sure it scared the hell out of her."

They thought they had a great album. But then, in the spring of 1989, Lee called them out of the blue and said she didn't want it released.

"It was a huge setback for us," Rudman says, "since we had structured the project as a limited partnership, and we had investors out there anxious for a release. But what we decided—and Ken and I have years of experience working with artists—was just to be cool about it and not in any way pressure her, which we knew would backfire.

"We also did this because we knew that she had taken incredible risks on the project. It was one of the first true jazz albums—at least insofar as recording songs new to her—that she had made since *Mink Jazz*, twenty-five years before. The Arlen songs were anything but conventional; they were killer-dillers. They required total nakedness in performance. From the beginning, that's what attracted her to the project. But embracing a project is not the same thing as embracing your work on it and knowing when to let go. She was sixty-eight when we recorded her—and as neurotic and brilliant and transcendent as ever."

The pair has various theories about Lee's cold feet. Predominant is the possibility that the first versions she heard, straight out of the studio, weren't as smooth as she thought they could be. There was talk of astrologers' advice, but Lee was not known to be wedded to astrology, nor would the stars' alignment explain the years that stretched on. Ken Bloom and Bill Rudman chalked it up to fate, and waited faithfully—for three years—for the phone to ring.

F ueled, perhaps, by the Arlen project, despite her apparent dissatisfaction with the final product, Peggy Lee still found a way to sing the blues. For her Ballroom appearance in 1989, she wrote a whole new section of the show: the history of the blues. As Lee's personal notes from the time, written in her own hand, indicate, the script, choreography, and music for this part of her show were as tightly scripted as . . . well, a Broadway show. But this time, she was returning to the true roots of her music, not of her life. It was a very bluesy journey indeed, and an ambitious move for a sixty-nine-year-old woman who could have come in and "Mañanaed" them to death:

> The quintette takes applause, bows, and is seated. Lights down. Peggy enters in spot on stage right. Pauses. Continues (underscoring by Mike until she is seated center stage).
>
> *PL:* Good evening: Are you enjoying yourselves? That's the whole idea. (Wind chimes as light goes down to black. Pin spot on PL's face and Jay's hands on bass playing root theme.)
>
> *PL:* I love the blues. They're happy, sad . . . they're lighthearted and downhearted. They came out of the jails . . . in from the fields . . . little snatches of life . . . and sometimes, it helped to sing . . . it was a release . . . an expression of the soul . . . and the street vendors were a part of it. . . . (ensemble underscoring)
>
> *Jay:* Get your sweet blackberries . . . crawfish . . . get your red-hot crawfish. . . .

The journey takes us back to the places that, on the inside, she'd never really left—to New Orleans, for example. "You knew jazz was alive," she narrates, "when you heard Louis Armstrong playing 'Struttin' with Some Barbecue' . . . or maybe you hear Jack Teagarden playing the trombone . . . or maybe you'd hear some real old-time singing from Petie Wheatstraw, or Blind Lemon Jefferson . . . oh yes . . . and Ma Rainey, and Bessie Smith, and Lil Green—dear Lil Green . . . (*PL ad-libs some humming*)."

After a nod to the music of the chain gangs, where the script calls for "hammer on steel, sounds of chains and footsteps of convicts," she took the occasion to give her final public salute to the people who had written the music that had launched her career:

"Those people who wrote, and are still writing, these blues— artists, they are, just as surely as the French painters who exchanged ideas and colors from their palettes."

Throughout the narration, various songs were interwoven, from "Amazing Grace" to "When the Saints Go Marching In," from "Basin Street Blues" to "Baby, Won't You Please Come Home."

"The more cerebral section of the act," Rex Reed wrote in *The New York Observer*, "was devoted to the blues. She imitates the wail of the street vendors, the pain of the chain gangs and the passionate obsession of the gospel singers. It's the homesick blues . . . that showcase the indelible, honey-dripping, nectar-sipping Peggy Lee style at its zenith. . . . I've never heard her sing more securely in tune. I've never seen her make more direct contact with her musicians or her material. The woman has been through hell, but she deserves her rightful place as one of America's natural treasures."

Now Lee looked to another part of her past to pull off one of her last, and most lasting, artistic triumphs. She had been recently asked to do promotional work for the Disney video of *Lady and the Tramp*. And in examining the contract, she noticed that in her 1952 agreement with the studio, Disney had been barred from releasing "phonograph transcripts" of the songs for profit. She also couldn't help noticing that video sales of the film were enormous—and no wonder. In a culture increasingly swamped by the crass, the Disney cartoon offered parents and kids alike a diversion that met everyone's standards: a funny, creative, engaging tale that had lost none of its appeal—and never would, testimony in large part to Peggy Lee's innate ability, and long-stated objective, to create lyrics for songs that were beholden to no particular time or place. Songs that could stand forever.

Now copies of the movie, first released in 1955, were jumping off the shelves—a movie whose signature song involved a couple of Siamese cats. "The Siamese Cat Song" was one of the six she'd cowritten that made it into the movie. She'd also contributed voices for four characters, including "Peg," the dog from the wrong side of the tracks.

In November 1988, at a Manhattan news conference, Peggy Lee announced that she was suing Disney for $25 million. She'd been paid no more than $3,500 for the original work, she said—and $500 for the promotional work: "My hairdresser makes more than that," Lee said. Walt would never have allowed this to happen, she told her listeners. All she wanted was for Disney to do right.

Two years later, her case went to trial in the Superior Court for the County of Los Angeles. Lee appeared at the trial in a wheelchair, with her oxygen bottle strapped to the back of the chair. Her attorneys were now asking for $9 million. Disney was offering $400,000. The final award, in April 1991, was $2.3 million. The award was twice appealed, and twice upheld.

"They say, 'Don't mess with the Mouse,'" she told *People* magazine. "I'm glad that my rights were vindicated."

"I'm not being a saint—saying I don't want the money," she told *The New York Times*. "I want it. But there is a larger purpose. I think it is shameful when artists can't share financially in the success of their work. That's how we make our living."

If Disney had been reluctant to acknowledge Peggy's contributions—at least to her satisfaction—the American Society of Composers, Authors and Publishers (ASCAP) was not. In March 1990, ASCAP announced that Peggy Lee would join a fraternity that included Frank Sinatra, Ella Fitzgerald, and Lena Horne when it awarded her its Pied Piper Award, the highest achievement the organization bestows, signifying lifetime achievement. At the awards dinner in Washington, various entertainers sang a selection of the more than one hundred songs Lee had written lyrics for.

Paul Horner was in attendance. Despite everything, he remained an admirer of her artistry. But none of the songs that the two had worked on together were included in the special performance. After the show, a mutual friend approached Lee to chastise her for ignoring Horner's work. Horner stayed out of the picture, but sent her a letter.

"I'm sure she thought I was going to say, 'You cow, how dare you not include me,'" Horner says, "but I didn't. I wrote her a letter just saying, 'Dear Peggy, it was so good to see you up and about again.' It was, 'Congratulations.'

"I got a phone call the night she got it. She said, 'Paul, Paul, can you forgive me?'"

"I said, 'Oh, Peg, what's to forgive?' And I do forgive."

In the spring of 1992, Bill Rudman received the phone call he'd been waiting three years for. "She just called us out of the blue and said, 'You know, dear, I've been listening to the tape, and it's pretty good. I don't see any reason why you can't put it out if you want to.' We weren't surprised; we totally believed in the work and knew she'd eventually come around."

The problem, she said in an interview, was with the early mix of the songs. "[My voice] is a center core with rings of overtones.

If they don't record it properly, it just picks up the center core, and it shaves off the layers of overtones."

Angel Records released *Love Held Lightly* just a few months before Peggy's seventy-third birthday. It was her sixty-fourth album.

By some standards—by many standards, allowing for the limitations in her instrument—*Love Held Lightly* was as good an album as Peggy Lee had ever recorded. Her voice was by now a whisper of the old Peggy Lee voice, even when it was whispering. But the material and the artist were so well matched that even a fading instrument couldn't get in the way. Rudman and Bloom's mixing work had to be given great credit, and the musicians were superb. Chiodini's blues guitar had never been better. And the horn section under Ingham's arranging were playing true jazz, not parlor jazz or perfunctory jazz.

But Lee was the marvel here, and it was no wonder: She was singing from a songbook that she loved and knew as well as anyone alive. Not only had Rudman and Bloom shown her a path back to the days of her glory, she'd been given material that no one else had had a shot at in decades. Her stroll through four decades of Arlen was effortless, like donning a well-worn gown from her golden days and finding that it still fit perfectly.

The fare ran the complete gamut from Broadway froth to serious blues.

"She was the first of the cool, laid-back singers, and so I tried to get away from those show-bizzy Las Vegas arrangements," Keith Ingham recalls. "I think 'sophisticated' is what I was aiming for. I wanted to give people solos in moderation. I remember that she thought I should add percussion on a few things— 'ethereal' was the word she used for what she wanted in all of the percussion, and of course, here Grady was a tower of strength. She liked impressionistic things that would add a little color.

"Eight of these songs had never been recorded before, and it was a big undertaking for her. She adored Harold Arlen, and she wanted to do the best she could. And she really got into these lyrics. It was amazing. With the voice, we had to take a chance, but the sense of art was all still there. To me her instincts were always spot on. She knew how to interpret a song, so well."

An Arlen-Mercer number called "Got to Wear You Off My Weary Mind," bumped from a film musical in 1944 called *Here Come the Waves,* was nothing but bow-your-head-at-the-table-with-the-fifth-martini-glass-staring-up-at-you blues, flavored by terrific solos, the wailing saxes, the muted trumpet. Equally effective was "I Had a Love Once," written by Arlen on the occasion of his wife's death. Its emotion is pure heartbreak. So is Lee's rendition of the final song Arlen ever wrote, and Peggy's favorite on the record:

> *I had a love once*
> *I too was strong once*
> *Strong as a mighty oak*
> *Tall as a mountain*
> *Touched by a silver stream*
> *Soothed by a silver stream*
> *Bathed by a silver stream*
> *So roll on you rivers*
> *Wind on you valleys*
> *Gone is my loved one.*
> *Gone, gone this day.*

But the coolest tunes on this very cool record belong to the unique club of Peggy Lee classics that fall under the "autobiography" heading—the songs that come to life because they cut so close to home. The first is "Happy with the Blues," the song she had a chance to rewrite the lyrics for. It's a contrary piece, a snappy blues tune. The upbeat bass line by Leonhart describes the pace of a man walking briskly down a side street, maybe whistling, Hey, it ain't all so bad—a snap-fingered good feel, underlain by blues.

But what's telling is the message, and it went for both Arlen and Lee: If you're endowed with—and cursed with, and blessed with—the blues, if they're your unavoidable and preordained station in life, then you either learn to live them, or chuck it all. And if you can make a life of celebrating that melancholic state, so much the better:

> *My one and only*
> *Has left me lonely*
> *And he was really the man I would choose*
> *But he is gone now*
> *No "from now on" now*
> *He left me happy with the blues.*

But for pure coda, a moody film noir rainy midnight-streets thing called "Come On Midnight," with words by Martin Charnin, is so haunting as to be downright spooky. Chiodini's guitar shared the stage with Charnin's dark, sparse verse, and it spoke worlds:

> *Midnight*
> *Midnight*
> *Bring me*
> *Cover*
> *Come on, midnight*
> *Close in*
> *Call it a day.*

The reviews were enthusiastic. Writing in *LA Weekly*, the hip alternative paper, Chris Cuffaro said, "This was one of those perfect ideas: unrecorded songs written by Harold Arlen, one of the greats of Golden Era songcraft, performed by the only living person who could pull it off. And even rarer than a perfect idea is its combination with perfect execution, which is what we have here."

But it was *Entertainment Weekly*, in awarding the album a B-plus rating, that made the most astute observation. After praising "the care that Peggy Lee and producers Bill Rudman, Ken Bloom and Keith Ingham invested in this unusual new Harold Arlen songbook," the writer notes, "Here, her age is an asset"—the ultimate compliment for a woman finally learning how to grow old gracefully.

By now, Rudman and Lee had become friends, good enough friends for late-night phone calls. "We had lucid, witty conversations, they all had a late-night mood to them. She'd tell jokes, she'd sing. She'd do the voices of little furry woodland creatures with different accents and pitches and tics for each one, much like the creatures she voiced for Disney in the old days. Only in this song, the furry little woodland creatures were doing very nasty things to each other."

Another night, Rudman asked, "So why do you think you waited so long to give us the go-ahead?"

"Well, you know me," she answered. "I'm always looking for the Holy Grail."

"Do you think you'd know it," Rudman asked, "if you found it?"

"She paused," Rudman recalls. "Then she said, 'Probably not,' followed by that patented, extremely self-aware Peggy Lee laugh."

Then she'd breathe the words she always finished her late-night conversations with: "Angels on your pillow."

And then, having been unable to find them in her waking life, she'd fall asleep, hoping to meet them in her dreams.

"Peggy was a walking tragedy," Bill Rudman says now, "who was able to channel that into something that transcends the tragedy. Of course, she took perverse delight in recounting the tragedy, that's true. But ultimately? She was the ultimate beautiful human being."

In November 1989, Peggy and the combo— minus Grady Tate— went back into the studio to record her penultimate record, *The Peggy Lee Songbook: There'll Be Another Spring*, a collection of songs written or cowritten by Peggy, sung by Peggy, and interpreted by Peggy. The compositions were all post-Barbour. Some were old classics, and she did them as proud as she could; where her voice wasn't up to the old notes, this new small-combo arrangement lent a whole new feel to such once-lavishly-produced classics as "Sans Souci" and "Johnny Guitar."

But the highlights were the new stuff—"Circle in the Sky" and four songs she'd written with Chiodini—transferred from a four-track, of course. Chiodini and Lee seemed to have a sublime songwriting vibe; his melodies were light and catchy, but they never strayed far from the blues, and her lyrics had a whole new sense of playfulness, and a whole lot fewer of the easy rhymes she'd fallen back on in the past. On the whole, the four Chiodini songs represented the best lyrics she'd written in decades.

The words to a light waltz called "I Just Want to Dance All Night" rang true enough: "Make the music play all night / 'Cause I don't want to go home." Another offering gives a delightful blues-infused piece of humor, with the lady taking a laughing look at her oft-reconstructed self: from her nose, to her lips ("Aren't they sublime? . . . try them out sometime . . ."), to the famous mole. Everything, she sings, was assembled "one by one by two . . . I'd like to give it all / I'll give it all to you."

A thing called "Boomerang" gave her the chance to get funky: She adopts a canine persona for her playful metaphor here: "I will follow you, just like the hound dog do."

The keeper, the top cut, her last memorable composition, is a Chiodini-Lee tune called "Over the Wheel," a nice, smooth, major-key three-quarter waltz whose message comes straight from her spiritual lesson books: It's part Ernest Holmes, part Scattered Brotherhood, part the new Peggy Lee, trying to learn to relinquish the past, trying to put all of the pain of a lifetime behind her: "Over the wheel, darlin' / Let it go, let it go, over the wheel, darlin' / let it all go away, over the wheel."

The reviews were more than simply appreciative. The consensus seemed to be that she was going out at the top of her game.

"Peggy Lee is an American icon," said *Time* magazine in its review. "Her singing, no longer as seemingly effortless as it once was, now combines its sultry smokiness with the quality of having lived life with a capital 'L.' These songs have been recorded with a knockout team of studio musicians. Lee fans should pounce." *People* magazine praised the "dreamy intimate album."

Jazz Link magazine opined, "Her words are true poetry. . . . This is vintage Lee." And this was *Stereo Review:* "There's a refreshingly uncynical, perennially forward-looking and springlike tang to all these songs."

The album rightfully earned Peggy Lee her final Grammy nomination.

Chiodini and Lee kept writing. Today, John Chiodini safeguards the tapes of fourteen unreleased songs in a little strongbox that he keeps in his home studio. As of this writing, three have been mixed, with instruments added.

"Most of All I Love You" is a pleasant ditty, light as air, a whistleable thing, featuring a typical Lee lyric, "I love Sundays, and walks in the park / I love Mondays, and loving in the dark."

But the other two are pure blues. In "I've Been Too Lonely for Too Long," the title says it all. And "I've Got a Brand-New Baby" is a swaying, major-keyed blues vamp, double-entendred to the hilt: "We've got a way of loving that makes our world go round / And you should hear our music—it makes a brand-new sound."

"Hear that?" John Chiodini says now, as he plays the song on the sound system in his living room, nodding to the blues that fill the air: "That's where she *lives.*" He is not aware of having lapsed into the present tense, four years after her death.

Peggy was recording on her own, too. Well, one song, anyway. On his eightieth birthday, Billy Harbach, now very happily married again, received a cassette in the mail at his home in Fairfield, Connecticut, from Bellagio Road. It was Peggy's latest version of "Just for a Thrill." Her voice was in fabulous form, but she'd changed the words to "Just for our Bill."

As Harbach plays it, years later, his tears flow copiously and unashamedly.

THIRTY

Take Me Back to Manhattan

LEE HAD ONE more Manhattan nightclub left in her. It was in a hotel, of course—an ugly monolithic tower planted in midtown Manhattan, soaring over a blighted mid–West Side that hadn't yet been theme-parked, the New York Hilton was an eyesore.

Lee wasn't in such great shape herself: For a year, she had suffered from a painful condition called polymyalgia rheumatica, as well as an inflammation of her nerve endings caused by neuropathy, a result of her diabetes. None of it was about to keep her from a good booking in New York—in a small venue, the Club 53. So she headed east in August 1992 to say goodbye in style—and to meet the last of the Peggy Lee men, that unusual breed of camp followers and genuine, loving devotees of Norma *and*

Peggy, men who ranged from the brilliant to the eccentric to the indescribable.

And in Alexander Theroux, she had them all in one man.

If Alexander Theroux's career had been marked by anything, it was the diversity of his constant quest for enlightenment. In a previous time and place he'd have been characterized as a Renaissance man—author, painter, teacher. He was in love not only with music and art, but also with sports, literature, and religion. He was interested in the pursuit of new ideas and ways of thinking, and had spent a couple of years in a monastery. He was a man whose everyday discourse, whose simplest sentences, might be sprinkled with references to Plato, Pete Rose, William Blake, and Dinah Washington. He was a man as intriguing as the most brilliant college professor you ever had—complete with the requisite cloud of thoughts swarming around his thatch of long, unruly hair.

Throughout his life in public, Alexander Theroux had been overshadowed by the fame of his brother, the writer Paul Theroux. But it had never been fame that Alexander sought. If it was recognition and riches he'd been after, he'd have written novels whose sentences didn't, on occasion, require a Sherpa guide to help most of us reach their summit. He'd written novels praised for their brilliance (*The Adulterer*) and others criticized for their impenetrability (*Darcanville's Cat*). The latter was notable not only for the density of its text but also for its cover—an oil portrait of exquisite styling, evocative of the old masters. It was painted by Alexander Theroux.

It was *Darcanville's Cat* that prompted, out of the blue, the postcard that arrived in Theroux's Cape Cod mailbox one day in 1991, from one of his favorite singers of all time.

"You have a wonderful talent," wrote Peggy Lee. She'd read

Darcanville and had been moved to drop a note. He was stunned; as fate would have it, he'd been reading her autobiography. An aficionado of the music of the fifties, Theroux considered Peggy Lee the artist among artists in his favorite musical era. He answered Lee's communication with a letter of his own. Her answer to his answer included a phone number.

And so, one day, feeling nervous as hell, and making sure he'd shaved—even though he was only picking up the phone—Theroux called Peggy Lee. Therein began a yearlong dialogue conducted mostly by phone. They spoke three or four times a week.

And there were letters. "I've never put this much on paper in my life," she wrote in the middle of one particularly philosophical musing. "I rarely even write my family. . . . What have you done to me?"

He was delighted to find that she was intellectually curious, as eager as he to delve into all sorts of matters. Her gossip took him back to a time he'd only glimpsed in his own pursuits. As he recalls, she talked about how downright dumb Benny Goodman was; about her dislike of Billie Holiday; about how Robert Meservy of Newton, Massachusetts—Robert Preston—had been one of her truest loves. They talked about writing, singers, books, and God: a great deal of talk about God. Lee's spirituality was underscored, quite bluntly, in her response to his gift of a book of poems he'd written—some of which contained images she found offensive.

"My dear Alex," she wrote. "I don't even know how to begin, except to say my heart is . . . broken, or at least cracked. . . . Your book of poetry arrived today, and while much of it is up to what I thought your magnificent standard is, some is not at all. Jesus would never resort to such vulgarity."

Theroux wasn't sure exactly why she was attracted to him. The word "Yale" on his résumé? His search for faith? His youth? For his part, he was attracted not only by the woman whom he'd always considered the musical goddess of the fifties—and not just as a singer, but as a lyricist, an art he held in the highest regard—but also by the woman who so willingly and ably accompanied him on his spiritual quest.

"I adored the woman," Theroux says now. "I didn't mind being an acolyte. I genuinely found her perceptive, theologically hip, a real seeker. She was a quester. She had an intellectual hunger. And her verbal gifts were amazing."

When Peggy told him in the spring of 1992 that she was going to appear at the Hilton in New York, it was time to meet in person. She'd have a room for him in the hotel, she said. He journeyed to the city and checked in to his room before heading up to her suite to meet her.

They had a drink. She was not scheduled to perform for another two days, and Peggy invited Theroux to come up the next morning, and they could talk.

And they did. For hours and hours. The entire day. Of North Dakota. Of Hollywood. Of Mercer and Sinatra. Of her stepmother. Of Preston, "the love of her life."

They also spoke of Disney, and how she'd pleaded with Walt to let Old Trusty live. She took a break only once, to call California so that one of her household staff could hold her cat Baby to the phone and Peggy could hear her heartbeat.

Finally, at about seven o'clock, Theroux said he was too tired to continue and was going down to his own room. "Boom—she suddenly trigger-snapped at me: 'Go ahead, then! Get out!'"

Stunned, bewildered, and exhausted, Theroux retired to his room. "And then she called me within five minutes and apologized. She was obviously contrite, but she didn't allude to what had just happened. She just said, 'I hope you have a good night's sleep, Alex.' She was contrite immediately. I think she felt I'd betrayed her."

The next day, no mention was made of the incident. Theroux helped her with her wheelchair down to the first performance, and joined her in her dressing room afterward, where he watched a seemingly endless procession of well-wishers line up in the hallway, patiently awaiting their moment with the Queen: "It was like she was an archbishop, or a cardinal."

After the line had finally disappeared, they went up to her suite, where Theroux, standing at her side wearing his best suit, was privy to a different procession. In her private sanctum, the profiles were a tad higher, and he was given an unanticipated glimpse of life behind the curtain.

"There were thirty-five people in her bedroom. Al Pacino had come in with some flowers. Madonna came up with Jellybean Benitez to talk to Peggy about 'Fever,' which she was about to record. Peggy said, 'Do you know Alexander Theroux, the famous writer?' I was a little goober from Boston. But Madonna sees me with a beautiful suit, and doesn't know me, and shook hands with me like I was the wizard of Oz."

Peggy's Hilton engagement delighted the faithful and convinced the skeptics. "It was like there was a vacuum in that room except for this one piercing ray of light," according to singer k. d. lang, "which was her voice and her presence."

The critics were equally kind. The *Times,* noting the "wobble" in her voice and her failing eyesight, nonetheless opined that "her willpower, musicality and professionalism enable her to project . . . the old magic. The evening's ballads . . . were infused with an autumnal dreaminess, as though the singer were contemplating past loves from a wistful, almost otherworldly distance."

The *New York Post*'s Jerry Tallmer, though, threw all caution to the wind: " 'Indomitable.' Write that down. Then write down: 'Peggy Lee.' She sang a reflective and subdued ' 'S Wonderful,' rocking slightly from side to side, and when she came to 'you've made my life so glamorous,' I thought, 'My God, how long has she been making all our lives just a little bit, just a lot more glamorous?' She sang fast and light and up-tempo; she sang several lovely ballads—including her own—in which she seemed, or made us think she seemed, to go inside herself. . . . And, of course, she sang her trademark songs, as pure, hot, light, strong, powerful as ever. . . . The voice holds, only the vessel has changed."

Most impressed of all was Gary Giddins. It had been a lifetime since *The Village Voice*'s heralded jazz critic had first mistaken her for Billie on a Goodman record. It had been two decades since he'd panned her Waldorf shows. Now he came full circle in the *Voice*, calling her "still gloriously Lee . . . in an absolutely riveting set that will be talked about for years."

"She was astonishing," Giddins says now. "I wish every singer in the world could have seen what she did. Her range was narrow, but her timing was infallible. She sold every song. I remember that people were actually crying."

Of course, no Peggy Lee engagement could be a classic Peggy Lee evening without a healthy dose of self-reference. In this case, after she'd made clear how miraculous it was that she was even appearing on the stage, after a year of ill health, she touted her Disney victory—but couldn't help remarking that she hadn't seen any coin yet.

"If they're waiting for me to die," she said, "good luck!"

Over the next few days, Theroux stayed by Peggy's side. There were no more marathon sessions; she had rehearsals and performances to attend to. He saw her put on her makeup, he saw her prepare for the performances. He saw her put on her wigs. On the day that happened to be Theroux's birthday, she gave him a plush blue bathrobe from Lord & Taylor.

At the end of the engagement, she extended an invitation for him to visit her in California. And while over the coming years they continued to talk often on the telephone, and she continually extended the invitation, Theroux never took her up on her offer; that one flash of anger had scared him away. A man who'd spent his life examining human nature for its foibles and strengths, a man who'd created characters on the page and on the canvas, sensed that a line had to be drawn.

"I never wanted to go because . . . she did have a dark side," Theroux says now. "The lash of her petulance was scary to me. She could get so mad, and so upredictably irked, and I have no defenses against that kind of woman."

Theroux's defense against falling into what Peggy's old manager Brian Panella had once termed "her web" was the safe remove of the telephone. But even at a distance—or perhaps because of it— the relationship stayed intimate. They were girlfriend and boy-friend.

"Three times a day, there was a period I'd talk to her. And there was a period when you really start to think, 'This is kind of a romance.' Not in a sexual sense. But I was kind of dependent on this call."

Peggy asked him to write an autobiography of Baby, her cat. He asked Peggy to write a book of remembrances of composers. Neither happened. She sent him a copy of her own privately pub-lished collection of poetry.

She'd read aloud passages from his books that she particularly liked. And, of course, she'd sing to him. Theroux had a soft spot for songs about the West; "Along the Colorado Trail" once brought him to tears. She sang "The Cowboy and the Bearded Lady" and told Theroux she'd written it for him, although Ther-oux suspected she already had it in the can. But he didn't protest.

There'd be overnighted packages, too, like the one containing a signed Sinatra photograph. Theroux, the music junkie, thought he'd be getting a photo with an authentic Sinatra autograph on it.

When he mentioned on the phone that the signature looked as if it had been written with an autopen, Peggy was miffed:

"That is Frank's signature," she wrote in a letter. "I have a file full of letters from Frank, if they have not been stolen. . . . No one is trying to take advantage of you, I promise. It hurts me that you think that. . . . I don't remember berating you. I may have been very firm in trying to convince you of the authenticity, but I certainly didn't mean to berate you! We *are* frank and candid friends, as I said to you on the telephone. . . . You see, Alex, a great many people have taken advantage of me and hurt me deeply in my life, and sometimes I think I should just become a recluse. Please wipe the slate clean."

She finished the letter with the words "I love you."

Of course, she'd detail her ailments. Her obsession with her infirmities increasingly struck Theroux as unusual. "There's no question she needed her illnesses for pity," he recalls. "I think it's a survivor syndrome: 'I've been through a lot, and I can still sit up here and sing.'"

But Theroux had another suspicion: that to counter her aloneness, she had created another Peggy as company. "In a way she was her own baby—her own child," he says now. "She had a daughter, of course, but it was almost like she was taking care of herself as if she were another figure."

She spoke of what she'd been through, too. She talked of times of too much cognac. Of being "estranged" from her daughter. Of unnamed men.

"I always had the suspicion that she had affairs with everybody," Theroux says, although she would never be able to count Theroux among them. "I'm talking black, white, green. They would be devotees to her. I can easily see her being married, and getting so petulant over nothing, and causing these guys to leave. Peggy had that Janus quality; when she turned that other face, she was terrifying.

"I think she diverted herself with these mad marriages, with drinking, with indolence. . . . She always had a kind of sleepiness about her. It was attributed as cool, and it *was* cool, but I don't think Peggy Lee was driven to get up in the morning and crank out stuff.

"See, I think it's a trope for the great singers to be irresponsible elsewhere. I swear—it's part of the blues. The lush-life syndrome. The blues open up the lush-life world: smoking, drinking, dives, darkness, infidelity. The lower worlds. When you are a singer with a band, you've gotta take cognac, you do take drugs, you have to have affairs: That's your world.

"She had her demons. But the one thing you can polish in a life that's a mess—divorces, slammed doors, screaming emotions at ten at night—is the persona of the figure. No matter what happened, if you can put the platinum wig on and snap your fingers. . . . Peggy could maintain Miss Peggy Lee and the figure—the mural, the persona, the mask—in the face of all the chaos. The rest of the house doesn't matter. It's the art that matters. That's the temptation among famous people: They don't have to give a shit about anything but the performance. So it doesn't matter how many times you're married, how much of a buffoon you might be. Sinatra is a good example. He was great at what he did. Why did we put up with Wagner's ego? Because he gave us *Tristan and Isolde*. That's what they bank on: that you'll forgive them for what they do. The chaos around them doesn't matter if their art is good. The populace is willing to forgive them if they're good."

In a letter, Alexander Theroux, who is now married, offered these final, professorial thoughts about the woman—about the two women:

"She found an uneasy, plaguing sort of dichotomy between the decadent nightclub world and the ascetic intuition she had, and cherished, so much. 'Blakean' is a good word here—

innocence versus experience. But remember that Blake points out that the true Sons of Loss achieve 'organized innocence': they go through experience with their innocence and achieve the mastery that the frightened and inexperienced innocent never reaches, because those persons do not dare to seek. Peggy richly sought."

On July 31, 1993, Lee performed at the Concord Jazz Festival in California. Marian McPartland recalls the show vividly. Despite the sunglasses and the wheelchair, McPartland found herself entranced: "Her voice was sinuous and soft and beguiling. You could hear every word. It wasn't loud. In contrast to the way some people now think they have to shriek to get over.

"I remember she had on this beautiful headdress, or headband. . . . She just looked gorgeous. I don't know if they had a fan in back, but there were feathers in the hat that gently blew in the wind. She really made a very attractive picture, and she did a very good show.

"Needless to say, there were millions of people milling around, wanting to give her a hug. I was pleased that she was so glad to see me. That might have been the last time I saw her."

The most memorable performance of Peggy Lee's last years took place in a hotel ballroom. She sang two songs. No one who heard them has forgotten them.

On May 9, 1994, Peggy was given the Lifetime Achievement Award of the Society of Singers in a gala ceremony at the Beverly Hilton Hotel. The Society of Singers had been founded in 1984 with the express purpose of raising funds to help musicians who, for one reason or another, had fallen on hard times. The not-for-profit organization had founded its Lifetime Achievement Award in 1989, naming Ella Fitzgerald its first recipient—and thereafter bestowing the name "Ella" on the award. Frank Sinatra and eighty-year-old balladeer Tony Martin had been awarded Ellas. Now it was Peg's turn to be so honored.

For two hours, she sat at the central table in the huge room, a white Buddha—impassive, eyes hidden behind wraparound shades, fur collar framing her expressionless face, as her life swirled and paraded before her eyes—live, in film clips, in tributes.

The video montage featured everything from *Stage Door Canteen* and *Pete Kelly's Blues* to a rare video from a TV special on the making of *Lady and the Tramp* narrated by Walt himself—featuring a very buff Peggy playing finger cymbals as she sang "He's a Tramp" in the studio.

And here was Peggy with a roster of all-stars on various television spots over the years. With Hope and Sinatra and Nat King Cole. In a rare clip with Dave, singing "Mañana"—Dave crosslegged on the floor, head hidden by a large sombrero. With Benny and Ella and Sarah. With Dean. With Sammy. With Judy and with Lena.

Through the clips, as the years rolled on, her looks morphed through several changes, but the voice never did. From show to show, as the others variously stretched, wailed, belted, oversang, undersang, and generally took the TV cameras casually, Peggy never did. In not a single song did she waver. On one video clip, featuring Peggy with Vic Damone and Lena Horne, Damone tried to go operatic. Horne was belting hard and aggressively. Peggy just sang.

The live entertainment that night was equally entrancing, and enthusiastic. Natalie Cole jazzed up a version of "I'm a Woman," and it was sensational. Rosemary Clooney's "You Gotta Have Heart" swept the room away with its samba sway; Clooney, the good soldier, the true survivor of the era—after an appearance on the cover of *Time* magazine in the fifties, she'd descended into a private hell of addiction and spent time in a psych ward before pulling herself together and rising again to the top, with the Concord label—had seldom been in better form; she was having a ball.

The highlight of the night, though, belonged to the truest female voice of the new generation: the torch who carries the flame. Singing "Black Coffee," k.d. lang stood the room of black-tied and sequin-gowned Hollywood stars on its head. Even veterans of k.d.'s shows, accustomed to her extraordinary energy and range of emotion, knew that on this night, beneath a blue spot, she was going the extra mile. The chill started with the first syllable, and didn't wane until she'd finished.

Now the spotlight hit Peggy, in her wheelchair, and someone handed her a microphone. The room hushed.

"You know," she said, in tones as conversational and matter-of-fact as if she were talking to a tiny, intimate room instead of a huge ballroom, "it's been said by many great philosophers that love is the greatest force in the universe, and I think I've felt and heard more love here in this room tonight. . . . I know that that is the shining truth . . . and when I think about these singers and musicians and what they go through, getting started . . . all the rough, rough things you go through on the road . . . well, Emerson said, 'God will not have his work done by cowards,' and that's the truth too. . . .

"I think you can imagine what I'm feeling about this, to have all of this magnificent talent. . . . From my heart I thank you . . . and I don't think I'd better say much more, or I'll cry. So I'll try singing."

The first song was a quiet, slow samba version of Gershwin's " 'S Wonderful.' " For two hours, the Society of Singers orchestra, the various singers, had all been brassing the room away; each arrangement had been bigger and bolder and jazzier and louder than the last.

And now, in the huge ballroom, you could hear a pin drop.

"For about five minutes, she was thirty-five years younger," Artie Butler says now. "She cast a spell over the whole room. The spell was her secret weapon, you know. It was like watching an old movie. We still talk about that performance. She put a hurt on us that night. I mean a good one. In a tiny voice, she did more with that song than I ever heard anyone do with a song in my life."

She finished with "Here's to You," the song she'd written for Cary Grant to sing to his daughter some thirty years ago, a haunting simple poem whose lyrics consisted, for the most part, of farewells uttered in several languages: *À votre santé; Vaya con dios; Shalom; Salut, Ciao; Pace; L'chaim;* and, finally, the spoken words "Angels on Your Pillows."

It was a salute. It was a goodbye. The standing ovation went on for a long time.

Peggy Lee's final major public performance, on August 2, 1995, at the Hollywood Bowl, where she shared the marquee with George Shearing and Mel Tormé, proved a fittingly bittersweet finale to her sixty-year career. Emil Palame remembers rehearsing duets for Tormé and Peggy at Peggy's house, and counts the moment as one of the highlights of his life. But he—as well as others—remembers Tormé and Shearing both giving Peggy the cold shoulder, for reasons lost to history. (Tormé is no longer alive; Shearing declined to speak about Peggy.) Tormé refused to appear with her in the second set. "I think Peggy got so much attention," Palame says now, "that it bugged him."

"She said to me that night, 'Neither one of these guys is talking to me,'" Stella Castellucci recalls. "The two were in cahoots about something."

But Lee performed another song that night, and it brought a personal farewell from a random fan that stands as an appropriate final review of Peggy Lee the singer. It was the old Walter Spriggs blues tune "You Don't Know": the simplest blues song she'd ever sung. It had been ignored as the flip side of the "Fever" single. It had disappeared on the second side of the album *Big Spender.*

"After the concert was over, the line to come back and see her was two or three hours long," Stella Castellucci recalls. "She insisted on seeing everyone. She wouldn't turn anyone away.

"I'll never forget one of them: this big husky black man, very pleasant, very down to earth, they were talking and yakking. And he said, 'Well, Miss Lee, I got to tell you: When you do the blues, they're done.'

"And that just did something to her," Castellucci says now. "She said, 'Oh, thank you!' It just lit her up for the rest of her evening. She went to bed that night, and she was lying there looking at TV, and I'm lying on the chaise longue in her room.

" 'Did you hear what that man said to me?' she said. I said, 'I did, Peg.' She said, 'Yeah.' Then she went to sleep."

Peggy's relationship with Alexander Theroux continued. "Angels on your pillow" were invariably her final words in each call. Most often, the common thread was religion, and by now Theroux sensed her need for salvation.

"In our talks of God," he says, "she had a lot of the 'wormturns' quality to her. You knew she'd come from darkness to God. I always knew there was sort of a contrition involved in her faith. She knew she was coming to the end. I remember being wistfully sad when I talked to her in the last year."

One night in October 1998, Alexander Theroux called, and was told that Peggy had fallen ill.

On October 23, 1998, Peggy Lee was at home, but her cat Baby was in the hospital. Lee asked Kathy Levy to go check on Baby;

the cat wasn't eating. Levy followed orders, and phoned from the vet's: "Of course she won't eat," Kathy told Peggy. "She has an orange plastic bowl, and they're playing country music."

Levy persuaded the vet to let her take the cat home to Lee. Levy noticed that Peggy was "quiet, and absorbed."

Four days later, on October 27, 1998, Peggy Lee suffered a massive stroke. She was seventy-eight.

Peggy's mind remained sharp. As Quincy Jones puts it now, "The stroke just kept her from getting to her antenna." Struck mute, struck down, the voice finally silenced, Peggy Lee pulled off one of the more wondrous triumphs of her life.

By all accounts, the stroke effected a remarkable transformation in a lady who had been so demanding of others, so impatient, so often intolerant: The anger left her. The ego was calmed. The high, sometimes unrealistic expectations of others now gave way to an understanding. Her personality, say those who knew her well, actually changed. When friends walked into the room, she would light up. She was capable of the occasional word or two—if she had to think about saying something, friends recall, she couldn't get it out, but she could still blurt out the occasional good-natured expletive at her own frustration—but she communicated effectively: with a squeeze of a hand, with the look in her eyes. Above all, she was easy to be with.

And, more remarkably, faced with the sudden inability to express herself—in effect, trapped inside her physical infirmity—by all accounts she handled it not only with grace, but with triumph. Communication had been her life. And now she could communicate as powerfully and effectively with a brush of a finger into the palm of a friend's hand as she ever had with her music.

It was all the more remarkable considering that, of all of the afflictions that could have visited her at the end, it was a stroke—whose most deleterious effect was the complete silencing of her instrument. For seven decades, it had been Peggy Lee's voice that had brought her the fame she'd sought. Her songs had not only entranced a nation, they had muted her insecurities as well. It was through song that Peggy Lee had been able to reach the world. It was in response to her voice that the world had reached out to her and given her the love she'd always sought.

But without it, she now seemed as whole, as complete as she'd ever been. And it is difficult not to wonder, if just a little, whether the quieting of the voice of Peggy Lee—and with it, the disappearance of Miss Peggy Lee—allowed Norma Deloris Egstrom to find some peace.

The final year was difficult for all. Peggy's living will made it clear that she did not want the doctors to terminate her life. She was on feeding tubes, and an artificial respirator for the final year, along with a talking tracheostomy; but when the synapses don't work, the talking tracheostomy doesn't help.

But she did her best to communicate with her loved ones. In the summer of 2001, Quincy Jones paid a visit to Bellagio Road.

"Nicki told me, 'Don't pretend you understand mother, Quincy,'" Jones says now. "But I'd worked with Peggy in creative moments. I could hear that mind still trying to work. I could feel the wit, but she couldn't get the words out. It was funny, because we still went to our original kind of relationship.

"She had on a white turban, and the bed had been all dolled up, and she had lipstick on. We always used to fuck with each other with jokes and stuff—that was always part of our relationship—and this time she tried to say something, but I didn't know what she was talking about. She knew exactly who I was. She pulled her turban off—almost like, 'Fuck it'—she didn't say that, but—then she pulled her teeth out. Nicki said, *'Mother!'* We all cracked up."

In the first week of January 2002, after months in the hospital, on artificial-life-support systems, Peggy's doctor sent her home. Two weeks later, lying in her own bed, in her "Peach Palace," on an ordinary day, with the bedroom shutters open to furnish a view of her favorite rose bush, Peggy Lee suffered a fatal heart attack.

She was cremated, and her remains were interred in a bench in a cemetery in Westwood, in a section called the Garden of Serenity.

The legacy of Peggy Lee's work is undisputed. As an artist, she was without parallel. The only unanswered question—a question that must be asked—is whether Norma Deloris Egstrom was, at the end, a happy woman.

"Yes," Kathy Levy answers, quickly and surely. "She had her own little happiness, and her happiness was in her gift: her love of music. And of mankind. She really did care about the smallest person; if I'd called her when she was talking with the president, she'd have taken my call. She really did have a love of mankind; her voice smiled."

The final sentiment must be offered by a musician. A pianist, of course.

"I hope to God," says Artie Butler, "that she's singing for someone now."

Acknowledgments

I have chosen to acknowledge and thank many of the sources for this book in the notes section to follow. But I would like to take this opportunity to extend special thanks to Will Friedwald, Bill Rudman, David Torresen, Ivan Santiago, and Freeman Gunter for their help in reviewing the manuscript; Phoebe Jacobs, Stella Castellucci, and John Chiodini for their generous time, hospitality and insight; and Kate Stevenson, the keeper of the flame in Jamestown, North Dakota.

In addition, I extend my grateful thanks to the staff at the Institute of Jazz Studies at the Newark, New Jersey, campus of Rutgers University. The IJS is an extraordinary treasure, and this book would not have been possible without its considerable resources or the enthusiasm of its staff; I would like to thank Tad Hershorn in particular. Also, I thank Carol Bursack, the librarian for the Fargo *Forum*, and Wes Anderson of the Barnes County Historical Society in Valley City, North Dakota.

As always, I thank Esther Newberg at ICM. I am also grateful for the efforts of my tireless editor, George Hodgman, who came up with the idea for this book, and who is therefore one of the two people responsible for it. The other cannot read this acknowledgment, but I must thank her nonetheless. It was through my brief friendship with the extraordinary Rosemary Clooney that I was first introduced to the music of this time, and it was the memory of Rosemary's effervescence, graciousness, and remarkable love of life that gave me the confidence to take on this project when George Hodgman proposed it. Thanks, Rosemary.

Notes

In researching this book, I drew upon hundreds of contemporaneous newspaper and magazine accounts. Only the most significant are cited. In addition, I drew extensively on archival material and recordings at the Institute of Jazz Studies at the Newark, N.J., campus of Rutgers University. In addition, I screened several videotapes at the Museum of Television and Radio in both its New York and Los Angeles locations. For dates of Lee's recordings, as well as the musicians involved, detailed background information about the recordings, and reviews of various performances, I relied extensively on David Torresen's definitive and exhaustive Web site, www.peggylee.com.

For information on popular music in the twentieth century, I consulted numerous books, but extensively and most notably *Jazz Singing*, by Will Friedwald (Da Capo Press, 1992). For information on musicians and music of the Big Band era, I relied on several books, most notably *The Big Bands*, by George T. Simon (Macmillan Publishing Company, 1967). For information about Benny Goodman's band during Peggy's era, I turned to *Benny Goodman: Listen to His Legacy,* by D. Russell Connor (Scarecrow Press and the Institute of Jazz Studies, Metuchen, N.J., 1988). I also drew on Peggy's own autobiography, *Miss Peggy Lee* (Berkley Publishing Group, 1989; Bloomsbury Publishing, London, 1990), which remains the definitive account of the lady's life.

Prologue: White Night

For the Basin Street East section, I relied extensively on interviews with Phoebe Jacobs, who was the publicist for the club at the time; an interview with Quincy Jones; and interviews with several musicians, including bassist Max Bennett, guitarist Mundell Lowe, drummer Grady Tate, and the late pianist Joe Harnell.

In addition, I referred to accounts of the Basin Street engagements that appeared in various periodicals, including *The New Yorker,* and newspapers, including *The New York Times,* the *New York Journal-American,* and the *Toronto Telegram.*

For descriptions and details of New York City and its weather at the time, I consulted primarily *The New Yorker* and the *Times.*

I also drew on Gary Giddins's landmark biography of Bing Crosby, *A Pocketful of Dreams* (Little, Brown and Company, 2001).

In addition, I relied on two recordings of Peggy at Basin Street: *Basin Street East Proudly Presents Miss Peggy Lee* (Capitol) and *Peggy at Basin Street East* (Collector's Choice), in describing Lee's performance.

Invaluable information for this section, and for several of the subsequent chapters, also came from David Torresen's Web site on Miss Lee (www.peggylee.com).

According to the liner notes of the Collector's Choice album, the blizzard of 1961 occurred on the night of the recording, but this is in dispute. However, if the recording did not take place on the night of the snowstorm, but within the following few days, Miss Lee's set list would likely have been virtually identical.

One: In Dakota

Much of the detail on Peggy's childhood in Jamestown and Nortonville, North Dakota, is from the author's visits to the area. In addition, I relied on Kate Stevenson's documents, including birth and death records, videos, and extensive research on Miss Lee's life. For additional and corroborative information on Lee's upbringing, as well as information on other parts of her life, I referred to music author Gene Lees's definitive liner notes for the 1998 Capitol Records four-CD compilation, *Miss Peggy Lee*. Further information on her childhood came from numerous interviews Peggy gave throughout her life to several dozen journalists, as well as accounts in various periodicals, including *The Jamestown Sun*.

In addition, for details about Nortonville and Jamestown as well as remembrances of Peggy's father and stepmother, I interviewed several residents. I am thankful for George Spangler's guided tour, as well as for his wealth of information. For details about life at the time in these towns and in rural North Dakota in general, I referred to published accounts of the histories of both Jamestown and Nortonville, including *Century of Stories: Jamestown and Stutsman County*, published by the Fort Seward Historical Society in 1983. For details of Peggy's mother's funeral, I relied on newspaper accounts. For information on Barnes County, I consulted the wealth of documentation at the Barnes County Historical Museum in Valley City, which included clips from the Valley City *Times-Record*, as well as video archives, including an interview with Pearl Buck.

For information on the Midland Continental Railroad, I relied on several histories, most prominently two documents written by railroad historian F. Stewart Mitchell: an article in *Trains* magazine, and his research in support of an application for National Register of Historic Places status for the Wimbledon MCRR depot. General information on railroads and those riding the rails during the Depression comes from *Riding the Rails,* the award-winning PBS documentary by filmmaker Michael Uys and his wife, Lexy Lovell.

Two: **Pick Up Your Telephone**

For Peggy's years in Wimbledon and Valley City, in addition to the author's visits to the town and to the Midland depot where she lived, I relied on interviews with classmates, including Ethelyn Olson, for whose thoughts I am particularly grateful. I also thank Peggy Rose for her vivid recollections of Wimbledon. For Peggy's graduation poem and the recollections of William Brenner, as well as information on the railroad, I relied on documents and correspondence provided by Myrna Bultema, the curator of the unofficial Peggy Lee museum housed in the old depot in Wimbledon.

Interviews with residents of Wimbledon and Valley City provided information on KVOC and Doc Haines, with special thanks to members of the Ingstad and Ginsberg families, Edith Butcher, Mary Rose, Leo and Louverne Radke, and Curt Olson. For information about the Jack Wardlaw band, I interviewed members of the Wardlaw family. In addition, I referred to accounts in the *Grand Forks Herald* and the Fargo *Forum*.

For general information about life in North Dakota during the Depression, I am thankful for the memories and hospitality of Geraldine Westley. I also relied on several written accounts, including *Journal of the Northern Plains,* published by the State Historical Society of North Dakota. I also drew on Eric Sevareid's autobiography, *Not So Wild a Dream.* For more information on North Dakota life, I thank the music and pop-culture author Chuck Klosterman, a North Dakota native, whose book *Fargo Rock City* remains the seminal history of heavy metal.

Three: The Most Beautiful Street West of Minneapolis

For Peggy's experiences in Jamestown following high school, I am grateful to Red Homuth for his vivid recollections of Peggy, the Gladstone Hotel, and life in Jamestown. For information on Jamestown in the twenties and thirties, *Century of Stories: Jamestown and Stutsman County* was invaluable. I thank Jamestown's Mary Young, a font of knowledge on her town's history. I relied also on several Internet accounts, including that found at Fargo-history.com, as well as an interview in *Interview* magazine.

For accounts of Peggy's time at WDAY in Fargo, I interviewed members of the Sydness family for recollections of Ken Kennedy. I thank Joseph Grant for his accounts of Peggy's days as his family's neighbor and friend, and Bill Snyder for his memories of WDAY. I also thank Edith Butcher for her recollections.

For accounts of the "Milkman's Matinee" radio program, I referred to a *Time* magazine account. Information on the jazz scene in Los Angeles is drawn from several books, as well as Internet sites about L.A. history. For the route of Peggy's train trip, I consulted period railroad timetables.

Four: The Magic Aquarium

For information on Peggy's stint at the Powers Hotel, I relied on interviews with Lloyd Collins, and am grateful for his time and enthusiasm. For information on Peggy's relationship with Johnny Quam, I am grateful to Mr. Quam for his memories. For information on the Powers Hotel, in addition to the author's visit, I relied on an October 1937 article from *Hotel Monthly* magazine. For information on Sev Olson's band, I relied on the memories of Lloyd Luckman, Sev's trumpet player. Background on Minneapolis in the late thirties is drawn from various historical Web sites. For general information about big-band music and big-band life, I am grateful to Jean Bach, the producer of *A Great Day in Harlem,* the superb 1994 documentary film about the remarkable Art Kane photograph of jazz musicians in Harlem from the January 1959 issue of *Esquire* magazine.

Five: Benny Blows In

For information on the Will Osborne band, I relied on liner notes from Osborne's records, newspaper and trade magazine accounts from the Institute of Jazz Studies, and accounts in the Stutsman County *Record* and the Fargo *Forum.* For information on the Doll House in Palm Springs, I relied on memories of the late Ethel Harutun, as well as Internet histories of Palm Springs. Descriptions of Frank Bering are based on Internet photo archives of Chicago newspapers. For information on the Buttery and the Ambassador hotels, in addition to the author's visit, I relied on interviews with Marian McPartland.

For detailed information on Benny Goodman, I relied on *The Kingdom of Swing* by Benny Goodman; *Benny Goodman* by D. Russell Connor; *Swing, Swing, Swing* by Ross Firestone; Geoffrey Ward's *Jazz;* the documentary film *Benny Goodman: Adventures in the Kingdom of Swing,* directed and produced by Oren Jacoby; "John Hammond on Record"; archives from IJS; the autobiography *High Times, Hard Times* by Anita O'Day; and *I Had the Craziest Dream,* Helen Forrest's autobiography. Further information on Benny was obtained from periodicals.

For information on Mel Powell, I consulted a profile of Powell by Whitney Balliett in *The New Yorker.* The account of Benny's Carnegie Hall concert is based on a recording of the evening on the Giants of Jazz label.

Eight: **Do Right**

For information on Peggy's two years with Benny, in addition to the
sources cited in chapter five, I relied extensively on her 1993 interview
with Bill Rudman and Ken Bloom from the files of the Institute of Jazz
Studies, especially back issues of *Metronome* and *Down Beat;* newspaper
clippings; musician biographies; back issues of *Esquire* magazine; a *Look*
magazine interview; a *Zoo World* magazine interview; and liner notes. I
also relied on accounts in various newspapers, including the Fargo *Forum.*
In addition, I relied on interviews with the guitarist Bucky Pizzarelli, to
whom I am particularly grateful; pianist Artie Butler; and Phoebe Jacobs.

Information on Harold Arlen was supplied by his son Sam, to whom
I am grateful. I also consulted *Happy with the Blues* by Edward Jablon-
ski and *Skylark: The Life and Times of Johnny Mercer* by Philip Furia.
Information on Johnny Mercer was gained from interviews with Billy
Harbach and Gene Schlatter, from Gene Lees's biography of Mercer,
Portrait of Johnny, and from Furia's biography cited above.

In addition to Whitney Balliett's *New Yorker* profile of Mel Powell, I
relied on Peggy's interview with Powell in *Miss Peggy Lee.*

For information about the Hotel New Yorker, I relied on the hotel's
archives, which included documents, artifacts, and histories of the hotel.

For the section on the film *Stage Door Canteen,* as well as for information on many of the other films cited in this book, I relied on the Web
site imdb.com, the Internet Movie Database.

Nine: **Our Little Dream Castle**

For information on Dave Barbour, I relied largely on interviews with
several musicians, including André Previn, Pete Candoli, and Jack
Costanzo, as well as on several of the books previously cited. In addition, I had the benefit of the narrative sections from a bootleg recording
of *Peg,* Lee's 1983 musical, and the unreleased demo recordings of the
score of the show, provided by pianist Paul Horner. Peggy's recollections
of her early Capitol years are from the audio interview with Lee conducted by Bill Rudman and Ken Bloom in 1989.

For histories of Capitol Records, I consulted Lees's *Portrait of
Johnny* and Furia's *Skylark.* For recollections of Peggy's first efforts
with Capitol, I relied on the first-person account of Dave Dexter in the
liner notes of *Peggy Lee with the David Barbour and Billy May Bands,*
issued by Hindsight Records in 1977. Information on the "Mañana"

lawsuit is drawn from the Associated Press account in the *Chicago Daily News*. Recollections of Carlos Gastel were provided by, among others, George Schlatter in an interview.

For information about Ernest Holmes, I consulted primarily *That Was Ernest*, a biography of Holmes by Reginald C. Armor. In describing Peggy's relationship to the church, I drew from a 1987 article from *Science of Mind* magazine. For information on religious trends at the time, I relied on a paper presented by Philip Jenkins at a Center for Studies on New Religions (CESNUR) conference in 1999. For further detail, I relied on a *Life* magazine feature story from March 1948.

Ten: On Air

For information on Bob Hope and the early history of radio, I relied on William Robert Faith's *Bob Hope: A Life in Comedy* (Harper Collins, 1985). Information on Peggy and her career in this era was supplied in interviews with Bucky Pizzarelli. Further information came from various newspapers and periodicals including *The New York Mirror*, the Fargo *Forum*, *Down Beat* magazine, and other publications from the records of the IJS.

Eleven: Borderline

For information on Peggy in the late forties, I relied on several periodical accounts, including those from *Cue* magazine, August 1948; *American* magazine, October 1948; *Melody Maker*, September 1949; *Senior Scholastic* magazine, October 1949; *Life* magazine; *Click* magazine; *Metronome* magazine; and *Newsweek*. In addition, I relied on the previously cited 1989 Lee interview with Bill Rudman and Ken Bloom, and on a personal interview with Lorraine Feather, the daughter of Leonard and Jane Feather, to whom I am particularly grateful.

Accounts of nightlife in Los Angeles at the time come from, among other sources, the Tanner-Gray Line bus company's *This Week in Los Angeles* magazine of July 1948. I also referred to an interview in *Cue* magazine.

Twelve: You Was

For information on Bing Crosby, and his relationship with Peggy, I drew upon Gary Giddins's *A Pocketful of Miracles*, as well as interviews with Mr. Giddins. Descriptions of Peggy's appearance on Bing Crosby's radio show with Crosby and Louis Armstrong are based on the recording of the show in the catalog of the Museum of Television and Radio in New York (hereafter referred to as MTR).

For information on Bob Hope, I relied on William Robert Faith's *Bob Hope: A Life in Comedy.* Details of Peggy's first television appearance with Hope are based on the recording of the show at MTR in New York.

For descriptions of Peggy's trip to St. Louis, I relied on Rudman and Bloom's 1989 interview. Accounts of her father's trip to Los Angeles are from *Miss Peggy Lee* (hereafter referred to as *MPL*).

For perspective on musical trends at the time, I referred to composer Aaron Copland's fascinating *Music and Imagination,* a compilation of Copland's lectures at Harvard in 1951–52.

Thirteen: Home

For information on the North Dakota Winter Carnival, I relied extensively on video footage and written material from the Barnes County Historical Society, as well as accounts in the Fargo *Forum* and the recollections of Lois Brier and the family of Belle May Ginsberg. The account of Peggy's final day with her father is from *MPL*. Information on Peggy's role in *Mr. Music* is derived from an interview with Marge Champion, to whom I extend thanks. Additionally, I drew on wire-service interviews and accounts in the Fargo *Forum*.

Information on Robert Preston is derived from *MPL* as well as from interviews with Phoebe Jacobs, Alexander Theroux, and Stella Castellucci. Extensive information on Dave and Peggy comes from a *Metronome* magazine profile.

Accounts of Steve Allen are based on personal interviews with his widow, Jayne Meadows, to whom I am particularly grateful, and Leonard Stern, a writer on the show, and a most gracious contributor of insight relating to Allen. The accounts of the television show are from the recording in MTR in New York. Information on the last days of Peggy's marriage to Dave Barbour is from, among other sources, the Valley City *Times-Record* and wire-service accounts.

Information on Peggy's last days at Capitol comes from Will Friedwald's extensive and thorough liner notes to the Peggy Lee singles collection issued by Capitol in 2002.

Fourteen: **Lovers**

The re-creation of Peggy's radio shows is based on a recording of two shows issued by Jasmine Records (London) in 1986. Accounts of Peggy's time at the Copa rely on published reports, specifically in *The New York Herald,* and an interview with the late Joe Harnell. For Peggy's memories of the creation of her version of Richard Rodgers's "Lover," I relied on her 1989 interview with Bill Rudman and Ken Bloom, as well as her own accounts in *MPL* and various periodicals including *Down Beat, Theatre Arts* magazine, and *The New York Times.*

The Robert Preston information comes from Phoebe Jacobs and Alexander Theroux. For information on Peggy's relationship with Jimmy Rowles, I am particularly grateful for Tad Hershorn's manuscript about the life of Rowles. In addition, Stella Castellucci's memories of Rowles and Peggy were very helpful.

For the section on Ciro's, I am indebted to Sheila Weller. I am also grateful to George Schlatter for his lively memories of the time and the place and the woman. I also thank trumpeter Pete Candoli and drummer Jack Costanzo. For the section on Mel Ferrer, I relied on an interview written by Don Freeman for *The San Diego Union,* as well as information from other periodicals including the *New York Post.*

I am also thankful for the memories of recording-industry giant Ahmet Ertegun. And I am grateful to Stella Castellucci for all of her help on this as well as many other chapters.

Fifteen: **Modern Screen**

For information on the making of *The Jazz Singer,* I am thankful for the detailed and extensive recollections of Leonard Stern, a credited writer on the movie. I also relied on periodical accounts, including *Down Beat* and the *New York World Telegram.* For information on Brad Dexter, I drew on several sources, including interviews with Stella Castellucci, Jack Costanzo, and Pete Candoli. I also thank Corky Hale for her recollections of Lee and Dexter's wedding. Additional written sources include Gay Talese's legendary profile of Frank Sinatra in the April 1966 issue of *Esquire* magazine.

The account of the Academy Award performance is based on a screening of the show at MTR in New York. For further information on Lee's life, I drew on a profile in the New York *Daily News.*

I am also grateful for the memories of Mary Bennett, who provided information and insight regarding Peggy's marriage to Brad Dexter in this chapter, as well as other valuable memories.

Sixteen: Coffee Break

For Peggy's performances at La Vie en Rose, I am grateful for the memories, humor, and talent of Dolph Traymon, proprietor and pianist at the Fife 'n Drum in Kent, Connecticut, for more than three decades. I also thank actor Don Hastings, star of the soap-opera stage. In addition, I relied on reviews from *The New Yorker.*

For information on the recording of the Decca album *Black Coffee,* I am thankful for the accounts of Pete Candoli. In addition, I drew upon interviews and stories by Ralph Gleason that appeared in *Down Beat.* For the Natalie Wood anecdote, I consulted Suzanne Finstad's *Natasha: The Biography of Natalie Wood.*

Descriptions of Peggy's appearance on the Sid Caesar program are based on the video of the show on file at MTR in New York. Accounts of Peggy's work on *Lady and the Tramp* are based on the video clip featuring Walt Disney and Peggy that was shown at the Society of Singers tribute to Peggy later in her life; I am grateful for the generosity of pianist and arranger Artie Butler for providing the tape, as well as personal information for several details in later chapters. I also relied on accounts in *Cosmopolitan* magazine and several newspapers.

Seventeen: Kelly Girl

For the history of the making of *Pete Kelly's Blues,* I relied as heavily on the recollections of Arthur Hamilton as the film relied on his wonderful songs. For Mr. Hamilton's gracious interview, I am grateful and appreciative. For Peggy's candid assessment of her film career following *Pete Kelly's Blues,* I referred to a thorough and entertaining profile written by Shaun Considine in the June 1974 issue of *After Dark* magazine. Peggy's frank discussion of her life at the time is from a story by Kirtley Baskette in the April 1995 issue of *Redbook,* the best magazine profile ever written of Lee.

For the section concerning Peggy's houseguests on Kimridge Avenue in the mid-fifties, I am particularly indebted to two of Peggy's musicians at the time, who granted multiple interviews and offered gracious hospitality to boot. Pianist Gene DiNovi was generous with his time and his memory, and his recollections of Jimmy Marino, among other subjects, were invaluable. I am also thankful, again, to Stella Castellucci.

Eighteen: **High on a Hill**

The description of Peggy's rendition of "Johnny Guitar" on the Colgate television show in 1954 is based on the videotape of the show on file at MTR in New York. For the story of Peggy and Dewey Martin's courtship, I relied on an article from 1957 entitled "Peggy Lee and Dewey Martin: Their Love Story" available on the Internet at www.peggylee.com/library/570000.html, with source and author unknown. Peggy's remarks about the album *Dream Street* are from various periodical interviews, including John Tynan's interview in *Down Beat* in 1957.

Impressions of pianist Lou Levy are drawn from an interview with Peggy's close friend Kathy Levy, to whom I am particularly grateful, as well as the remembrances of several of Peggy's musicians, including guitarist Mundell Lowe. For memories of her engagements in Las Vegas, I am thankful for the recollections of Stella Castellucci, Jack Costanza, and Max Bennett.

Details about Peggy's musical collaboration and personal relationship with Frank Sinatra came from many sources, including interviews with Phoebe Jacobs. Stella Castellucci was helpful in providing insight into the recording of "The Man I Love." For the section on Peggy's duets with Sinatra, I relied on the American Public Television broadcast of *Sinatra: The Classic Duets.*

Nineteen: **Things Are Swingin'**

For the story of the creation of Peggy's version of "Fever," I am particularly grateful to bass player Max Bennett—as I am for all of his assistance, his time, and his insight. The Jimmy Scott reference to Little Willie John is from David Ritz's biography of Scott, *Faith in Time.* For the discussion of the song and the growing genre of rock and roll, I referred to stories from *Metronome.* Information on Peggy's divorce from Dewey Martin is from wire-service accounts.

For information about the Copa and about Peggy at this time, as well as about her relationship with Dewey Martin, I am grateful for the memories of the late Joe Harnell, her pianist. Harnell's contributions and insights were copious, about the woman, her music, her life, and her personality. I am sorry not to have had the opportunity to thank him more thoroughly before his passing.

For information about the television show *Swing into Spring,* as well as for all of his other memories, I am grateful that André Previn took time from his full schedule to share his thoughts. For details of that show, I referred to the videotape on file at MTR in Los Angeles. For further insight into Billy May at the time of the album *Pretty Eyes,* I relied on Will Friedwald's biography of Frank Sinatra and on Friedwald's personal recollections.

For more information on Peggy's relationship to Dewey Martin and her other husbands, I referred to the fine profile of Miss Lee by the late Maurice Zolotow in the July 1983 issue of *Los Angeles* magazine.

For thoughts on Peggy, I am particularly thankful to Jayne Meadows for her time, her thoughts, and her hospitality—as well as her introduction to Bill Harbach, an extraordinarily gracious individual, whom I must also thank: for memories, for music, for books, for kindness, and for hospitality. Peggy was fortunate to have had his friendship.

Twenty: **Rainy Nights in London Town**

For the section concerning Peggy's relationship with Patrick Catling, I relied on Catling's extraordinarily entertaining autobiography, *Better Than Working,* and conversations with Mr. Catling himself, whose life has been as fascinating as Miss Lee's.

The Bing Crosby show re-created in this chapter is available for screening at MTR in New York. There is no more spectacular television show from this golden age of entertainment, and it is worth going out of one's way to visit this extraordinary museum to view this particular hour of musical heaven.

For the information on Peggy's relationship with Quincy Jones, I thank Mr. Jones for his time, his recollections, and his hospitality. I also referred to Mr. Jones's autobiography, *Q: The Autobiography of Quincy Jones* (Doubleday, 2001).

For insight into Peggy and her music at this time, I am grateful for the thoughts and memories of singer Jack Jones.

In particular, for her memories of Peggy during all of her Basin Street engagements, I cannot thank Phoebe Jacobs enough.

Twenty-one: **The Best Is Yet to Come**

For information on JFK's birthday celebration at Madison Square Garden, I referred to various Kennedy biographies and Web sites. Recollections of Jack del Rio were supplied by Phoebe Jacobs, and several musicians including Stella Castellucci and Jack Costanzo. For information on Peggy's income, I relied on wire-service reports that appeared in the Fargo *Forum*.

For the details about the creation of "I'm a Woman," I am grateful for the time, energy, humor, hospitality, and wholehearted cooperation of Jerry Leiber and Mike Stoller, without whom much of this book would not have been possible—as indeed without whom the direction of modern music would have taken a very different, and diminished, turn. No single songwriting team has influenced modern American music so delightfully; we are all enriched by their talents.

For personal information about Peggy and her music in this and all subsequent chapters, I am very grateful for the memories and insights of the extraordinary Grady Tate, jazzman nonpareil.

For personal information about Peggy for this chapter and all subsequent chapters, I am grateful for the memories of her dear friend Kathy Levy.

The performance of Peggy singing with the Righteous Brothers on the Ed Sullivan show was re-created from a video anthology of several Sullivan clips provided by Kate Stevenson.

For details about the recording of "The Shining Sea," as well as several subsequent insights, I thank Johnny Mandel.

Twenty-two: **All There Was**
Jerry Leiber and Mike Stoller provided the bulk of the story about the writing and recording of "Is That All There Is?" Guitarist Mundell Lowe also provided significant background.

I am also grateful to Peter Levinson, Peggy's former publicist and the author of two distinctive biographies of the music of the time: *Trumpet Blues: The Life of Harry James* and *September in the Rain: The Life of Nelson Riddle*. For his expertise, his generous assistance, and his insights into the lady, I am indebted to Mr. Levinson.

For Peggy's engagement at the International Hotel, I relied on several biographies of Barbra Streisand, as well as the recollections of Artie Butler, whose memories of Peggy proved invaluable, whose hospitality was equally generous—and whose immortal piano arrangement on Joe Cocker's "Feelin' Alright" cannot go unmentioned. I also relied on Mike Stoller's thoughts.

Twenty-three: **Grand Tour**

For reviews of Peggy's London engagement, I referred to David Torresen's Web site, peggylee.com. For the account of the party at Peggy's house as she prepared for her Waldorf engagement, I relied on Eugene Boe's account in *Cue* magazine, April 1969.

For information about her appearances at the Empire Room at the Waldorf, I am indebted to several people. Grady Tate, as always, provided tremendous insight into Peggy's performances. Freeman Gunter, Peggy's friend, was gracious, insightful, and generous with documents as well as memories, and I am grateful for all of his help and hospitality. Robert Richards, Peggy's friend and collaborator, provided time, energy, documents, and insight, as well as gracious hospitality and boundless enthusiasm.

Brian Panella, Peggy's former manager, was generous with his time and his thoughts, and his understanding of Peggy Lee added tremendously to this book.

Twenty-four: **Diplomacy**

The re-creation of Peggy's engagement at the White House was possible because of a bootlegged CD of that evening's performance. I am indebted to Peter Levinson for recollections of the evening, as well as to Grady Tate for additional perspective on the events. I am grateful to Leonard Garment for his memories of the cultural atmosphere of the Nixon White House, and would highly recommend to aficionados of both politics and music Mr. Garment's entertaining autobiography, *Crazy Rhythm*. Background on the political situation was taken from various biographies. The newspaper accounts of the evening are taken from Vera Glaser's article in the *Chicago Daily News* as well as later articles in *The New York Times*.

I am grateful, again, to Brian Panella for his detailed accounts of Peggy's performances, financial situation, and state of mind. Kathy Levy, Mary Bennett, and trombonist Alan Kaplan added insight to this chapter. I am grateful to Irv Cowan, proprietor of the Diplomat Hotel and producer of Lee's Broadway show, for his memories of Peggy and her parties at this time. Accounts of Peggy's performance at Louis Armstrong's funeral are taken from the front-page *New York Times* story on the event.

I again thank Artie Butler for his contribution to the section on Lee's album *Norma Deloris Egstrom from Jamestown, North Dakota*.

For accounts of the taping of Quincy Jones's Duke Ellington television special I thank Robert Richards. Freeman Gunter's recollections added dimension to this chapter as well. Accounts of Peggy's appearance with Paul McCartney are drawn from *Zoo World,* July 1974, as well as from *The New York Times.*

I thank Gary Giddins for his personal insights. I drew upon Giddins's review from *The Village Voice* for this chapter. The review of Lee's Waldorf performance by David Tipmore is drawn from an article available on the Internet at www.peggylee.com/library/740926.html; the forum of its original appearance in print is unknown.

Accounts and details of Robert Richards's relationship with Peggy at this time are drawn from several interviews with Mr. Richards.

Twenty-five: **Mirrors**
For accounts of the recording of *Mirrors,* I am grateful to Jerry Leiber and Mike Stoller, primarily, for their enthusiastic recollections and extensive background. Johnny Mandel aided greatly with his own thoughts, as did Kathy Levy. Peter Levinson's recollections and insights fleshed out this chapter.

For Peggy's involvement in Transcendental Meditation at the time, I relied on a newspaper account written by Sandra Pesman that appeared in the *Chicago Daily News.*

For accounts of Peggy's appearances in Las Vegas, I relied on Kathy Levy's memories. For her state of mind at the time, as well as her preparation routines, I am thankful, again, for Freeman Gunter's thoughts.

For the circumstances of Peggy's separation from the William Morris agency, I relied on documents provided by Robert Richards.

For accounts of her fall in the hallway of the Waldorf, I drew on the recollections of Freeman Gunter and Robert Richards, as well as Peggy's own later accounts in various periodicals.

For the re-creation of her performance at the Waldorf, I referred to a bootleg CD recording.

Twenty-six: **Piano Players**
For information about Peggy's performances with Bill Basie, I am thankful for the account provided by Tom Cassidy. I am also grateful for the information about her Australian tour, as well as insight into the lady herself, furnished by Irving Arthur.

For further information on Peggy at the time, I relied on interviews with Robert Richards. For documents pertaining to her relationship with Shigeru Okada and Mitsukoshi Ltd., and to the menu of the dinner party and an account of the evening, I am also grateful to Mr. Richards.

For information on Peggy's spiritual quests, I am particularly thankful for Kathy Levy's insight and Freeman Gunter's memories. All quotations from *Letters of the Scattered Brotherhood* are taken from the Harper & Brothers 1948 edition of the book, which I would recommend to any reader interested in pursuing some of the spiritual paths that Peggy took; even for skeptics, it is an unusual, and in many ways enlightening, volume.

For accounts of Peggy's recording of *Close Enough for Love,* as well as her broad and insightful remarks on jazz in general, I am grateful for the astounding Marian McPartland's generous cooperation. On a personal note, I would like to add that being able to interview Ms. McPartland was one of the highlights of my professional life.

I am particularly and especially grateful to John Chiodini for information about the recording of the album *Close Enough for Love,* about Peggy, and about music, as well as for his hospitality, generosity, and all-around all-star attitude. His demeanor, decorum, and generosity are extraordinary.

Twenty-seven: One-Woman Show

For information about the musical *Peg,* I relied on several sources, including Irv Cowan, Bucky Pizzarelli, Grady Tate, Jay Leonhart, Mike Renzi, Bill Luce, and Phoebe Jacobs; innumerable periodical accounts; and the *Playbill* magazine for the show. I also referred to various published sources for the history of the Lunt-Fontanne Theater. For further details, I consulted Maurice Zolotow's July 1983 profile of Peggy in *Los Angeles* magazine.

In particular, I thank Paul Horner, the composer of the original music for the show, not only for his memories and cooperation, including his accounts of the theater engagement in Detroit that led to the production of the musical, but for his generosity in allowing me to listen to unreleased recordings of the songs that did not make the show. His insights into the woman were extraordinary and invaluable.

I also referred to *TheatreGoer* magazine for information on the Sondheim show.

For information on her lawsuit against the Waldorf and Johnson Wax, I am particularly grateful for Freeman Gunter's memories.

For reviews of the show, I referred to peggylee.com.

I thank Allen Bardin for his memories of the dinner party at Peggy's apartment, as well as Freeman Gunter for his own recollections.

For further insight into Peggy at the time, I referred to an interview in *Interview* magazine, which was particularly insightful.

Twenty-eight: Hip Angel

For information regarding Peggy at this time, I must take this opportunity to thank pianist Mike Renzi for his considerable time, energy, cooperation, and good humor, as well as his deep insight into the woman. Renzi's contributions have been invaluable to this project. In addition, I am grateful for the thoughts and memories of her bass player Jay Leonhart. To whatever degree this book captures the essence of Peggy in her later years, it was through the generous collective wisdom and joy of Renzi, Chiodini, Leonhart, and Tate.

I am also indebted to Emil Palame for his memories, his time, and his insights, and for specific details about the writing of "Circle in the Sky."

For details of the Westwood Playhouse performance, I thank Deborah Kelman for her contributions.

For information on string theory, I am grateful for the scientific acuity of Ted Klein, copy editor at *GQ* magazine, who helped me understand *The Elegant Universe,* Brian Greene's seminal tome on the new physics of the cosmos.

Accounts of Peggy's performances at the Ballroom rely on several sources, foremost the recollections of Peggy's band. In addition, James Gavin's account in his terrific book *Intimate Nights* was a great help, as was the article written by Rob Hoerburger for *The New York Times Magazine.* Further sources included *The New Yorker, The New York Observer,* and *The New York Times.*

Twenty-nine: I Won't Dance

For information on Peggy's heart surgery in New Orleans, I relied on John Chiodini's recollections. Jay Leonhart's insights added depth to this chapter, as did those of the extraordinary pianist Michael Feinstein, to whom I am also grateful. A lengthy interview from the Los Angeles *Daily News* was essential to this section of the chapter.

Information about the recording of *Peggy Sings the Blues* comes primarily from the memories of the band.

For information about the genesis, planning, and recording of *Love Held Lightly,* as well for immeasurably helpful reflections on Peggy and for documents, archival interview materials, support, hospitality, graciousness, encouragement, enthusiasm, and general above-and-beyond-the-call-of-duty effort, I cannot thank Bill Rudman and Ken Bloom enough. They are two of the most important keepers of the flame, and without them, this book would not have been possible. I also thank them for furnishing reviews of the album, which came from several sources, including *L.A. Weekly* and *Entertainment Weekly.* I also thank pianist Keith Ingham for his time, his memories, and his enthusiasm for this project, for Harold Arlen, and for Peggy Lee.

For descriptions of Peggy's blues show at the Ballroom, I drew upon Rex Reed's review in *The New York Observer.*

For memories of the Pied Piper award ceremony, I thank Paul Horner.

For information about the recording of *The Peggy Lee Songbook: There'll Be Another Spring,* I again thank John Chiodini, who generously allowed me to listen to several songs, yet unreleased, that he and Peggy wrote for Boudoir Productions. I also thank him for providing review materials, which came from, among other sources, *Stereo Review* and *Jazz Link.*

Finally, I am again grateful to Billy Harbach for allowing me to hear Peggy's birthday tribute for his eightieth birthday, one of the most poignant songs she ever recorded.

Thirty: **Take Me Back to Manhattan**

For much of the information in this chapter, I am grateful for the assistance of Alexander Theroux, whose own artistry with words defies further description. I must thank Theroux for his time, his personal documents, his letters, and, above all, his exceptional insight into Peggy Lee. He was instrumental in providing the final chapter, literally and figuratively, in this exploration of the extraordinarily talented and complicated woman who was Peggy Lee.

For further details of Peg's engagement at the New York Hilton, I relied on published accounts.

For the re-creation of the Society of Singers tribute to Peggy, I am grateful for the videotape provided by Artie Butler, as well as—as always—for his insights.

For other accounts of Peg's final days, I thank Kathy Levy, Stella Castellucci, and Quincy Jones.

Index

Aandahl, Fred, 226–27
Abbott and Costello, 298
Addams, Jane, 93
Adulterer, The (Theroux), 499
After Dark, 289, 410
"Afterglow," 435, 436–38
"Aintcha Glad," 32
"Ain't Goin' No Place," 169
Alcoholics Anonymous, 229, 290
Alexander, Willard, 97, 104
All Around the World (Little Willie
    John album), 315
Allen, Peter, 433–34, 443
Allen, Steve, 235–36, 260, 272, 329, 330
"All of Me," 243, 311
"Almost Like Being in Love," 394
"Along the Colorado Trail," 504
"Alright, Okay, You Win," 317
"Always," 408
A&M, 415
American Federation of Musicians,
    117, 154
American magazine, 206
American pop
    Arlen-Mercer team and, 131–36
    development of, in 1930s, 55–57
    John Hammond and, 30–32
    Mount Rushmore of, 10
American Society of Composers,
    Authors and Publishers (ASCAP),
    490

"Am I in Love," 265
Amis, Kingsley, 342
Anderson, Florence, 45
Anderson, Judith, 157
Andrews, Anna, 61
Angel Records, 491
"Any Old Time," 205
Appeal of Jazz, The (Mendl), 29
"April in Paris," 37
"Aren't You Glad You're You," 212
Arlen, Harold, 32, 33, 190, 302, 357
    background of, 131–21
    Lee records trunk songs of, 481–84,
        485–86, 490–95
    songwriting with Mercer, 131–36
    writes "Blues in the Night,"
        135–36
Arlen, Sam, 132
Armstrong, Louis, 4, 29, 85, 105, 155,
    202, 204, 205, 311, 331, 404, 488
    Henderson and, 94
    influence of, on Crosby, 96, 183
    influence of, on Goodman, 93, 101
    Lee first hears on radio, 25
    Lee meets, 138
    Lee sings at funeral of, 399–400
    on Lee's singing, 399
    on Mount Rushmore of jazz singing,
        10
    on radio with Crosby and Lee,
        208–11

Armstrong, Louis *(continued)*
  records with Dorsey and Crosby, 65
  on TV with Crosby, 334–35
Arnaz, Desi, 243
Arthur, Irving, 428–29, 469
"As Long as I Live," 357
Asphalt Jungle (film), 261
"As Time Goes By," 346
As You Like It (Shakespeare), 52
Atlantic Jazz Singers (compilation
  album), 388
Auld, Georgie, 304
"Avalon," 102

Babes in Arms (musical), 136
Bacall, Lauren, 197, 415
Backus, Jim, 295
Bailey, Mildred, 29, 95, 134, 155, 182,
  210, 303, 372
Bailey, Pearl, 312, 483
Baker, Josephine, 45
"Bali Ha'i," 216
Balliett, Whitney, 470
Ballroom club appearances, 469–70,
  475–77, 482, 487–89
Bandera, La (film), 244
Bankhead, Tallulah, 157, 279, 484
Banquet of Melody (film), 178
Barbour, Dave (first husband), 52,
  272
  background of, 154–55
  bop music, 202–3
  credited for "I Don't Know Enough
    About You," 178
  death of, 366
  "Don't Smoke in Bed" and, 196–97
  drinking, 172, 179, 196–97, 199, 216,
    289–90, 403, 446
  film *Mr. Music* and, 231–32
  film *Secret Fury* and, 254
  friendship with Lee after divorce,
    292, 294
  Hollywood Hills house and, 188
  illness and near death of, 190–92
  Latin music and, 201–2
  Lee divorces, 236–39
  Lee marries, 160, 163–68
  Lee meets, 154

Lee's love for, and "Johnny Guitar"
    lyric, 298–99
  Lee's marriage to Dexter and, 261
  Lee's performances with, 212
  Lee's sale of Denslow house and, 269
  Lee's TV appearances with, 508
  "MaZana" and, 193–99
  "MaZana," plagiarism lawsuit for,
    195, 198–99
  marriage problems, 188, 190–92,
    193–94, 197–99, 203, 205, 206,
    211, 216, 222, 403, 410–11
  Metronome interview of, 233–34
  mother of, 172, 191–92
  musicianship of, 180
  painting and, 175, 179
  personality of, 164, 179, 188, 261
  portrayal of, in *Peg*, 446, 448, 450,
    456
  Previn and, 180
  records for Capitol, 166
  records hit "Golden Earrings" with
    Lee, 194
  records own music, 206
  records "Waiting for a Train" with
    Lee, 176–77
  refuses to go to AA, 229
  songwriting with Lee, 169–70, 184,
    189–90, 193–99, 238, 439
  songwriting with Lee, rights to
    songs, 348–49
  stops touring as drinking gets out of
    hand, 213–14
  visits North Dakota with Lee,
    224–27
Barbour, Nicki (later Foster, Nicki),
    344, 348
  birth and childhood of, 165–66, 172,
    174, 186, 191, 197, 205, 206, 237,
    247, 292
  Denslow house and, 268
  Kimridge house and, 271–72, 294
  Lee's marriage to Dexter and, 261,
    266, 299
  Lee's relationship with, 322
  marries Dick Foster, 358, 363–64
  Sinatra and, 309
Bardin, Allen, 458–59

Barnet, Charlie, 92, 116, 167, 234
Basie, Count Bill, 3, 29, 33, 51, 67, 105,
    115, 121, 130, 158, 166, 250, 272,
    275, 277, 304, 406
  compliment to Lee, 138
  performs with Lee, 427–28
"Basin Street Blues," 480
Basin Street East club, 324–25
  Lee's appearances, 325–28, 347, 348,
    349–51, 359, 360–62, 362, 364,
    435–36, 456
  February 4, 1961, 1–8, 325–26, 337
  live album of 1961, 338
Baskette, Kirtley, 291
"Baubles, Bangles and Beads," 334–35
Bautzer, Greg, 261
Beat movement, 317, 319, 334,
    335–36
Beatles, 407
"Because I Love Him So," 328
"Because You're Mine," 263
Beiderbecke, Bix, 29, 85, 133–34,
    182–83, 435
"Bella Notte," 281
Benitez, Jellybean, 502
Bennett, Max, 6, 7, 304–5, 314, 316,
    357, 438, 439, 463
Bennett, Tony, 4, 304, 339, 385, 389
Benny, Jack, 87–88, 100, 200, 218, 356,
    367
Benny, Mary, 367
Berg, Billy, 176, 202, 250
Berg, George, 147–48, 149
Berigan, Bunny, 96, 98, 155
Bering, Frank, 88–89, 108
Berle, Milton, 219
Berlin, Irving, 96, 131, 198, 408
"Best Is Yet to Come, The," 357
Better Than Working (Catling), 340
"Bewitched, Bothered and
    Bewildered," 220–21, 299
Big Broadcast of 1937, The (film), 99
Big Sky (film), 300
"Big Spender," 456
Big Spender (album), 370, 511
Billboard, 200, 337, 357
  names Lee number one vocalist of
    1948, 211–12

Bing Crosby Show, The (TV show),
    333–36
"Black Coffee," 275–76, 319, 439, 509
Black Coffee (album), 274–78, 305
black music and musicians
  Arlen-Mercer songs and, 131–32,
    133
  Crosby and Armstrong and, 209–10
  influence of, on Crosby, 183
  influence of, on Lee, 153
  mixed bands and Goodman, 32, 99,
    104
  L.A. and, 65
  ODT buses and, 151
  progressive jazz and, 141
Blake, William, 506–7
Blitz, Fred, 23
Block, Martin, 176
Bloom, Ken, 5, 196, 308, 481–84,
    485–86, 490–95
Blue Devils of Minneapolis, 33
blues, 123, 131, 153, 176, 239, 276, 370,
    487–88, 511
  late albums of, 479–81, 491, 495
Blues Cross Country (album), 479
"Blues for Benny," 273
"Blues in the Night," 131, 135–36
Blues in the Night (film), 483
"Blue Skies," 96, 180
Boardner, Steve, 65–66
"Body and Soul," 82, 102
Bogart, Humphrey, 197, 415
Bolger, Ray, 157
"Bombshell from Brooklyn," 158
Bontemps, Arna, 65
"Boomerang," 496
Borzage, Frank, 158
Boswell, Connie, 200
Boulanger, Nadia, 347
"Bouquet of Blues," 284
Bourgeois, Jess, 224
Brando, Marlon, 265
Brandt, Mattie, 20
Breen, Michael, 287
Brenner, George, 140
Brenner, William, 36, 43–44
Brier, Lois, 227
British Gramophone magazine, 31

Broadway Limited (train), 129
Brodszky, Nicholas, 265
Bronson, Charles, 269
Brooks, Jack, 87
Broonzy, Big Bill, 153
Brown, Georgia, 376
Brown, James, 316
Brown, Ruth , 388
Brubeck, Dave, 272, 435
Bryant, Mike, 214
Buck, Pearl (first piano teacher), 25, 26
Bufman, Zev, 446–47, 453, 454
Burke, Johnny, 212, 230, 328, 346, 436
Burke, Sonny, 209, 243, 245, 249,
    281–82
Burton, Richard, 446, 454
Bushkin, Joe, 333–34, 341
Butcher, Edith, 40, 42, 61
Butler, Artie, 385, 404, 510, 514
Buttery club (Ambassador West,
    Chicago), 89–91, 108–9

Caesar, Sid, 279–80, 283
Caesar's Hour (TV show), 279–80
Cagney, James, 87
Cahn, Sammy, 7, 265, 333
Callas, Maria, 356
"Call Me Darling," 6
Cavalcade of Stars (TV show), 217
"Calypso Blues," 320
Camel Caravan (radio show), 101
Candoli, Pete, 207, 255–56, 267, 275,
    276
Cannon, Dyan, 364
"Cannonball Express, The," 238
Cantor, Eddie, 100
"Can't We Be Friends?," 312
Capitol Jazzmen, 169
Capitol News, The, 166
Capitol Records, 187, 190, 196, 213,
    216, 316, 338, 383, 415
  Lee returns to, 306–7, 365
  Lee signs with, 166–71, 403–5
  Lee's contract not renewed, 238, 243,
    243
Capote, Truman, 483
Capri, George, 336–37, 337
"Caravan," 67

Carlisle, Una Mae, 121
Carmichael, Hoagy, 120, 134, 143, 210,
    346
Carney, Art, 4, 8, 349
Carpenter, Karen, 404
Carpenter, Ken, 209, 218
Carroll, Earl, 252
Carter, Benny, 117, 150, 202–3, 238,
    346, 357, 361
Casablanca (film), 258, 259, 266
Case, Russ, 240, 248–49
"Case of MJ, The," 418
Cash Box, 357–58
Cassidy, Tom, 427–28
Castellucci, Louis, 256, 257
Castellucci, Stella, 251, 257–58, 266–67,
    269, 293, 300, 301, 302, 305, 310,
    336, 346, 358–59, 510–11
Catlett, Big Sid, 105, 107, 169
Catling, Patrick Skene, 339–42, 343,
    358
"Cavalier of the Boulevard, The," 276
Cavanaugh, Dave, 306, 323, 361, 383
Champion, Gower, 230–32
Champion, Marge, 230–33
Charles, Ray, 3, 7, 331, 338–39, 344,
    388, 389, 406, 456
  Lee's tribute for, 7, 338–39, 364
Charnin, Martin, 483, 493
Chennault, Claire, 143
Chevalier, Maurice, 100, 371
Chicago Daily News, 397, 420–21
Chicago Sunday Herald-American,
    120
Chicago Sun-Times, 212
Chicago Tribune, 450
Chicago Women's Symphony
    Orchestra, 114
Chiodini, John, 409, 439–40, 462–63,
    464, 466–68, 472–73, 476–77,
    479–80, 481, 485, 491
  songwriting with Lee, 495–96
Chittison, Herman, 155
Christian, Charlie, 105–6, 107
Christian Science Monitor, 384
"Circle in the Sky," 478, 495
Ciro's, 251–52, 252–56, 258, 261, 285,
    291, 293, 294, 299, 314–15, 331

"Clarinade," 242
"Clarinet a la King," 116–17
Clark, Buddy, 91
Click magazine, 142
Clinton, Larry, 92
Clooney, Rosemary, 9, 195, 238, 265, 280, 508–9
Close Enough for Love (album), 438–40, 479
"Clown Party," 444
Cole, Natalie, 508
Cole, Nat King, 135, 167, 170, 248, 277, 294, 320, 508
Coleman, Cy, 357, 364, 448–55
Colgate Comedy Hour (TV show), 298
College Inn restaurant (Chicago, Sherman Hotel), 88–89, 92
    Lee plays, with Goodman, 109–10
Collins, Lloyd, 71–77, 88, 135, 442
Coltrane, John, 1
Columbia Records, 94, 112, 153–54, 166
"Come On Midnight," 493
"Come Onna My House," 195
"Come Rain or Come Shine," 280, 359
Como, Perry, 204, 240
Concord Jazz Festival, 405–6, 507
Connor, Russ, 147
Cooley, Ed, 315
Cooper, Gary, 87, 265
Copacabana, 242–43, 246, 290, 320–23, 371
Cornell, Katharine, 157
Costanzo, Jack, 299, 358
    on Barbour, 170, 180
    on Dexter, 261
    on "Is That All There Is," 383–84
    on Lee and music vs. men, 305–6
Cousteau, Jacques, 484
Cowan, Irv, 371, 401–2, 443–45
Coward, Noël, 120
"Cowboy and the Bearded Lady, The," 504
Crawford, Joan, 4, 230, 261, 298
Crosby, Bing, 10, 29, 57, 95–96, 125, 134, 171, 195, 241, 265, 283, 311, 330, 366
    Armstrong and, 65

background of, 182–84
films with Lee, 230–33
friendship with Lee, 181–82, 191, 200–201, 210–11
hits, 202
on Mount Rushmore of jazz singing, 10
radio and, 218
radio with Lee, 199–201, 208–11
TV with Lee, 333–36
tape recording and, 200
Crosby, John (reviewer), 219
Crosby, Stills & Nash, 399
"Cubana Bop," 212
Cuban music, 201–2, 243
Cue magazine, 194, 390, 422
Cuffaro, Chris, 498
Cugat, Xavier, 95, 158, 243
Curtiz, Michael, 258–59, 261, 266
Cuthbert, Dr., 69
Cutshall (trombone acc), 136

da Costa, Modie, 168
"Daddy Was a Railroad Man," 456, 457
Dailey, Frank, 115, 116, 121
Damone, Vic, 508
Daniels, Billy, 265
"Danny Boy," 235–36
Darcanville's Cat (Theroux), 499–500
Darin, Bobby, 298
Darkenwald, Chad, 45
Davenport, Johnny, 315
Daves, Delmer, 157–58
Davis, Miles, 317, 406
Davis, Sammy, Jr., 4, 8, 251, 311, 349, 508
Davis, Wild Bill, 363
Dawson, Greg, 469
Day, Doris, 9, 258–59
"Day In, Day Out," 5
Dean, James, 293
Dearie, Blossom, 475
Debussy, Claude, 106, 152, 266
Decca Records, 166
    Lee leaves, for Capitol, 306
    Lee records for, 243–45, 246, 274–78, 288

Deery, Bob, 53–54
de la Renta, Oscar, 484–85
Del Rio, Jack (fourth husband),
    358–59, 369
Delta Rhythm Boys, 178
Depression, 23–24, 49–50, 56, 63
DeProng, Louis, 66
DeSylva, Buddy, 166
Dexter, Brad (second husband, Boris
    Velijko Milanovich, Barry
    Mitchell), 261–62, 263, 266–69
Dexter, Dave "Dex," 121, 166–69
Dietrich, Marlene, 3, 377–78
DiNovi, Gene, 292–96
"Dippermouth Blues," 65
Disillusionment (Mann), 375
Disney, Walt, 5, 281–82, 283, 344, 501,
    508
    Lee lawsuit vs., 488–89
"Dixieland Band, The," 134
Doc Haines Orchestra, 41
Dodds, Baby, 122
"Do I Love You?," 297, 323
Doll House (Palm Springs) perfor-
    mances, 87–89
"Don't Be So Mean to Baby," 184
"Don't Be That Way," 64, 101
"Don't Explain," 389
"Don't Let Me Be Lonely Tonight,"
    388, 408
"Don't Smoke In Bed," 196–97, 255
Dorsey, Jimmy, 31, 65, 151, 243
Dorsey, Tommy, 57, 81, 100, 115, 125,
    151, 159, 328, 334
Down Beat, 92, 111, 120, 121, 157,
    163–64, 238, 248, 259, 264, 273,
    277, 302–3, 326
    Lee named Number One Girl Singer
        of 1946, 187
    Lee second to Ella for Female Singer
        of 1953, 277
"Down by the River," 211
"Down in the Valley," 480
"Down South Camp Meeting," 116
Dragnet (TV series), 286, 287
Dream Street (album), recorded by Lee
    for Decca, 301–3
Dubin, Al, 158

Duckworth, George, 110
Duckworth, Lady Alice Hammond,
    108–9, 114–15
Duke, Doris, 443
Durante, Jimmy, 4, 171, 195, 198, 200,
    241, 356

Earl Carroll's Vanities of 1932 (revue),
    32, 132
"Easy Evil," 408
"Easy to Love," 205
Ebony concerto (Stravinsky), 250
Eckstine, Billy, 272, 406
Eddy, Mary Baker, 174
Eden, Anthony, 341
Edison, Harry, 233
Egstrom, Clair (brother), 20, 24, 74, 78,
    119
Egstrom, Della (sister), 19, 24, 69, 74,
    119, 164
Egstrom, Jean (sister), 18–19, 74
Egstrom, Leonard (brother), 78
Egstrom, Marianne (sister), 19, 20, 24,
    69, 74, 119, 164, 227
    on Lee, 291
Egstrom, Marvin (father), 17–21, 28,
    34–40, 53
    death of, 221–23, 227–29
Egstrom, Milford (brother), 222,
    227–28
Egstrom, Min Schaumberg
    (stepmother), 35, 37, 43, 222
    abuse of Lee as child, 18, 21, 24,
        27–28, 38, 222, 223
    Lee gains compassion for, 460–61
    marries Marvin, 18–21
    portrayal of, in *Peg*, 450
Egstrom, Norma Debris (original
    name). *See also* Lee, Peggy
    changes name to Peggy Lee,
        60–61
    personality of, endures, 10
    Nortonville performance of 1930,
        15–16
Egstrom, Selma Anderson (mother),
    18–19, 43
Egstrom, Tyke (nephew), 74
"Eight, Nine and Ten," 190

Einstein, Albert, 293, 463, 468
Eldridge, Roy, 59
Elegant Universe, The, 468
Elichman, Marty, 385
Ellington, Duke, 2, 7, 25, 29, 33, 66, 98,
    101, 124, 212, 272, 275, 340
  Lee meets, 138
  on Lee, 406
"Elmer's Tune," 112–14
Emerson, Ralph Waldo, *ix,* 174, 509
Empire Room, 390–92, 398, 406–7,
    421–23, 442
  fall and lawsuit, 433–24, 449
Entertainment Weekly, 494
Erickson family, 34–36
Ertegun, Ahmet, 388
Esquire, 109
Etri, Bus, 116
Evans, Ray, 194
Everybody Comes to Rick's
    (unproduced film), 266
Extra Special! (album), 370

Fairbanks, Douglas, 219
Falcon Crest (TV show), 254
Fargo *Forum,* 163–64, 226–27, 237,
    266, 410
Fargo-Moorhead Twins (baseball
    team), 55
Feather, Leonard, 76, 273, 327, 388, 463
  friendship with Lee, 76, 143
  Metronome blindfold song test by,
    204
Fehr, Henry, 43
Feinstein, Michael, 473
Feller, Bob, 91
Ferlinghetti, Lawrence, 3, 274
Ferrer, José, 265
Ferrer, Mel, 254–55
"Fever," 5, 7, 339, 370, 455, 502,
    511
  Lee has hit with, 315–16, 318–21
Fields, Dorothy, 241, 357
Fields, Shep, 202
Fifth Dimension, 399, 401
Firestone, Ross, 32
Fitzgerald, Ella, 3, 9, 150, 202–3, 205,
    217, 276, 284, 311, 312, 316, 325,
    356, 362, 367, 400, 490, 507, 508
  influence of, on Lee, 51
  Lee named second to, 277
  Lee sings with, 202–3
  Pete Kelly's Blues and, 286
  style of, vs. Lee, 124
Flack, Roberta, 406
"Fly Me to the Moon," 328
"Foggy Day in London Town, A,"
    311
"Folks Who Live on the Hill, The," 52,
    309–10, 436, 464
Fontanne, Lynn, 157, 454
"Forever Nicki," 206
"Forever Paganini," 206
"For People Who Are Not
    Sentimental," 234
Forrest, Helen, 89, 103–4, 108–14, 116,
    118, 202
Foster, David (grandson), 365, 366,
    468
Foster, Dick (son-in-law), 363–65
Foster, Holly (granddaughter), 366,
    472, 485
Foster, Michael (grandson), 365–66
Foster, Nicki Barbour (daughter,
    formerly Barbour, Nicki), 165–66,
    236, 271–72, 363–64, 467, 472, 513
  relationship with Lee, 365, 421, 430
Foxx, Redd, 472
Franklin, Aretha, 370, 388, 406
"Freckle-Faced Gertie," 58
Friedwald, Will, 170, 197, 237, 306,
    308, 323, 327, 328, 346
Friesen, Gil, 415
Frombach, Estelle, 173–74
Fun Zone carnival, 63, 64

Gabin, Jean, 244
Gabler, Milt, 245, 275
Gaillard, Slim, 204, 250
Gardner, Ava, 87, 251, 261
Garland, Judy, 3–4, 197, 200, 322, 349,
    362, 371–372, 401, 508
Garner, Erroll, 331
Gastel, Carlos, 199, 213, 214
  as Barbour's manager, 170–71,
    213

Gastel, Carlos (continued)
 becomes Lee's manager, 188
 Lee replaces, with Kelly, 268
Gavin, James, 469
George Gobel Show, The, 319
"Georgia on My Mind," 26
Geronimi, Clyde, 281
Gershwin, George, 64, 67, 127, 131,
 200, 243, 257, 305, 509
Gershwin, Ira, 64, 67, 127, 143, 197
"Get Happy," 132–33
Getz, Stan, 304, 380
"Ghost Riders in the Sky," 213
Giddins, Gary, 182–84, 199, 366,
 409–10, 503
Gilbert, Henry, 198
Gillespie, Dizzy, 175, 202, 212
Ginsberg, Allen, 274, 319
Ginsberg, Belle May, 41, 48, 226
Gleason, Jackie, 349
Gleason, Ralph, 277
"God Bless the Child," 480
Godfrey, Arthur, 218
Godfrey, Cy, 316
Goetz, Bill, 197
"Golden Earrings," 194, 202, 212
Golson, Bennie, 357
"Goodbye," 242
"Good Enough to Keep," 180
Goodman, Benny, 4, 40–41, 51, 56–57,
 64, 81, 302, 315, 334, 341, 409,
 500, 508
 background of, 92, 92–102
 Barbour and, 155
 Basin Street East and, 324–25,
 326–27
 on bop, 202
 Carnegie Hall concert, 100–102
 drugs, alcohol and, 115–16
 girl singers and, 102–5
 Hammond signs, to record with
 black musicians, 31–32, 94
 Henderson and, 96
 McPartland on, 436
 Paramount show of 1942, 151–54
 perfectionism of, 141–42
 personality of, 94, 104–5, 141, 152,
 326, 437

Powell leaves, 155–56
Sinatra introduced by, 160
Stage Door Canteen and, 158–59
 tour of 1935, and explosion of swing,
 97–99
Goodman, Benny (hits of), 135
 records "Blues in the Night" with
 Lee in 1942, 135–36
 with Forrest of "Man I Love," 89
 with Lee, of "I Got It Bad," 124–25
 with Lee, of "Why Don't You Do
 Right," 157
Goodman, Benny (and Lee) hires Lee,
 105–7, 108–12
 hit with Lee, of "I Got It Bad,"
 124–25
 hit with Lee, of "Why Don't You
 Do Right," 157
 Lee begins to thrive with, 123–24
 Lee leaves, to marry Barbour, 160
 Lee performs with Barbour and, in
 San Francisco, 172
 Lee's first recordings with, 111–14,
 122–23, 126–27
 Lee's first recording without, 169
 Lee's songwriting promoted by,
 120–21
 meets Lee, 92
 performs with Lee, 277
 radio with Lee, 241–42
 records "Blues in the Night" with
 Lee in 1942, 135–38
 relationship with Lee, 139–43
 tour with Lee of 1941, 114–21
 tour with Lee of 1942, 146–57
 TV appearance with Lee, 325
Goodman, Ethel, 105
Goodman, Eugene, 104–5
Goodman, Fred, 105, 117, 139, 141,
 148
Goodman, Harry, 93–94, 104
Goodman, Irving, 104
"Goody, Goody," 57, 135
Gore, Tipper, 474
Gorme, Eydie, 339, 443
Gottlieb, Robert, 328
"Got to Wear You Off My Weary
 Mind," 492

Grace, Princess of Monaco, 342, 396
Grammy Awards, 399, 481, 496
Granata, Hugo, 327
Grant, Cary, 4, 8, 251, 364, 366, 401, 510
Grant, Duane Lee, 58–60
Grant, Edna, 58
Grant, Joseph William, 57–60
Grant, Magda Christina "Peggy," 58–61
Great American Popular Singers, The (Pleasants), 135
Great American Songbook, 8–11, 120, 320, 387
Greatest Show on Earth, The (film), 265
Green, Lil, 152–53, 156, 488
Grier, Howard, 261
Grusin, Dave, 408
Guadalajara Trio, 87, 89
Gunter, Freeman, 391–92, 406–7, 422, 449, 458–59

Haines, Lyle "Doc," 40–43
Hamilton, Arthur, 284–86, 438
Hammerstein, Oscar, II, 309
Hammond, John
  Goodman and, 31–32, 94–96, 99, 104, 105, 108–9
  Lee's first recording and, 112–14
Hampton, Lionel, 32, 99, 102, 106, 118, 325
Hancock, Herbie, 464
"Happiness Is a Thing Called Joe," 190
"Happy with the Blues," 483, 492–93
Harbach, Bill, 330–31, 358, 497
Harbach, Otto, 330
Harburg, Yip, 133, 190, 302, 483
"Hard Day's Night, A," 365, 407
"Hard-Hearted Hannah," 273
Harlem jazz, 31, 96, 182
Harlow, Jean, 287
Harnell, Joe, 6, 321–23, 337–38, 343–44, 448
Harrison, George, 388
Hart, Lorenz, 67, 134, 136, 244, 263
Hartford, Huntington, 252

Hastings, Don, 272–73
Hatfield, Bobby, 365
Hawkins, Coleman, 96, 435
Haydn, Richard, 230
Hayes, Helen, 157
Hayloft Jamboree, 58
Haymes, Dick, 150
Heart Is a Lonely Hunter, The (film), 408–9
Heider, Wally, 382
"He Is the One," 408
Henderson, Fletcher, 29, 33, 94, 96–99, 190, 250
Henderson, Florence, 334
Hendricks, Lillie Mae, 262, 292, 294, 390, 352, 440, 443
"He Needs Me," 288
Hepburn, Audrey, 254
Hepburn, Katharine, 158, 484
Here Comes the Waves (film), 492
"Here's That Rainy Day," 346, 435–36
"Here's to You," 510
Herman, Woody, 89, 151, 170, 212, 250, 268, 304
Hershorn, Tad, 251
"He's a Tramp," 281, 508
High Fidelity magazine, 389
High Noon (film), 265
"High Society," 335
Hines, Earl, 105
Hoefer, George, 302–3
Hoerburger, Rob, 475
Hoffenstein, Samuel, 395–96
Holiday, Billie, 9, 41, 124, 167, 202, 204, 212, 234, 279, 334, 340, 341, 372, 389, 398, 409, 436, 500
  influence of, on Lee, 51, 157
Hollywood Hotel (film), 134
Holm, Celeste, 265
Holmes, Ernest, 173, 174–75, 189, 216, 262, 266–67, 432, 496
Holmes, Hazel, 175, 189, 266–67
Homuth, Red, 52–54
"Honeysuckle Rose," 101
"Hooray for Hollywood," 134, 265
Hooray for What! (Broadway show), 483
Hoover, J. Edgar, 279

Hope, Bob, 100, 200, 265, 283, 508
  TV shows, 218–21, 231
Horne, Lena, 3, 273, 296, 311–12, 449,
  490, 508
Horner, Paul, 464, 490
  writes *Peg* with Lee, 441–55
Hot Nocturne (film), 133
"Hound Dog," 360, 381
Hour Glass (TV show), 218
House of Flowers (musical), 483
Hovde, Ossie, 74
Hover, Herman, 252, 254
"How Long Has This Been Going
  On," 127
Hughes, Howard, 251, 261
Hundling, Lloyd, 116
Hunt, Pee Wee, 277
Huston, John, 261

"I Can't Give You Anything but
  Love," 83, 96
"I Don't Know Enough About You,"
  178–81
"I Dream of Jeannie with the Light
  Brown Hair," 74
"I Get Along Without You Very Well,"
  346
"I Got a Man," 7
"I Got It Bad," 124–25, 466
"I Got Rhythm," 201
"I Gotta Right to Sing the Blues," 32,
  132
"I Had a Love Once," 492
I Had the Craziest Dream (Forrest),
  104
"I Just Want to Dance All Night,"
  495
"I Let a Song Go Out of My Heart,"
  212
"I Lost My Sugar in Salt Lake City,"
  323
"I Love Being Here with You," 355
"I Never Knew Why," 456
"I See a Million People," 121
"I Thought About You," 74, 135
"I Won't Dance," 357
"If I Could Be with You," 241, 335
If You Go (album), 346–47

"I'll Be Seeing You," 405, 478
"I'm a Woman," 359–62, 439, 508
I'm a Woman (album), 359–62
"I'm Fine," 444
"I'm Gonna Go Fishin'," 7, 339
"I'm in the Mood for Love," 76
"I'm Ready to Begin Again," 416
"In Other Words," 328
Inge, Adele, 130
Ingham, Keith, 481–82, 485, 491–92,
  494
Ingstad, Bob, 41–42, 53–54
Ingstad, Don, 53
Institute of Religious Science, 173
International Hotel (Las Vegas)
  appearances, 420
Interview magazine, 56, 460
Intimate Nights (Gavin), 469
IRS, 402
Irving, Val, 207
"Is That All There Is?," 309, 390, 394,
  396, 415, 424–25
  Lee records, 374–86
  wins Grammy, 392, 399
Isley Brothers, 399
"It Could Happen to You," 328
"It Don't Mean a Thing If It Ain't Got
  That Swing," 98
"It Had to Be You," 89
"It Was a Lover and His Lass," 52
"It's a Big Wide Wonderful World,"
  357
"It's a Good, Good Night," 317
"It's a Good Day," 212, 225, 240, 249,
  264, 275, 317, 439
  Lee records, 185–86, 191, 200
  Lee writes with Barbour, 184–85
"It's a Wonderful World," 317
"It's De-Lovely," 67, 85–86
"I've Been Too Lonely for Too Long,"
  497
"I've Got a Brand-New Baby," 497
"I've Got a Crush on You," 201
"I've Got You Under My Skin," 257,
  276, 311

Jablonski, Edward, 481
Jabuti (trombonist), 66

Jackson, Wilfred, 281
Jacobs, Phoebe, 247, 307–8, 310–11,
    331–32, 338, 344–45, 347–51, 358,
    368, 473
Jacobs, Suzy, 344
Jade club, 66–68, 87
James, Dennis, 219
James, Harry, 92, 102, 105, 112, 130,
    151, 379
jazz
    arranged, 31
    bop, 175, 202–3, 212, 272
    Cubop, 243
    changes in, of 1940s, 175, 202–3
    "Cool School," 272
    Crosby show of 1960 and, 335
    difficulty of, in late 1970s, 434
    Dixieland, 284
    Goodman and, 96–99
    Lee as jazz singer, 204–5, 217,
        276–77, 303, 436, 465
    Los Angeles and, 65, 67
    New Orleans and, 65, 132
    in 1920s and 1930s, 28–33, 55–57
    popular, 8–11
    progressive, 175–76, 234
    resurgence of, with Beats, 317
    touring and lifestyle of musicians,
        115–19
    West Fifty-second Street and, 30, 138
Jazz Link magazine, 496
Jazz Singer, The (film, remake), 258–64,
    283, 289, 299
Jefferson, Blind Lemon, 488
Jenkins, Allen, 158–59
Jenkins, Gordon, 242, 245
"Jersey Bounce," 151
Jessel, George, 157
Jewison, Norman, 372
Joey Bishop Show, The, 383, 390
John, Little Willie, 315–16, 318
"Johnny Guitar," 298–99, 422, 495
Johnny Guitar (film), 298–99
Johnson, Rev. Joseph, 18
Jolson, Al, 200, 220, 258–259
Jones, Isham, 89
Jones, Quincy, 4, 344–47, 358, 363,
    364, 372, 405–6, 476, 479, 512–513

"Jubilee Stomp," 340
"Just for a Thrill," 7, 331, 339, 405,
    497
Just for You (film), 265
"Just One of Those Things," 438–39

Kane, Art, 435
"Kansas City," 480
Kaye, Danny, 100
Kelly, Ed
    becomes Lee's agent, 268
    on Lee, 291
Kelly, Gene, 251
Kelman, Deborah, 463–64
Kemp, Hal, 117, 155
Kennedy, John F., 356
Kennedy, Ken (Sydness), 55–58, 60, 80,
    82, 109, 225
Kenton, Stan, 170, 234
Kerkorian, Kirk, 384, 420
Kern, Jerome, 309, 357
Kerouac, Jack, 3, 274, 317, 334
Kimball, Robert, 328
King, B. B., 370
King, Wayne, 91
"King Porter Stomp," 98
Kitt, Eartha, 475
Klee, Harry, 357
Koehler, Ted, 32, 132–33, 357
Kopler, Harold, 213–14
Koussevitzky, Serge, 234
Kraft Music Hall (radio show), 181–84,
    199
Krupa, Gene, 64, 92, 94–99, 101, 105,
    328
Kubrick, Stanley, 226
Kyser, Kay, 158

Ladd, Frank, 144
Lady and the Tramp (Disney film),
    281–82, 292, 508
    Lees sues for royalties for, 488–89
Lady Fatima (film), 260
Lafferty, Bernard, 443
Laine, Frankie, 238
"La La Lu," 281
Lamond, Dan, 385
Lamour, Dorothy, 251

lang, k. d., 502, 509
Larkin, Al, 169
Larson, Alice, 188
Lastfogel, Abe, 403
"Last Night When We Were Young,"
    302
Latin ala Lee (album), 407
Latin rhythms, 193, 195, 198, 201–2,
    243–44, 276
"Laughing Song," 198
Laugh-In (TV show), 137
"La Vie en Rose," 243
La Vie en Rose club, 278
LA Weekly, 494
Lawrence, Steve, 339, 443
"Lazybones," 134, 210
Leader of the Band (Lees), 268
"Lean on Me," 389
Lee, Gypsy Rose, 158
Lee, Peggy (appearance of), 458–59
    beauty and sex appeal, 5, 6, 111, 124,
        131, 187, 275
    distinctive jaw, 28
    Meadows on, 329–30
    plastic surgery and makeup,
        422–23
    as teen, 36, 67, 72
    weight problems, 36, 280, 371, 406,
        453, 469, 473
Lee, Peggy (awards and honors of)
    ASCAP Pied Piper Award, 490
    Billboard number one vocalist of
        1948, 211–12
    Down Beat Number One Girl
        Singer of 1946, 187
    Grammy for "Folks on the Hill,"
        309
    Grammy for "Is That All There Is?,"
        392, 399
    Grammy nomination for *Miss Peggy
        Lee Sings the Blues*, 481
    Grammy nomination for *Peggy Lee
        Songbook*, 496
    honorary doctorate from North
        Dakota State University, 461
    Lifetime Achievement Award of
        Society of Singers, 507–11
    named "Queen" by Ellington, 2

Oscar nomination for *Pete Kelly's
        Blues*, 5, 289
    Peter Allen's tribute to, 434
    second to Ella as *Down Beat* Female
        Singer of Year for 1953, 277
Lee, Peggy (band musicians and)
    hires drummer Grady Tate,
        362–63
    hires guitarist John Chiodini,
        439–40
    hires Rowles as musical director,
        250–51
    likes company with musicians on
        tour, 369
    musical love affair between singer
        and accompanist, 295–96,
        322–23
    in 1980s, 462–70, 475–79
    Quincy Jones becomes arranger for,
        344–47
    relationships with, 304–6, 321–22
    threatened by other women and
        wives of musicians, 428–29
Lee, Peggy (childhood and family)
    abuse of, by stepmother, 18, 21, 24,
        27–28, 38, 448, 451–52
    birth of, with name Norma Deloris
        Egstrom, 10
    death of father and, 221–23, 227–29
    death of mother, as child, 18
    death of younger sister Jean, 18–19
    dream of being in show business,
        26
    dreams of singing with band, in
        Fargo, 75
    early life in Nortonville, North
        Dakota, 21–28, 34–35
    early musical talent and piano
        playing of, 19–20, 25–26, 28–30,
        36–40
    education of, 24–25, 43, 47–48
    education of, Dale Carnegie course,
        72, 75
    father visits, in California in 1950,
        221–23
    high school glee club, 39–40
    job as waitress in Jamestown, ND,
        51–55

lacks exposure to jazz, 29–30, 33
meets friends from ND, during
  Terrace Room triumph, 140
moves to Fargo to sing for WDAY
  radio, 55–58
moves to Jamestown after high
  school graduation, 47–48,
  49–52
moves to Wimbledon with family as
  teen, 34–38
press interviews on, in late 1940s,
  212
railroad and, 23
railroad depot run by, as teen, 35–36,
  39, 44
relationship with father, 35
relationship with stepmother as teen,
  35
teen years in Wimbledon, 34–48
visits father in North Dakota, in
  1950, 227–29
visits siblings while on tour break
  with Goodman, 119
Lee, Peggy (daughter Nicki and), 421,
  430
  birth of Nicki, 165–66
  grandchildren and, 366
Lee, Peggy (early career)
  changes name to Peggy Lee, 57–61
  debut of, at Valley City Eagles'
    Lodge, 42–43
  Goodman hires, in Chicago, 92,
    105–7, 108–12
  Goodman band and, begins to thrive
    in 1941 tour, 123–25
  Goodman 1941 tour and Terrace
    Room appearances of, 123–33,
    136–45
  Goodman 1942 tour and Paramount
    triumph, 146–56
  leaves Goodman band to marry
    Barbour, 160
  moves to Los Angeles as teen to try
    to become star, 61
  Palomar Ballroom with Goodman,
    96–99
  Panther Room, in Chicago, 88–89,
    112

returns to California and sings at
  Doll House with Max Schall,
  87–89
returns to Fargo after tonsillectomy,
  69
sings as teen, in L.A. Jade club and
  Fun Zone, 64–68
sings as teen, with Jack Wardlaw
  Orchestra, 46
sings in Chicago at Buttery, 89–91
sings in Fargo at Powers Hotel, on
  return from L.A., 70–80
sings in Minneapolis at Flame
  Room, 80–83
sings on KRMC radio after high
  school, 50
sings on KVOC radio and Doc
  Haines in Valley City, 40–45
sings on WDAY radio in Fargo,
  55–61
sings with Lloyd Collins in Fargo,
  71–76
tours with Osborne band in 1939,
  82–83, 84–86
Lee, Peggy (films)
  film projects unmade, 266
  Jazz Singer remake, 258–64
  Lady and the Tramp voices, 281–82
  Mr. Music with Crosby, 230–33
  Pete Kelly's Blues and stops making
    films, 283–91, 294
  State Door Canteen, 157–59
Lee, Peggy (finances and business side
  of career)
  agent Rockwell and, 268
  Capitol left by, 237–38
  Capitol signs, 169
  earnings in 1948, 205
  fees at Basin Street East, 326
  hits of 1949, 211–12
  Lady and the Tramp rights, 282,
    488–89
  lawsuit vs. Waldorf from fall, 449
  manager Gastel and, 171
  manager Gastel fired and replaced by
    Kelly, 268
  manager Panella and, 402–3
  money problems with Barbour, 188

Lee, Peggy (finances and business side
  of career) *(continued)*
  Mr. McGoo records, 295
  need for money and fear of poverty,
    90, 392, 402, 411
  plagiarism lawsuit vs., for
    "MaZana," 195, 198–99
  returns to Capitol to record *Man I
    love*, 307–8, 309–10
  rights to songs written with Barbour,
    348–49
  sale of Denslow house, 268
  staff waits to be paid, 430
  stardom of, 9, 98
  tour with Goodman and pay, 150
  touring and recording vs. films,
    290
  William Morris signs, 90
  William Morris drops, 424
Lee, Peggy (friendships)
  with Alexander Theroux, 499–507,
    511
  with Benny Goodman, 138–41, 152,
    159
  with Bill Rudman, 494–95
  with Bill Sawyer, 54–55
  with Bing Crosby, 181–82, 191,
    200–201, 210–11
  with Bobby Darin, 298
  with Cary Grant, 363, 366
  with Emil Palame, 464–65
  with Ernest Holmes, 189
  with Frank Sinatra, 186, 307–10
  with Gene DiNovi, 292–96
  with Harold Arlen, 132
  with Jane Leslie, 76, 90, 142
  with Jimmy Marino, 293–96
  with Johnny Mercer, 132
  with Kathy Levy, 366–70
  with Leonard Feather, 76
  with Lillie Mae Hendricks, 262
  with Lou Levy, 367–68
  with Phoebe Jacobs, 310–11
  with Ray Charles, 347
  with Robert Richards, 411–12,
    428–29
  with suicidal RAF pilot of 1942,
    138–39

Lee, Peggy (health of), 505
  alcohol and, 63–64, 79, 206–7,
    278–79, 290, 296, 380, 394–95, 473
  death of, 513–14
  double pneumonia and lung damage
    in NYC, 347–49
  early problems of, 27
  fainting, 172–73, 431
  heart problems, 292
  heart surgery in New Orleans,
    308–9, 471–75
  illnesses and stroke of, in old age,
    498, 511–13
  pills and, 430
  pneumonia, after St. Louis, 216
  psychosomatic illness and spiritual
    guidance, 195, 216
  throat operation and broken teeth,
    ends Osborne job, 86–87
  tonsillitis and botched tonsillectomy,
    69
  vitamin injections, 343
Lee, Peggy (live performances)
  at Armstrong funeral, 399–400
  Australia tour of 1979, 428–29
  Ballroom, 469–70, 475–77, 482
  Ballroom show on history of blues,
    487–89
  Basie refuses to appear with, after
    Detroit shows, 428
  Basin Street East, 1–8, 325–28,
    337–39, 347, 348, 349–51, 360–62,
    435–36, 456
  Central Park Schaefer Jazz Festival,
    405
  Ciro's, 251–56, 261, 285, 291–292,
    294, 299, 314–15, 331
  club act in 1957–58 and relationship
    with musicians, 304–6
  Club 53 in New York Hilton, in old
    age, 498–99, 502–4
  Concord Jazz Festival performance
    (1993), 507
  Copacabana, 242–43, 246, 290,
    320–23, 371
  with Crosby, 200
  Diplomat Hotel Café Crystal
    (Miami), 371, 407

Empire Room at Waldorf-Astoria,
390–92, 398, 406–7, 421–23, 442
Empire Room appearances end with
fall, 433–24, 449
Ferrer helps with theatricality of act,
254–56
Hickory House, 434, 436
Hollywood Bowl final performance
of 1995, 510–11
Hollywood Palladium, 160, 190
JFK birthday concert, 356
La Vie en Rose as musical pinnacle,
272–73
Las Vegas, and *Mirrors* material, 420
Las Vegas, and tiff with Streisand,
385–86
London, 339, 389
New Orleans, final appearances in,
471–73
North Dakota Winter Carnival and
1950 homecoming, 224–29
pre-show ritual, 4
returns to Las Vegas after Grammy,
400–401
St. Louis trip of 1949 and learns to
manage own affairs, 213–15
shows laid out in detail, after St.
Louis 1949 problems, 213–14
touring and exhaustion, in 1950s,
290–91
touring in early 1970s, 405–6
tours England after closing of *Peg*,
460
Venetian Room (1954), 277
war-bond rallies, 150–51
Westbury Music Fair, 402–3
Westwood Theater, 463–64,
474–475
at White House for Reagan, 285,
484–85
at White House for Nixon and
bombs, 393–98
Lee, Peggy (marriages)
finds love in career rather than
relationships, 269
marriage and relationship problems,
and personality of, 5, 306, 324,
505–7

marries and divorces Jack del Rio,
358–59
Lee, Peggy (marriages: Dave Barbour),
154–55, 160, 163–68
celebrity and pull of career after
marriage, 166
death of Barbour and, 366
desire to be full time wife and
mother, 171–72
divorces Barbour, 236–39
Mexican vacation, 193–95
marriage problems, 172, 179, 188,
190–94,197–99, 203, 205–06, 211,
216, 222, 229, 403, 410–11
relationship after divorce, 411
Lee, Peggy (marriages: Brad Dexter),
261–63, 266–67 divorces, 267–69
Lee, Peggy (marriages: Dewey Martin),
299–301, 314, 316
abuse of, 316, 322
divorces, 324
Lee, Peggy (musical style and
influences)
accessibility of, 295
Arlen–Mercer team and, 132
artistry of, as jazz singer, 8–11
attempt to translate rock songs for
her audience, 387–90
blues style develops during marriage
to Barbour, 176
bop music and, 202–3, 212
critic Gleason on, as jazz singer,
277–78
critics begin to be less impressed, in
1970s, 409–10
discovers power of softness, 88
eccentricities of, on stage, 254
favorite women singers of, 51
genius of, 10
influences on, 51–52, 234
influences on, during childhood and
teens, 22, 25–30, 37, 40–41, 51–52
jukeboxes in L.A. of 1930s and, 64
Latin music and, 201–2
legacy of, 514
mentored by Mel Powell, 112–14
Metronome interview on, with
Barbour, 233–34

Lee, Peggy (musical style and
   influences) *(continued)*
minimalism of, developed with
   Goodman, 123–24
minimalism of, recorded in "Where
   or When," 137
music as disease and, 278
music theory and, 29
of late 1940s, 211–13
perfectionism of, 189–90, 305
performing difficulties at end of
   1970s, 427–28
performing looseleafs, 390
performing style of, 4–7, 72, 351
poetry reciting, 395–96
rehearsing and perfectionism of,
   141–42
singing style of, 72–75, 82, 177
timing and rhythm of, 123–24,
   243–45, 465–66
versatility as jazz–pop singer, 319
Lee, Peggy (personality of), 9–10, 72,
   75–76, 89–90, 241
abusive side of, 451, 501
addiction of, to audience adulation,
   216
aging and, 422–23, 426–28, 469
childhood and suicidal thoughts,
   26–27
closing of *Peg*, reaction to, 458–59
color and sound waves theory of,
   293
craziness and vortex of, 466–67
dark, moody side of, 302
determination and self–reliance of,
   28
dichotomy between North Dakota
   girl and Miss Peggy Lee image of,
   10
emotions and search for peace, 432
hard work of, and lack of mother,
   291
hostess and late nights, 349–51
humor of, 26, 54, 78, 148–49, 168,
   318, 330–31, 369, 396, 444, 484
intellectual curiosity of, 48, 463, 500
narcissism hides insecurity and
   romantic longings, 437–38

need for affection from audience,
   278–79
poetry by, 411
public image of, and victim
   personality, 186
relationships with men, 321–22
sadness in relationships vs. happiness
   in music, 306
Sinatra's vs., 307–8, 312–13
vulnerability of, 5
Lee, Peggy (personal life, homes,
   entertaining, and hobbies of)
after shows, and in–suite performances, 8, 398–99
becomes follower of Holmes and
   Divine Science, 173–75
Bellagio Road house, 440, 462–63
Blair Drive house built with
   Barbour, 188
cooking, 350
Denslow Street house, 197, 201, 207,
   262, 268
domesticity of, 309
entertaining and love of company,
   207, 232, 266–67, 272, 303,
   349–51, 401–2, 429–30, 443–44
escapes sex traffickers as teen, in
   L.A., 67–68
favorite foods, 285, 295, 305, 485
gardening and, 188, 205
home life and creative projects of,
   266
Kimridge home, and live-in
   characters, 271–72, 292–98, 307,
   314, 342–43, 349–51, 358
moves to New York after divorce,
   268
painting and designer fabric deal,
   429–32
painting by, 175, 266, 411–12
penthouse parties in L.A., 363–64
pet dogs, 126
press interviews, in 1970s, 409–10
sells Kimridge house and moves to
   penthouse apartment, 358
spirituality and, 189, 213–214,
   262, 266–67, 419, 421, 432–33,
   445, 511

Tower Grove Road home, 365–66, 378, 401–2

Transcendental Meditation and, 419, 421

Lee, Peggy (radio), 195
with Crosby and Armstrong, from Marine Memorial Auditorium, 208–11
with Crosby on Philco show, 200–201
with Goodman, from Meadowbrook:(1941), 120–22
Kraft Music Hall, 181–84
Let's Dance, 95
listening to, during childhood, 25–30, 33
national broadcast from Panther Room with Goodman, 112
own show on CBS sponsored by Rexall, 192–93
reads poetry on, 248–49
See also Lee, Peggy (early career)

Lee, Peggy (recordings)
album *If You Go* with Jones, 346–47
Arlen trunk songs for Rudman and Bloom, *Love Held Lightly,* 481–84, 485–86, 490–95
Black Coffee for Decca, 274–78
"Blues in the Night," 131, 135–38
"Don't Be So Mean to Me Baby" and "It's a Good Day," 184–86
"Don't Smoke In Bed" written with Barbour and Robison, 196–97
Dream Street for Decca, 301–3
"Fever," 315–16, 318–20, 321
final album for Capitol, *Norma Deloris Egstrom from Jamestown, North Dakota,* 403–5
first hit, "I Got It Bad," 124–25
first recordings with Goodman, 111–14, 121–23
for Capitol, 190
for Capitol, during 1940s, 196
"Golden Earrings" and "Manama," 202
hits diminish in 1950s, 238
hits of, 5
hits of 1949, 211–12

I'm a Woman, 359–62
"Is That All There Is," 373, 374–86
late albums *Miss Peggy Lee Sings the Blues,* 479–81
Let's Love album with title song by McCartney, 407–8
"live" album at Miami Beach Ambassador Hotel, 323
"Lover" for Decca with Burke, 244–46, 248
lull in recording career from 1964–67, 370
Man I love produced by Sinatra 307–10
with Martin and Torme as career plateaus, 216
Mirrors, 413–19
Natural Woman, 389–90
New American Jazz for Capitol (1943), 166–69
Pass Me By with rock songs, 365
penultimate album *The Peggy Lee Songbook: There'll Be Another Spring,* 495–96
Pretty Eyes with Billy May, 327–28
"Somebody Else" with Goodman, 137–38
"Somebody Nobody Loves" and "How Long Has This Been Going On" with Goodman, 126–27
Sugar 'n' Spice and *Mink Jazz* for Capitol, 357
"That Did It, Marie" with Goodman, 137–38
Things Are Swingin' for Decca, 316–19
"Waitin' for the Train to Come In," 176
"What More Can a Woman Do?" and "You Was Right, Baby" with Barbour, 171
"Where or When," 136–37
"Why Don't You Do Right," 152–53, 157–59

Lee, Peggy (romances)
affairs and loneliness of, 379
after divorce from Dexter, 292–96
career vs., 359, 369

Lee, Peggy (romances) *(continued)*
distrust of men and relationships,
403
in Fargo, 75–77
with Bill Harbach, 330–31
with Buddy Clark, 91
with Frank Ladd, 143–45
with George Capri, 336–37
with Greg Bautzer, 261
with Johnny Quam, 77–80
with Patrick Catling, 339, 342–43
with Quincy Jones, 344–47, 372
with Red Homuth, 52–54
with Robert Preston, 233, 246–48,
328
with Sev Olson, 81–83, 144
Lee, Peggy (songwriting), 266
Arlen and, 492
artistry of lyrics, 9
with Barbour, 169–70, 177–78,
184–85, 189–90, 238
with Barbour, for "MaZana" hit,
193–95
"Because I Love Him So," 328
with Burke for *Lady and the Tramp*,
281–82
with Burke produces hits, 245
with Chiodini, 495–96
"Circle in the Sky" with Palame, 487
early, 37, 40
"Fever" and, 318–19
first song on death of mother, 19
Goodman promotes, 119–21
"Heart Is a Lonely Hunter" with
Grusin, 408–9
with Horner for one–woman show,
Peg, 236–37, 441–58
"I'm Gonna Go Fishin'," 7
for "It's a Good, Good Night," 317
for *Jazz Singer*, 263
for *Johnny Guitar*, 298–99
lyrics first published with "Success
Awaits at Labor's Gate," 46–47
with McPartland and album *Close
Enough for Love*, 347–52
mentored by Johnny Mercer, 178
for Mr. Magoo, 295
for "Shining Sea," 372

originality of, 302
for penultimate album, 495–96
talent of, 305
for "Things Are Swingin'," 316
See also specific song and album
titles)
Lee, Peggy (television), 508
Academy Awards, with Mercer,
265
Bing Crosby show (1960), 333–36
Caesar show (1954), 279–80
Ellington tribute, 405–6
of early 1950s, 217–21
of "Fever," 319
with Goodman on *Swing into
Spring*, 325
with Hope on *Star–Spangled Revue*
(1950), 219–21
Joey Bishop Show, 383
"Johnny Guitar" for *Colgate
Comedy Hour*, 298–99
of late 1960s, 371
with Sinatra, 311–13
Steve Allen show, 235–36
Sullivan show, 355–56, 365
Lees, Gene, 166, 268
Leiber, Jerry, 360–62, 374–86, 413–20
Leigh, Carolyn, 357, 365
Leigh, Janet, 284, 286
Leigh, Vivien, 342
"Lemon Drop," 212
Lewis, Jerry, 484
Lenya, Lotte, 377
Leonhart, Jay, 324, 454–55, 460, 465,
468, 473, 485, 493
Leslie, Jane, 69, 76, 90, 110, 142
"Let Me Go, Lover!," 284
"Let's Bring Back World War One,"
414–15
"Let's Dance," 101
Let's Dance (radio show), 95, 98
"Let's Do It," 121–22
"Let's Love," 407–8
Let's Love (album), 407–8
*Letters of the Scattered Brother-hood,
The*, 432, 467
Levant, Oscar, 197
Levinson, Peter, 379, 383, 394, 418–19

Levy, Kathy, 366–70, 419–20, 430, 433, 511–12, 514
Levy, Lou "Good Gray Fox," 304, 316, 357, 367–68, 390, 398, 464
Lewis, Jerry, 251
Lewis, Ted, 22
"Life Is So Peculiar," 232
Life magazine, 202, 205
Link, Harry, 249
"Listen to the Glissen," 85
"Little Fool," 120
"Little Sir Echo," 59
"Little White Ship," 417–18
Live at Basin Street East (album), 362
Live at the Blackhawk (Miles Davis album), 317
Livingston, Alan, 237–38
"Loch Lomond," 52, 481
Locket, Edith, 44
Loewy, Raymond, 129
Lombardo, Guy, 40, 45–46, 158
London, Art (later Lund), 137, 150
London Times, 389
"Lonely Woman," 203
Long, Jack, 206
"Long and Winding Road, The," 407
Look magazine, 121, 226
Loper, Don, 321
Lorre, Peter, 87
Los Angeles *Daily News*, 474
Los Angeles magazine, 450
Los Angeles Times, 463
Louis, Jean, 356
Love Held Lightly (album), 308, 490–95
Love Me Tonight (film), 244
"Lover," 5, 243–46, 255–56, 273, 279, 294, 338, 339
  Lee films, in *Jazz Singer*, 263
  Lee records, 243–45
Lowe, Mundell, 304, 348–49, 373, 374–75, 389, 391
Luce, Bill, 446, 448, 451, 453
Luckman, Lloyd, 81–82, 88
Lund, Art (London), 137, 150
Lunt, Alfred, 454
Luske, Hamilton, 281

McCartney, Linda, 407
McCartney, Paul, 407–8
McClintock, Harry (Hats McKay), 198–99
McCoo, Marilyn, 443
McCoy, Joe, 153
MacCrae, Gordon, 367
McGarity, Lou, 136–37, 147–48, 245
McHugh, Jimmy, 96
McKenzie, Red, 56
"Mack the Knife," 334
McPartland, Jimmy, 435, 437
McPartland, Marian, 272, 507
  writes with Lee, 434–38
McQueen, Steve, 269
McRae, Carmen, 250, 390
Madonna, 502
Madwoman of Chaillot, The (play), 416
Magnificent Seven, The (film), 269
Maid of Salem (film), 106
"Make the Man Love Me," 241
Malneck, Matty, 178
Mambo Jambo (Barbour album), 233
"Man I Love, The," 64, 89, 309
Man I Love, The (album), 207–8, 309–10
"MaZana," 197–99, 205, 211–12, 225, 238, 243, 508
  lawsuit, 195, 198–99
  Lee writes with Barbour, 193–95
Manchester, Melissa, 408
Mandel, Fred, 88–90
Mandel, Johnny, 372, 388, 413–15, 418
Manilow, Barry, 404
Mann, Thomas, 375
Mann Act, 68
Manne, Shelley, 318–19
Manone, Wingy, 56, 154–55, 328
Marable, Fate, 85
March, Hal, 66
Marino, Jimmy, 293–94, 296, 298
Mariosa, Princess, 321
Marks, Gerald, 243
Marsala, Joe, 340
Marshall, Jack, 316–18

Martin, Dean, 216, 251, 253, 311, 356, 508
Martin, Dewey (third husband)
Lee divorces, 324
Lee marries, 299–301, 307, 314, 316, 322
Martin, Freddy, 158
Martin, Jeanne, 356
Martin, Tony, 508
Marvell, Holt, 249
Marvin, Lee, 286
Marx, Groucho, 200
May, Billy, 167, 170, 317, 327–28
Meadowbrook Ballroom, 116, 119–21, 167
Meadows, Jayne, 236, 272, 329–30
Medley, Bill, 365
Melody Maker magazine, 31, 320
"Melody of Love" (Lee's first song), 19
Melvoin, Mike, 361
Mendl, R. W. S., 29
Menuhin, Yehudi, 158
Mercer, Ginger Mehan, 134
Mercer, Johnny, 5, 47, 74, 131–36, 143, 149, 210, 265, 316, 330, 483, 492
at Academy Awards with Lee, 265
background of, 133–36
Capital records and, 166–67
helps Lee with songwriting, 178
leaves Capitol, 237–38
Lee and Barbour record for, 170–71
writes "Blues in the Night," 135
Mercer, Mabel, 272
Merman, Ethel, 158
Metronome magazine, 92, 107, 110, 112, 115, 122, 127, 137, 140, 142, 151, 156, 201, 203, 233–34
blindfold song test, 204
interview with Barbour and Lee, 203, 233–34
"Jimmy Bracken" column, 142
"Mexicali Rose," 62
Midland Continental Railroad, 34–35, 44–47
Midler, Bette, 484
"Midnight," 301–2
"Midnight on the Ocean," 198

"Milkman's Matinee" (radio program), 62
Miller, Glenn, 91, 94, 100, 112, 115, 130, 155–56, 167
Miller, Seymour, 126
Milner, Martin, 286
Mink Jazz (album), 357–58, 486
Miranda, Carmen, 194–95
Mirrors (album)413–19
"Mirrors and Marble," 444–45
Mississippi (film), 211
Miss Peggy Lee (memoir), 20, 90, 195, 238, 364, 450, 458
Miss Peggy Lee Sings the Blues
Grammy nomination, 481
recorded, 479–80
Mitchum, Robert, 341
Mitsukoshi fabric deal, 429–30
Mitterand, François, 484–85
Monaco, James, 158
Mondragon, Joe, 257, 275, 318
Monk, Thelonius, 435
Monroe, Marilyn, 251, 269, 341, 356
Monroe, Vaughn, 190–91, 213
Montgomery, Wes, 399
"Moonglow," 37
"Moonlight in Vermont," 312
Morgan, Helen, 266
Morgan, Tom, 136, 154
Morton, Jelly Roll, 65
"Most Beautiful Man in the World, The," 6, 394
"Most of All I Love You," 497
Moten, Benny, 33, 250
Moulin Rouge (film), 265
"Mr. Magoo Does the Cha Cha Cha," 295
Mr. Music (film), 230–33, 283
Mullen, John, 200
Muni, Paul, 157
Murray, Kel, 95
"Music Goes Round and Round, The," 57
Music Man, The (musical), 247, 328
Musso, Vido, 147
"My Blue Heaven," 26
"My Funny Valentine," 67

"My Heart Belongs to Daddy," 276
"My Old Flame," 302, 410
"My Way," 304

Nathanson, Wynn, 101
Natural Woman (album), 389–90
Nelson, Gene, 84
Nelson, Mrs. Gene, 84
New American Jazz (album), 168
New York Herald Tribune, 219, 242
New York Journal-American, 326
New York magazine, 459
New York Mirror, 186
New York Observer, 488
New York Post, 502–3
New York Times, 103, 398, 400, 457,
    468, 469–70, 475, 480–81, 502
New York World Telegram, 101
New Yorker magazine, 2, 273–74, 321,
    337, 361, 470
Newman, Randy, 378–79
Newsweek magazine, 200
"Nice Work If You Can Get It," 313
Nichols, Red, 94
"Night and Day," 26
Nilsson, Harry, 399
Nixon, Richard M., 393–98
"Nobody Knows You When You're
    Down and Out," 205
None but the Brave (film), 269
Noonday Variety Show (radio show),
    58
*Norma Debris Egstrom from James-
    town, North Dakota* (album),
    403–5
Norman, Mary, 67
Norvo, Red, 56, 95, 155, 247, 272
Nureyev, Rudolf, 485

Obcron, Merle, 157
O'Brien, Edmond, 284, 286
O'Day, Anita, 9, 102–3, 217, 269–70,
    304, 376, 409
Oelsner, Dr. Tom, 472
Okada, Shigeru, 429–31
"Old Master Painter, The," 216
Oldrate, Johnny, 252

Oliver, Sy, 7
Olson, Ethelyn, 36–38
Olson, Marti, 83
Olson, Ole, 21, 126
Olson, Sev, 81–83, 115, 121, 144
"On Broadway," 360–61
"One Beating a Day," 448, 451–52
"One O'Clock Jump," 67, 114, 118
On the Road (Kerouac), 334
"On the Sunny Side of the Street," 22
Oppenheimer, J. Robert, 293
Oppenheimer, Mme., 90
Osborne, Will, 82–86, 115, 121
"Over the Rainbow," 133
"Over the Wheel," 496

Pacino, Al, 502
Page, Patti, 9, 339
Palame, Emil, 464–65, 472–73, 477–79,
    510
Paleface (film), 265
"Pale Moon Shinin'," 335
Palitz, Morty, 245–46
"Panama," 210
Panella, Brian, 383, 385, 391–92, 399,
    400–401, 504
"Paper Moon," 133
Paramount performances, 100–102,
    151–54, 159–60, 186, 233
Parker, Charlie, 175, 212, 272, 315
"Pass Me By," 365
Pass Me By (album), 365
Paul, Les, 244
"Peace on Earth," 281
Peg (Broadway show), 441–58
*Peggy Lee Songbook: There'll Be
    Another Spring, The* (album),
    495–96
"Peggy Lee Stories for Girls"
    (Andrews series), 61–62
"Peggy Lee: Too Good for Her Own
    Good" (Hoefer), 302–3
"Pennies from Heaven," 57
People magazine, 489, 496
Pete Kelly's Blues (film), 283–91, 294,
    427, 438, 508
    soundtrack album, 289

Peterson, Willy, 82
Petrillo, James, 154
Philco, 200–201
Phillipe, Gerard, 276
Piano Jazz (NPR radio show), 436
Pizzarelli, Bucky, 191, 454–56, 463
Pleasants, Henry, 135
Pollack, Ben, 93–94
Pollock, Jackson, 3, 274
Pompidou, Georges, 393–94, 397
Porter, Cole, 67, 86, 120, 122, 131, 134,
    257, 263, 276, 316 438–39
Potter, Larry, 65–68
Potter, Mrs., 67
Powell, Bud, 202
Powell, Mel (Epstein), 106–7, 109, 136,
    148, 151, 169, 172, 242, 446
  leaves Goodman, 155–56
  mentors Lee, 111–17
Powers, Tom, 225
Powers Girl, The (film), 229
Powers Hotel, 70–76
Prado, José, 440, 443, 462
Prado, Perez, 202
Presley, Elvis, 311, 360, 420
Preston, Robert, 233
    romance with Lee, 246–48, 301, 328,
    500
Pretty Eyes (album), 327–28
Previn, André, 325, 463
  on Lee's style, 123–24
  plays with Barbour, 180
Private Lives (play), 454
Punch magazine, 339–40
"Purple Hills in the Sunset," 40

Qaddafi, Muammar al-, 393
Quam, Johnny, 77–80

race records, 133
Radke, Leo, 43
Rainey, Ma, 488
"Rain Sometimes," 438
Ralston, Frank, 444
Ramone, Phil, 374
Randolph, Popsie, 142, 152
Raskin, Milt, 180, 328
Rasmussen, Gladys, 61–63

Ravel, Maurice, 256
"Razor," 405
RCA records, 166
Reading Lyrics (Kimball and Gott-
    lieb), 328
Reagan, Ronald, 285, 473, 484–85
Rebel Without a Cause (film), 276,
    295
Redbook magazine, 290–91
Redman, Don, 96
Reed, Rex, 488
Reiner, Carl, 279
Rendezvous with Peggy Lee (album),
    187
Renzi, Mike, 452, 455, 460, 462,
    465–67, 475–76, 481
Rexall radio show, 192–93
Reynolds, Debbie, 287
Rich, Buddy, 1, 125, 202, 272
Rich, Frank, 457
Richards, Robert, 411–12, 423–24,
    429–34, 449
Rickles, Don, 402–3
Riddle, Nelson, 30, 307, 310, 327, 379
"Riding on the Rails," 443
"Ridin' High," 317
Righteous Brothers, 365
Rinker, Al, 29, 95, 182
Rivera, Diego, 90
Robbins, Jerome, 319
Roberts, Howard, 318
Robin, Leo, 265
Robison, Willard, 196–97, 212, 234,
    243, 276
"Rock Me to Sleep," 238
rock music, 11, 217, 320, 339, 360, 365,
    387, 474
Rockwell, Tom, 268
Rodgers, Richard, 3, 67, 136, 244, 248,
    263
Rogers, Dick (singer), 85
Rollini, Adrian, 154
Rollins, Sonny, 435
Rooney, Mickey, 200
Roosevelt, Eleanor, 52
Roosevelt, Franklin D., 50, 106,
    183–84
Rose, Billy, 82, 94–95